Reopening the Word

Reopening the Word

Reading Mark as Theology in the Context of Early Judaism

MARIE NOONAN SABIN

OXFORD
UNIVERSITY PRESS

OXFORD
UNIVERSITY PRESS

Oxford University Press, Inc., publishes works that further
Oxford University's objective of excellence
in research, scholarship, and education.

Oxford   New York
Auckland   Cape Town   Dar es Salaam   Hong Kong   Karachi
Kuala Lumpur   Madrid   Melbourne   Mexico City   Nairobi
New Delhi   Shanghai   Taipei   Toronto

With offices in
Argentina   Austria   Brazil   Chile   Czech Republic   France   Greece
Guatemala   Hungary   Italy   Japan   Poland   Portugal   Singapore
South Korea   Switzerland   Thailand   Turkey   Ukraine   Vietnam

Published by Oxford University Press, Inc.
198 Madison Avenue, New York, New York 10016
www.oup.com

Oxford is a registered trademark of Oxford University Press

First issued as an Oxford University Press paperback, 2012

Library of Congress Cataloging-in-Publication Data
Sabin, Marie Noonan
Reopening the Word : reading Mark as theology in the context of early Judaism /
Marie Noonan Sabin.
p. cm.
Includes bibliographical references and index.
ISBN 978-0-19-514359-1 (hardcover); 978-0-19-989574-8 (paperback)
1. Bible. N.T. Mark—Criticism, interpretation, etc.   2. Bible N.T. Mark—
Theology.   3. Bible. O.T.—Theology.   4. Christianity—Origin.   5. Christianity and
other religions—Judaism   6. Judaism—Relations—Christianity.   I. Title.
BS2585.52 S33 2001
226.3'06—dc21   00-065229

Excerpts from Morna D. Hooker, *The Gospel According to Saint Mark*, are reprinted by
permission of Continuum International Publishing Group Inc.

Excerpts from *Mark, II, Ancient Christian Commentary on Scripture*, edited by Thomas C.
Oden and Christopher A. Hall. © 1998 by the Institute of Classical Christian Studies
(ICCS), Thomas C. Oden and Christopher A. Hall. Used with permission from
InterVarsity Press, P.O. Box 1400, Downers Grove, IL 60515.

Parts of chapter 2 originally appeared as "Reading Mark 4 as Midrash," *Journal for the
Study of the New Testament* 45 (1992). Reprinted by permission of Sheffield Academic
Press Limited.

Part of chapter 6 originally appeared as "Woman Transformed: The Ending of Mark Is the
Beginning of Wisdom," *Cross Currents* 48/2, Summer 1998. Reprinted by permission.

Printed in the United States of America
on acid-free paper

To W.A.S.

Preface

Kosuke Koyama, emeritus professor of ecumenics at Union Theological Seminary, used to startle (and humble) his classes by proclaiming, "*Theologian gives job description to God!*" The gift of Koyama's proclamation was that it threw his students off balance, for perceived that way, the whole enterprise of systematic Christian theology seemed like an enormous act of hubris. Koyama's challenge was not to our beliefs but to our methods. Once able to get out of the box, as it were, of our habitual modes of talking about God, we were freed to consider other ways of speaking about the transcendent.

It was a necessary freedom for exploring the non-Christian theologies of Hinduism and Islam, and even the nontheology of Buddhism. We did not, in Koyama's courses, consider Judaism—probably because the connections between Christianity and Judaism were taken up elsewhere. Nonetheless, this exercise in detached engagement with other forms of religious discourse was an invaluable preparation, I found, for trying to learn the language of religious Jews.

Had I confined my study of Judaism to the courses at Union Theological Seminary, however, I might not have noticed that I was still trying to understand "Jewish theology" in Christian terms. Instead I availed myself of the opportunity to study across the street at Jewish Theological Seminary, where I entered an entirely different culture. There I found myself in a world that was, first of all, more professedly religious than any I had experienced since my Catholic school and college: these young men and women preparing for the rabbinate were careful about keeping the Sabbath, intense in their debates about the meaning of Scripture and Mishnah, deeply and totally committed to their faith. I respected that commitment because it resonated with my own.

That respect, in turn, prepared me to accept what was otherwise very troubling—the instances (not by any means the rule, but frequent enough to be upsetting) in which I was regarded as suspect because I was a Christian. I wanted many times to explain that I was there only out of a desire to understand Judaism, not to co-opt it, but there was no time or place to address this subtle issue—I had simply to accept the suffering of being misunderstood. Yet the experience of being a stranger had its own salutary effect: I began to realize how a serious commitment to one's own religion may easily result in the misinterpretation of that of another. I began to hear more keenly the ways Christians misinterpret Jews. The subjective experience bore theological fruit, for it taught me how much is involved in truly hearing the religious language of another.

The rightful hearing of another, I discovered, involves layers within layers of listening. When, for example, I studied Justin Martyr's *Dialogue With Trypho* in a class jointly composed of Jews and Christians, I assumed that my Jewish classmates would know that I was as appalled as they by Justin's disdain for the Jews; it was a deep shock to realize that instead they thought that I—and all Christians—shared his contempt. I knew that a modern Christian speaking as Justin did would be condemned by the post-Shoah church and that Justin's judgment of the Jewish Bible as a crude composition only revealed his own ignorance. Yet since my Jewish classmates were not engaged in the study of Christianity, they had no way of distinguishing my attitudes and thought-processes from Justin's. I began to see the ongoing effects of mutual ignorance.

Justin thought he understood the Bible of the Jews better than the Jews themselves. How many Christians, I wondered, still think the same? What, in fact, are the differences between the way we each read Genesis, for example, or Isaiah? I brought my questions to my courses in Scripture at both seminaries. Biblical courses at Union, for the most part, were heavily self-conscious in respect to method: we did not merely study the Bible; we studied *how* to study it. I was intrigued by the fact that the Jewish approach to Scripture was both more direct and more concerned with the way the Bible relates to itself. In teaching the Psalms, for example, Rabbi Yohanan Muffs perceived each one as a nexus of allusions to myriad other passages in Scripture: intertextuality was not a concept but an experience. In that way our Bible study was both meditation and game, and we came to see the Bible as a whole—and wholly relevant, both to itself and to us. We never questioned whether the Bible was meaningful today: we assumed that it was and zealously dissected every part of it, pursuing the interrelationships as joyously as we might a piece of music.

Midrash was considered a separate discipline from Scripture, but I found in those classes the same intense engagement with the biblical text. We pored over the words, parsed the phrases, stared between the lines, and explored the gaps. I came to appreciate firsthand the saying of the ancient rabbi: "Turn it [the Bible] round and round. Everything is in it."[1]

What was omitted was also significant: we never spoke of different kinds of theologies, much less the relationship between theology and the Bible. I had entered a world in which one did not talk about God but rather how one related to him. The intellectual debates were not directed at God's existence or nature; they were focused on human understanding. It was accepted, moreover, that while God is One, the ways of human understanding are multiple.

I discovered that in arguing for one interpretation over another, the ancient rabbis tended to make use of stories; when speaking of God, they went by way of analogy, using the formulas of "like" and "as it were." I began to learn a different kind of religious language— one that tended to speak of the divine by way of poetry and the human by way of narrative.

My initial instinct was to translate this other language back into my own: to change the metaphors for God into concepts and the human stories into precepts. I strove, moreover, to make these abstractions consistent and orderly. Doing so, I had to work to make sense of the biblical contradictions: How could God at the same time be loving and angry, creator and destroyer? How could Abraham be both patriarch and liar? How could Moses be God's chosen leader and yet too disobedient to enter the Promised Land? How could one prophet tell the people to beat their spears into ploughshares while another gave the opposite message?

In my own training, theological and ethical understandings formed a logical system that I applied as a tool for interpreting the Bible; I used the Bible to support and illustrate what I already thought and believed. Some kind of abstract theology, in other words, came first, and I made the Bible fit. But in the thought-processes of religious Jews, I discovered, the Bible cannot be subsumed into some other category. In itself it represents a point of engagement between human beings and the divine being, and to be "theological" is to enter its world of reality.

This discovery shed light on Justin's misbegotten disdain for the Jews. Justin came to the Hebrew Bible, as he did to his Christian faith, by way of Stoic philosophy; as he had trained disciples in Greek thought before his conversion, so he tried to turn Christianity into a school of philosophy. In the process he proposed that the Stoic idea of the Logos or Reason was the same as the Hebrew *dabar* (which carries the implications of action) and "the Word made flesh" of John. Because he believed that Reason was the supreme value, he sought to bring all perspectives together in a tidy conceptual schema. The root of the scorn he expressed toward Trypho the Jew stemmed from Trypho's refusal to read the Hebrew Bible the way he did. I recognized something of my own training in Justin's insistence on placing schema before text, and the recognition led to a further question: To what extent was the very language in which Justin framed his thoughts responsible for furthering the rift between Christians and Jews?

Justin translated the language of the texts before him into the context with which he was familiar; beyond his intentions, the imposition of one context upon another did violence to the integrity of the first, and its consequences have been far-reaching.

Justin believed the truth of the Platonic construction of reality— that is, a universe of absolute and ideal forms that are merely reflected or copied in the world we see. Identifying Jesus as the Logos (that is, Reason) he perceived him as the Platonic Truth and everything else as pale reflection. Applying this construction directly to the reading of Scripture, Justin read Christian Scripture as presenting the absolute truth and Jewish Scripture as the limited copy.

Justin, of course, was not alone in doing this: he clearly drew support from the idealized language of John ("I am the Way, the Truth, and the Life"), and he might have known the contemporaneous Letter to the Hebrews, which uses explicitly Platonic language: "Christ did not enter a sanctuary made by human hands, a mere copy of the true one" (9:24); and "the law has only a shadow of the good things to come and not the true form of these realities" (10:1). I reflected that in all three instances this language had practical consequences: in all three cases, it resulted in feelings of Christian superiority and concomitant scorn for the Jews.

I observed that this language, moreover, has continued to be operative in modern Christianity—even though the Platonic schema from which it came has long since been abandoned and the disdain it implies is no longer intended. Yet many Christians still understand the Scriptures in the language of an outmoded philosophy. In some instances, traditional language is preserved without regard for contemporary consequences. In others, the consequences dominate, and in an attempt to make the Scriptures "relevant," words are forced into modern molds. Awareness of these distortions led me to ask the questions Justin never did: How did Jews of the first century read their own Bible? How did they talk about it?

Much scholarship has been exerted in recent times to retrieve the Jewishness of Jesus: scholars have explored the history, the economy, the social strata of first-century Palestine. Yet it seemed to me that the nature of Jesus' theological discourse had been slighted. I felt compelled to ask: Is not Jesus' way of doing theology—his very theological language—his primary context?

I could see, moreover, that theological language does bear—for both good and ill—pragmatic fruit, and so I was moved to consider: If we retrieve the theological language of first-century Jews, what implications might it have for Christian understanding—both of the Gospel and of Judaism? Might a new understanding of the Gospel offer a new model for modern Christian discourse? What added dimensions might result for Christian faith itself? Because I care both about historical contexts and modern consequences, I decided to pursue the nature of theological discourse in Early Judaism.

Thus I began with a question: How might the earliest Gospel have sounded to those first followers of Jesus who were pious Jews? I proposed to discover, or uncover, the theological understandings of the first Jews who followed the teachings of Jesus and who yet saw themselves as Jews; I sought to understand those early members of "the Jesus movement" who in fact saw Jesus' teachings as confirmation of the Torah. I have been concerned with history to the extent that history frames the theological context of the first century; I have been concerned with Christian belief not as it has been articulated in later centuries but as it first emerged from the matrix of Early Judaism.[2]

I am not alone in doing this but responding to the challenge proposed by many recent scholars to read the New Testament differently, in the light of new understandings of Hebrew Scripture and Jewish exegesis. Bruce Chilton has pleaded both with Christian scholars not to assume that Jesus departed from Judaism and with Jewish scholars not to "force early Judaism into the mold of later, rabbinic theology"; he asks both to make a fresh start.[3] Jacob Neusner has also spoken of the importance of Oral Torah for Christian origins and the need for a new exegesis of the New Testament with a new understanding of the multiple Judaisms of the first century.[4] Paul van Buren, in his three-volume work *A Theology of the Jewish-Christian Reality*[5] and a fourth book, *According to the Scriptures*, argued that the Jewish Scriptures were sacred to the first followers of Jesus not only because they were Jews but because "they provided the language, images, and idiom with which those Jews learned to speak of Jesus."[6] James Sanders has suggested "comparative midrash" as a relevant and evocative method for reading the New Testament.[7]

Most significant of all, Rolf Rendtorff has called for biblical theologians to "study the New Testament first of all as written by Jews who stood in an immediate and unbroken continuity with the Bible (in Hebrew or Aramaic, or even in Greek) and who never had the idea to be something else than Jews." Noting that New Testament theologians usually begin their interpretation with the opposite premise, he called for a more ecumenical starting point, namely, "the close relationship between the Old Testament and the writings of the originally Jewish group that later developed out of Judaism and was then called Christianity."[8]

The purpose of my study is thus to delineate, in a new way, the theological location of the earliest Gospel, assuming this locus to be neither identical with later Christianity nor with later Judaism, but rather with some fluid moment before they broke apart and codified their respective ways.

My motives for doing so arise from my own theological landscape. I bring to my study of the Gospel text an admitted desire to find it not contemptuous of Judaism, because contempt for another represents for me the very antithesis of gospel meaning. It is in fact my own Christian (Catholic) faith that leads me to believe that Christians are called to an inclusive dialogue with all faiths, but especially with the faith-tradition that formed the heritage of Jesus and the first evangelists. I also write as a Christian seeking to connect my understanding of Mark with the ancient church criteria of continuity with "the apostolic witness" and congruence with "the rule of faith." These criteria are somewhat circular and not inherently transparent: what constitutes "the apostolic witness" is determined by how one reads the Gospels, and "the rule of faith" is consequent upon that reading. Only Augustine's insight seems irrefutable: that the essential rule and witness is love of God and love of neighbor, and any interpretation that violates these two great commands is suspect.[9]

If that rule is taken as measure, then the Christian community of the present time seems compelled to note that a contradiction has emerged from within Christian tradition that is simultaneously ethical and exegetical. It is a contradiction revealed by the genocidal horror of our age—the Shoah: an exercise in neighborly hatred of such seismic proportions that it has disclosed a fault line in the Christian community's self-understanding as one founded on neighborly love.

There are those who argue that the ones who perpetrated this genocide could hardly be called "Christian," but that is begging the question; the fact remains that a "Christian" society permitted genocide to happen in its midst, and while it is true that some individuals did indeed protest, it is sadly remarkable that they stand out as the exception. It is also true that others even "justified" the killing of Jews on the basis of their understanding of the Gospels. These facts raise urgent questions about the Christian tradition: If even a single Christian could imagine "justifying" such a flagrant violation of "the rule of faith"—which Augustine identifies as the rule of love—does it not suggest that in some way Christians have not been reading, teaching, or preaching the apostolic witness correctly? Do we not have reason to suspect some kind of systemic distortion here? Can we retrieve an earlier witness that will serve as a corrective?

The underlying motivations for this study are thus issues of faith. I believe that the ugly revelation of the Shoah makes it urgent for Christians to rethink their attitudes toward Judaism. It is a matter of urgency because Christian silence in the face of Hitler's planned annihilation of the Jews reveals a serious contradiction in witness to the revelation Christians claim in Jesus Christ of God's totally inclusive love. This claim is basic to all aspects of Christian belief; it constitutes its essential "rule of faith." The Shoah revealed a self-contradiction in Christian witness that is particularly located in its triumphalist repudiation of the Jewish witness to the divine. I believe it is urgent, therefore, for Christians to retrieve the Jewish witness of the first century and reconsider its relationship to the apostolic witness.

Issues of faith, therefore, are what led me first to study how Jews of the first century interpreted their Scripture; what I learned is what led me to reopen Mark in the context of Early Judaism. The results, I believe, delineate a new identity for Mark's Gospel: clearly in respect to generic discourse; possibly in respect to date and author; most compellingly in respect to theology.

Acknowledgments

The idea for this book came out of the convergence of two important parts of my life: a love for language and literature that led to my writing a doctoral dissertation on the richly varied generic sources of *The Canterbury Tales*; a happy interfaith marriage that led to my taking courses at the Institute for Judaeo-Christian Studies founded by John M. Oesterreicher. The first experience educated me in trying to see texts freshly and read them closely; the second opened my eyes to the riches of Judaism and the principles of interfaith dialogue. Both experiences contained seeds that came to a slow ripening at Union Theological Seminary when I began to pursue the Jewish roots of the earliest Gospel. In the course of bringing the initial thesis from a bare idea to its present state, I have had the help and support of many people whom I would like to thank.

I am deeply indebted to two scholars no longer living: John Oesterreicher, who taught me that many things that I had considered uniquely Christian in fact were Jewish first; and Paul van Buren, who took time from his last book, *According to the Scriptures*, to talk with me about some early chapters of my manuscript. I am sorry that neither one of these scholars, so dedicated to interfaith dialogue, is around for further conversation.

There are scholars who have read the manuscript in the past year to whom I feel especially grateful. Most particularly, I would like to thank W. D. Davies, who gave me the benefit of his wide-ranging scholarship and deeply probing insights. Along the way, he pointed out to me the parallel between my thesis in chapter 5 that Mark presents Jesus as a living *mashal* and his own argument that Paul saw Jesus as "a kind of equivalent of . . . the oral tradition in Judaism as the clue to the scriptures." That he might consider this book to be in his tradition, even in part, is an honor indeed. In short, I feel blessed to have had his interest, his criticism, and his praise.

I feel greatly indebted, as well, to Gerard Sloyan, who made painstakingly detailed comments on every chapter and footnote, and then reviewed the revisions. I know this book is better for his careful scholarship, and I am grateful for the generosity with which he lavished so much time. (It is only fitting that I add the appropriate disclaimer here: the faults that assuredly remain are all my own.)

I would also like to express my particular gratitude to Calum Carmichael, whose critique was extremely helpful and whose support has been especially bolstering.

My heartfelt thanks also go to Charles M. Murphy, who gave me valuable insights into improving my final draft.

There are also scholars who read early versions of the manuscript who aided me enormously. My special appreciation goes to Ellen Davis, whose courses at Union Theological Seminary gave me a rich understanding of the joys of reading the Hebrew Bible. She kindly read parts of my work and encouraged me to continue. I am grateful to Bernard Lee, who not only endorsed the whole enterprise but articulated the ways in which my biblical findings dovetailed with his theological explorations of the differences between Greek and Hebrew modes of thinking. I would like to express special thanks as well to Bill Birmingham, Nancy Malone, and Joe Cunneen, the editors at *Cross Currents* who helped me shape part of chapter 6 into the article entitled "Women Transformed: The Ending of Mark Is the Beginning of Wisdom." Their encouragement, along with their expertise, marked a turning point in my efforts.

Many other friends have provided a continual source of strength throughout the duration of my research and writing. I am grateful to Pat Brückmann, who was one of the first to read the whole draft and encourage its publication. My particular thanks go to Hope Crawley, who read every draft of every chapter over the past seven years, including all twenty versions of what started as an introduction and is now chapter 1. Thanks, too, are owed to those who, without reading the manuscript, nonetheless supported it every step of the way: to Eva Fleischner, whose own commitment to interfaith work has always been an inspiration; special thanks as well to Father George Lutz, Georgia Dunn, Barbara Langan, and Trina Paulus—the small community at St. Peter Claver Church in Montclair, New Jersey, who engaged me every morning in a dialogue homily, patiently heard out all my ideas, and enthusiastically encouraged my work.

Last but far from least, I am grateful to members of my family whose presence lives between the lines: to my parents, John and

Marie Noonan, who nurtured me not only in my Christian faith but in respect for all persons and traditions; to my brother John, whose own work has provided continual inspiration and who has offered continuous encouragement to mine; and to my children—Margaret and Kate, Chris and Jim, John and his wife Kathy—who have so generously applauded my endeavors. Above all, I would like to express my deep gratitude to Bill, who has given tirelessly of his professional skills as an editor as well as his constant loving support as a spouse to help me bring this book to birth. It is to him, cherished husband, editor, and friend, that this book is gratefully dedicated.

Contents

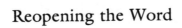

Reopening the Word

1

The Theological Context of Mark

Searching for the Origins of Mark

Before any scholarly discussion of the Gospel of Mark can begin, one must confront the most basic set of questions that can be asked about any document: Who is "Mark"? Where and when, and even why and how, did he compose? And finally, *what* did he compose— what is the literary construct we designate as "gospel"? These questions are so intertwined that the answer to one becomes dependent on the answers one gives to all the others. Since, moreover, the answer to every one of these questions is uncertain, controversial, and to some extent subjective, I will try to weigh the alternative evidence and arguments before offering my own assumptions and conclusions.

Who Is Mark?

The simplest answer is that we do not know. Raymond Brown sums up the scholarly consensus: "None of the Gospels mentions an author's name, and it is quite possible that none was actually written by the one whose name was attached to it."[1] There is, however, an early church tradition based on Eusebius's fourth-century *Ecclesiastical History* that cites a fragment from the second-century bishop Papias, who posited "Mark" as the author of the earliest gospel and linked him to Peter. Many second-century church fathers corroborate this view. Irenaeus (135–202 C.E.) speaks of Mark as "the interpreter

3

of Peter" (*Against Heresies* 3.1.2). Again according to Eusebius, Clement of Alexandria (150–215 C.E.) goes so far as to suggest that Mark recorded Peter's words while Peter was still alive (*History of the Church* 6.14.6) and that Peter "ratified the writing for reading in the Churches" (*History of the Church* 2.15.2). In still another passage, Clement states that "Mark, the follower of Peter, while Peter was preaching publicly the gospel at Rome in the presence of certain of Caesar's knights and was putting forward many testimonies concerning Christ, being requested by them that they might be able to commit to memory the things that were being spoken, wrote from the things which were spoken by Peter the Gospel which is called according to Mark" (*Adumbrations in 1 Peter 5:13*). Origen (185–254 C.E.) also supports the Papias tradition by citing verse 13 in the first letter of Peter, where he speaks of "Mark my son." In addition, the anonymous Anti-Marcionite Prologue to Mark's Gospel, arguably going back to the second century, speaks of Mark as "Peter's interpreter" and says that "after the death of Peter himself he wrote down this same gospel in the regions of Italy."[2] By the fourth century the tradition seems to have been well accepted: Jerome (347–420 C.E.) paraphrases Eusebius's quote from Papias (although he changes Papias' venue from Phrygia to Alexandria; *Commentary on Matthew, Book 4, Prosemium 6*).[3]

Many modern scholars have assessed the evidence as too fragmentary to be reliable and dismissed it, frequently suggesting that the early church was disposed to use any evidence that connected a gospel to one of the apostles. Recently W. R. Telford dismissed the Papias tradition on internal grounds as well, saying that "the author of our text shows unfamiliarity with the geography of Palestine . . . Jewish customs . . . and even the Jewish leadership groups . . . and offers harsh criticism of Jews and Judaism."[4] Yet others have continued to find the tradition persuasive. Vincent Taylor, for example, in his classic commentary on Mark, says in his preface that he finds the Papias tradition "so sound, that if we did not possess it, we should be compelled to postulate something very much like it."[5] Martin Hengel writes:

> Presumably this tradition from Papias and Irenaeus rests on an old tradition which we can trust. For the usual explanation, that Papias' note about Mark was meant to guarantee the apostolic derivation of the Second Gospel, is not convincing. His comments on Mark (and on Matthew) are far too detached and critical for that.[6]

Moreover, in respect to internal evidence, Taylor comments: "The Semitic background of Mark is unmistakable and the only questions for consideration are whether the Gospel is a translation of an Aramaic original or whether the Greek suggests dependence on Aramaic tradition."[7] In addition, Hengel asserts: "There can be no question that Mark . . . reproduces the 'historical contours' of Palestinian Judaism before the destruction of the temple more accurately than the later evangelists."[8]

Persisting as part of the Christian tradition, the Papias testimony demands, I think, at least to be considered. We have, after all, nothing else to offer in its place: either one accepts the testimony that Mark composed on the basis of Peter's teachings and preachings or one acknowledges that one has no idea who composed the work at hand.

The testimony in question is admittedly a complex series of quotes within quotes. What we actually possess is Eusebius's partial citation of Papias, who in turn cites the brief opinion of an unknown "John the Elder" (or Presbyter), to the effect that

> Mark, having become the interpreter of Peter, wrote down accurately whatever he remembered of the things said or done by the Lord, however not in order. For neither did he hear the Lord nor did he follow him, but afterwards, as I said, Peter, who adapted his teachings to the needs [of the hearers], but not as though he were drawing up a connected account of the Lord's oracles. So then Mark made no mistake in thus recording some things just as he remembered them, for he made it his care to omit nothing that he had heard and to make no false comment therein. (*History of the Church* 3.39.15)[9]

Even those who readily accept the idea that Peter might have had a scribe named "Mark" find phrases here that are troubling: What is meant by calling Mark Peter's *interpreter* (*ermeneutes*)? Why the lack of chronological order? (And is that Mark's lack of order, or Peter's, or both?) And what is implied by saying that Peter "adapted his teachings to the needs" (*pros tas chreias epoieito tas didaskalias*)? And is it correct to assume that "his hearers" are what he was adapting to? These questions are clearly linked to the further questions of where, when, and why Mark composed.

Where, When, and Why?

Those who accept the Papias tradition have searched the New Testament for further evidence that Mark and Peter were historically linked. Like Origen, many cite the verse in 1 Peter where he speaks of Mark as "my son." In addition, they point to the passage in Acts where Peter visits the home in Jerusalem of "John whose other name was Mark" (Acts 12:12) and the further one where "Barnabas and Saul returned to Jerusalem and brought with them John, whose other name was Mark" (Acts 12:25). Telford (along with others), however, points to contrary evidence: 1 Peter is now widely regarded as pseudonymous and so "the most that can be said is that it too witnesses to a late first-century or early second-century tradition that associated the apostle with a 'Mark.'" Telford suggests that Papias might even have been speculating on the basis of 1 Peter.[10] Others note that "Markos" was such a common Greek name that one cannot be certain that any of the other New Testament references to "Mark" (or "John Mark") indicate the same person as the composer of the Gospel.[11]

Both sides of the argument have some merit and neither one has certainty. Subjectivity enters the argument in connection with the scholar's view of the Jewishness of the Gospel. Telford, who finds Mark's Gospel to be "harsh" in its attitude toward Jews and Judaism, cannot easily relate it to Peter; Taylor and Hengel, who find it to be rooted in Judaism, see the link with Peter to be highly plausible.

These divergent assessments carry over into the theories regarding the Gospel's provenance. Those who link the Gospel to Peter tend to place its composition in Rome, where 1 Peter is thought to have been written—largely because of the assumption that the "Babylon" of its final greeting (from "your sister church in Babylon") must refer to Rome. They find support in the Anti-Marcionite Prologue's reference to Italy, Clement of Alexandria's elaborate suggestion of "Caesar's knights" asking for written testimony concerning Christ, and the fact that Irenaeus gives the founding of the church in Rome and the preaching of both Peter and Paul as the context for the writing of Matthew's Gospel. Irenaeus concludes: "And after the death of these Mark, the disciple and interpreter of Peter, also transmitted to us in writing the things preached by Peter" (*Against Heresies* 3.1.2.). Irenaeus does not exactly say that Mark did the transmitting in Rome, but many draw that inference. Telford, who does not link Mark with Peter, lists Galilee, Antioch, and Syria as alternative possibilities, arguing for each one on the basis of internal evidence and concluding that "while Rome is still the most popular of all these alternatives, the question of provenance is clearly still an open one."[12]

The dating of the Gospel has similar circularity. Those who choose to rely on Clement of Alexandria place the date in the lifetime of Peter, while those who prefer to use Irenaeus and the Anti-Marcionite Prologue place it after the death of Peter. Or one could say that how one dates the Gospel from internal evidence determines which statement one uses. Today the most controversial internal evidence centers around the prophecy of the Temple's destruction in Mark 13, and most scholars accordingly date the Gospel shortly before or after the year 70 C.E.

Why Mark wrote the Gospel is obviously related to all this speculation about when and where (and vice versa). Is Mark's Gospel so tied to Peter in Rome that one must assume it was written for an audience similar to that addressed in 1 Peter—that is, Gentile communities of rural Asia Minor? Or to "Caesar's knights," as Clement of Alexandria says? Or could one speculate that Mark's link to Peter has nothing to do with 1 Peter and therefore nothing to do with Rome? Might the link suggest instead "the Jerusalem church" (Acts 15) or at least a Jewish audience?

Taylor comments that "there is nothing strange in the supposition that in the earliest Jerusalem days Mark heard the Apostle tell of the events of the ministry and death of Jesus."[13] This view coincides with Taylor's internal findings that "the Semitic background of Mark is unmistakable" and that "Mark's Greek is 'translation-Greek' or at least is strongly coloured by Aramaic tradition."[14] Similarly Hengel, who also trusts Papias, finds linguistic evidence that Mark was a Jew: "He was a Greek-speaking Jewish Christian who also understood Aramaic. I do not know any other work in Greek which has as many Aramaic or Hebrew words and formulae in so narrow a space as does the second Gospel."[15] Telford, on the other hand, who does not trust Papias, asserts that "the Gospel was written in Greek with Gentiles in mind." He proceeds to offer as proof the very Arámaic translations (3:17; 5:41; 7:11; 7:34; 14:36; and 15:22, 34)[16] that Taylor and Hengel see as evidence of Mark's Aramaic mindset. In other words, all three critics ultimately rely on the same internal evidence but evaluate it differently.

It is worth pausing over this difference in evaluation. Those who think the translated Aramaic words are proof of a Gentile audience argue that it is obvious that if the author felt the need to explain Aramaic meanings, then his audience could not have been Jewish (or at least not Palestinian). Those on the other side of the argument put these words together with the numerous semitisms of Mark's style and think that altogether they indicate that the author's primary language was Aramaic, which, despite a later translation into Greek, comes through as in a palimpsest.

Those who argue for a Gentile milieu make a lot of the strange passage at the beginning of chapter 7 where Mark purports to be explaining Jewish customs to a Gentile audience:

> For the Pharisees, and all the Jews, do not eat unless they have washed themselves [with the] fist [*sic*] carrying out the tradition of the elders, and they do not eat from the marketplace, unless they immerse themselves, and there are many other traditions which they carry out, the immersing of cups and pots and bronze vessels [and beds]. (7:3–4)[17]

This literal translation indicates, just to begin with, how fraught the text is with obscure phrases and ideas. No one knows what to do with the word for "fist": "with the" is sometimes added to make grammatical sense, or some translators simply interpret and turn this into "wash their hands." Similarly the last phrase, "and beds," seems nonsensical and is usually omitted. What is even stranger is the fact that the verb used for the washing of cups and pots (as well as for people) is *baptizō*: since Mark uses *baptizō* at the beginning of his work to indicate a ritual of repentance and change of heart (1:4, 8), is it likely that he would have applied it to the washing of pots? Of course a writer unfamiliar with Greek might have confused *baptizō* with *baptō*, which is the the general word for covering something with fluid, but it is worth noting that the usual Greek word for the Jewish ritual of washing is *aponizō* or *aponiptō*—as in Matthew 27:24. All these peculiarities have led many scholars to conclude that this passage did not come from Mark but was interpolated at a later time, and by a Gentile author who was himself so ignorant of Jewish rituals that he did not know how to explain them intelligently.[18] Most translations recognize the problems inherent in the passage by placing it in parentheses, and there is no question but that the text reads more coherently if one omits verses 2b–4.[19] Some scholars have used this passage as an indication that Mark was addressing a Gentile audience, but it seems poor evidence to use as the basis for proving the provenance of the Gospel.

At the same time, the underlying semitisms often provide a key to theological meaning. Thus, for example, when Jesus invites his disciples to "come apart into a desert place [or wilderness] and rest awhile" (6:31), it is worth knowing that the word for "rest" in the sense of leisure is rarely found in classical Greek: Mark's use of it in that sense, particularly in conjunction with the "wilderness," suggests that he is thinking of the *Sabbath rest* in the book of Exodus.[20] Or to give another example, when Jesus instructs the crowd to sit before he feeds them with the five loaves, Mark's words are literally as follows: "And he commanded them all to recline in meal-sharing groups upon the green grass. And they reclined in garden-plots by hundreds and by fifties" (6:39–40). Here the repeated word *recline* suggests the symbolic posture of those eating a Passover meal, a connotation reinforced by their gathering in "meal-eating groups."[21] The strange and unusual word "garden-plots" does not seem to make much sense in Greek but arguably would be suggestive in Hebrew of the garden of Genesis. The repetitious phrasing here, in which the second verse offers a slight variation on the first ("garden-plots" for "green grass" and "hundreds and fifties" for "meal-eating groups"), is typical of the couplets of Hebrew verse.[22]

We cannot be sure of the language of the orginal because the earliest extant manuscript dates from the fourth century. It is possible (although not provable) that it was translated by someone other than the author or that the author wrote it one way and later translated it himself. These suppositions seem to be supported by the fact that Mark's Greek is crude while his narrative design is sophisticated. Is it possible that the same author could have composed so brilliantly on one level and so poorly on another?[23] An argument can certainly be made that whoever wrote it in Greek was not comfortable with the language and continued to think in Aramaic. Why, then, he would have written in Greek at all is also a matter of speculation: Was it because of his specific audience, or because the church at large had become mostly Gentile, or because Greek was the language of the educated? Whatever the reason, it is particularly striking that he did not express himself in classical Greek but in the language of the common people: in *koine* Greek—a word that means both "common" and "unclean." When one considers (as we will later) how much Mark stresses Jesus' outreach to those labled as "unclean," one wonders: could the use of koine Greek have been not just a practical but also a *theological* choice?

Why one thinks Mark wrote is further connected, inevitably, to *how* one evaluates the way he wrote. To return to Papias's statement about the Gospel's lack of order, Taylor, like Hengel, assumes that the comments about Mark's lack of order are disparaging ones; unlike Hengel, however, he suggests that Papias is making excuses for Mark by noting that he himself was not an eyewitness and that Peter had concerns other than chronology.[24] Underlying the whole discussion, of course, is the assumption that chronological order is the normal, expected one. Thus Taylor and Hengel (and also Papias and the Elder) assume that the genre of Mark's work requires a chronological record of events. What if, however, Mark composed in a genre where chronology was not important?

Similarly, the phrase describing Mark as Peter's "interpreter" is troubling to those who assume that Mark should be slavishly recording Peter's words, not elaborating on them. Some would even turn "interpreter" into "translator" in order to make the phrase more acceptable to modern norms. But what if Mark was following a custom different from the ones known to Western history?

Finally, the statement about Peter's "adaptation" of his teachings to "the needs" is susceptible to different understandings. Does it mean that he addressed the needs of his audience, or of the particular situation at hand, or, more generally, of the times? Did he "adapt" his actual teaching or his method of presenting it? Any kind of adaptation may seem a bit laissez-faire to those used to dogmatic authority, but what if Peter's flexible approach was rooted in a different kind of teaching (or preaching) than the ones we know? In short, the questions of Mark's identity and the Gospel's provenance are inextricably linked to the question of genre, and in the circular pattern of evidence that I have been following, the answer to that, too, depends on how one reads the internal evidence. As I begin to present my own speculations and hypothesis, I ask the reader to understand that I can be no more historically certain than any other reader of Mark and that it will take me the rest of the book to provide all the internal evidence that I think supports my conclusion.

What Is the Gospel?

One of the most thorough studies of the genre of the gospels was undertaken in recent years by Richard Burridge.[25] He comes to different conclusions from this book, but he begins with a discussion of genre that is extremely helpful. He traces the different theories of the gospel genre in the last century, noting the shifts in focus from the text in itself (the form critics) to the author (the redaction critics) to the reader (the proponents of reader-response theory).[26] He also gives the broad outline of genre theory in general, from the classical period to the twentieth century, pointing out the change from prescriptive to descriptive approaches.[27] He notes the modern preference for speaking of rhetorical "conventions" rather than rules and for subsequently translating conventions into "expectations." Citing the work of E. D. Hirsch, Jr., who calls genre "a system of expectations,"[28] and applying this statement to the gospels, Burridge comments succinctly: "Very different expectations will arise from considering their genre as lectionary or aretology."[29] He is accordingly insistent on the importance of identifying the genre of a work in order to understand it, citing Alistair Fowler: "It is an instrument not of classification or prescription, but of meaning."[30] In further assessing the nature of genre, he argues that every genre involves literary relationships between one work and a kindred family of works, and that a genre must always be set in its historical context so that one can determine "which genres were actually available at the time."[31] I find all this discussion a helpful reminder that the question of the gospel's genre should not be bypassed but needs to be addressed. Thus while I disagree with Burridge's conclusion that the gospel genre is Graeco-Roman biography, I propose to use his principles to lead the reader in a different direction.

One of the most penetrating comments about genre is Fowler's observation that "in reality genre is much less of a pigeon hole than a pigeon."[32] Fowler's comment highlights the organic nature of a genre, the way it embodies a whole culture. Chaucer dramatizes this fact in his *Canterbury Tales* by making each pilgrim incarnate the genre he chooses as the vehicle of his story. Thus the Knight, for example, not only tells a tale of courtly love but exemplifies the perspectives of the genre in his very being, while the Miller's ribald parody similarly encapsulates the attitudes of his whole way of life. Chaucer dealt with whole pigeons. To put it another way, one might say that while every genre expresses itelf through particular rhetorical forms, it cannot be narrowly reduced to them, because it also embraces a whole frame of reference—that is, the frame that gives ultimate meaning to the culture that produces it.

What was the cultural frame of reference that produced the composition of Mark? Most would agree, I think, that it was first and foremost *religious*. No one proposes that Mark was a purely secular document; therefore, it does not make sense to look to a genre that comes from a purely secular context. If that can be agreed upon, the next question arises: Where did the religious framework come from? There was a period in the nineteenth century, as Burridge notes, when Christian scholars insisted that the gospel writings were sui generis, but a developed sense of the nature and function of language has led modern scholars (like Burridge himself) to discard that theory on the grounds that no literary work is created ex nihilo: rather it is inevitably related to what has gone before.[33] What religious framework, then, most naturally provided the matrix for Mark's composition? Burridge argues that the Graeco-Roman biography was a genre available in the first century. But was it available as a vehicle for *religious thought*? Certainly not to religious Jews, who had a different religious heritage to draw on. Nor was it the obvious mode to Greeks and Romans as a vehicle for religious reflection: for that, they had traditions of philosophy and mythology.

To take the argument to its most extreme, let us assume that Mark was a Gentile writing for Gentiles: even then it seems improbable that he would have departed so totally from his tradition as to choose, as a vehicle for theology, a genre usually associated with secular purposes. Even supposing that he was a Gentile stretching the boundaries of his tradition, yet it seems more likely that he would have stayed within the general expectations of his world and composed something recognizably philosophical or mythological. But I do not think that any Christian scholar today would argue that Mark's composition is either one of those.

On the other hand, suppose that Mark was either a Jew trying to express himself theologically or a Gentile trying to communicate what he had learned from a Jewish teacher. What religious genres would he have had at hand?

A study of first-century Judaism discloses that all religious Jewish composition of the time (both oral and written) was oriented toward Scripture; further, it tended to imitate the genres found within the Bible. Thus a religious Jew had a wide range of rhetorical forms available, from chronological narrative to poetry, prophecy, and parable. At the same time, the overarching cultural framework informed every genre with a scriptural perspective. This framework and this mix of rhetorical forms aptly describe what we find in the Gospel of Mark. Moreover, when one considers that Jesus and his first followers were Jews, it seems unthinkable that they would have presented religious teaching in a rhetorical form separated, and even alienated, from their own religious, biblical culture. Nor does it seem likely that the earliest follower to set down these teachings would have done so either. With these general thoughts about genre in mind, Papias's statement needs to be revisited.

Papias Revisited

Earlier I noted that there are certain aspects to Papias's statement
that have troubled even its adherents: namely, that Mark was Peter's
"interpreter," that Mark recorded what Peter remembered about the
sayings and doings of Jesus but "not in order," and that Peter in fact
"adapted" his teachings "to the needs" of either his audience or the
moment and did not present them "as though he were drawing up
a connected account of the Lord's oracles." And I also suggested
earlier that the questions raised about these phrases indicate that the
commentator (from Papias himself to Hengel) had different expectations of Mark's document. If we accept Hirsch's definition of
genre as "a system of expectations," then we must also consider that
all these commentators, from the second century to the present,
have been expecting a different genre. But, as I intend to show, all
the words that Papias uses, while not fitting the Graeco-Roman idea
of history or biography or philosophy or chronicle of any kind, are
aptly descriptive of Jewish religious thought in the first century.

First of all, when Papias refers to Mark as Peter's *interpreter*, he
is using a word that Nehemiah uses about Ezra (Neh. 8:8) and that
is often cited by Jewish scholars as referring to midrashic (that is,
Jewish hermeneutical) practices. Second, when Papias differentiates
Mark's style from the chronological ordering he expected, he describes a contrast that suggests the difference between the Western
idea of the historical genre as the *factual record* of events, and the
Jewish idea of the historical genre as an *interpretation* of them. Finally, when Papias describes Peter's preaching as a matter of "adapting his teaching to the needs," he gives a description that does not
match the Graeco-Roman notion of logically ordered exposition but
does describe the Jewish exegetical practices of the first century,
where the aim was to *adapt* one's preaching to *the needs* of the
community. If Papias's statement is read carefully, it supports the
view that the composition of Mark's Gospel makes use of the techniques typical of first-century Jewish religious discourse.

Retrieving the Jewish Context

Since virtually nothing is known about the particular author *Mark*,
I have striven instead to retrieve the religious milieu out of which
a composition like "the gospel" might have come. I have accordingly
turned to the religious traditions that were operative in the first
century of the Common Era, and I have studied what Jewish scholars have had to say about their own methods of conveying religious
insights. In so doing, I encountered the theological discourse of
midrash, generally unfamiliar to Christians and in the last century
almost lost as an exegetical method even to Jews.[34] I am aware that

in referring to midrash as a way of doing *theology*, I am using a term that is conventionally applied to the Christian study of God and is not usually used by Jews. I use it deliberately here (and in my subtitle) to suggest that this Jewish way of talking about God, while quite different from the Christian method of erecting a schema or system of concepts about God, is nonetheless a form of theological speech and should be recognized as such. While it has been natural for Christian readers to assume that the first followers of Jesus received catechetical instruction in a systematic, conceptual way,[35] it seems to me that they might rethink this assumption if they were familiar with the theological thought-patterns of first-century Judaism. Because I believe understanding midrash is a key to understanding Mark's Gospel, I think it warrants some detailed description.

What Is Midrash?

Midrash is the term Jews use for their most ancient way of interpreting the Bible. It is a difficult term to pin down because it is used in different ways in different contexts. Geoffrey Hartman notes that the term indicates "both the genre of biblical exegesis and compilations of it."[36] The compilations of "the Midrash" are Rabbinic texts that date from the fourth century C.E. and later. The genre "midrash," however, may refer to hermeneutical techniques and attitudes that first appear in the Bible itself and then are reproduced in the "Oral Torah," which interpreted the Bible from the time of Ezra in the fifth century B.C.E. What complicates the understanding of midrash as a genre is the fact that in the process of interpreting Scripture, it mimics its various forms. Thus what is most surprising to one trained in Christian exegesis is the fact that this kind of interpretation is not directly expository but makes use of the whole range of the Bible's own narrative and poetic and even riddling shapes. Michael Fishbane speaks of midrash as a kind of "imagination,"[37] thus transcending any narrow discussion of midrash as conforming to a set of rules or conventions, and suggesting how it indicates a way of reading Scripture and even a way of reading life.

In this book I use the term in all three senses—texts, techniques, imagination. When I cite Rabbinic texts, I do so with caution, aware that their content might be anachronistic. I use them for the most part to exemplify hermeneutical techniques, about which I feel on more certain ground, basing my confidence on Fishbane's argument for "inner-biblical exegesis," his perception that "the Hebrew Bible has an exegetical dimension in its own right" and is "the repository of a vast store of hermeutical techniques which long preceded early Jewish exegesis."[38] But first and foremost, I emphasize midrash as a kind of imagination because grasping it that way, I think, engenders an understanding of it as a cultural frame rather than as just a series of rhetorical strategies. Indeed, I think that those scholars who have dismissed the idea that Mark's Gospel belongs to the midrashic tradition have done so without a full understanding of the kind of imaginative theology it represents.[39] How, then, does it form "a kind of imagination"?

Midrash as a Kind of Theological Imagination

Michael Fishbane introduces his monumental work on biblical interpretation with the observation that "[o]ne of the most remarkable features of the great world religions is the emergence to independent dignity of traditions and commentaries which supplement the original authoritative teachings." In this context he goes on to suggest that *interpretation* is, in itself, "a cultural form of the first magnitude . . . transforming the foundational revelations" of one group into those of another."[40] As he proceeds to talk about the Jewish practices of interpreting Scripture, he in fact touches on something much larger—namely, the Jewish attitude toward interpretation, which extends it from technique to a whole way of thinking and being. What Fishbane points out, not only in this work but in subsequent articles and books, and with increasing clarity, is that Jews have never received God's word uncritically; each faith-community within Judaism has made the word its own by interpreting it anew for its own context. This reinterpretation of the text, Fishbane shows, is also creative, resulting not only in new laws but new narratives. The impulse to appropriate (or reappropriate) meaning, he suggests, underlies both biblical composition and the community's response to it.

There are three key elements in Fishbane's analysis of this process of reappropriation. The first is the principle of intertextuality: he perceives each biblical text building on another through conscious allusion and deliberate reworking of narrative.[41] In terms of an immediate hermeneutic, this perception changes the way we regard certain peculiarities of the biblical text: verbal echoes, repeating images, or reworked narratives are not seen as accidents of random authorship or textual happenstance but rather as conscious patterns of design. The nature of Scripture is shown to be self-reflexive, constantly echoing and reinterpreting itself.

The second key element is what Fishbane calls "the religious duty . . . to *reactualize* the ancient word of God for the present hour."[42] The term *reactualization* comprehends both the role of history and the theological belief that God's purpose, transcending time, is reenacted in different moments in history, albeit in differing ways. Thus the intertextuality involved is not the simple act of a community taking over an old tradition and making it its own; rather, it is a creedal gesture—the act of acknowledging that God continues to act in history and indeed is acting now, making this moment God's own. In this view, two versions of the same story (e.g., the exodus) are not to be taken as a random collation but rather regarded as purposeful interpretations; an altered or even conflicting use of an original story is not seen as a careless or repudiating appropriation but rather as a way of showing how, in spite of differences, past word and present moment are relevant to one another.[43] Scripture and history are constantly intersecting, each disclosing new meanings through, and for, the other.

The act of perceiving this intersection is interpretive, theological, and innovative all at once. It is theological discourse expressed as new narrative or the reworking of metaphor. It is a theological response to Scripture that becomes itself Scripture. Thus the third key element in Fishbane's thesis is the recognition that interpretation "partakes of the sanctity of Scripture even as it further reveals it." In fact, as Fishbane ponders the implications of sacred interpretation generating new sacred text, he is moved to ask, "Do we in fact cross a great divide from the Hebrew Bible to its rabbinic interpreters, or is the foundation text already an interpreted document—despite all initial impressions to the contrary?"[44] In effect, he is asking if the Bible contains an *uninterpreted* word.

The question reverberates, in itself opening up new horizons of meaning, not only within the biblical text but within the faith-communities that are engaged with it. Once said, the truth of the observation appears transparent: of course God's word cannot be fully received by any single individual or faith-community; human reception is always limited, imperfect, interpretive. The written text necessarily involves a hermeneutic; the "received text" is an interpreted text. Those of us who struggle to interpret the text for our own time are wrestling with a sacred word that is already a sacred interpretation. *Interpretation* becomes the overarching genre of the Bible.

If the Bible is viewed as sacred interpretation of God's word rather than as a perfect transcription, the task of theology changes. It changes because the Bible so understood becomes a model of theological discourse that is *dialogical*, and that perception shifts the focus from isolated meanings to meanings *in relationship*. The midrashic model recognizes that the biblical word does not represent simply the divine speech but rather an exchange between God's word and the human interpreter. On the one hand, it acknowledges God's word as the overarching context, the primary frame of reference and essential orientation; on the other, it recognizes that the human speakers of the word have heard its truth in a particular moment, in a particular community, in relation to a specific act or moral choice. To interpret the word again in the present requires struggling both with past meaning and with immediate context.

Underlying the struggle is the tacit acknowledgment that human words are always limited and human hearing always partial. No single interpretation can thus be considered final; midrashic hermeneutic allows for a never-ending conversation between God and humanity. Implicit as well in this conversational model is the recognition that God is ceaselessly disclosing new meanings. Midrashic theology allows for God's ongoing creativity and revelation; it "reflect[s] the dynamic nature of God."[45]

Acknowledgment of this dynamic unfolding simultaneously serves as an invitation to human beings to enter into the dialogue; theological meaning is not seen as fixed and foreclosed but participatory and open-ended. The midrashic model points as well to the need for ongoing conversation between one interpreter and another. The act of interpreting, in effect, becomes part of a great conversation that spans the generations.

Midrash as a Way of Reading

Once midrash is grasped in terms of its large implications, one can more readily understand its particular hermeneutical practices. Essentially there are three general ways midrash interprets Scripture: it rewrites the biblical text by changing it not entirely but enough to shift its focus; it creates a new text by mimicking an old one; it juxtaposes different biblical texts, thus exposing either their harmony or their discord and thereby shifting the meaning of the central text.

Midrash is most easily identified when it occurs as the *rewriting* of an earlier biblical narrative or image, such as can be found within the Bible itself: the several versions of the story of the exodus, for example, or the series of rewritings revolving around the land promised to Abraham. Viewed in Genesis as his inheritance (Gen. 15:7), this land becomes variously imaged as the entrance to God's sanctuary (Exod. 15:17) or participation in God's "rest" (Ps. 132:7–8).[46]

Strategies for transforming the biblical text for theological purposes, however, can also take other forms. Fishbane talks about the "ongoing process of legal clarification" evident in subtle additions made to the Decalogue in narratives that, *mimicking the language* of Exodus 20:18–21, "report divine prohibitions of food-gathering (and baking or boiling foods) or wood-gathering on the Sabbath day (Exod. 16:4–27; Num. 15:32–36)."[47]

More subtle still is the example Fishbane cites from 2 Chronicles 15:2–7. In this case, meaning is transformed through the technique of *recontextualization*. The passage is purportedly an oracle delivered to King Asa of Judah by Azzariah ben Oded:

2. "YHWH will be with you when you are with Him: for if you seek Him, He will be present to you; but if you abandon Him, He will

abandon you. 3. Now for a long time Israel was without a true God, without an instructing priest and without Torah. 4. But when in distress Israel turned to YHWH, God of Israel, and sought Him, He was present to them. 5. Of those times there was no peace for those who went out or came in [from battle] for tremendous disturbances assailed the inhabitants of the lands. 6. And nations and cities smashed each other to bits, for God confounded them with every distress. 7. But now: be you strong and do not slacken: for there is recompense for your deeds."

Fishbane explains how this passage, which to the uninitiated might look like a single speech, has in fact "woven together several strands of tradition."[48] Both the opening words, "YHWH will be with you," and the closing words, "be you strong," he suggests, echo earlier sources, where the exhortation is to enter military service. In this case, however, the speaker is not promoting a military lifestyle—in fact, being in a state of battle seems to be a metaphor for being confounded by God. Instead, he is exhorting his reader to seek God and to study Torah so that God "will be present to you." Fishbane concludes: "The old military language has been thoroughly subordinated, even transformed, by being juxtaposed to spiritual-covenantal concerns."[49] At the same time, I might add, the spiritual-covenantal concerns are given a special urgency by the old military frame.

It is easy to observe the transformation of a text through its reformulation, but perceiving its transformation by means of its *juxtaposition to other texts* requires both memory of the whole Bible (the legacy of an oral culture) and the poetic imagination to grasp how the mere arrangement of parts can convey meaning. For this exegetical strategy to work, the reader also has to understand how brief allusions can serve to evoke whole passages or biblical books, or, in Fishbane's words, how allusions function as "metonyms."[50] Midrash, therefore, must also be understood in terms of its rhetorical effects.

Midrash as a Way of Writing

There are several kinds of rhetorical effects one can expect from midrashic writing, all of which serve to link one biblical text with another. In addition to using biblical allusions and echoes as interpretive metonyms, the midrashist may interpret by means of repeating keywords, by tallying words from different contexts, by creating a "lexicon" through the juxtaposition of harmonious passages on the same theme, or by creating a dialectic through the juxtaposition of those that are discordant.

Illustrating the last technique, Daniel Boyarin discusses the midrash on Exodus 15.22: "And Moses removed Israel from the Red Sea." The biblical text calls for comment because it seems to contradict earlier texts in which God is always in command. Rabbi

Eliezer gives two different interpretations. In his first interpretation he suggests that God continues to remain in command and the verse in question is only there to emphasize the people's faith in Moses. He does not say this directly but presents his interpretation by bringing together two other texts: first, an earlier passage in Exodus where, when God tells the people to return and retrace their steps, the Midrash attributes their obedience to the leadership of Moses, and second, a passage in Jeremiah that praises the people for their faithfulness in the desert. In his second interpretation R. Eliezer juxtaposes an entirely different set of texts (Num. 14:4 and Neh. 9:17–18) that in effect suggest that the phrase means "Moses led them with a stick against their wills."

Boyarin summarizes the significance of Eliezer's contradictory readings by pointing out that they faithfully mirror the contradictory traditions about Israel in the desert (Israel as faithful, Israel as faithless) that are found within the Bible itself. He points out that the contradictory *midrashim* constitute a dialectic centered on the word *return*: in one sense to be taken as a word of faith as contextualized in Exodus 14.4 and Jeremiah 2.2; in another sense to be taken as a word of rebellion as contextualized by Numbers 14.4 and Nehemiah 9.17–18. Thus, he suggests, the dialectic of Eliezer is not sophistry but "an echo of the dual voices of the Torah and of its interpretive traditions within the canon."[51]

What the example shows most clearly is that no one sentence can be excerpted from a midrashic text as the full explication. Midrash does not seek to lock up the text in neat explanations but to unlock its rich ambiguity. Boyarin suggests that it is by reenacting the "axiological ambiguity of the biblical story" that midrash serves to create structures that are simultaneously disruptive and regenerative.[52] Midrash performs this function not by glossing over the "double-voiced" text but by revealing it:

> Looked at from a literary-critical perspective (synchrony) rather than a literary-historical perspective (diachrony) the text is polyphonic. Built into its very structure is contradiction and opposition. Here and all through the canon, there is a dialogue of voices evaluating the wilderness period, a voice which proclaims that it was the time of the greatest love of Israel for her God and a voice which cries out that under the very marriage canopy, as it were, Israel was unfaithful to her Groom. Each tanna [rabbinic interpreter] hears only one of these voices.[53]

Boyarin suggests that by exposing the many voices of the text, midrash disrupts the domination of any single voice and preserves "the polyphony of the Torah."[54]

In addition, as a byproduct of these juxtapositions, the midrashist may create a third narrative that is plotlike in shape but exegetical in origin and purpose. The prototype of this "third narrative" is the parable, or *mashal*. Examples of all of these rhetorical effects can be found in Rabbinic texts, especially those of midrashic homilies.

In the linking techniques of the midrashic homily, seemingly unrelated verses are brought together through the tallying of keywords or catch-words—a process that seems to be the vestige of a time when transmission was committed to memory.[55] In the written examples that are extant, we find that the opening verses from the Prophets and the Writings are chosen to tally with the reading from the Pentateuch, either thematically or linguistically or both. In one instance, for example, when Numbers 1:1 was the central text— "The Lord spoke unto Moses in the wilderness of Sinai"—the homily was opened by Hosea 2:16: "Therefore, behold, I will allure her, and bring her into the *wilderness* and *speak* tenderly to her."[56]

The words echo, the contexts seemingly conflict: the "wilderness" of Hosea is the place of God's abduction of Israel, the "tender" speech is the meltdown of God's anger; yet the echoing words are a reminder that the first "wilderness" was the locus of God's liberation, and the first laws of the Lord, the beginning of freedom. The homilist, free to choose his opening, tallied words but juxtaposed discordant meanings; the difference-in-sameness points to the many-faceted experience of being God's chosen.

In some cases past homiletic interpretation may have provided a hidden basis for the tally, as in the matching of Exodus 3:1, "Now Moses was keeping the flock of his father-in-law," with Isaiah 40:11, "He will feed his flock like a shepherd." While the verbal tally of "flock" appears to be the only link here, the connection is deepened by a long tradition of imaging Moses as God's surrogate shepherd. Once again the contextual distance between the verses is first apparent; the harmony has to be revealed. This example also shows the homilist reading the texts synchronically, indifferent to the historical order: the passage in which God promises to return his people from exile is placed before the narrative of God's first call to Moses, thus making the later image of God's shepherding color Moses' naive activity.

Between the opening verse (or verses) and the ending one were often a series of other scriptural allusions, strung "like pearls on a string" one on top of the other; the form, called *haruzin* ("beads"), may well also have been developed as an aid to the homilist's memory.[57] In any event they were linked together by the homilist so as to form a narrative "journey," a "plot-like" structure from Prophets to Pentateuch.[58]

Such homilies assumed an audience versed well enough in Scripture to hear the echoes and remember the contexts; the homilist did not spell out the connections but rather engaged his hearers in the process of interpretation.[59] The techniques developed for an oral culture resulted in homilies that stimulated continual theologizing;

the audience as well as the homilist was drawn into wrestling with the implications of the texts. Thus not only was the midrashic homily dialectical in form; it insisted on a dialogical process for speaker and listener alike. The medium was consonant with multiple views and only one message—that of an ongoing dialogue between God and his people.[60]

At the heart of this participatory process was the device of the *mashal*, the exegetical parable (not to be confused with the illustrative parable)—a compact exegetical narrative constructed out of elliptical scriptural allusions, in a compressed way imitating the allusive fabric and the dialectical arrangement of the large homily.[61] Because of its brevity and ellipses, it sometimes appears to be a riddle, more-difficult to understand than the texts it is constructed to elucidate. At other times its succinct narrative form exhibits a deceptive simplicity so that the hearer (reader) is tempted to overlook its complex relationship to the larger homiletical structure. Yet just as that large structure demands an audience alert to scriptural allusion and awake to its tensions, so this microcosmic structure requires theologically sensitive hearers to complete its meaning.

To give an example, the Genesis Rabbah (that is, the Genesis Midrash) contains the story of a king who says to an admirer: "Offer up your son on my table." The admirer brings his son forthwith, knife in hand. At that point the king exclaims, "Did I tell you, 'offer him up'—so as to eat him? I said to you, 'Offer him up'—for love." The story concludes, "This is what is written: 'it never came into my mind.' (Jer. 19:5)—this refers to Isaac" (Gen. R. 56.8).[62] This short story, like the large midrashic homily, juxtaposes a text from the Pentateuch with a text from Jeremiah. To make sense, it requires an audience familiar with the context in Jeremiah as well as with Genesis 22 and also with the longstanding debate within Judaism over the meaning of God's command to Abraham. So much is compressed in these few lines, and so much knowledge of both Scripture and exegesis is assumed, that without such background the story might appear either to be a dark riddle or a simplified parallel to the binding of Isaac. But an audience grasping all its elements would be neither mystified nor talked down to but engaged in a new perspective. The full context from Jeremiah shows God reproaching Israel "Because the people have forsaken me, and have profaned this place by burning incense in it to other gods . . . and have built the high places of Ba'al to burn their sons in the fire as burnt offerings to Ba'al, which I did not command or decree—*it never came into my mind.*" The homiletic effect of the *mashal* lies in the way it compels reflection on the dissonance between Genesis and Jeremiah—a reflection that each audience must further interpret in relation to its own life-context.

Midrash as a Way of Reading Life

The relationship between text and life is the final way the midrashic homily engaged the participation of its audience. In fact, the overriding function of all midrashic activity is consistent with this purpose—to show God's word relevant in changing times. From the differing accounts of the exodus to the pages of Rabbinic dispute, the aim remains the same: to reinterpret God's ancient word according to the exigencies of the present. In this reinterpretation there was always an exchange: a critical situation or event was viewed through the lens of Scripture; the meaning of Scripture was "reactualized" by the exegesis of the event. In the synagogue, the formulaic word for this reactualization was "fulfillment": the reading from the Prophets was introduced as the "fulfillment" of the teaching of Moses.[63] Thus the midrashic homily allowed for the "fulfillment" of God's word not once but many times.

James Kugel suggests that the midrashist takes up the void left by the cessation of prophecy; as "the divine word was increasingly a text," so "God's human intermediaries become by necessity students of old scrolls" and interpreters of the written form of the divine word.[64] Because of this mediating function, the midrashist addresses a community of participating interpreters. Midrash therefore not only fills in gaps left by the text but also works to bridge the gaps between believers. It thus creates not only a dialogue of texts but a conversation among interpreters. This conversation, obviously, is not always one of consensus but often one of conflict. Gerald Bruns asserts that the House [or school] of Midrash "is the place where disputes are meant to go on, where there is always room for another interpretation, or for more dialogue, where interpretation is more a condition of being than an act of consciousness."[65] It is this participatory, argumentative "condition of being" that Bruns sees as particularly defining Jewish identity. It is the overriding importance of communal participation that lead Bruns to assert: "Midrash is not method but form of life."[66]

Is the Midrashic Tradition Relevant to the Gospels?

Are these findings applicable to the Gospels? To answer that question, I need to distinguish between historical data and literary-theological patterns. In respect to historical data, we must acknowledge that we are on uncertain ground. Much of the foregoing analysis is based on Rabbinic texts that postdate the Gospels by one to four centuries. In particular, the synagogue sermon, which David Stern finds "prototypical," is known only from fourth-century examples or later. It is not possible to make a claim of direct kinship between the gospels and the Midrash on strictly historical terms.

On the other hand (as already noted), Jewish scholars see the midrashic tradition starting much earlier than the extant textual evidence indicates. Joseph Heinemann dates the work of the Tannaitic sages from 70 C.E. and places the origin of midrashic narratives "as far back as the middle of the Second Temple period."[67] Kugel pushes back the beginnings even further: "The midrashist's biography could safely begin at the end of the biblical period, in the last few centuries before the common era. But his true genealogy goes back much further, to the time of Israel's great prophets."[68] In fact, Kugel—like Fishbane—sees the elements of midrashic interpretation beginning within the Bible itself.

If we consider that the gospel narrative was composed in a Jewish milieu between the exegetical narratives of the Bible and the exegetical, "plot-like" journeys of the synagogue homily, then it seems not unreasonable to think that Mark's narrative flows within the general stream of midrashic tradition. Jewish scholars have themselves discerned the relationship. In the middle of the last century, David Daube compiled a pioneering book rich in parallels between the content and methods of the New Testament and Rabbinic Judaism.[69] His work illuminates both the Jewish context of much of Jesus' teaching and some of the structures embedded in the gospel narrative. More recently, David Flusser proposed that Jesus' parables and Rabbinic parables share compositional similarities that indicate that they belong to the same genre.[70] David Stern, citing Flusser, issues caveats about not "importing anachronistic ideas into earlier texts" but is sufficiently intrigued by the similarities to devote a number of pages to analyzing the parabolic form of Jesus.[71] Kugel goes so far as to list New Testament texts among his sources for constructing *The Bible As It Was*, noting that they "everywhere bear witness to the exegetical traditions current among Jews in the first century C.E."[72] From his perspective, the New Testament writings are sufficiently Jewish that they can provide evidence of Jewish hermeneutic functioning in the time of Jesus. They belong to the large patterns of Jewish literary-theological discourse.

Jewish Theological Discourse and the Gospel of Mark

To return to Papias one more time in the light of the previous discussion, when Papias calls Mark Peter's "interpreter," could he not be suggesting that Mark was midrashically exegeting what he had heard? When Papias notes that Mark "wrote down accurately whatever he remembered . . . however not in order," could he not be describing (unwittingly) the synchronic order preferred by the midrashist? And when he notes that Peter himself did not "draw up a connected account of the Lord's oracles" but "adapted his teachings to the needs" [of someone or something], could he not be describing the homiletic purpose that organizes so much Jewish exegesis? In any event, it is the intent of this book to demonstrate how Mark's Gospel fits the large literary-theological patterns of the midrashic imagination: in particular, the technique of juxtaposing biblical texts so as to open up new meanings in them, and overall, the theologically imaginative, rhetorical method of creating a plot-like exegetical journey that "reactualizes the word for the present hour."

Connecting With Christian Tradition

Does linking Mark to Jewish religious thought somehow make it less "Christian"? Some Christian scholars (particularly in the nineteenth century) seem to have been disposed to think so. But in the long history of the Christian church, in spite of the polemic, persecutions, pogroms, and Shoah (none of which I wish to overlook, minimize, or sanction) there also recurs the opposite strain of yearning to stay connected to Jewish roots. The evidence, to be sure, is mixed, revealing a house divided; yet for present purposes, I propose reviewing it as a glass half full.

However one views Mark's use of Aramaic words, one must nonetheless conclude from them a desire to stay connected to the language of Jesus and Peter. The New Testament texts outside of Mark reveal a complex relationship, strained to the point of split identity. Matthew's fierce polemic against the Pharisees (23:13–33), for example, is countered by his insistence that Jesus came to fulfill the Torah (5:17–18). The Acts of the Apostles historicizes the protesting alienation from Judaism of the originally Jewish community of Jesus-followers and its controversial turning to Gentile converts. The Gospel of John, which is received today as accusatory of "the Jews," nonetheless frames its narrative with Jewish feasts and even proclaims, at one point, that "salvation is from the Jews" (4:22). Paul, to be sure, when confronted with the question of holding Gentile converts to the whole Mosaic law, contrasted Judaism with Christianity as "the child of the bondwoman" against "the child of the free woman" (Gal. 4:22–31), yet when confronted by the first evidence of Christians boasting of their superiority to Jews, he denounced such triumphalism and proclaimed that Christianity should view itself as "the wild olive branch" grafted onto the original and never-superseded vine of Judaism (Rom. 11:17–18).

The Letter to the Hebrews is a particularly significant example of mixed signals. Platonic terminology allows the author to set up a framework of "real" things and shadowy copies; applying the framework to Scripture, he perceives the first testament as the pale "copy" or "type" of the "reality" to come in the second (8:5; 9:24; 10:1). The base theological worldview is not that of Scripture but of Plato;

the hermeneutic is not one that draws meaning out of the scriptural word but rather one that imposes on it a philosophical consistency. This approach effectively begins the separation of Christian hermeneutic from the common Jewish method of interpreting Hebrew Scripture. As Bruce Chilton has argued, it is a first step toward removing Christianity from its original Jewish ethos.[73] The explicit argument of Hebrews—that Jesus "in speaking of a new covenant . . . treats the first as obsolete" (8:13) or that Jesus "abolishes the first in order to establish the second" (10:9)—thus articulates a repudiation of Judaism that is made possible by its philosophical (rather than its religious) frame. Yet some might argue that the Platonic frame is also the one used by Philo, who might have been the only Jewish writer on Scripture that the Hellenic author knew and understood.[74] In a similarly complex way the letter's chapter 11 holds up as models many names from Hebrew Scripture. If one studies this list carefully, as Pamela Eisenbaum has, one finds that while the author extols these figures, he does so in such a way as to show both their alienation from Israel's history and their inferiority to those of Christian faith.[75] Read closely, this chapter without question demeans Jewish faith. Yet ironically it also functioned to keep some parts of Israel's story in Christian tradition.

Much of second-century Christian thought was galvanized by the proposal of Marcion, who, arguing that the God of the Old Testament was a "god of wrath" in contrast to the "God of love" in the New Testament, wanted to remove the whole of the Hebrew Scripture from the Christian canon. Intuitively denouncing this proposal as heresy, the church fathers then struggled to bolster their intuition. One can read this struggle negatively, noting how much injury they did to the Jewish texts in the process of trying to save them. Or one can look at the other side and see how hard they worked to hold onto their Jewish heritage.

Justin Martyr, educated as a Greek philosopher and unfamiliar with traditional Jewish exegesis, knew no way to counter Marcion except to interpret both testaments as Greek philosophy linked by Logos. Like Barnabas in his Epistle, Justin assumes that this indeed is the only way to interpret Scripture, and so he also disparagingly asserts that Jews have not understood their own sacred texts. Although his most famous exercise in biblical exegesis is titled "*Dialogue* With Trypho," the attitude of superiority he assumes and the gratuitous insults he heaps on his Jewish opponent would be impossible to justify today by any fair-minded standard of interfaith exchange.[76] On the other hand, one could argue that ironically, in spite of its anti-Jewish polemic, the "Dialogue" was nonetheless one of the documents that helped preserve the Jewish Scriptures for the Christian church.

Similarly, when Irenaeus acted to reinstate the sacredness of the Hebrew Bible, he did it a mixed service by using the typological method as the principle of preservation. On the one hand, Irenaeus insisted on there being one and the same God in both testaments, arguing not only against Marcion but also against the Gnostic Valentinians who assigned the writing of the Torah to an inferior divinity called the "demiurge";[77] on the other, he posited that Scripture is a hidden revelation whose meaning is known only to Christians. Believing that all the Scriptures prefigured Christ and that "every prophecy is enigmatic and ambiguous for human minds before it is fulfilled," Irenaeus argued that "[t]his is the reason that the law resembles a fable when it is read by Jews at the present time" (*Against Heresies* 4. 26.1).[78] That argument, on the one hand, certainly demeaned what the Scriptures meant to the Jews; yet on the other, it proclaimed the permanent value of the Torah revelation. One must assume that Irenaeus believed the latter and used the only method he knew to prove it.

In general, the various hermeneutical schools that mark the time of the church fathers reveal a desire to preserve the importance of the Jewish Scriptures. Both the allegorical exegesis of the Alexandrines and the literal-historical exegesis of the Antiochenes take that principle as their point of departure. They did not read the Jewish Bible the way Jews did, yet in a limited way they mimicked Jewish interpretive methods. The patristic habit of interweaving scriptural passages, for example, may owe something to the similar ancient Jewish practice.[79] In Philo's allegorizing of Jewish Scripture, the Alexandrians found a way to bridge their understanding of the revelation they had experienced in Christ with the revelation they affirmed in the Jewish Bible (but did not understand as an independent entity): they made use of Philo's allegorical methods to support their presuppositions about the christocentric meaning of all Scripture. As Philo interpreted Homer through Moses, they interpreted Moses through Christ.

Origen, the best known of the Alexandrians, developed his allegorical system of threefold meanings in Scripture from his initial desire to see both testaments as part of the same spiritual entity. Thinking that in both testaments there are some events that cannot be taken literally, he asserts:

> Because the principal aim was to announce the connection that exists among spiritual events, those that have already happened and those that are yet to come to pass, whenever the Word found that things which had happened in history could be harmonized with these mystical events he used them, concealing from the multitude their deeper meaning." (*First Principles* 4.2.9)[80]

It is important to note that Origen does not find all the historical events to be Jewish and all the mystical ones to be Christian but rather finds both testaments to contain both levels of meaning. He speaks of them together: "from Scriptures that we believe to be divine, the so-called Old as well as the New Testament, we adduce testimonies as witnesses to that which we consider a convincing proof of our statements" (*First Principles* 1.1). Like Irenaeus, he argues directly against the Gnostics, who posit a lesser god as the one "whom the Jews worship" (*First Principles* 2.1). He considers that "the reason for the false opinions, the impious attitudes, and the amateurish talk about God on the part of those groups just mentioned seems to be no other than that Scripture is not understood in its spiritual sense but is interpreted according to the mere letter" (*First Principles* 2.2). He bases his threefold method on Hebrew Scripture itself, citing Proverbs 22:20–21: "And you, write down those things threefold in your counsel and wisdom that you may reply with word of truth to those who ask you" (*First Principles* 2.4). To be sure, when he develops his method, he speaks, like the author of Hebrews, of "the heavenly realities, whose copy and shadow the 'Jews according to the flesh' were worshipping" (*First Principles* 2.6); yet he never suggests that the testament of the Jews is "obsolete" but rather posits "the same Spirit and coming from the same God" in both testaments (*First Principles* 2.9). Striving to keep that unity and yet to acknowledge differences, Origen cites Paul's distinction between "children of the flesh" and "children of God": "'For it is not the children of the flesh who are the children of God', and 'not all who are descended from Israel are Israel'" (Rom. 9:8, 6), and "He is a Jew who is one inwardly, and real circumcision is a matter of the heart; in the spirit, not the letter" (Rom. 2:28–29). Origen comments: "Now, if the criterion for the Jew is found in something inward, we must understand that just as there is a race of the Jews in the flesh, there is also a nation of Jews inwardly, the soul having acquired this noble lineage through certain ineffable words" (*First Principles* 3.6.). One discerns here a clear desire on Origen's part to connect with those who are "inward Jews." He works out the relationship spiritually and anagogically, to be sure, rather than directly or historically, and most Jews would be wary of such a spiritualization of their racial being, yet nonetheless it must be acknowledged he is seeking a connection. Although he uses the Platonic language of "shadow" and "fulfillment," he does not make an invidious contrast between Jews and Christians. When he speaks of Christ's second coming as an "advent" in which "the type of Deuteronomy will find its fulfillment, when all the saints will live by the law of that eternal gospel in the kingdom of heaven" (*First Principles* 3.13), his use of the term "saints" seems to include both.

The Antiochene school reacted against the excesses it found in the Alexandrian methods of allegorical exegesis, insisting, as Diodore of Tarsus does in the prologue to his Commentary on the Psalms, on the importance of "the historical substance and the plain literal sense."[81] At the same time, it allowed for a deeper spiritual meaning that Diodore called *theōria*: "we will not disparage anagogy and the higher *theōria*. For history is not opposed to *theōria*. On the contrary, it proves to be the foundation and the basis of the higher senses . . . [yet] *theōria* must never be understood as doing away with the underlying sense; it would then no longer be *theōria* but allegory." Diodore is scornful of the allegorists:

> Those who pretend to "improve" Scripture and who are wise in their own conceit have introduced allegory because they are careless about the historical substance, or they simply abuse it. They follow not the apostle's intention but their own vain imagination, forcing the reader to take one thing for another. Thus they read "demon" for abyss, "devil" for dragon, and so on.

In the preface to his Commentary on Psalm 118, Diodore explains that Paul's use and application of the word "allegory" is "different from that of the Greeks" who use it "when something is understood in one way but said in another."

Diodore's insistence on keeping the historical level of meaning was not motivated by knowledge of Jewish methods of exegesis (which he reduced to pure literalism), but it had the effect, nonetheless, of preserving the Jewish contexts of the biblical texts. When he comments on Psalms 29 and 84, for example, Diodore is at pains to explain the Jewish setting first: "Historically, Psalm 29 was spoken by Hezekiah at the occasion of his deliverance from an illness and from the threat of war with the Assyrians. . . . In the same way, Psalm 84 was pronounced in the person of those Israelites who had returned from Babylon." Diodore then goes on to apply these psalms to Christians freed from death by "the promised resurrection," but he does not suggest that the second meaning wipes out the first. On the contrary, he argues that each psalm "is a statement adaptable to many situations according to the grace of him who gives it power," and he speaks with deep respect of the Jews who prayed it: "This great, rich, and beautiful psalm was pronounced in the person of the saints in Babylon who were longing to return to Jerusalem on account of the divine laws and the holy mysteries celebrated there, and who were emboldened to make such petitions by their pious lives."

In general, the church fathers from the second through the fourth centuries can be aligned on one side or the other of the allegorical/historical divide. What unites them is the constant desire to find a way to keep the so-called Old Testament for the church. The typology, the allegory, and the *theōria* all arose from this basic impulse. A similar impulse, perhaps, although ironic in its effects, drew some of the early Christian exegetes to develop *testimonia*—books of Old Testament verses topically arranged as prooftexts for Christian faith.

Here indeed is a classic case of the house divided: on the one hand, these books were used polemically to demean Jewish faith; yet they provided still another method of maintaining the Jewish Scriptures in Christian tradition.

Tyconius the Donatist, who influenced Augustine, made use of these *testimonia* in writing his *Book of Rules* for reading Scripture. In his case, the resulting hermeneutic is one that attempts to separate two orders of being, that of "the law" from that of "the promise" or "faith." Tyconius does not, however, disparage those who live according to the law. On the contrary, he asks, "Who would be so impious, so inflated by senseless pride as to assert that Moses, the prophets, and all the saints (of old) did not fulfill the law or were not justified?" (3.1)[82] He quotes Paul in Romans 4:21 exclaiming "Is then the law contrary to the promise? By no means!" and he comments: "We see that the law does not touch the promise. Rather than impinging upon one another, each of the two preserves its own order. For just as the law never hindered faith, so faith never destroyed the law" (3.3). At length Tyconius makes it clear that he equates "the law" with "works," and "faith" or "the promise" with grace. He thinks that no one can be justified by works alone (3.12), but he also believes that grace has always been present—in the Israelites as well as after Christ (3.9). He goes on to make a distinction similar to Origen's between those who are Jews of the flesh and those who are inwardly Jews, saying: "not all who are from Abraham are children of Abraham, and not all who are from Israel are Israel . . . but the only seed of Abraham were those who, like Isaac, were children of faith and promise" (3.21, 22). The argument is badly strained, but in its tension we can discern a tremendous struggle to justify the writer's own belief in the order of Christian grace without cutting himself off from those whom he perceives as his forefathers in faith.

Jerome and Augustine, those two great doctors of the early church, further illustrate this continuing theme. Jerome began as an allegorist but, under the influence of the school of Antioch, came to insist on "the Hebrew truth" of Scripture. Augustine, on the other hand, was initially turned off from Christianity because he was repelled by the literalistic reading of the Hebrew Bible given by the Manichees; he was converted by Ambrose's allegorical exegesis. Yet in the end, Augustine, too, came to allow for literal as well as figurative levels of meaning and to insist on the need to understand the context of the author. He eventually formulated the essential criterion for reading Scripture that should reverberate through any mode of exegesis—the "rule of faith," which demands that all interpretation serve the two great commandments of love of God and love of neighbor.

To return to the original question—Does linking Mark to Jewish religious thought somehow make it less "Christian"?—I hope even this brief survey will show that on the contrary, the search for that link is an essential part of early Christian tradition. The way I propose to argue for that link will be different from that of the church fathers, because the studies of the past century have provided modern exegetes with greater understanding of Judaism itself, of Jewish exegesis, and of the Jewish contexts in which the Gospel took shape. Similarly, the desire to preserve the Jewish roots of the Gospel has different motivation today from that in the early centuries of the church, yet my search for the Gospel's Jewish origins is not unrelated to the tradition of Irenaeus, Origen, Diodore, and Tyconius. As Jerome sought "the Hebrew truth" of what he called the "Old" Testament, so this book seeks the Hebrew truth of the New. In so doing, it also strives to follow Augustine's general rule that exegesis serve the love of neighbor and his particular suggestion that the exegete attempt some dialogue with the mind of the author by searching out the context of his words.

Dialoguing With the Text

In trying to elucidate the Gospel of Mark, I am trying to follow the principle that is basic to interreligious dialogue—that is, to seek to understand the other according to that person's self-understanding. That principle, in turn, has yielded two components of hermeneutical method: retrieval and dialogue. By *retrieval* I mean the attempt to rediscover what this text might have meant to its original author and audience; by *dialogue* I mean the attempt to relate to that original meaning in ways that involve openness to a different culture and an exchange between the past and the present.

Both terms need further clarification. In contemporary discussion the "hermeneutics of retrieval" is paired with the "hermeneutics of suspicion," the implication being that the current reader is "suspicious" that some later interpretations may have obscured, in various ways and for various reasons, the essential or original meaning of the text, which now stands in need of being "retrieved" for the present.[83] Although the phrasing suggests the opposite, David Tracy describes this hermeneutical attitude toward Scripture as in fact a profound act of *trust*—that is, "to do so is to trust that the Spirit is present to the church in spite of the church's errors."[84] Tracy further links this trust to the "risk" that Hans-Georg Gadamer implies is undertaken by the good interpreter, the "to-and-fro" movement that constitutes both "game" and "conversation" with the text.[85]

"Suspicion" and "retrieval" are part of this "to-and-fro" movement. "Suspicion" functions first: before the conversation between text and interpreter can take place, the interpreter must try to "locate the systemic distortions in both the preunderstanding of the interpreter and in the classic texts and traditions of the culture."[86]

Nonetheless, what will be "retrieved" is always at risk: "As in any genuine conversation, one cannot determine the outcome before the actual interpretation," and

> once that concrete interpretation begins, all earlier situational analyses are also put at risk by the conversation itself. It is not only our present answers but also our questions which are risked when we enter a conversation with a classic text. . . . There is no way, prior to the conversation itself, to determine the "correct" theological interpretation of the biblical texts.[87]

Further complicating the conversation is the theologian's need "to establish mutually critical correlations between an interpretation of the Christian tradition and an interpretation of the contemporary situation"[88] and to make this correlation between text and present need as a believing member of a faith community. Tracy also believes that this open and multilevel conversation must take place with reference to a norm, which for him is "the apostolic witness." Yet what is ultimately and definitively meant by that norm is left deliberately ambiguous, for Tracy does not want to limit it by an a priori definition but rather to seek its meaning through wide-ranging and ongoing conversation. He calls for "the whole community of interpreters in all disciplines to engage in authentic conversation" about how to understand the biblical text.[89] The conversation itself becomes for him the locus of biblical meaning.

The "hermeneutics of suspicion" functions here in my refusal to accept the repudiation of Jews and Judaism as intrinsic to the gospel witness. Retrieving the witness of the earliest Gospel thus requires, I think, risking any past assumptions that Jesus and his first followers preached in a theological context that was either alien to, or alienated from, Judaism. I believe that retrieving the witness of the Gospel necessitates acknowledging the truth of the Jewish witness to God—both before and after and at the time of Jesus—and risking its retrieval. Such risking requires a willingness to surrender our prior certainties about the meaning of the text. It requires restraint. It requires not being quick to read into this primary text the teachings of the later church but rather trying to grasp what theological meaning the words might have had for religious, first-century Jews.

In reviewing the large patterns of first-century Jewish culture, I have taken note that Jewish thought of the time was radically bibliocentric and that Jewish theology involved reopening Scripture in the light of the present moment. Jewish theological discourse perceived a constant intersection between Scripture and current events. Current history was understood through the perspective of Scripture, while at the same time current history opened up a new understanding of the biblical word. In Fishbane's words, the task of the exegete was to "reactualize the past word for the present hour."

In continually finding new understandings of Scripture, moreover, Jews did not construct a logically ordered, systematic theology but rather gave an ad hoc response to the biblical word. In articulating these new understandings, they did not employ straightforward exposition but used artful and poetic—sometimes even playful— means of expression.

These artful expressions were derived from Scripture in a variety of ways that pointed to ancient meanings and at the same time showed them to have new relevance. The methods that were used to do this, moreover, were themselves derived from rhetorical structures found within the Bible: the patterns of intertextual allusion, the reworking of an earlier narrative, and the purposeful juxtaposition of both harmonious and dissonant passages that served to recontextualize and illuminate the original meaning. The overall effect of these methods (both within the Bible and in the commentary on it) was to set up a "conversation," as it were, between one part of the Bible and another and between the reading community and the text.

In this book I propose to set up a similar kind of conversation. Basic to this conversation is the assumption that in different times and places various Christian communities have brought different frames of reference to the reading of the gospels. To my knowledge there is no evidence that any of these communities brought to bear the presuppositions that functioned in first-century Jewish exegesis. Such a fact is hardly surprising in view of the speed with which the Christian church became largely Gentile. But today Christian scholars have both a heightened consciousness of how cultural frameworks condition our understanding and a greater grasp of the characteristics of first-century Jewish composition. Today, therefore, it seems both possible and desirable to reconstruct those earlier presuppositions and use them as a lens for reading first-century texts. Emboldened by other scholars who have worked along these lines and strengthened by their research, I propose to attempt such a reconstruction.

I further propose to juxtapose such a reconstruction with other frames that have been used for reading Mark's Gospel. In this way readers can see for themselves the different kinds of results that each framework yields. For the other frameworks I have chosen passages from the church fathers and from Morna Hooker's 1991 commentary.[90] I have chosen commentaries I particularly respect because, in the midrashic spirit, I would like to allow for multiple readings that are valid. What I hope to persuade the reader is not that the midrashic reading I attempt to reconstruct is the only correct one but rather that no matter how fruitful another approach may be, reading Mark as midrash greatly enhances its meaning.[91]

Thus while I plan to "risk" the midrashic view by placing it into a three-way conversation about the meaning of Mark's text, I also plan to argue for the midrashic reading as forcefully as I can. When

I say "the midrashic reading," I mean that I will, first of all, consider Mark's text to be *interpretive* of Scripture (not just allusive to it) and so pay careful attention to the *function*, both of the scriptural references and of the echoes the text contains. Second, I will look for the kinds of structures Boyarin describes: a "lexicon" of verses centered on a given motif; the dialectical juxtaposition of contradictory verses; the interaction of particular texts with the "cultural code" of its time. In respect to the last, I will be concerned with the way that the scriptural exegesis intersects with history. Last but far from least, I will try to show how Mark's text, perceived in this way, unlocks the rich ambiguity of Hebrew Scripture.

I am trying for a double "reopening" here: I hope to reopen Mark's Gospel in order to show the ways in which it, in turn, reopens the Hebrew Bible. By so doing, I hope to open up new meanings in Mark's text that have long been frozen in the formulas of other kinds of discourse.

I am also trying to create (in the words of David Tracy) "a community of interpreters" through the artifice of setting up a textual dialogue between different kinds of readers of Mark's text. I hope that the "to and fro" will also draw the readers of this book into taking part in the conversation.

Rereading Mark as Theology in the Context of Early Judaism

It is difficult to describe the end of a journey before one has taken it, but nonetheless I would like to try to give the reader some idea of why it is worth the effort. Retrieving the Jewish context of the Gospel reopens for modern Christians the riches of their Jewish heritage. Discovering the bibliocentric world of the first century brings one into a culture where scriptural exegesis and theology are not separate disciplines but essentially one and the same; as such the ancient Jewish hermeneutic may offer a model for modern Christian thought. As a matter of fact, it is a model surprisingly contemporary in nature, offering a way of doing theology that makes the realities of history and faith relevant to one another and that, at any given time, insists on both the ongoing revelation of God and the ongoing participation of the faith-community. It is at once historical and spiritually imaginative, dialogical and open-ended.

To retrieve this Jewish mode of reading Scripture is also to retrieve the distinctive theological voice of Mark with its particular fruits. Looking at the Jewish biblical contexts, one finds that Mark is deeply steeped in the values of the Wisdom traditions: the recognition that God is present in everyday situations and accessible to ordinary people; the acknowledgment of uncertainty and the prizing of watchfulness; the celebration of the feminine aspects of the divine;

and the perspective of Creation theology by which God is constantly in action to recycle, nurture, and transform. One perceives Mark's distinctive presentation of Jesus to be that of a Wisdom parable— in himself revealing *what God is like.* One sees that we are not presented here with a biography but with a rhetorical-theological construct, something that cannnot be simplistically grasped as the tale of a hero but must be exegeted like a text. Mark presents Jesus as a living *mashal,* a person whose life, death, and resurrection is itself an exegesis of the Jewish Scriptures, one whose meaning is not obvious but riddling and richly ambiguous, unfolding in time. In the framework of the Wisdom traditions, Mark invites his readers into further dialogue with this riddling text, not giving answers but calling them to be humbly uncertain and prayerfully on the watch.

2

Scripture Interpreting Scripture: Reopening the Word

This chapter has two main goals: first, to illustrate how Mark uses Scripture in a dialogical, interpretive way, using one or more passages (or allusions to them) to provide the framework of meaning; second, to set up a "conversation," as it were, between this midrashic approach and other reading frames that have been used to exegete the Gospel. To do this, I propose to deal with two specific places in Mark—the opening verse of chapter 1 and the seed parables of chapter 4—and to provide three or more different commentaries on them. One or more will be ancient, and one new; beside them I will set what I consider a plausible midrashic exegesis. By setting forth the contrasts, I hope to engage the reader in the dialogue.

The Opening Verse

archē tou euaggeliou iesou christou [huiou theou]

The opening verse of Mark appears straightforwardly simple in the usual translations that treat it as almost the title of Mark's work: "The beginning of the good news of Jesus Christ, the Son of God" (*NRSV*). The phrase that appears in brackets in the Greek ("Son of God") is acknowledged by a footnote saying that some ancient authorities lack it. The apparent simplicity, however, is deceptive; different exegetes have found different meanings implicit here. I shall look at the possible exegesis of each word of this opening verse.

The Multiple Meanings of archē

Origen's Reading of archē (185–253/4 C.E.)

> The gospel [euaggeliou] is primarily concerned with Christ Jesus, who is head of the whole body of those who are being saved. Mark conveys this point when he says, "The beginning of the gospel concerning Christ Jesus." ... In its unfolding the gospel has a beginning, a continuing middle and an end. The beginning can be viewed either as the entire Old Testament, with John the Baptist being its summarizing type, or (because he stands at the juncture of the new with the old) the final stages of the old covenant. This runs counter to those who would assign the two different covenants to two different Gods. (*Commentary on John* 1:14 [ACC, 2])

Morna Hooker's Reading of archē

> Since Mark heads his work the beginning of the good news of Jesus Christ, it might be possible to take this title for the whole work, and to understand him to mean that his whole account of the life and ministry of Jesus is the beginning or basis (archē) of the good news. But since Jesus himself proclaims the good news in v. 14, it seems clear that it is the activity of John the Baptist that is to be regarded as its beginning. (*The Gospel According to Saint Mark*, & BNTC 2; [Peabody, Mass.: Hendrickson, 1991], 33)

It is interesting to observe the points these two exegetes have in common, despite the difference of seventeen centuries. Understandably enough, both immediately read the words before them in the light of church teaching: Origen instantly translates "beginning" into Jesus as the head of the church, Hooker into the "basis of the good news." Both, on second thought, looking further into the text, correct their first theological impulses with what they see to be the logic of the narrative and propose that John the Baptist must be considered what Mark had in mind as the "beginning." For Hooker, the reason for this shift is primarily a syntactical one, although she is also aware of other commentators who treat the scripture quotation in verses 2–3 as a parenthesis and translate the opening as "The beginning of the good news ... was John the Baptist." For Origen, it has the added advantage of countering the anti-Judaic tendencies of his time by pointing to "the entire Old Testament" as the beginning.

Rereading archē in a Jewish Context

In the midrashic tradition, opening with the word *Beginning*, especially without either "a" or "the" before it, would have signaled the opening of Genesis. This, in turn, would have triggered much further reflection, because in the midrashic interpretation the "Beginning" of

Genesis became a codeword for Wisdom. Thus "In the beginning, God created" is rendered interpretatively: "In *wisdom* God created." The practical cause for this substitution was the grammatical oddity of the Hebrew phrase (*b'reshit*), which, being in the construct state, strictly means "In the beginning of . . . ." If one reads that as "in the beginning of *God*," neither one's understanding of God as beyond beginnings nor the rest of the sentence, makes any sense. The ancient Jewish interpreters of the Bible found a solution in personified Wisdom's speech in Proverbs: "The Lord created me as the beginning of his work, the first of his acts of long ago . . . then I was beside him, like a master-worker" (8:22–30). In that phrasing and image lay the kernel of many others: that Wisdom preexisted Creation, that Wisdom was God's cocreator, that Wisdom was, in fact, the creating energy of God.[1]

These ideas are found elsewhere in the Bible and contemporary texts: Psalm 104 declares, "O Lord, how manifold are your works! In wisdom you have made them all" (v. 24), while Jeremiah describes God as the one "who established the world by his wisdom" (10:12). An identical phrase is found in the Dead Sea Scroll entitled "Hymn to the Creator": "Blessed is he who created the earth with his power, who established the world with his wisdom" (11Q5 Psalms Scroll[a]). The Targums (interpretative translations of the Hebrew Bible into Aramaic, dating from the first century C.E.) repeat and extend the idea. The Fragmentary Targum on Genesis simply makes the substitution—"In Wisdom the Lord created"; the Targum Neophyti identifies Wisdom with the Torah—"Two thousand years before the world was created, [God] created the Torah."[2]

The Rabbinic Midrash develops these interpretations still further. One comments, "You find that by (or 'in') wisdom, the Holy One, blessed be he, created the heaven and the earth" (Tanhuma Buber i:11), while another reflects, "Torah, because it was loved more than all things, was created before all things, as it is written, 'The Lord possessed me, the beginning of his ways'" (Sifre on Deut. 11:10). The Genesis Rabbah imagines God using the Torah as a blueprint: "God looked into the Torah and created the world" (1:1). Still another passage from the Genesis Rabbah portrays the Bible as itself a midrash on Creation.[3]

When one reflects still further that Wisdom became personified in Jewish writings—in Proverbs (roughly dated in the postexilic period), in Sirach (second century B.C.E.), and in the Wisdom of Solomon (first century B.C.E.)—one must consider that to an audience steeped in Jewish traditions, the opening word *archē* was full of multiple possibilities.

If one lets the text speak out of the context of its own time, one is confronted by meanings that are rich in their ambiguity. Instead of a familiar catechetical summary, one encounters language that opens up new meanings. If we keep from assuming we know what Mark is going to say and wait to discover it, we will hear that Jesus is linked both with the first Creation and with Wisdom personified, although we have not yet heard what this means.

The Roots of Euaggeliou

Origen's and Hooker's Readings of Euaggeliou

As shown, Origen simply translates this according to Christian convention as "gospel"; Hooker elaborates on her choice of "good news":

> The Greek word *euaggeliou* is normally translated "gospel" but we have chosen to translate it 'good news' because in Mark's time the term was not yet a technical term meaning a document. It was no false instinct that later led to Mark's book being termed a "gospel," but as far as we know, nobody before Mark had written a "gospel," and his first readers would have understood him to be referring to a message—the good news which was proclaimed by the early Christian preachers—not to a particular literary form. The book is not in itself "a gospel"; rather it contains the gospel, which is something to be believed (1:15). The background of the term *euaggeliou* is to be found in the LXX, where the cognate verb (*euaggelizō*) means "to proclaim the good news." In particular, we find it used several times in Isa. 40–66, where the good news that is proclaimed is the imminent salvation which God is going to work for his people.... By using this term, Mark claims that this salvation has come in Jesus. (pp. 33–34)

It is interesting to see how in this case, Hooker does not simply accept a familiar word, but pauses to consider how it might have been first received. In searching out its etymological background, she discovers that the Greek noun appears to derive from a cognate verb that means the whole phrase "to proclaim the good news."

Rereading Euaggeliou *in a Jewish Context*

If one pushes this process one step further and considers what the LXX was translating from the Hebrew, one finds that the words *good news* do not appear at all in the Hebrew text of Isaiah but only the verb (*basar*) that in itself implies the whole action of bringing joyful announcements. For example, in Isaiah 52:7 ("How beautiful upon the mountains are the feet of him who *brings good tidings*") or again in Isaiah 61:6 ("The Spirit of the Lord is upon me. He has anointed me *to preach glad tidings* to the poor"), the verb encompasses the whole idea that the news is good. In short, the noun *euaggeliou* that we see in the LXX is a Greek derivative from a Greek verb; the noun does not exist in Hebrew. The emphasis in Isaiah is not on "the message" but on *the action of bringing* good news. If Mark is writing in Greek but thinking in Hebrew (a possibility suggested by his "translation" mastery of the Greek language and the numerous places where "semitisms" poke through his awkward vocabulary),[4] then what he may be emphasizing here are the dynamics by which God's creation unfolds and God's wisdom is received.

Rereading iesou christou [huiou theou] *in a Jewish Context*

It is quite natural that both Origen and Hooker assume here that the end of the opening sentence should be read as a creedal proclamation: "Jesus Christ, Son of God." However, since the capitalization and the comma that support this reading were not in place in the original manuscript, one can at least imagine an alternative way of understanding these words. Translating them back into a Hebrew mindset, one might hear instead "Yeshua, anointed son of God." In this understanding, the word "anointed" (*mashiah* in Hebrew) would certainly signal a special agent of God but not a title, and "son of God" (which, in fact, is missing from some manuscripts) would indicate the kind of special relationship to God that, in terms of the Hebrew Bible, had always belonged to Israel.

Origen follows Pauline rhetoric in making "Christ" so much a part of Jesus' name that he inverts the Markan order and speaks of "Christ Jesus." Hooker, too, sees no need to probe the meaning of *christos*. But many scholars have. John Donahue notes the "growing consensus that Jesus in his lifetime did not claim to be the Messiah."[5] Raymond Brown comments that while Jesus was named *christos* "with astounding frequency" after his resurrection, "the scenes in the Gospel in which Jesus is addressed or acknowledged as the Messiah are very few" and that "Jesus, confronted with the identification, responded ambivalently."[6] Even though Mark is using the post-resurrection convention of the Christian community, he is also the evangelist who most stresses, later in his text, this ambivalence of Jesus (8:29–33). What makes the issue important is the fact that it has been conventional in popular Christian thought to assume that there was a monolithic expectation of "the messiah" in Judaism at this time. The 1992 symposium at Princeton, however, headed by James Charlesworth, came to the conclusion that "there was no single, discernible role description for a 'Messiah' into which a historical figure like Jesus could be fit. Rather, each group which entertained a messianic hope interpreted 'Messiah' in light of its historical experiences and reinterpreted Scripture accordingly."[7] Are we right, then, to assume that *christos* here is a title when the term had multiple meanings in Early Judaism—ones that Mark's narrative, in fact, continues to explore? If we translate *christos* as "anointed," without capitals or assumptions, we leave open the possibilities of this exploration.

In summary, if we are willing to put aside all the later conventional formulas about Jesus and probe the words of Mark in the context of Jewish theological discourse, we can receive the opening verse with slightly different resonances, hearing it not flatly but polyphonically—as: "Beginning (*first Creation/Wisdom*) of the (*bringing of*) good news, of Jesus, anointed son of God." In that hearing every word opens up a poetic trajectory that simultaneously points back to Scripture and forward to Mark's narrative. Here Mark sets up the scriptural frame his narrative is designed to interpret: Genesis and the Wisdom writings; the biblical traditions concerning the creative dynamic of God's word; the varied literature of messianic hope; the scriptural meaning of "son of God." It is only by letting his narrative unfold that we can discern how he relates Jesus to the interpretation of each of them.

The Seed Parables

In many ways the parables of chapter 4 contain the seed of Mark's whole gospel. As such they are a particularly interesting section to ponder according to different reading frames. Once again I will cite the interpretations of them by one of the church fathers and then Morna Hooker before offering what I see as a midrashic view.

The Parable of the Sower (4:2–8)

And he taught them many things in parables, and he said to them in his teaching: "Hear! See! A sower went out to sow. And it happened in the sowing that, on the one hand, it fell along the way and the birds came and consumed it, while on the other hand, it fell upon rocky ground where it did not have much soil. It rose up straightway because the ground did not have much depth, but when the sun rose it was scorched and because it had no root, it withered. Other seed fell in the thorn-plants and the thorns rose up and throttled it and it did not yield fruit. But other [seed] fell on good soil and yielded fruit, rising up and spreading and bringing forth thirtyfold and sixtyfold and hundredfold."

Chrysostom's Reading (347–407 C.E.) of the Sower

As the sower fairly and indiscriminately disperses seed broadly over all his field, so does God offer gifts to all, making no distinction between rich and poor, wise and foolish, lazy or diligent, brave or cowardly. . . . For it is the way of the Lord never to stop sowing the seed, even when he knows beforehand that some of it will not respond. But how can it be reasonable, one asks, to sow among the thorns, or on the rock, or alongside the road? Maybe it is not reasonable insofar as it pertains only to seeds and earth, for the bare rock is not likely to turn into tillable soil, and the roadside will remain roadside and the thorns, thorns. But in the case of free wills and their reasonable instruction, this kind of sowing is praiseworthy. For the rocky soil can in time turn into rich soil. . . . When the Word is choked, it is not merely due to the thorns as such, but to the negligence of those allowing them to spring up. . . . Let us not place the blame on what we possess, but on our own corrupt mind. For it is possible to be rich and not be deceived. It is possible to be in this world and not be choked with cares. (*The Gospel of St. Matthew, Homily* 44.5.1 [ACC, 52])

Hooker's Reading of the Sower

A parable involves a comparison and, once the comparison is made, then something or somebody in the parable is in a sense 'identified' with a thing or person in the real world. . . . Most of the parables found in Mark are very brief, often amounting to little more than pithy sayings. Only two of them are of any length—those about the Sower and the Vineyard. Mark's use of the former suggests that he sees it, not simply as a key to the teaching of Jesus (4:13), but as a key to his whole ministry. This is brought out in the explanation of the parable in vv. 13–20: the seed represents the word proclaimed by Jesus, the crop the response of men and women to him. The end of the story is told in the parable of the Vineyard, where the failure to respond to the messengers ultimately leads to the death (and resurrection!) of the son of the owner of the vineyard. The fact that each parable is placed immediately after a challenge by the Jerusalem religious authorities concerning the nature of Jesus' authority (3:20–35; 11:27–33), as well as at the head of a block of teaching linked with the theme of the parable, suggests that Mark regarded both of them as allegories of Israel's response and rejection of Jesus. Taken together, they encapsulate the whole story of the ministry. (pp. 121–22)

Aside from the fact that both Chrysostom and Hooker assume (in passages not quoted here) that the Sower is Jesus, the two exegetes are worlds apart. Chrysostom is intent on finding the parable's moral relevance to his hearers; Hooker wants to find its place in the overall perspective of Mark. In applying the parable to himself and his community, Chrysostom notably resists the idea that the qualities of "soil"—which he identifies as qualities of soul—are fixed or predetermined entities. Instead, he proposes that the rocky soil could be transformed. He carries this idea over even into his reading of the allegorical explanation that follows the parable (vv. 13–20), insisting on the primacy of free will and nuancing the evils of riches and worldly cares. In effect, he makes the parable fit his moral theology, in which intention and choice are paramount.

Hooker, on the other hand, reads the parable as part of a pattern in Mark that she sees as having two fixed players—Jesus and Israel. In order to do this, she argues that all parables involve allegorical referents and then links this parable to the allegory of the Vineyard parable. She justifies this link in two ways: first, by making use of the allegorical explanation that follows the parable (vv. 13–20), and second, by saying that "each is placed immediately after a challenge by the Jerusalem authorities." I need to consider each of these links in turn.

Rereading the Sower in a Jewish Context

First of all, while the explanation that follows the parable is certainly an *allegorical reading* of it, that does not mean that the parable itself was *written* as an allegory. David Stern, discussing the *mashal* form at length, goes out of his way to distinguish it both from the Greek parable, which he describes as "an illustrative tale," and from allegory per se. While he concedes it may have, at times, some "allegorical characteristics," he insists that the *mashal* functions "neither to offer a proof in argument nor to disguise or personify abstract concepts in more concrete forms" but as "an allusive tale"—that is, he sees it as always alluding to, and interpreting, Scripture.

It is also important to keep in mind the distinction between allegory and metaphor. A metaphor is a comparison between two objects otherwise unlike; the comparison is suggestive rather than definitive, and elliptical rather than comprehensive. As such it points to meaning rather than defining it, opening up meaning rather than limiting it. Thus when the poet says "my love is like a red, red rose," he compares his beloved to a rose in a metaphorical way that is suggestive but not precise. The allegorist, in contrast, works out a definite, point-for-point comparison between one object and another. The comparison is logically, explicitly, and comprehensively developed. The interpretation of an allegory is thus tightly circumscribed by the writer's intention. In the medieval *Roman de la Rose*, for example, the writer objectifies and personifies every emotion of the lady he is pursuing. There is both drama and subtlety in the interrelationship of the emotions but no mystery about what represents what. Applying these distinctions to Mark's parables here, one must note that there is nothing inherently allegorical about the first parable: it can be read, as Chrysostom's rendering shows, as a series of suggestive metaphors.

The allegorical explanation may well have been—as some scholars think—a later interpolation.[8] In any case, the fixed, point-for-point explanation is a different style from that of the *mashal* itself. So either one sees this exposition as a later intrusion into Mark's text or one perceives the stylistic shift as Mark's way of underscoring the theological implications. Another possibility is that the explanation may simply be considered a *nimshal*—that is, something added on to the *mashal* to indicate its historic context (in this case, a "persecution").

What about Hooker's argument that the Sower parable should be linked to the Vineyard parable because each is placed in the immediate context of a challenge to Jesus' authority? In fact, the challenge referred to (3:20–30) is not its immediate context but is separated from that episode not only by six verses but by the tenor of Jesus' teaching. Jesus' immediate response to the challenge is an emphasis on the possibility of forgiveness and, in the succeeding episode (vv. 31–35), on the inclusiveness of his community. In this instance, it appears that Hooker is making the parable fit her own view of where Jesus (or Mark) stands vis-à-vis Israel.

Setting this parable in a midrashic context offers a different perspective from that provided by either of these exegetes, both on certain details of its construction and on its larger function. If we consider the parable as, first of all, scripturally oriented, we would recognize that it is based on the biblical trope of God the Sower creating through his word. The trope of God the Sower begins in the first book of Genesis, where God's word—*dabar* in Hebrew, meaning "to act" as well as "to say"—effects ongoing motion. In the lyrical, rhythmic prose of Genesis 1, God uses speech to fill the earth with seed-bearing plants and trees, and the heavens, earth, and seas with self-propagating creatures. God's word creates a universe that will go on creating itself.

Similarly, in Isaiah 55:10–11 God's word is described as a dynamic energy with a creative purpose:

> For as the rain and snow come down from heaven, and do not return there until they have watered the earth, making it bring forth and sprout, giving seed to the sower and bread to the eater, so shall my word be that goes forth from my mouth; it shall not return to me empty, but it shall accomplish that which I purpose, and succeed in the thing for which I sent it.

In Jeremiah 31:27–28, God the Sower promises to sow again to renew creation:

> The days are surely coming, says the Lord, when I will sow the house of Israel and the house of Judah with the seed of humans and the seed of animals. And just as I have watched over them to pluck up and break down . . . so I will watch over them to build and to plant, says the Lord.

If we read the parable of the Sower against this background of God's insistent desire to create and re-create, we will be given pause by the way the narrative here is shaped to suggest predestined doom as well as fruitfulness. This kind of eschatology is suggestive of some apocalyptic writings of the period. It is particularly instructive to observe a similar use of the seed-sower trope in 4 Ezra. In Ezra's first vision there is a discussion between Ezra and the angel Uriel about the causes of Israel's defeats in history. Ezra asks "why Israel has been given over to the Gentiles as a reproach" (4:23), and the angel replies with a seed analogy: "For a grain of evil seed was sown in Adam's heart from the beginning, and how much ungodliness it has produced until now, and will produce until the time of threshing comes!" (4:30–31) In the second vision Ezra ponders the implications of the analogy and grieves over the fate of the evil seed, which he perceives to encompass most of humanity. The angel indeed affirms, "Many have been created, but few will be saved" (8:3). Ezra then implores God to have mercy, noting that "in truth there is no one among those who have been born who has not acted wickedly" (8:35). The angel replies that he cannot worry about the damned but "will rejoice over the creation of the righteous." He continues by reciting a seed parable that bears a striking similarity to Mark's: "For just as the farmer sows many seeds upon the ground and plants a multitude of seedlings, and yet not all that have been sown will come up in due season, and not all that were planted will take root; so all those who have been sown in the world will not be saved" (8:41).[9] Since 4 Ezra is dated considerably later than Mark's Gospel (around 100 C.E.), there is no possibility that Mark had this text before him;[10] the similarity of ideas suggests that what we have here is a stock trope. If we are looking at the parable as "an allusive tale," then we might fairly conclude that what is being alluded to is this kind of eschatological perspective.

In a way similar to Ezra's seed analogy but more expanded, this parable starkly contrasts two options through the use of three verbs of intense destruction (*consume, scorch, throttle*) pitted against three verbs of intense fruitfulness (*rise up, spread, bring forth*). It would appear that through no fault of their own, the fate of the seeds is predetermined. Chrysostom tries to get around the harsh determinism implied by arguing that souls, unlike soils, are transformable; Hooker seems to accept the idea of predestined punishment or reward and to apply it to Jews versus Christians. Looking at the parable as part of a larger midrashic construction, however, one can find another way of seeing it.

If one is familiar with the way the midrash tends to juxtapose different scriptural passages on the same theme, sometimes to form a harmonious "lexicon" and sometimes to show dissonance, one would look to see how the first seed parable relates to the succeeding two, responding not to any one of them in isolation, but to the whole composite. Since no commentator I have seen attempts to read all three parables as commenting on each other, I will look first at other readings of the second two seed parables and then return to what I see happening if all three are perceived as an interrelated structure.

Parable of the Seed Growing Secretly (4:26–29)

And he said: "Like this is the kingdom of God: as though someone were to throw seed on the ground and sleep and rise, night and day, while the seed sprouts and grows—how, he does not know. Automatically, the earth bears fruit: first the shoot, then the full-grown head of grain. But when the harvest is delivered up straightway he sends [in] the sickle because the harvest has showed itself."

Tertullian's Reading (Second Century C.E.) of the Seed Growing Secretly (4:26–29)

> Observe how the created order has advanced little by little toward fruitfuness. . . . In just this way has righteousness grown in history. . . . [God's] righteousness first emerged in a rudimentary stage as an undeveloped natural apprehension in the presence of the holy One. Then it advanced through the law and the prophets to childhood. At long last through the gospel, God's righteousness has been personally manifested with the vital energies of youth. Now through the paraclete, righteousness is being manifested in its mature stage. (*On the Veiling of the Virgins* 1 [ACC, 60])

Parable of the Mustard Seed (4:30–32)

And he said: "How shall we compare the kingdom of God, or in what parable shall we describe it? As a mustard seed which, when sown upon the earth, is the smallest of all the seeds on the earth, and [yet] when sown, rises up and becomes the greatest of all the vegetable-plants and yields large branches so that under its shade the birds of heaven can dwell."

Clement of Alexandria's Reading (c. 150–c. 215 C.E.) of the Mustard Seed (4:30–32)

> The word which proclaims the kingdom of heaven is sharp and pungent as mustard. It represses bile (anger) and checks inflammation (pride). From this word flows the soul's true vitality and fitness for eternity. To such increased size did the growth of the tree which sprang from it (that is the Church of Christ now being established over the whole earth) fill the world, so that the birds of the air (that is, holy angels and lofty souls) dwelt in its branches. (Fragments from *the Catena of Nicetas*, Bishop of Heraclea 4 [ACC, 61])

Hooker's Reading of the Seed Growing Secretly and the Mustard Seed

Mark now gives us two parables which—unlike that of the sower—are specifically about the Kingdom of God. The first, in vv. 26–29, has no parallel in the other gospels. . . . The concluding words . . . echo Joel 3.13, which refers to the final judgement. The second parable, in vv. 30–32, forms a pair with the first, but the new introduction, "And he said," shows that it circulated independently in the tradition. . . . The opening formula, with its parallel phrases, may be compared with similar introductions to parables in Jewish sources. Mustard seed was apparently proverbial for smallness . . . but "when it is sown, it springs up and grows bigger than any other plant." It grows so large "that the birds of the air can build nests there." . . . Like the conclusion of the previous parable, these words echo Old Testament imagery. . . . If the Markan parable also is interpreted allegorically, the birds may represent the Gentiles, who will one day have a place in the Kingdom—and indeed, in Mark's day, are perhaps already flocking in; but the important point is the contrast between the almost invisible seed and the enormous bush. . . . It is significant that the parables are about the Kingdom of God. One would naturally expect the Kingdom to be spoken of in terms of judgement, of setting things right, and of obedience to God's will; instead, we have parables which imply that the Kingdom is present and yet not present. . . . Just as the harvest comes from the grain sown in the earth, and the mustard bush springs from the almost invisible seed, so the Kingdom will follow from the ministry of Jesus. Unlike the parable of the sower, there is no hint here of even partial failure. (pp. 135–37)

Not surprisingly, both of the ancient commentators cited here approach the parables from the perspective of the church, intent on using them to show its greatness. Thus Tertullian reads the parable of the Seed Growing Secretly as an allegory of the evolution of God's righteousness from the Creation to the formation of the church through the Holy Spirit, while Clement of Alexandria identifies the church with the great tree sprung up from the mustard seed. It is not part of their concern to take notice of scriptural echoes or references or to comment on any difference between the two seed parables and the parable of the Sower.

Hooker, on the contrary, is quick to see that these parables are "unlike that of the sower" in being "about the Kingdom of God" and in giving "no hint of even partial failure." She suggests that "one would naturally expect the Kingdom to be spoken of in terms of judgement" while instead we have something else here. She does not appear to notice the seeming contradiction to what she has said earlier when she notes that the allusion to Joel 3:13 "refers to the final judgement," but she could have supported her conclusion about the

nonjudgmental quality of this parable by pointing out that the citation from Joel is only half given: the judgmental part—the words that
speak of treading down the wicked—is in fact omitted here.

Unlike the ancient commentators, she is sensitive to the Jewish
character of the parables and to their scriptural allusions. She observes,
for example, that the phrasing about the tree grown so large "that the
birds of the air can make nests in in its shade" echoes passages in
Ezekiel and Daniel. She notes that in these passages the tree stands
for a kingdom and then, combining this fact with her thesis that all
parables have allegorical referents, she interprets "the birds of the air"
as repesenting the Gentiles "flocking in" to the Christian community.

Rereading the Seed Parables in a Jewish Context

A different way of reading these allusions, however, can be argued
if one approaches the parable as an exegetical form, one whose
primary function is not just to cite Scripture but to *interpret* it. If,
further, one applies the midrashic pattern of juxtaposing dissonant
passages, not only from Scripture itself but also from various interpretations of it, one finds a different way of seeing these three
parables about a sower and seed, strung together here "like pearls
on a string."

First of all, one would notice that the second parable views the
sower-seed topos from a perspective surprisingly different from that
of the first, where the sower is clearly God and a moral burden is
placed on the soil that receives the seed. In the second parable the
importance of both sower and soil recede and the emphasis shifts to
the innate and independent purposefulness of the seed. Juxtaposed
with the first, this second parable reads like a comic antitype: the
farmer scatters the seed and ignores it; almost in spite of him, the
earth "goes on automatic" and brings the seed to ripeness. Even
the rhythm imitates the "automatic" quality it describes in the alternating pattern of "sleep and rise" and "night and day."

This *mashal* is not a stock one; there is no known precedent. But
there is a text that is related to it. In Ecclesiastes 11 we find this
admonition to living without calculation:

> Whoever observes the wind will not sow; and whoever regards the
> clouds will not reap. Just as you do not know how the breath comes
> to the bones in the mother's womb, so you do not know the work of
> God, who makes everything. In the morning sow your seed, and at
> evening do not let your hands be idle; for you do not know which will
> prosper, this or that, or whether both alike will be good. (vv. 5–6)

In this context, sowing without calculation is a virtue; the image
of the breath passing unforeseen into the womb inculcates trust in
the power and goodness of God.

The juxtaposition alters the significance of the harvest. Although the final line—"But when the grain is ripe, at once he puts in the sickle" (v. 29)—echoes Joel's description of the "harvest" as a time of God's vengeance (Joel 3:13), the grim aspects are omitted here and the passage from Ecclesiastes undercuts its fierce perspective: in Ecclesiastes God moves, in spite of human ignorance, to bring life, not death.

The second *mashal*, then, juxtaposes a biblical tradition that contrasts with the first. The effect of this juxtaposition is just what has been shown happening before in midrashic discourse: contradictory perspectives are brought together in tension to unlock the ambiguity of the Hebrew Bible. The Sower parable offers the uncomplicated view of good and evil, reward and punishment, that we find in Deuteronomy or Psalm 1: the righteous will prosper while the wicked will wither away. Placed in an Endtime setting, the unbending logic of this choice is intensified. The Wisdom literature that contextualizes the second parable responds to the question of evil with less certainty and more trust. So here, the grain ripens for the sower, "he knows not how." This second *mashal* describes a process that is the exact reversal of the first: there the harvest is a direct result of the quality of the receiving soil, while here it does not matter—the seed's power cannot be stopped. In the first parable, the abundance of the harvest is miraculous, but the process of arriving at it is one of natural cause and effect; in the second parable, the law of cause and effect is disregarded, and the process of growth itself appears to be the miracle. In the first there is clear division between good and evil; in the second there is only acknowledgment of good. The first emphasizes the stages of withering or growth; in the second, "ripeness is all." The first points to a final End where God and Satan battle for the outcome; the second moves swiftly to an eschatological fulfillment, the End Time of God's kingdom. Contrasting traditions within Early Judaism are reflected in these contrasting parables.

The third parable is different again. It opens with a conventional formula indicating its function as analogy—"With what can we compare . . . or what parable shall we use for it?" It is linked to the second parable through its focus on the kingdom of God and to both previous parables through its use of the seed analogy. Within itself it weaves together different traditions.

The mustard seed as "the smallest of seeds" was proverbial in Jewish folklore, so the *mashal* begins with a common bit of folk wisdom. The concluding metaphor—of the plant with branches large enough to provide shade and dwelling for the birds of heaven—involves a complex reworking of visionary images in both Ezekiel and Daniel. The abrupt transition from common proverb to visionary literature is a rhetorical shift that parallels the graphics of going from the "smallest of seeds" to the "greatest of plants." Yet the parable is more than a simple simile of contrast. To understand its full richness one must look at the texts it is reworking.

Two chapters in Ezekiel are relevant. Chapter 17 opens with the Lord commanding Ezekiel to "put forth a riddle and speak a *mashal.*" The parable then given to Ezekiel by the Lord is a story of eagles and cedars. One eagle plants a sprig of cedar "in fertile soil . . . beside abundant waters," and it becomes a "low-spreading vine" (vv. 5–6). A second eagle then transplants the vine. He also takes it to "good soil by abundant waters" (v. 8), but here God questions its survival, asking if it will be withered by the east wind (v. 10). A concluding *nimshal* then indicates the historical context for the story: the struggles between Jerusalem and Babylon, Babylon and Egypt. In a third narrative it is God who plants the sprig of cedar high above the mountain so that it becomes "a noble cedar," and "beasts and birds dwell in its shade" (vv. 22–23). The cedar here is clearly a symbol of the Davidic kingdom, which, after many vicissitudes, is finally planted by the Lord for all time. In chapter 31, however, the cedar symbol is given a different twist. Here God (speaking through the prophet) compares Pharaoh to a "cedar in Lebanon . . . of great height" (31:3) whose branches grew so large that "[a]ll the birds of the air made their nests in its boughs; under its branches all the beasts of the field brought forth their young; and under its shadow dwelt all great nations" (v. 6).

God says it was more beautiful than any tree in his garden, so that "all the trees of Eden envied it" (vv. 7–9). Nevertheless, God goes on to say that because "it towered high . . . and its heart was proud of its height," he will give it to the "most terrible of nations" to cut down (v. 12). Then the peoples of the earth will leave it, and the birds of the air will "dwell upon its ruin" (vv. 12–13). Here the cedar symbolizes the antithesis of God's kingdom and becomes a symbol of earthly pride. The tall cedar—in other words, the bird-sheltering tree—is an ambivalent symbol, and its contradictory traditions are exposed through Ezekiel's double-voiced use of them.

The book of Daniel constructs Nebuchadnezzar's dream out of this ambivalence. In chapter 4 Nebuchadnezzar describes to Daniel a dream that made him fearful:

> I saw and behold, a tree in the midst of the earth; and its height was great. The tree grew and became strong, and its top reached to heaven and it was visible to the end of the whole earth. Its leaves were fair and its fruit abundant, and in it was food for all. The beasts of the field found shade under it, and the birds of the air dwelt in its branches, and all flesh was fed from it. (vv. 10b–12)

The tree "in the midst of the earth" suggests the forbidden tree of Genesis 2, while its heaven-reaching top and nourishing of all flesh suggest the tree of life sealed off in the garden. The dream continues much like the parable given to Pharaoh. In spite of the magnificence of the tree (or because of it?) a "holy one" arrives and cries out, "Hew down the tree and cut off its branches, strip off its leaves and scatter its fruit; let the beasts flee from under it and the birds from its branches" (v. 14). Unlike the tree of Pharaoh, however, the tree here does not end in total destruction. Rather, the holy one leaves "the stump of its roots in the earth" (v. 15), and Daniel interpreting the dream sees this as the promise of eventual restoration (v. 26).

In both Ezekiel and Daniel, in other words, the bird-sheltering tree is an Endtime symbol. In both it is also two-sided, implying either doom or renewal. In Ezekiel these contradictory aspects are separated as two different messages addressed to two different persons or peoples, yet connected by the very fact of imagery: one side appears to be the mirror image of the other. In the book of Daniel these reverse images are brought together in the one dream.

The parable of the Mustard Seed, then, is making use of an ambivalent symbol, one that has been used to signify both final judgment and creation, both Davidic certainty and prophetic ambiguity. As such it is a link between the two preceding parables, exposing the tension between them. More than that, the parable does not simply take over the symbol passively but reworks it so as to give it fresh meaning. This reworking involves the choice of the mustard seed itself.

First of all, a fine but plausible connection between the "bird-sheltering tree" and the seed analogies needs exploring. Nebuchadnezzar's dream, I have noted, concludes with a hint of his restored kingdom (symbolized by the tree) in the holy one's instruction to "leave the stump" of the tree intact. This "stump" echoes the place in Isaiah's call story when God instructs him in the ironic aspects of his mission—"Go and say to the people: "Hear and hear, but do not understand" (6:9). Isaiah asks, "How long, O Lord?" (6:11) and God replies with a description that foresees a long process of devastation and then renewal:

> Until cities lie waste without inhabitant, and houses without men, and the land is utterly desolate. and the Lord removes men far away, and the forsaken places are many in the midst of the land. And though a tenth remain in it, it will be burned again, like a terebinth or an oak, whose stump remains standing when it is felled. The holy seed is its stump. (6:11b–13)

The implication is that despite all appearances, the stump is not the end but rather the "holy seed" from which new life will spring. Thus the bird-sheltering tree, symbol of worldly greatness and/or God's kingdom on earth, is linked to a renewable stump—which, in another context, is holy seed. The same dynamic seems to be at work here in the suggestion of God's kingdom implicit in a tiny seed.

Next, the choice of mustard seed—the specificity of it—must be explored. In no other seed analogy is the species of seed named; why here? The first answer is the obvious one contained in the text: it emphasizes its smallness. But a second effect is the suggestion of commonness, of ordinariness. Surely nothing as awe-inspiring as a "noble cedar" or a tree whose top touches the vault of heaven would come from such common seed. And in fact Mark does not use the word "tree" to describe its final growth but rather *lachana*, which literally means "garden plants" or "vegetables." To the reader versed in all the great trees of Scripture, this surely comes as a jolt or a joke. The birds of heaven are taking shelter here under a tree about eight feet high. The great tree of God's kingdom has gone domestic.

The third parable thus embraces the ambivalence of the sower-seed traditions—judgment-fulfillment—and reinterprets them by translating their central symbol into a familiar herb, effectively changing the scenario of the Endtime harvest into a garden scene—itself suggestive of the original state of Creation.

In this midrashic dialectic, no single parable stands alone; each must be seen in relation to the others. The first presents an eschatological view in which there is a final and absolute sorting out of good and evil. The second presents a comic antithesis to the first by depicting an unwitting sower and an automatic harvest. The third takes the comedy still further by reducing the harvest to an edible vegetable-plant. The total effect is to undermine the grim view of God as a rigid predestiner and the concomitant possibility of irreversible tragedy for human beings who do not meet the soil-test standards. Instead, the second parable indicates the inevitability of God's goodness coming to harvest, and the third parable suggests that this goodness is ordinary and accessible.

A knowledge of midrashic exegesis suggests that here is a structure typical of its patterns. A series of parables is woven out of divergent scriptural contexts and strung together on the common motif of seeds. The Pentateuchal text here is Genesis 1—the description of God's creating word. The texts from the Prophets are Isaiah 6 (Isaiah's call to preach to those who will not see or hear), the eschatological harvest of Joel 3:13, and the great tree of Genesis, Ezekiel, and Daniel, as well as Isaiah's "stump" that bears "holy seed." The text from the Writings is the passage about the trusting sower of Ecclesiastes. When Jesus is questioned about the first parable—based on Genesis—he exclaims, "Do you not understand this parable? How then will you understand all the parables?" (v. 13) He then proceeds to "make a journey" from passage to passage in order to illuminate the meaning of the primary text. He makes this journey by constructing a "lexicon" of passages on the theme of seeds, turning it about from all different angles—the process of sowing, the attitude of the sower, the nature of the yield. As he juxtaposes one passage with another, he shifts the meaning of God as sower from a certain and absolute interpretation (parable one) to a flexible and open-ended interpretation (parable three). Crucial to this shift is the passage from Ecclesiastes, which offers a perspective of total nonknowing, noncalculating trust in the goodness of God. By means of this turning point the Markan Jesus shifts the perspective on God's kingdom from a fixed time of final judgment to an unceasing process of growth.

An essential element of this shift is an openness to the gradual unfolding of God's mystery. The passages that link the parables bear out this emphasis.[11] The first and second parables are linked by the sayings about the lamp and the importance of bringing hidden things into the open (vv. 21, 22); the admonition to hear (v. 23); and the observation that "for the one who has, to him it will be given" (vv. 24, 25). All of these remarks take their meaning from the context of biblical exegesis. In biblical tradition the "lamp" is repeatedly associated with biblical teaching.[12] Perhaps most to the point is the suggestion in the Song of Songs Rabbah that the parable form is a lamp by which one can read the Bible more clearly:

> Do not let this *mashal* be light in your eyes, for by means of this *mashal* one comes to comprehend the words of Torah. A *mashal* to a king who has lost a golden coin from his house or a precious pearl—does he not find it by means of a wick worth a penny?[13]

If the lamp here is understood as a metaphor for the *parable/ mashal*, Jesus' words can then be seen as a direct commentary on his exegetical method: "Is a lamp brought in so that it may be placed under a bushel or under a bed, and not so that it may be placed on a lampstand? For nothing is hidden except in order to be made manifest, nor become secret but in order that it may be brought out into the open." To paraphrase, he appears to be asking, *"Is a parable brought forward in order to hide meaning? For nothing is hidden in the scriptural text except in order to be made clear."* He is, in other words, articulating here the theory of midrashic exegesis—the use of midrash, especially the parable (the "lamp"), to uncover new meanings hidden in the biblical text. He continues at this point with the injunction to "hear" and the talmudic observation that the more one has heard the word of God, the more one will continue to hear.[14]

The theory itself indicates an attitude toward Scripture that perceives it not as obvious or singly defined in meaning but rather as full of multiple meanings that are to be gradually uncovered. In this perspective God's kingdom, like Scripture, is not a special "secret" to be given to a special few but an inclusive mystery whose meaning unfolds in time; the human grasp of it is never complete but always in process. In the midrashic perspective, to speak in parables is to engage in a discourse in which God's meaning is never finalized but always to be revealed.

3

Scripture Intersecting History:
Mark's Eschatology

Chapter 4 is sometimes cited as evidence of Mark's "apocalyptic" theology because of the Sower parable with its intimations of a predetermined harvest, because of its allusions to eschatological passages in Joel, Ezekiel, and Daniel, and because of Jesus' speech about the "mystery" or "secret" of the kingdom. But as I have just shown, if the three seed parables are read in relation to each other, it appears that the Markan Jesus was not proclaiming a deterministic or exclusive eschatology but rather creating a dialectical structure in which contrasting images serve as commentary.

The structure and perspective of chapter 4 bear an affinity to chapter 13, which is the key to any discussion of Mark's eschatology. It is sometimes referred to as the Little Apocalypse, a name originally coined in 1864 by T. Colani, who thought that apocalyptic motifs were peculiarly Jewish and, wanting to separate Christian theology from any vestige of Judaism, proposed that the whole chapter was a misplaced interpolation.[1] The descriptive phrase was later adopted by Rudolph Bultmann, who saw the chapter as belonging to Mark but, assuming that a "Christian apocalypse" must be different from a "Jewish apocalypse," defined the chapter as "a Jewish apocalypse with a Christian ending."[2] Some have read the chapter as the *ipsissima verba* of the historical Jesus;[3] others, taking note of its multiple echoes of Hebrew Scripture, have proposed that it was a midrash on Daniel[4] or a speech composed in the tradition of the "farewell discourses" of Jacob, David, and Moses.[5]

A few critical voices have qualified the "apocalyptic" designation. Elisabeth Schüssler Fiorenza notes that the chapter does not fit the SBL definition of the apocalyptic genre.[6] Donald Sneen perceives that the emphasis in the chapter is on redemption, not judgment.[7] Hugh Anderson finds the chapter to be "a parenesis against apocalyptic fanaticism,"[8] while Charles C. Torrey patiently lists the elements conventionally considered to be "apocalyptic" that are absent from Mark.[9] George Beasley-Murray makes careful distinctions, noting the difference between "apocalyptic literature" and "apocalyptic eschatology," also pointing out the close affinity between what has been termed "apocalyptic" and the eschatology of the prophets.[10]

Once again I hope to engage the reader in different ways of seeing Mark's text by offering for comparison both ancient and current commentary. In doing so, I would like to ask the reader to follow along with my perception that chapter 13 is constructed with interlocking frames. The overarching frame opens with a statement about the destruction of the Temple (vv. 1–2) and closes with the parable of the lord away from home (vv. 34–37); the inner frame opens with the disciples asking when the end will take place (v. 4) and closes with Jesus saying that "no one knows" (v. 32). The first two parts of the following discussion take up the commentary on each of these frames; the next two deal with the discourse inside of them—in particular, "the desolating sacrilege" and the paradoxical images of hope. In a final section I will attempt to draw all the parts together.

The Outer Frame of Chapter 13

The Destruction of the Temple (Verses 1–3)

And going out of the Temple, one of his disciples said to him, "Teacher, what stones and what buildings!" And Jesus said to him, "Do you see these great buildings? There will not be stone upon stone left here that will not be completely destroyed."

Origen's Reading (185–253/4 C.E.)

The temple was not overthrown all at once, but gradually as time went by. Similarly, everyone who welcomes the Word of God into himself is something like a temple. If, after committing sin he does not completely fall away from the Word of God, but still partially preserves in himself traces of faith and accountability to God's commands, he is a temple partly destroyed, partly standing. But he who after sinning has no care for himself but is always prone to depart from faith and from life according to the gospel, till he completely departs from the living God, he is a temple in which no stone of doctrine is left upon any stone and not thrown down. (*Commentary on Matthew* 29 [ACC, 181])

Cyril of Jerusalem's Reading (*315–86* C.E.)

Antichrist will come at such a time as there shall not be left of the temple of the Jews "one stone upon another," to quote the sentence pronounced by the Savior. For it is not until all the stones are overthrown . . . and I do not mean merely the stone of the inner walls, but the floor of the inner temple where the cherubim were, that the Antichrist will come "with all signs and lying wonders" treating all the idols with disdain. (*Catechetical Lectures* 15.15 [ACC, 181])

Hooker's Reading

The exclamation here ["Look, teacher, what huge stones and what wonderful buildings!"] sums up the sense of security felt by the Jews, confident that God would protect his own people, and encouraged by the sight of these wonderful buildings—the symbol of his presence with them (cf. Jer. 7.4).

Jesus' answer is a prophecy of the temple's destruction. This saying has a good claim to be an authentic utterance of Jesus, since it is found . . . in several contexts. . . . In the Matthean and Markan accounts of Jesus' trial, he is accused of saying that he himself will destroy the temple, but this accusation is said to be false. . . . There is nothing particularly surprising in Jesus' words. According to a tradition in the Talmud, Rabbi Johanan ben Zakkai, a contemporary of Jesus, also foretold the destruction of the temple forty years before it occurred (B. Yoma 39b). Perhaps the political intrigues of the time and threats of revolt by extreme patriots made a Roman retaliation seem inevitable. Perhaps Jesus thought only of the divine judgement which must fall on Israel because of her refusal to hear his message. Certainly prophecy of the temple's destruction was in keeping with the prophetic tradition: cf. Jer. 7:14; 26:6; Mic. 3.12. Such statements were never popular. They sounded like disloyalty—even blasphemy, since the temple symbolized the presence of God with his people. . . . There is no reason to suppose that Jesus' quarrel was with the temple itself: indeed, in Matthew this passage follows Jesus' lament over Jerusalem and the temple (Matt. 23.37-9; cf. Luke 13.34). His complaint was against the nation, and the destruction of the temple is part of their punishment. . . . The mode of destruction is not important: what matters is that Israel's punishment is complete. (pp. 304–5)

Although proceeding from different vantage points, the two ancient commentators are alike in adapting the loss of the Temple to Christian concerns and at the same time showing respect for the Temple's existence. Both see the destruction of the Temple as a gradual process. Origen, using the Jewish Temple as a symbol of the interior state of the Christian soul, appears to be making a parallel between a weakening of Christian faith and what he sees as a weakening of Jewish faith that brought on the loss of the Temple. Cyril, linking the destruction of the Temple to the coming of the Antichrist, seems to consider the *standing* of certain parts of the Temple to be a good sign for Christians: it is only when the last remnant is gone that the Antichrist will come.

Hooker, too, evinces a certain regard for the Temple's existence, pointing out more than once that it was a symbol of God's presence with his people. She is also quick to argue that the report that Jesus said *he* would destroy the temple is termed (by Mark) to be a false accusation. She thus makes an important distinction between *prophesying* an event and *willing* it. As proof of the difference, she notes that the Talmud reports a similar prophecy from the mouth of Rabbi Johanan ben Zakkai (one of the fathers of modern Judaism) and observes how much "prophecy of the temple's destruction was in keeping with the prophetic tradition." She concludes that "there is no reason to suppose that Jesus' quarrel was with the temple itself." Yet, although she thus argues at length that Jesus' statements here are in the tradition of those most staunch in upholding Judaism, she also sees Jesus as condemning Judaism: "Perhaps Jesus thought only of the divine judgement which must fall on Israel because of her refusal to hear his message. . . . His complaint was against the nation, and the destruction of the temple is part of their punishment."

Rereading Mark 13:1–3 in a Jewish Context

Another way of seeing Mark 13 is to perceive it as a text in which scriptural allusions intersect with historical events. In this perspective one finds that, as in the parables in chapter 4, Mark absorbs and resignifies multiple texts, midrashically constructing a dialogue between eschatological viewpoints.

Hooker is the only one of the commentators to mention the scriptural tradition here, twice mentioning Jeremiah 7 and also taking note of Jeremiah 26 and Micah 3. Jeremiah 7 is conventionally known as "the Temple sermon," the place where, in the name of God, Jeremiah particularly chides the people for violating the Covenant. The thrust of his remarks is that the Temple or Temple worship should not be regarded as security that God is with you: God cannot be confined to a building but dwells with those who do God's will. Hence Jeremiah says: "Do not trust in these deceptive words, 'This is the Temple of the Lord, the Temple of the Lord, the Temple of the Lord'" (v. 4). Jeremiah spells out what the people need to do if they want God to dwell with them: "if you do not oppress the alien, the orphan, and the widow, or shed innocent blood in this place, and if you do not go after other gods to your own hurt, then I will dwell with you in this place" (vv. 6–7). If, however, the people go on breaking the commandments—stealing, murdering, commiting adultery, swearing falsely (v. 8)—then God will do to the Temple what he did to the shrine at Shiloh, namely, destroy it (v. 14). The threat is repeated later in 26:6. A similar threat in Micah is addressed to "you rulers of the house of Jacob and chiefs of the house of Israel, who abhor justice and pervert all equity" (3:9). Micah specifies their sins: "its rulers give judgment for a bribe, its priests teach for a price, its prophets give oracles for money; yet they lean upon the Lord and say, 'Surely the Lord is with us! No harm shall come upon us.'" Like Jeremiah, Micah points out the hypocrisy of those who defy God's laws and then claim God as their support. Like Jeremiah, Micah concludes with a threat: "Zion shall be plowed as a field; Jerusalem shall become a heap of ruins" (3:12).

There are several questions surrounding these passages that we need to probe further. First, what is the whole scriptural tradition to which these passages belong? Is there also a scriptural tradition of revoking the threat? Second, what were the historical circumstances in which these threats were uttered? In what way does this scriptural tradition intersect with historical events at the time of Jesus and Mark? And finally, how does Mark present this intersection?

The biblical introduction to the building of the Temple, like the earlier proposal of an Israelite monarchy (1 Sam. 8), is fraught with tension. The prophet Nathan is initially enthusiastic about David's plan to build a house for God, but his naiveté is corrected by God, who points out that God has hitherto flourished in a moveable dwelling (2 Sam. 7:5–7). In the exchange that follows between God and David, there is considerable play on the word "house": God implies that God can create a structure that can contain David, but not the other way round. When God finally gives in and promises that David's son, whose house God will establish, will "build a house for my name," there is still the overriding implication that God remains in charge: God is agreeing to a structure that will honor his name but not to one that restricts his freedom. The biblical writer thus leaves open the door to the prophetic metaphor that God abandons the Temple when it no longer honors him.

The prophetic critique of both monarchy and Temple is a continuing theme in the Hebrew Bible: beginning with Samuel's doubts about the monarchy (1 Sam. 8:11–18), it takes on a homiletic function when Nathan calls David to repentance (2 Sam. 12:1–15). With Solomon's building of the Temple, monarchy and cult were linked, and the prophetic voice was raised simultaneously against injustice and idolatry. The prophetic role also grows from denunciation of specific actions (as in Elijah's reproofs of Ahab's idolatrous deeds) to sermons that reproach the people's complacency toward a status quo that fosters social injustice, defining such injustice as the true violation of Temple worship. The prophetic sermon perceives the loss of both kingdom and Temple to be the consequence of sin and offers visions of both restored to holiness.

It is important to realize that while the prophets may justify the destruction of the Temple, they never rejoice in it or perceive it as a moment of final judgment. On the contrary, they weep over its loss and project images of its restoration: God will take back his faithless bride (Hos. 11), renew the Covenant (Jer. 31), rebuild the Temple (Ezek. 40–42), restore Jerusalem (Mic. 4 and 7, Zech. 14), remake his people as a new creation (Isa. 11, 27–30, 35, 40–66). Thus to cite the prophetic tradition is not to invoke a one-sided judgment but rather a perspective in which God may be angry but always relents, may destroy but always restores.

This double-sided view becomes clearer if we consider the historical circumstances in which each prophet composed. It is worth noting that for almost every prophet, the historical context involved some takeover of Jerusalem by foreign, pagan forces. Thus First Isaiah (chs. 1–39) relates to the period in which Assyria had annexed the Northern Kingdom of Israel and subdued the Southern Kingdom of Judah (742–687 B.C.E.). Similarly, both Hosea and Micah speak after the Assyrian conquest (733–32 B.C.E.). Jeremiah is usually dated before 587 B.C.E., when Jerusalem was ransacked by Babylon and the people taken into exile, although there are some scholars who think it was written afterward, as ex eventu prophecy. Ezekiel (593–563 B.C.E.) is known as the prophet who preached to the exiles. Second Isaiah (chs. 40–66) recounts the return of the people to Jerusalem and the rebuilding of the Temple under Cyrus of Persia (539 B.C.E.)—whom Isaiah terms a "messiah." In short, the prophetic warnings of the doom of Jerusalem are related to historic fact, and whether they were composed before or after the disastrous event, one of their basic functions is "to justify the ways of God to man." Similarly, their projections of a restored Jerualem and Temple are connected to historical hopes and, in some cases, may even have been set down after these hopes were realized.

All this needs to be kept in mind in considering the implications of the prophecy here. First of all, are the words of prophecy the *ipsissima verba* of Jesus (in which case they would have been uttered, like those of Johanan ben Zakkai, some forty years before the Temple's destruction) or are they a rhetorical speech that Mark places in the mouth of Jesus? If the latter, is Mark using the tradition to make a threat about the future of Jerusalem, or is he composing ex eventu in an attempt to explain what has happened? In either case, if he is invoking the prophetic tradition, he is reminding the Jewish people of other circumstances in which they not only broke the Covenant but also were overrun by foreign powers and idolatries. What was the historical situation of the Temple in the time of Jesus and of Mark?

After their sixth-century return from exile in Babylon, the Jews were allowed to rebuild their Temple but not to reestablish their monarchy. The high priest thus became the sole center of Jewish power, with all the attendant temptations and corruptions one might expect. To sketch the development of the high priest's role from the sixth to the first century is to reveal the increasing power and secularization of the Temple authority. With the third-century conquest by Alexander III, the high priest took on the function of collecting taxes for the conqueror. In the next century, Antiochus IV, the Seleucid governor of Palestine, made the Greek constitution the operative norm instead of the Torah, placed his own statue in the Temple (where even graven images of God were not allowed), and systematically and brutally attempted to destroy the Jewish religion. Not the least of his actions was to remove the office of the high priest from even a semblance of sacredness and crudely put it up for sale. When a man named Menelaus subsequently outbid his brother for the job, he also stole the Temple treasures for his own pocket, so that Jeremiah's poetic image of the Temple as "a den of thieves" (Jer. 7:11) shifted from metaphor to fact.[11] The direct consequence of such profanation was a fierce uprising of religious Jews—the Maccabean revolt, which freed Jewish Palestine from foreign occupation and established a new priestly dynasty. In this new (Hasmonean) dynasty, the high priest was also made king.

The result was a far more complicated situation than that under David or Solomon. On the one hand, the Maccabean achievement was hailed as the freeing of Jews from a secular, antireligious rule, and the continuing celebration of Hanukkah attests to Jewish rejoicing in the "purification" and restoration of the Temple. On the other hand, the tradition of prophetic critique was soon reenergized by the spectacle of a high priest who was also named "the King of the Jews," particularly one whose lineage was not linked to the biblical "sons of Aaron."[12] Predictably, Jews became divided in their response. The most dramatic reaction appears to have been the Essene withdrawal from "the Wicked Priest" and the setting up of a "new covenant" community in the wilderness—in a literal following of the admonitions of Isaiah 40.[13] The most thoughtful response was that of the Pharisees, who approached the Hasmoneans with the suggestion that they keep the power of the monarchy but yield the authority of the Temple. They were blocked by the Sadducees, however, who ingratiated themselves with the Hasmoneans. There were undoubtedly other Jews not easily categorized. Josephus documents the anger of at least one group of pious Jews when he describes how they pelted the Hasmonean high priest-king, Alexander, at a celebration of the Feast of Booths.[14]

What is undeniably clear is the incendiary nature of the issues of Temple and king in respect to Jewish religious identity. The coming of the Romans intensified the situation.[15] Augustus replaced the Hasmoneans with his own governors, who, though still nominally

Jews, were essentially secular. These "Herodians," as eager collaborators with Roman power, can hardly be considered models of the Torah-observant community. Herod Archelaus "the Great" (37–4 B.C.E.) changed the power base entirely by repudiating the Hasmoneans and creating a still different priestly aristocracy that he drew from outside Palestine. The Romans called him "King of the Jews," and his son, Herod Antipas (4 B.C.E.–39 C.E.), although technically a tetrarch, continued the tradition of this title. Josephus documents the popular feelings of pious outrage against the Romans—feelings that were exacerbated by two different Roman attempts (first that of Tiberius Caesar and then of Gaius Caesar) to set up self-images in the Temple.[16]

To sum up, shortly before and during the lifetime of Jesus, and continuing into the lifetime of Mark, the Temple had been taken over by foreign, pagan forces just as surely as during the lives of First Isaiah, Micah, and Jeremiah. The Roman profanation of the Temple is well documented. In warning that the Temple would be destroyed, a pious Jew of the time might well have meant that judgment was coming because of the actions of the *Romans*, as well as the actions of those Jews who, desirous of power, had violated the Covenant and sold out to them. Such a warning to Jewish leaders would have been well within the tradition of prophetic speech. It would not have been within the tradition for a prophet to completely repudiate his whole people or to predict destruction of the Temple without offering a balancing vision of hope. Is there any such balancing vision in the Markan discourse? I think it can be found in many different ways within the chapter but particularly in the concluding parable of the returning householder.

The Parable of the Returning Householder (Verses 34–36)

It is as though a man, having left his house, went away from home and giving to each of his servants the power to [do] his work, commanded the doorkeeper to watch: "Therefore, watch—you do not know when the lord of the house will come (in the evening, or at midnight, or at cockcrow, or in the early morning)—lest he come suddenly and find you sleeping."

The church fathers appear to be silent about this parable. Hooker links it to the preceding verse ("No one knows about that day or about that hour") and then discusses it.

Hooker's Reading

The parable in v. 34 illustrates the theme of v. 33. It presents a somewhat odd picture, since a man going on a journey in Palestine in the first century AD would not travel at night, and his servants could hardly be blamed for not waiting up for him. . . . Mark seems to have combined a parable about a man expected home at night with one about a man . . . away from home who entrusts his servants with various responsibilities (cf. Matt. 25.14–30 and Luke 19.11–27). The point of Mark's parable about the man who returns at night is not that his arrival is unexpected, but that his servants are given no warning about the precise time that he will come and must therefore be constantly vigilant. . . . Mark's allegorical interpretation of the parable is plain, and the moral is spelt out with only a thin disguise in v. 35: the disciples must keep watch, since they do not know when the master of the house is coming. This command suggests that he is already at hand, and the urgency here contrasts with the earlier part of the discourse which emphasized that the End could not be expected yet. (pp. 323–24)

Hooker concludes that Mark's main point is that "the disciples must keep watch since they do not know when the master of the house is coming." In arriving at this conclusion she uses two kinds of lenses that are typical of twentieth-century exegesis. On the one hand, she looks at the literal details of the parable to see if the story makes sense on a realistic level, and she finds that it does not. On the other, she searches for a parable in another gospel that might shed some light on this one and finds related parables in Matthew and Luke that emphasize watchfulness from a different angle. I think the particular meaning of Mark's emphasis on keeping awake becomes clearer if we return to the traditional biblical discourse about the Temple, because it reveals the link between the opening prophecy and the closing parable.

Rereading Mark 13:34–36 in a Jewish Context

At first glance there may seem to be no connection between the statement about the Temple's destruction and the parable of the absent master, but further reflection shows otherwise. In the writing of the prophets, God's response to the defilement of the Temple is envisioned two ways—both in his allowing the Temple to be shattered (Jeremiah) and in his taking leave of the Temple (Ezekiel). In the first metaphor, the Temple is regarded as a human structure that can be broken; in the second, the Temple is regarded as God's "house," in respect to which he is free to come and go. The second metaphor here, moreover, the parable about the house, picks up the image of the absent lord in the vineyard parable (12:1–11). As such it functions as a corrective: in this parable, the lord is away only temporarily and his loved possession is cared for by trusted servants (not by "hired hands"); the final thrust of the parable is the importance of keeping watch *because the lord will return*. Since "the Lord's house" is a metaphor for the Temple, the parable offers hope that the Temple will be once more inhabited by the divine presence. Thus the parable about the returning householder provides a merciful response not only to the disciples' question about the Temple's destruction but to their clear reverence for its ancient beauty and meaning. The cyclical life of the Temple, its destruction *and its restoration*, forms an *inclusio*, an outer frame to the whole eschatological discourse. It remains to see how this connects with the inner frame, which has to do with the disciples' question about the End.

The Inner Frame of Chapter 13

The Question and Answer About the End (Verses 4 and 32)

"Tell us when will this be, and what [will be] the sign that all these things are about to be brought to an end?" (v. 4)

"Concerning that day or hour no one knows, not even the angels in heaven or the son, but only the Father." (v. 32)

Irenaeus's Reading (c. 180 C.E.)

The gnostics presumptously assume acquaintance with the unspeakable mysteries of God. Remember that even the Lord, the very Son of God, allowed that the Father alone knows the very day and hour of judgment. . . . If then the Son was not ashamed to ascribe the knowledge of that day to the Father only, but declared what was true regarding the matter, neither let us be ashamed to reserve for God those enigmatic questions which come our way. (*Against Heresies* 2.27.6 [ACC, 194])

Augustine's Reading (354–430 C.E.)

It was not part of his office as our master that through him the day should become known to us. It remains true that the Father knows nothing that the Son does not know, since his Son, the Word, is his wisdom, and his wisdom is to know. But it was not for our good to know everything which was known to him. . . . It is according to this common form of speech that the Son is said "not to know" what he does not choose to teach. (*On the Psalms* 37.1 [ACC, 194])

Hooker's Reading

The question "when will these things happen?" is a natural one: these things (tauta) refer back to the temple's destruction. The next question, however, asking about the sign that all these things (tauta panta) are about to be fulfilled, suggests much more, and seems to look forward to the discourse that follows. . . . This saying's authenticity ["No one knows . . .", v. 32] has been endlessly debated. On the one hand, it has been argued that it must go back to Jesus, since no one would have attributed ignorance to him. . . . On the other hand, it seems unlikely that Jesus spoke of himself as the Son, since evidence that he did so is rare outside the Fourth Gospel. . . . One possible explanation is that an original saying by Jesus has been modified by the addition of the title. Whatever its origin, the verse serves here to warn Mark's readers about the folly of thinking one could predict the exact time of the End. . . . The need for constant vigilance is due to the fact that you do not know when the time will come. This suggests that there are no signs to warn the disciples of impending judgement, and it is this which makes it difficult to reconcile this paragraph with the previous one, where there are said to be clear signs of the End. (p. 323)

All three exegetes approach Jesus' response from the context of their respective periods. Irenaeus, seeking to confront the gnostics' claim to have special knowledge of the divine mysteries, is glad to point to Jesus' insistence on human uncertainty. Augustine, writing after the formulation of the Creed, wrestles with the seeming contradiction of the Son of God not sharing the knowledge of the Father. By relating the scriptural text to the growth of the inner self, Augustine finds some solution to his theological dilemma by considering that Jesus only spoke what is "for our good." Hooker, writing in a time of great interest in the historical Jesus, pauses over whether this saying might or might not represent his *ipsissima verba*. Also concerned about textual contradictions, she points out that it is difficult to reconcile Jesus' assertion of uncertainty about the End with his previous statements that there are "signs" of the End. All three exegetes agree that the overall thrust of Jesus' answer is acceptance of God's mystery. For Irenaeus that is a welcome emphasis, bolstering his argument against the gnostics. For Augustine and Hooker, however, this emphasis presents problems—a theological one for Augustine, historical and textual ones for Hooker.

Rereading Mark 13:4 and 13:32 in a Jewish Context

If we seek to bring Mark's own context to bear, we must look at the conventions of the apocalyptic writing of Early Judaism. In other eschatological writings of the time, a question about "the End" is responded to by a vision that includes a precise numerical revelation. When Daniel, for example, asks his angelic guide, "How long shall it be till the end of these wonders?" (12:6) he is told "one thousand two hundred and ninety days" and "one thousand three hundred and thirty-five days" (12:11–12). In 1 Enoch there is a vision of the history of the world that is schematized into "ten weeks": in the ninth week "the world is written down for destruction," and in the tenth, "the eternal judgment will be executed on the Watchers." The Book of Jubilees and the Qumran documents are concerned with calendars that calculate the precise moment time will end. In all these instances, there is a question and answer predicated on the belief that history is predetermined. In the context of these repeated patterns, the reply of Markan Jesus is even more striking: "Concerning that day or that hour no one knows, not even the angels in heaven or the son, but only the Father" (v. 32). The question the disciples express is a convention of apocalyptic writing, but Jesus responds with an atypical answer. In some works, moreover, the exact time of the End of things is treated as God's special "secret" that he confides to a select few. In Jesus' response there is no such secret or selectivity; the "mystery" of God is not a single piece of information but rather the vastness of what remains unknown. In Mark's handling of this conventional apocalyptic question, the mystery of uncertainty frames and qualifies everything else in the chapter 13 discourse. It remains to look at what is inside the frame.

Jesus' immediate response to his disciples here is indirect. He postpones the answer to their question and begins to speak instead about the nature of forthcoming tribulations. There are many parallel passages in the writings of Early Judaism. Just as Jesus here speaks of "wars and rumours of wars" and "kingdom against kingdom," for example, so we hear in 4 Ezra: "And they shall plan to make war against one another, city against city, place against place, people against people, and kingdom against kingdom" (13:31). In 1 Enoch we hear that "In those days the nations will be thrown into confusion" (99:14). The image of family betrayals appears in the Book of Jubilees: "And in that generation the sons will convict their fathers (v. 16). . . . And they will quarrel with one another, the young with the old" (v. 19). In 1 Enoch we are told, "they shall begin to fight among themselves. . . . A man shall not recognize his brother" (56:7). In 2 Baruch a general state of hatred is described as part of the final tribulation (70:3). The summarizing statement Mark cites as being that of Jesus (v. 19) is almost identical with that in Daniel: "And there shall be a time of trouble, such as never has been since there was a nation till that time" (Dan. 12:1).

In short, all these phrases are clichés of the period, common ways of expressing a general fear that the world is getting worse. If one is aware of this fact, one cannot read them as literal prophecy of the end of the world or as some special "apocalyptic" message of Jesus. Awareness that all these dire predictions are literary conventions of the time places them in a different perspective. What becomes important is not their substance but their function: *How* does Mark show Jesus making use of these conventions? *To what effect* is he using these eschatological clichés of his time? Is he allying himself with the perspective of Daniel or Qumran, or is he echoing these phrases in order to show his distance from them?

A careful reading shows that phrase after phrase is qualified here so as to offer reassurance. When Jesus speaks, for example, of "wars and rumors of wars," he adds, "Do not be alarmed; this must take place but the end is not yet" (v. 7). When he suggests the convergence of war, earthquake, and famine, he shifts the tone of doom by adding, "this is but the beginning of the birth-pangs" (v. 9)—an image used by the Prophets, the Pseudepigrapha, and the Midrash in connection with the coming of God's reign.[17] When he says, "Brother will deliver up brother to death," he goes on to say, "But he who endures to the end will be saved" (vv. 12–13). When he says, "in those days there will be such tribulation as has not been," he continues by noting that God will shorten the time of suffering (vv. 19–20).

What is perhaps even more striking is what the Markan Jesus is *not* doing: he is not pointing to these disasters as punishment for sin; he is not telling his disciples that if they are virtuous they will avoid them. Rather his warnings to his disciples are directed elsewhere: against being led astray by imposters of him (vv. 5–6); against being anxious at the moment of trial (v. 11); against being deceived by false prophets and false messiahs (vv. 21–22). Jesus' warnings, in other words, are not directed toward the issues of nation or cosmos but aimed at the pysche—its vulnerability, its desire to be in control, its susceptibility to deceit. Most remarkably, in terms of contemporary apocalyptic writings, Jesus does not ascribe the impending disasters to either God or Satan. On the contrary, the only concrete cause mentioned for all the misery is "the desolating sacrilege set up where it ought not to be" (v. 14). Since this is the core evil mentioned, it is worth looking at some ancient and modern commentary on it.

"The Desolating Sacrilege": The Core Evil

"The Desolating Sacrilege" (Verse 14)

But when you see the desolating sacrilege [or "the abomination of desolation"] set up where it [he?] ought not to be (let the reader understand), then let those in Judea flee to the mountains . . .

Origen's Reading (185–253/4 C.E.)

By the holy place ["set up where it ought not to be"] is to be understood every saying of divine Scripture spoken by the prophets from Moses onwards, and by the evangelists and apostles. In this holy place of all the Scriptures, Antichrist, the false Word, has often stood.

This is the abomination of desolation. (*Commentary on Matthew* 42 [ACC, 184])

Hooker's Reading

From general predictions about wars and catastrophes (vv. 5–8) and prophecies of persecution (vv. 9–15) we turn to a particular, local disaster. The pace of the discourse changes abruptly at this point, and we are at last given a "then" (*tote*) in response to the disciples' initial "when?" (*pote*). Until now, the message has been "Wait! Do not be overwhelmed. Endure!" But now the time for action has arrived.

The sign that this moment has arrived will be the appearance of "the abomination of desolation" or "desolating sacrilege" (*to bdelygma tēs eremōseōs*). This phrase comes from the LXX of Dan. 12.11, where it refers to the altar to Zeus which was set up on the altar of burnt offering by Antiochus Epiphanes in 168 BC (cf. 1 Mac. 1.54, 59). Anything connected with idolatry was an "abomination" to God, and this particular abomination put an end to temple worship and so caused its "desolation." . . . Many commentators believe that this event lay in the future for Mark as well as for Jesus, in which case the evangelist may have had in mind the threat by Caligula in AD 40 to erect his own statue in the temple. . . . If, as we have argued, Mark is writing after the destruction of Jerusalem, then he is presumably thinking of the desecration of the temple in AD 70 when, according to Josephus, the soldiers of Titus set up their standards in the temple and sacrificed to them, acclaiming Titus himself as Emperor (Wars, VI.6.1). The fact that Mark uses a masculine participle, "standing" (*estēkota*), with a neuter noun, suggests he was thinking of the person behind the symbol (perhaps Titus) rather than a statue or standard: the figure will stand "where it should not be. . . . Let the reader understand!" . . . the words are Mark's own parenthesis, a typical apocalyptic aside, alerting readers to the fact that his somewhat enigmatic language needs to be decoded. . . . The most likely explanation, however, is that Mark intends us to understand that what Jesus says is to take place in the temple is both the fulfillment of Daniel's prophecy, and also the sign of the arrival of the last things. The person who desecrates the temple is at one level a human being, but he is also the embodiment of evil, who came later to be known as the Antichrist. (pp. 313–15)

Origen continues to translate the Temple or "the holy place" into the Scriptures themselves. Then, thinking of Christ as "the Word of God," he finds the "false Word" to be "the Antichrist," or "the abomination of desolation." Hooker assumes that a definite historical event is intended and tries out various possibilities. Next, interpreting "Let the reader understand!" as an indication that Mark thought this phrase to be "enigmatic," and judging the parenthetical comment to be "a typical apocalyptic aside," she looks for an explanation in the book of Daniel. I would like to build on the scriptural references Hooker cites.

Rereading Mark 13:14 in a Jewish Context

The phrase "the desolating sacrilege" or "the abomination of desolation" is used in both Daniel and Maccabees to describe Antiochus's
act of defiling the Temple by placing his own image in it. In Daniel,
the phrase occurs in the vision of the last days accorded him by an
angelic figure; it is in fact a prophecy ex eventu, interpreting the
history the author has lived through. The climactic evil is the conquest and idolatry of Antiochus:

> Forces from him [Antiochus] shall appear and profane the temple and
> fortress, and shall take away the continual burnt offering. And they
> shall set up the abomination that makes desolate. He shall seduce with
> flattery those who violate the covenant; but the people who know their
> God shall stand firm and take action. (Dan. 11:31–32)

The first book of Maccabees, which recounts the same history,
repeats the phrase in the context of an expanded account of the deeds
of Antiochus:

> Then the king [Antiochus] wrote to his whole kingdom that all should
> give up his customs. . . . They were to make themselves abominable by
> everything unclean and profane, so that they should forget the law and
> change all the ordinances. . . . Now on the fifteenth day of Chislev, in
> the one hundred and forty-fifth year, they [Antiochus's men] erected
> a desolating sacrifice upon the altar of burnt offering. . . . According
> to the decree, they put to death the women who had their children
> circumcised, and their families and those who circumcised them; and
> they hung the infants from their mothers' necks. (1 Macc. 1:41, 48,
> 54, 60–61)

The second book of Maccabees, which is particularly given to a
theological interpretation of events, puts it this way:

> Harsh and utterly grievous was the onslaught of evil. For the temple
> was filled with debauchery and reveling by the Gentiles, who dallied
> with harlots and had intercourse with women within the sacred pre-
> cincts, and besides brought in things for sacrifice which were unfit.
> The altar was covered with abominable offerings which were forbid-
> den by the laws. A man could neither keep the sabbath, nor observe
> the feasts of his father, nor so much as confess himself a Jew. (2
> Macc. 6:3–6)

These lengthy quotations bear witness both to the extent of
Antiochus's attempt to destroy the religion of the Jews and to the
intensity of their feelings of outrage.

Since Antiochus and Maccabean history are not usually central to
Christian thinking, it is easy for Christian readers to underestimate
the force of the Markan Jesus' brief reference here to "the desolating sacrilege."[18] But if we translate Antiochus into "Hitler" and
recognize in his actions a similar attempt to systematically wipe out

the Jews as a religious people, then "the abomination of desolation" has the force of the modern "Auschwitz"—it is a catchword that summons up a whole world of anti-Jewish hatred and brutal religious oppression. The double echo here of Daniel and Maccabees, followed by the injunction, "Let the reader understand!" points unmistakably, I think, to these historical precedents as a symbol of the present religious oppression by the Romans, an oppression that, in Mark's lifetime, had taken several forms: the various attempts to turn the Temple into a place of worship of the Roman emperor, the more insidious destruction of Temple worship through the Roman system of appointing the Jewish high priests, and finally, its complete physical demolition. By not spelling this out but simply saying "Let the reader understand," Mark is only exercising, I think, a certain political prudence. The Roman reader (if there were any) would not have gotten the point, but the Jewish reader would have immediately sensed the link between the Jewish feelings of outrage against Antiochus and the feelings of revolt against the current Caesar.

The significance of the phrase is rhetorically highlighted by its placement at the center of Jesus' discourse. The very centrality of "the desolating sacrilege" distinguishes Jesus' discourse, I think, from any trace of "apocalyptic" eschatology because it makes the cause of human misery neither God's wrath nor Satanic victory but the ordinary human lust for power. This view of the source of evil is further developed by a network of scriptural allusions.

The subsequent imagery of distress follows the large patterns of Hebrew Scripture. The admonition to "flee to the mountains" and to not return to one's house to take anything away (vv. 14–15) echoes the instructions to Lot on the eve of the destruction of Sodom (Gen. 19:17). The lament for those who are with child is reminiscent of several places in Jeremiah where the prophet envisions God, angry at the violations of the Covenant, undoing creation: Zion is imagined gasping for breath like a woman giving birth who foresees death and not life as the end of her labors (Jer. 4:31); or the prophet sees the woman "who bore seven" swooning away (Jer. 15:9). The images of the darkened sun and moon also have precedent in the Prophets. In the oracle concerning the destruction of Babylon, Isaiah speaks of a day when "the stars of the heavens and their constellations will not give their light; the sun will be dark at its rising and the moon will not shed its light" (Isa. 13:10); the heavens will tremble and "the earth will be shaken out of its place" (Isa. 13:13). Joel imagines a day when "The sun and moon are darkened, and the stars withdraw their shining" (Joel 2:10).

In each instance the Hebrew Scripture also imagines a restoration: Abraham's story ultimately redeems the narrative of Lot; Rachel "weeping for her children" performs a redemptive act for Israel (Jer. 31:15); Isaiah foresees another day in which God "will swallow up death forever" (Isa. 25:8) and "create new heavens and a new earth" (Isa. 65:17); Joel sees beyond the day of darkness to a day when "the mountains shall drip sweet wine" and "a fountain shall come forth from the house of the Lord" (Joel 3:18). In the discourse of the Markan Jesus, the linking of the present distress with the biblical images of recurring tribulation points to the other end of the cycle, which is one of hope. Jesus' discourse in fact also concludes on a note of countering imagery.

Images of Hope

Jesus concludes his discourse with three images of hope: the son of man coming in clouds to "gather his elect from the four winds" (vv. 26–27); the fig tree putting forth its leaves (v. 28); and the parable of servants expecting their lord's homecoming (vv. 32–37).

The "Son of Man" (Verses 26–27)

Jesus' image here of himself as an ingathering "son of man" is the center of a triad: earlier it formed part of his self-identification before his disciples (8:38); later it will form part of his self-identification before the high priest (14:62). In the first instance Jesus speaks of himself coming "in the glory of his Father" but nonetheless containing in his being the reality of shameful death: "For whoever is ashamed of me and of my words in this adulterous and sinful generation, of him will the son of man also be ashamed, when he comes in the glory of his Father with the holy angels." In this instance, Jesus' words reinforce the essential link between his glory and the shameful cross. In the last instance, Jesus' self-description as "the son of man seated at the right hand of the Power" is linked to his assent to being "son of the Blessed"—a response related to his filial assent to the Father's will for his death (14:36). Both these qualifying contexts must be applied here, so that we perceive that "the son of man coming in clouds" is not an image of pure triumph but rather one of paradoxical tensions.

It is in the context of these tensions that Jesus describes himself as gathering "his elect from the four winds, from the ends of the earth to the ends of heaven." Many commentators have been puzzled by the fact that while Jesus appears to be acting as God's surrogate here, he does not—as in many of the apocalyptic writings of the time—act as a judge, and there is no mention of anyone being condemned.[19] But if the whole discourse is taken as conscious design, then the absence of judgment functions as one more way in which the Markan Jesus comments on other eschatological views: the idea of damnation is countered by the image of ingathering; the idea of an exclusive elect is countered by the image of an indeterminate gathering "from the four winds" and "from the ends of the earth to the ends of heaven"; the idea of God sending a triumphant superbeing as his surrogate is countered by this image of a "son of man" who has experienced shame, suffering, and death.

The Fig Tree (Verse 28)

The concluding images distinguish this eschatological discourse from those that tend toward an absolutizing of good and evil. The image of the fig tree becoming tender again is particularly significant and needs to be dealt with separately.

> "From the fig tree learn the parable: when its branch becomes tender and sprouts forth leaves, you know that summer is on the verge. And in the same way when you see these things happening, know that he/it is near, at the very door."

Hippolytus of Rome's Reading (d. 235 C.E.)

> The summer signifies the end of the world, because at that time fruits are gathered up and stored. (*On Matthew* [ACC, 189])

Hooker's Reading

> Luke takes it to be a parable about the Kingdom of God, and he may well be right (cf. Luke 11:20; 12:54–6). . . . Mark may perhaps have had another reason for adding the parable at this point. The parable is about a fig tree, and it was a fig tree that was cursed in chapter 11, when Jesus first pronounced judgment on Israel. It is significant that now, when Jesus has spelt out the nature of Israel's punishment and the final gathering of the elect, we have a story about another fig tree. The dormant tree, apparently dead, bursts into new life, and its young leaves are a promise of coming summer: hope, and not destruction, is the final word. "Learn a lesson from the fig tree": the fig tree is one of the commonest trees in Palestine. It is the most obvious harbinger of summer, since so many of the other trees are evergreen. Moreover, the fig tree was commonly used in Jewish literature to symbolize the joys of the messianic age. . . . "When you see these things happening": the awkwardness of the reference to "these things" (tauta) here betrays the fact that the parable is an addition. It is by no means clear what Mark had in mind. . . . [Perhaps] it is the destruction of the temple and the punishment of Israel which warn the Christian community that they must be constantly on the lookout. He is near: there is no subject in the Greek, and the verb (estin) can be translated equally well by "it is." Mark might mean "the Son of Man" or "the End." . . . "At the very door": this phrase . . . suggests that Mark has a person, rather than a thing in mind. (pp. 320–21)

Both exegetes see the fig tree as essentially a sign of hope. Both also connect it with the End Time—Hippolytus, it would seem, on purely natural grounds, Hooker on the grounds of its use in messianic literature. Hooker's conclusions about it are nonetheless contradictory. On the one hand she speaks about the fig tree symbolizing "the joys of the messianic age"; on the other she identifies the phrase that immediately follows, "these things," with "the destruction and punishment of Israel." In conclusion, she finds the parable and the phrase that follows it to be inconsistent and notes: "It is by no means clear what Mark had in mind." I would like to pursue the scriptural and midrashic uses of the fig tree and then attempt to place this parable into the larger context of the chapter.

Rereading Mark 13:28 in a Jewish Context

First of all, we need to consider why Mark has called this brief description of the blooming tree "a parable" (*mashal*): a *mashal* is not just a sign but a narrative, and not just any narrative, but one with an exegetical purpose. I think Hooker is right in linking this fig tree to the one in chapter 11 because if we do that, we find not just a single image but a connected story. It is a story in which the fig tree undergoes an entire life-cycle: from being cursed and withering to springing back into life. If we explore the scriptural life of the fig tree, we find that this story indeed has an exegetical function.

In Genesis 3:17 God curses the ground (which includes the fatal fig tree), but in the story of Noah, God promises never to do so again (Gen. 5:29 and Gen. 8:21). In Isaiah's visions of a new creation the specific curses of Genesis are reversed (Isa. 55:12–13, 65:17–25).[20] The Prophets, the Song of Songs, and the Midrash all speak of the return of the fig tree as a sign of an End Time envisioned as humanity restored to the Garden.

Isaiah, Jeremiah, Hosea, and Micah use the image of the barren fig tree as a metaphor for Israel when it has turned away from God (Isa. 28:4, Jer. 8:13, Hos. 9:10, Micah 7:1). By the same token, they describe the End Time as a coming age when the fig tree will bear fruit and each person will have his own vine and sit "under his own fig tree." The latter phrase first appears in 1 Kings 4:25 where it describes the prosperity of the days of Solomon; it is subsequently used as the image of future well-being in Isaiah 36:16, Joel 2:22, and Zechariah 3:10. The blossoming fig tree also appears in the Song of Songs as the sign that the winter is over and a new spring has come (2:13). When the fig tree appears here, therefore, revived and blooming, it points not to the destruction of Israel but to its Endtime restoration. The phrase "these things," I think, refers simply to the final stage of the fig tree story that has just been described.

The Parable of the Returning Householder Revisited
(Verses 34–36)

There is a further point about the traditional use of the Garden imagery in Hebrew Scripture that is worth pointing out: in biblical writings the primal Garden represents a holy space that blends imaginatively with the holy space of the Temple. Michael Fishbane has traced how, in the writing of the Prophets, the imagery of Eden merges with the vision of the Temple: Isaiah 11, where "the hope of exilic restoration to an edenic Zion is remarkably coupled with a projected reversal of the ancient curses of Genesis 3:16–19"; Ezekiel 40–42, where "the new Temple, on a mountain, is an Eden" and "waters of sustenance and life flow form the theshold and altar"; Zechariah 14, where "Ezekiel's eschatological vision of a new, historical Eden comes to firm expression"; and Joel 2, where the "vision is saturated with edenic images which accentuate the role of the Temple in a mythograph of renewed harmony and blessing."[21]

If we keep in mind that the Garden restored is an image of the Temple renewed, then we will see how the parable of the fig tree works together with the parable of the lord returning to his house. If we then review the whole structure of the discourse here, we find a remarkable coherence. The discourse is filled with images of Jewish sufferings taken from Hebrew Scripture, and at the center of them is an allusion to the desecration of the Temple at the hands of a foreign power. It is framed by the disciples' question about the Temple and Jesus' response, which combines giving a happy ending to the story of the fig tree with offering another suggestive narrative about a householder coming home. If Christian readers have had trouble, over the centuries, in seeing how clearly these stories point to the Temple's restoration, it may simply be because in time Christian catechesis came to view the Temple as the symbol of a hostile religion. But if Mark was writing in the early seventies, when the followers of Jesus still thought of their leader *as a religious Jew*, the destruction of the Temple would have been as shocking to them as to any other Jewish group. They would, I think, have seen Jesus as a reformer, but hardly a willful destroyer, of the ancient holy space.

Summary

It is clarifying to consider the shifts in time-frames here. The reference to Antiochus's blasphemous act would seem to place the time of tribulation in the past. Yet there are clearly passages that only make sense in the time of Mark. The prediction about being "beaten in synagogues" and bearing witness to Jesus' name before governors and kings (v. 9), as well as the suggestion that this will happen after

"the gospel" has been "preached to all the nations" (v. 10), all
suggest the early persecutions of the followers of Jesus. At the same
time, and most interesting of all, the particular warnings Jesus issues
to his disciples find immediate fulfillment in the Passion Narrative
that follows: the warnings about deceit, the betrayal of brother by
brother, the emphasis on false and mistaken identity, the call to
witness to Jesus' identity, the admonition to stay awake, even the
detail of the "cockcrow"—all point forward to what Mark will show
to be the immediate experience of the disciples. The ultimate effect
is the merging of these time-frames into a single, existential moment.
In that way, the cycles of betrayal and witness, destruction and restoration, are presented as timeless; the admonition to "watchfulness"
is not a special warning about a final "apocalyptic" crisis but rather
instruction about the ongoing need to respond to God's presence.

In summary, if one explores the way scriptural and historical allusions function here, and if one also takes into account the whole
structure into which they fit, one finds a discourse that coherently
undermines the apocalyptic perspective. The discourse is filled with
clichés of apocalyptic writing that are immediately modified by the
reassurances of Jesus. The echoes of contemporary passages concerning tribulation do not conclude with a judgment scene but with an
inclusive ingathering ("from the four winds"). At the center of the
evil time is not a battle between God and Satan but human desecration of the Temple. The initial observation about the loss of
the Temple is concluded by a parable about the householder's
homecoming. The initial "apocalyptic" question about the End is
given a double, nonapocalyptic answer: the hopeful image of the
fig tree in bloom; the acknowledgment of uncertainty and the
admonition to watchfulness. In effect, the discourse concludes with
eschatological viewpoints that are akin to the two kingdom parables
of chapter 4: the trustful, not-knowing wakefulness that is the thrust
of some of the Wisdom writings; and the Prophets' hope in the End
as a return to the Garden.

4

From the Temple to the Cross: An Exegetical Journey

The Temple, the Fig Tree, and the Vineyard

It is a tribute to the tightness with which Mark has constructed his Gospel that one cannot interpret one part without having it affect one's interpretation of another. I have chosen to deal with chapter 13 first because I think it provides a commentary on the events Mark describes in the chapters before and after it. Yet I am aware that my argument about the Temple in chapter 13 is incomplete without an analysis of the Temple's place in chapters 11 and 12 and 14 and 15. I will deal first with the linked episodes of the Temple, the Fig Tree, and the Vineyard parable; second, with the exegetical debates in the Temple; and third, with the journey Mark takes us on from false witness to revelation in the Temple. Once again I will begin the analysis of each section with citations from other commentaries.

The "Cleansing" of the Temple (11:15–17)

And he went out into Jerusalem and entered the Temple and began to cast out all the buyers and sellers in the Temple, and he overturned the tables of the money-changers and the seats of the pigeon-sellers, and he would not permit anyone to carry anything through the Temple. And he began to teach them, saying: "Is it not written, 'My house is called a house of prayer for all peoples'? But you have made it 'a den of robbers'!"

Bede's Reading (672–735 C.E.)

He scattered the fraudulent traders, and drove all of them out, together with the things that had to do with the carrying on of trade.
What, my beloved, do you think our Lord would do if he should
discover people involved in disputes, wasting time gossiping, indulg-
ing in unseemly laughter, or engaged in any other sort of wicked
actions? Remember: when he saw traders in the temple buying the
sacrificial offering meant to be made to him, he was prompt in getting rid of them. . . . These things should cause us great perturba-
tion, beloved; we should dread them exceedingly with well-deserved
fear, and carefully avoid them with painstaking diligence, lest he
come unexpectedly and find something evil in us, as a result of which
we should be rightly scourged and cast out of the church. (*Homilies on the Gospels* 2.1 [ACC, 161])

Hooker's Reading

In placing the story at the end of Jesus' life, Mark presents it as the
climax of Jesus' challenge to the Jewish religious authorities and of
his claim to authority: the incident sets the seal on Jesus' own fate
(and so on that of the nation). John, too, though he places the story
at the beginning of his narrative, links it with the death of Jesus; the
saying about the temple in John 2.19 ["Jesus answered them, 'Destroy this temple, and in three days I will raise it up.'"] is not just
a play on words but arises from the belief that the Jewish attempt to
destroy Jesus led to God's rejection of Jerusalem and its temple, and
the whole incident (like that of the marriage feast in Cana) symbolizes the replacement of Judaism by Christianity. . . . What was the
motive behind Jesus' action? Some have seen it as an attack on the
sacrificial system. But since the demand to offer sacrifice was included
in the commands of God, set out in the Torah, Jesus would hardly
have challenged the whole system. . . . Was it then the misuse of the
sacrificial system which Jesus was attacking? The complaint that the
authorities have prevented the temple from being a house of prayer
for all the nations supports this suggestion. . . . But Jesus' protest
may well have been wider than this. . . . It would have been in the
prophetic tradition for Jesus to protest about worship in the temple
which was hollow because it was offered by those whose behaviour
was unjust. . . . The quotation from Jer. 7:11 attributed to Jesus in
v. 17 does not refer in its original context to commercial transactions
in the temple. The people are there described as "robbers" or "brigands" because their behaviour outside the temple means that when
they enter the temple they cannot worship God sincerely. . . . The
temple had been cleansed in the past—by Josiah, who removed the
altars of other deities and deposed their priests (2 Kgs. 23), and by
Judas Maccabeus, after its desecration by Antiochus Epiphanes
(1 Macc. 4.36–59). . . . Since the temple symbolized the relationship
between God and his people, it was natural that hopes of renewal
should be linked with it. The Jewish hope of the End included the

expectation of a new temple, which would be built either by God himself or by his Messiah (e.g., 1 Enoch 90.28). Mal. 3.1–4 [alluded to in Mark 1:2] promises that the Lord will come to his temple and purge the priests and their offerings. Was Jesus, therefore, by his actions, demanding a thorough purging of both priests and people? Was this a symbolic action, equivalent to his proclamation: "The Kingdom of God is at hand: repent"? Clearly, as an act of reforming zeal, the incident would have to be judged a failure. . . . The evangelists, however, see Jesus' actions as much more than a mere gesture of protest: they are to be understood as prophetic actions, symbolizing a divine judgment which will be worked out in future events. (pp. 262–65)

In this instance, the two exegetes could not be further apart: Bede instantly applies the corruption in the Temple to himself and his congregation; Hooker applies it to the whole people of Israel. Although Hooker does not agree with the commonly held idea that Jesus was challenging the whole sacrificial system, and even though she goes on to discuss the parallel between Jesus' actions and those of the prophets, and although she notes that "the Jewish hope of the End included the expectation of a new temple," nonetheless, her analysis comes back to her basic perception that Jesus was expressing a divine judgment on Israel. Even though she observes that the Temple had a tradition of been "cleansed" by Jewish reformers and that such a cleansing by Judas Maccabeus after the desecration of Antiochus was celebrated annually by devout Jews, she still looks at the text through the lens of Christian replacement theology. Bede, by his internalizing of the text, offers instead a perspective in which corruption in Israel provides a mirror for the Christian conscience. I would like to offer a reading that, different from either, not only provides the historical context and the scriptural references but takes into account the way they interpret the story.

Rereading Mark 11:15–19 in a Jewish Context

Although there is a connected narrative in these chapters instead of a speech, I find that the narrative is not pure story but rather an exegetical construct composed out of the intersection of historical events with passages from Scripture. The historical events only tell *half* the story. Indeed, there are times, I think, when what may seem like history is in fact an allusion to a scriptural passage or a reenactment—a *reactualization*—of it. The pieces of Scripture that Mark interweaves with the narrative provide the interpretive spin. I propose to pay particular attention to those pieces of Scripture and to the way they are juxtaposed to one another and to the events Mark is recounting. By doing so, I think one finds a richer and more coherent meaning than if one reads the narrative as history alone.

As I have noted earlier, the initial Jewish ambivalence toward the Temple intensified in the third and second centuries B.C.E. when it was profaned by the takeover of pagan conquerors and their establishment of a political priesthood.[1] In this complex reality, the Temple both did and did not continue to function as the center of religious life. The traditional prophetic outrage at the desecration of the Temple then had twin targets: first, the foreigners who quite literally acted as Temple thieves and stole its treasures and who tried to place (again quite literally) idolatrous images in the Temple and second, those Jews in high places who acted *metaphorically* as Temple robbers and idolaters by collaborating with these pagans.

There is no historical warrant for indicting all the Jewish people in this kind of corruption. We need to keep in mind that devout Jews had a wide range of angry reactions to the political pollution of the priesthood and the Temple, from withdrawal to revolt. From the complex evidence available, the most nuanced response appears to have been that of the Pharisees, who, instead of following the extremes of flight or fight, began to reform Judaism from within, apparently by adapting Temple practices to the local synagogue and home. Thus when the Temple was in fact destroyed in 70, the Temple functionaries (mostly Sadducees), the outright revolutionaries (Zealots and brigands), and the apocalyptic purists (e.g., the Essenes) were largely destroyed along with it, while the moderate reformers had begun a system that allowed for religious survival.[2]

This reformist tradition had as its base the midrashic practices of reopening Scripture in the light of new events. To understand the complexity of attitudes toward the Temple in Mark, it is necessary to turn to those texts that provide the basis for the interpretation. In chapter 11 they involve the interweaving of Zecharaiah 9, 11, and 14 with Jeremiah 7 and Isaiah 56, as well as the history recounted in 1 Maccabees and the liturgy of the Feasts of Hanukkah and Booths.

The prophetic motif of restoring the Temple underlies the interpretive narrative of Simon Maccabeus retaking Jerusalem from Antiochus: "*He cast out of it all uncleanness*, and settled in it men who observed the law" (1 Macc. 13:48). Simon then expelled the idolaters "*and cleansed the citadel from its pollutions*" (1 Macc. 13:50).[3] He and his followers then entered the city in triumph— "*with praise and palm branches*" (1 Macc. 13:51). "And Simon decreed that every year they should celebrate this day with rejoicing" (1 Macc. 13:52). The Feast of Hanukkah (or Dedication) thus became an annual celebration of the restoration of Jerusalem, and especially of the Temple.

In itself, the union of "praise and palm branches" suggests the liturgical convergence of Scripture and historical fact. As far as we know, the word *hosanna* first appears in Psalm 118 as a cry to God to "save now"—its literal sense; its meaning changed when the recital of the psalm at the feasts of Booths and Hanukkah was accompanied by the waving of branches, and the branches became popularly known as "hosannas."[4] The liturgy thus condensed two meanings—a verbal plea for God's help and a gesture of praise anticipating God's gracious response; in time, the gesture of praise became the overriding thrust, and the waved branch and the "hosanna" were made one.

This ritual gesture and chant thus also unites two liturgies that celebrate the Temple—Hanukkah and Booths. The Feast of Booths or Tabernacles first appears in Leviticus (23:40) as a celebration of the harvest; it is a thanksgiving feast and a prototype of Endtime abundance. Further meaning comes from the fact that the Hebrew word for "booth" or "tabernacle" or "tent" indicates the dwelling place of God: in Exodus the word refers to the moveable tabernacle in which God chose to be present to his people; in the yearly feast it is represented by temporary shelters that the people erect with branches.

A perpetual Feast of Booths is celebrated in Zechariah's last chapter. There Zechariah announces that "a day of the Lord is coming" when the Lord will first "gather all the nations against Jerusalem to battle" and then, after the city is vanquished, will himself fight against those very nations (14:1–3). In this context Zechariah speaks of God's feet standing on the Mount of Olives and the Mount splitting in two (14:4). It is described as a frightening time when the people "shall flee as you fled from the earthquake in the days of Uzziah" (14:5), but it is also a time of new beginning when "living waters shall flow out" (as in Genesis 2:10–14) and God's kingdom will be established: "And the Lord will become king over all the earth; on that day the Lord will be one and his name one" (14:9). The remnant of people who survive the warfare shall come up to Jerusalem "year after year to worship the King, the Lord of hosts, and to keep the Feast of Booths" (14:16). Zechariah concludes with images of Jerusalem and the Temple fully restored to holiness. Building on an earlier image of false leaders as "false shepherds" who "buy and sell" their flock (Zech. 11:5), he here proclaims that "there shall no longer be a trader in the house of the Lord of hosts on that day" (14:21).

It is important to understand the theology of this final chapter in Zechariah in order to grasp how it is being used by Mark. Zechariah's theological purpose is in keeping with that of all the other prophets: to restore the Temple to its original holiness. The description of foreign nations attacking Jerusalem portrays the Temple weakened by idolatry; the plague that God then sends on the "peoples that wage war against Jerusalem" (14:12) suggests the need to purge the Temple of corrupting influences from without. Beyond the horrors of war and plague, however, the prophet has a vision of a holy society that has been purged of its sinfulness. It is in that holy society that there is a perpetual observance of the Feast of Booths (14:16). As the celebration of harvest and ingathering, this feast is an icon of the End Time. Still further, Zechariah's imagery of "living waters" suggests that the Temple in its restored condition is an analogue for the unspoiled Garden of Genesis; the perpetual festival in the new Temple also signifies the return to original wholeness in the sacred space of Eden.

All this mingled history and Scripture and liturgy provide Mark's framework for the Temple scene. In chapter 9, Mark sets Jesus' transfiguration on the Feast of Booths through the suggestion of Peter that they build three tents or booths on the mountain (9:5). Here, in chapter 11, Mark gives Jesus' entry into Jerusalem the liturgical setting of both Booths and Hanukkah by describing the crowds offering, as they did on both those feasts, "praise and palm branches" (11:8–10). He thus touches on two feasts of restoration—one of the End Time, the other of the Temple. When, at the same time, Mark describes Jesus entering the city on a colt, he would have reminded his Jewish listeners of Zechariah 9:9: "Lo, your king comes to you; triumphant and victorious is he, humble and riding on a donkey, on a colt, the foal of a donkey." In this passage Zechariah stresses not only the surprising humbleness of the conquering king but also his devotion to peace: "He will cut off the chariot from Ephraim and the war-horse from Jerusalem; and the battle bow shall be cut off, and he shall command peace to the nations" (9:10). Mark may be further adding to this paradox of victorious humility when he notes that "many people spread their cloaks on the ground": the usual context for this custom is that of beggars seeking alms.

These are the scriptural settings for Jesus' entry into the Temple: on the one hand, reminders of the End Time and of Simon Maccabeus triumphantly cleansing the Temple of its foreign polluters; on the other, reminders of Zechariah's humble king. Mark has juxtaposed discordant echoes, and until the whole narrative unfolds, we cannot be sure where it is going.

In this mixed setting, Mark further juxtaposes passages from the prophets: Isaiah 56:7 ("My house shall be called a house of prayer for all nations") and Jeremiah 7:11 ("You have made it [my house] a den of robbers"). I have already noted in the previous chapter the full setting for the quote from Jeremiah: Jeremiah equates stealing, murder, and adultery with the idolatrous action of offering sacrifices to Baal and in that context cries out, in God's name, "Has this house, which is called by name, become a den of robbers in your sight?" In short, Jeremiah is saying bluntly that any violation of the Ten Commandments is an act of idolatry, and any act of idolatry turns God's house into "a den of robbers." By specifically equating these actions to offerings to Baal, he is also acknowledging the pernicious influence of foreign gods on the religion of Israel. Whether or not we view him as preaching to the exiles in Babylon after the destruction of the first Temple in 587 B.C.E., we find here a double warning of threats to the Covenant: he is exhorting the people to be wary of two kinds of idolatry.

The passage from Isaiah 56, on the other hand, comes from a context that views foreigners benignly. Here Isaiah is envisioning a total restoration of God's blessing on all people. In Isaiah 55, God speaks of his word going forth like a fruitful seed (vv. 10–11) and the cursed ground of Genesis being restored to fruitfulness (v. 13). What follows is Isaiah's inclusive vision in which anyone who keeps the Covenant—foreigners as well as Jews—will be brought to God's "holy mountain" (another scriptural image of the Temple). "For," God concludes, "my house shall be called a house of prayer for all peoples" (v. 7). Mark thus shows Jesus quoting contrary traditions: a tradition that sees the Temple profaned and one that sees it restored; a tradition that views foreigners as profaners and a tradition that welcomes them into God's house.

By juxtaposing passages from Scripture, Mark develops his narrative in typical midrashic fashion. Given this intensely scriptural construct, Jesus' action of driving out "those who were selling and those who were buying in the temple" and overturning "the tables of the moneychangers" falls into place as a reminder of the prophetic imagery of "trading" in the Temple as a metaphor for its profanation, as well as a reenactment of Simon Maccabeus "cleansing" the Temple of pollution. In no way, however, does it suggest God's abandonment of Israel: the action of Simon Maccabeus is tied to the yearly feast celebrating the Temple restored; Isaiah and Zechariah speak of the Temple restored in connection with the Endtime return to Eden. There is tension between the contradictory voices of the biblical texts rather than a single-minded voice of condemnation. If we focus on only one of the voices, we get only half the picture. If, on the other hand, we allow both these voices to speak, what we hear is a complexity that is a faithful reflection of the complicated situation existing in first-century Jerusalem: a city on the one hand taken over by idolators and on the other the revered and ancient holy place.

Mark, writing some years (perhaps forty) after the death of Jesus, may have felt particularly strongly about how profaned the Temple worship had become. Yet the historical evidence suggests that there was no clear-cut separation between Jesus-followers and other Jews for a long time. The Romans thought of them as belonging to the same religion and initially persecuted them together. Even as late as the fourth century we find Chrysostom exhorting his congregation to stop attending synagogues.[5] Bede, writing later still (672–735), notably does not perceive Jesus' action in the Temple as a repudiation of Judaism. Yet somewhere in the Christian tradition this idea seems to have taken hold, and it appears to be a hard one to shake. To me, it does not seem conceivable that any devout Jew—including Jesus or his followers or Mark—would have wanted to see the city or Temple *destroyed*; at the same time, many, according to Josephus, viewed the Roman occupation and the Roman appointees (high priests and Herodian governors and tax collectors) as fosterers of idolatry and instruments of the Temple's pollution. Among other things, it is this *ambivalence* of feeling, I think, that is reflected through the juxtaposition of conflicting traditions here.

This general ambivalence is complicated further by the scriptural passages which Mark chooses to add to Jesus' entry into Jerusalem and to his action in the Temple. By playing off the echoes of Zechariah's nonviolent king against the reminders of Simon Maccabeus's soldierly triumph, Mark suggests that Jesus is both a reformer and a peacemaker. Similarly, by juxtaposing Jeremiah with Isaiah, Mark indicates that Jesus both wants to rid the Temple of foreign pollution and at the same time wants to include all foreigners in his Father's house.

When, therefore, Mark states that Jesus cast out "the sellers and the buyers in the Temple" and overturned "the tables of the money-changers and the seats of the pigeon-sellers" (11:15), he is not, I think, to be taken literally: he is using an ancient style of biblical metaphor. Mark is placing Jesus in the rhetorical tradition of prophetic "sign-acts"—of Jeremiah wearing a yoke around his neck to signify Israel's need to submit to Babylon or of Hosea marrying a prostitute to signify Israel's faithlessness as a wife to God.[6] Mark is linking Jesus to the ancient and honored tradition of the prophets denouncing the profanation of the Temple. With the hindsight of chapter 13, we know that the touchstone to this profanation is the idolatrous action of a foreign conqueror.

Moreover, as I have noted, the Jeremian denouncement of the Temple in its profaned state is placed in perspective by the Isaian vision of the Temple restored and inclusive. The note of restoration is deepened when Mark describes Jesus' action here as a "casting out," because the phrase echoes earlier scenes in which Jesus has "cast out" demons from those possessed only in order to restore these persons to the synagogue community (chs. 1 and 5).[7]

Many commentators read this scene in the Temple as an unambiguous condemnation of Israel because it is framed by the narrative of the withered fig tree. It is therefore necessary to look at that narrative next.

The Cursing of the Fig Tree (11:12–14, 20–25)

[handwritten margin note: "Not the Season" / "expectation"]

And on the next day when they came from Bethany he became hungry, and from a distance seeing a fig tree to have leaves, he went to see what he could find on it, and going, he found nothing on it but leaves, for it was not the season for figs. And he responded and said to it, "May no one eat fruit from you unto the age." And his disciples heard this. (vv. 12–14)

And passing by in the morning they saw the fig tree had withered away from its roots. And Peter remembered and said to him, "Rabbi, the fig tree that you cursed has withered." And Jesus answered and said to them, "Have faith in God. Truly, I say to you, whoever says to this mountain, 'Be lifted up and cast out into the sea' and does not hesitate in his heart, but trusts that what he has spoken will happen, it will be. Therefore I say to you, Everything that you pray and ask for yourself, trust that you have received and it will be yours. And whenever you stand praying, forgive if you have [anything] against someone, so that your Father who is in heaven may forgive you your transgressions." (vv. 20–25)

Cyril of Jerusalem's Reading (315–86 C.E.)

Remember at the time of Adam and Eve they clothed themelves—with what? Fig leaves. That was their first act after the fall. So now Jesus is making the same figure of the fig tree the very last of his wondrous signs. Just as he was headed toward the cross, he cursed the fig tree—not every fig tree, but that one alone for its symbolic significance—saying: "May no one ever eat fruit of you again." In this way the curse laid upon Adam and Eve was being reversed. For they had clothed themelves with fig leaves. (*Catechetical Lectures* 13.18 [ACC, 160])

Let it not come about that it should happen to us what happened to the barren fig tree in the Gospel. Let not Jesus come in these days and utter the same curse upon the fruitless. But instead may all of you say, "I am like a green olive tree in the house of God." (*Catechetical Lectures* 1.4 [ACC, 162])

Hooker's Reading

The incident of the fig tree is a difficult one. It is the only "negative" miracle in the gospels, for instead of pronouncing a word of salvation, which brings life, Jesus here utters a curse—apparently out of pique—which kills the tree.... The fig tree represents Israel, which has failed to produce the appropriate fruit when her Messiah looked for them. The background of this imagery is found in passages in the Old Testament which speak of the Lord looking in vain for grapes or figs on his vine or fig tree, and of the judgement which necessarily follows: especially relevant here are Hos. 9.10,

16f., Mic. 7.1, and Jer. 8.13. . . . This, then, is why Jesus curses the tree: not out of pique, but because it represents Israel, and Israel has fallen under the judgement of God.

Equally important is the expectation that in the messianic age the fig tree will bear fruit. . . . But why should Mark have included the comment that it was not the season for figs? It may be that this is a deliberate hint for us to take the story symbolically. . . . Because Israel does not recognize her Messiah she does not welcome him, and because she does not receive him, the messianic age—the season of figs—cannot arrive. (pp. 261–62)

The story continues on the following morning: the fig tree was not simply wilting, but completely destroyed, "withered from the roots." Peter's awestruck exclamation . . . underlines the fulfillment of Jesus' word of condemnation, and the word remembering makes doubly certain that we think back to vv. 12–14. The conclusion to the story is quickly told, but various sayings have been added to it—chiefly by word association, for the story itself has little to do with faith, prayer, or forgiveness. (pp. 268–69)

Cyril of Jerusalem views the fig tree from two different angles. In his second comment (which seems to bear no relation to his first) he follows the custom typical of much ancient commentary in applying the imagery to the inner state of the soul. In his first comment, however, he makes a connection between the fig tree in Mark and the fig tree in Genesis. In so doing, he implies that one valid way to read Mark is to see his words as a biblical allusion. Hooker also looks for relevant biblical passages, but they suggest nothing more to her than the motif she has already determined is the defining one—that "Israel has fallen under the judgement of God." Her certainty that this judgment is the overriding thrust of Mark's Gospel makes her confident about deciding that the story of the fig tree "has little to do with faith, prayer, or forgiveness." Although she eventually connects the fig tree here with the fig tree parable in chapter 13, she does not view the last as part of a connected narrative but rather as "a story about *another* fig tree" (italics mine).[8] Once again I think that reading these passages in Mark as midrashic discourse offers richer and more coherent meaning, because it points us toward seeing a single exegetical journey here.

Rereading Mark 11:12–14, 20–25 in a Jewish Context

Most commentators tend, like Hooker, to accept Peter's statement—"Rabbi, the fig tree which you cursed has withered" (11:21)—as indicating that Jesus has cheerfully damned the tree forever.[9] But several factors work against this reading. First of all, Mark says that Jesus finds no fruit on the fig tree "for it was not the season for figs" (v. 13)—a phrase that implies a temporary, not a permanent, condition. Second, Cyril is right, I think, in hearing a connection to Genesis. When Jesus forbids the tree from bearing fruit *"eis ton aiōna"* (v. 14) "unto the age" (i.e., "to the end of this age"), he is echoing God's curse of the ground in Genesis 3:17. The condemnation implied here, therefore, is not directed at Israel but is a reminder of the general condemnation originally laid on sinful humanity. And, with different nuances, I agree with Cyril that the ultimate implication here is indeed the *reversal* of that condemnation. As I noted earlier, in the story of Noah, God promises never to curse the ground again (Gen. 5:29 and Gen. 8:21), and in Isaiah's visions of a new creation the curses of Genesis are specifically reversed (Isa. 55:12–13, 65:17–25).[10]

It is in that tradition that the Prophets, the Song of Songs, and the Midrash speak of the return of the fig tree as a sign of God's kingdom. I agree with Hooker that this meaning is "fulfilled" here when Jesus points to the fig tree's blooming as a sign of the End Time (13:28). But I think it is straining the imagery to suggest that what we have here is the story of *another* fig tree instead of the expected denouement of this one. Altogether, the fig tree story, I think, has a meaning wider than that of Israel—I think it suggests that all humanity will be restored to the Garden. Of course, in that wide arc of redemption, the restored Temple is also included.

The reference to the fig tree in chapter 13 is generally not connected to the ones in chapter 11—perhaps because readers are used to looking for isolated messages rather than for patterns of imagery.[11] But in the midrashic linking style of Mark—and particularly given his fondness for patterns of three—the whole triad must be taken as metaphor and meaning.

Furthermore, although it is not usually understood this way, I think this reading of the fig tree passages is actually supported by the exchange that Mark gives between Jesus and Peter in verses 20–23. We are told that "the fig tree had withered away from its roots,"[12] and then Peter repeats, "Rabbi, the fig tree which you cursed has withered." Jesus responds, "Have faith in God. Whoever says to this mountain 'Be lifted up and cast into the sea,' and does not doubt in his heart, but believes that what he says will come to pass, it will be done for him." Most commentators, it seems, read the response of Jesus to imply that he is using his power to annihilate a living thing and is inviting Peter to do the same. But given the consistent choices the Markan Jesus makes for life, for healing, and for forgiveness, are we now to believe that Jesus is approving the use of power to destroy? If we read the passage in the full context of Mark's Gospel, we are bound to come to a different understanding. Perhaps we should remember that in Mark's characterization, Peter's perceptions are always somewhat obtuse. Certainly we should hear the echo from an earlier chapter in Mark where Jesus heals a man with a "withered"

arm (3:1–5). We also need to be aware of the large biblical contexts
Mark uses to provide the frame: the Isaian oak that burned down to
its roots and yet contained the "holy seed" (Isa. 6:13); above all, the
cursed fig tree of the primal Garden, which tradition asserted God
would restore. In these contexts, the Markan Jesus' response, "Have
faith," implies that in spite of all appearances, one can trust that God
will make the fig tree bloom again.

One might then see that Mark intended Peter's comment as a
lament, with Jesus' response as an encouragement. The fig tree,
not entirely dead, has leaves[13] but did not have fruit because "it
was not the season for figs" (v. 13); the seasonal imagery suggests
the perspective of Wisdom ("There is a season for everything under
heaven"), not a final judgment. Jesus' subsequent address to the tree
("May no one eat fruit from you to the end of this age"), precisely
because it echoes God's curse of the ground in Genesis, makes the
withering of the fig tree a symbol of the primal evil that God promises to reverse. Mark is suggesting that it is faith in the possibility of
this restoration to which Jesus urges Peter.[14]

Subsequently, Mark shows Jesus—in another speech to Peter—ex-
panding on the meaning of this faith: "Therefore I say to you, everything that you pray and ask for yourself, trust that you have received
and it will be yours" (v. 24). The exhortation to prayer echoes Jesus'
earlier remark about the need for prayer in "casting out" evil (9:29).
It is worth noting, finally, that Jesus immediately links this power
of prayer to forgiveness: "And whenever you stand praying, if you
have anything against someone, forgive, so that your Father who
is in heaven may forgive you your transgressions" (v. 25).[15] The
emphasis on forgiveness forecloses the possibility that Mark meant
us to conclude that Jesus desires or approves the withering of the
tree; instead, he quotes Jesus saying words that urge forgiveness
and imply restoration. And *forgiveness and renewal*, not judgment
and damnation, seem to me to be the key motifs in Mark's Gospel
as a whole.

The Parable of the Vineyard (12:1–11)

And he began to speak to them in parables: "A man planted a vineyard and placed a hedge around it and dug a trough for the juice,
and built a tower. He leased it out to tenant farmers and went on
a trip. And at the right season he sent a servant to take from them
some of the fruit of the vineyard. And taking him, they beat him and
sent him forth. And he again sent to them another servant, and that
one also they struck on the head and insulted. And he sent another,
and that one they killed. And many others—some they beat, some
killed. He had one more: he sent his beloved son to them last of all,
saying that 'My son will be respected.' But those tenants said to each
other, 'This one is the heir. Come, let us kill him and the inherit-

ance will be ours.' What will the lord of the vineyard do? He will come and destroy the tenants and give the vineyard to others. Have you not even read this Scripture: 'The stone which the builders rejected has become the cornerstone. This was the Lord's doing and it is wonderful in our eyes.'"

Ambrose of Milan's Reading (333–97 C.E.)

Matthew and Mark say: "He sent his only son, saying they will respect my son." . . . Was the Father deceived, or was he ignorant? Or was he powerless to give help? . . . Neither is the Father deceived nor does the Son deceive. It is the custom of holy Scriptures to speak in these many voices, as I have shown in many examples. In such instances, God feigns not to know what he does know. In this then is shown the unity of Godhead. A unity of character is shown to exist in the Father and the Son. For as God the Father seems to hide what is known to him, so also the Son, who is the image of God, seems to hide what is known to him. (*Of the Christian Faith*, 5.17.214–18 [ACC, 165])

Hooker's Reading

Certainly in its present context it demands to be read as an allegory of the failure of Israel's rulers to accept God's messengers . . . or perhaps, like the original image in Isaiah and Mark's own account of the withered fig tree, was intended as an indictment of Israel in general for her failure to produce fruit. . . . When the story was retold after the resurrection, however, then the death of the final messenger was interpreted allegorically of the crucifixion, and it seemed to Christians that something vitally important was missing from the story. . . . So the story was "rounded off" with a "proof-text" of the resurrection, the Old Testament citation in v. 10. . . . The parable is still an indictment of Israel and her leaders, but it is also a reassurance to Christians that they are the ones to whom the vineyard has been given, and so the legitimate tenants. . . . The proof-text from Ps. 118.22 . . . is quoted elsewhere in the New Testament (cf. Acts 4.11; 1 Pet. 2.7) but seems out of place in its present context, since the point of the parable is not the vindication and restoration of the wounded messengers, but the punishment of the tenants. . . . For Mark, the reference to the beloved son must have seemed a clear messianic claim on Jesus' part, however indirectly made: did he believe that the Jewish leaders also understood it in this way? If so, then this story, with the previous one [the Temple scene and the Fig Tree], is for Mark the real turning-point of the gospel, the moment at which the Jewish authorities reject their Messiah, and when his fate—and theirs—is sealed. (pp. 275–78)

Ambrose, born shortly after the Council of Nicaea (325 C.E.), assumes that by the "son" in the parable Mark means Jesus as the second person of the Trinity and so is totally caught up in what Mark may be saying about the relationships within the triune Godhead. Hooker (in a passage not quoted here) thinks the christological significance of "the son" would not have been in the original story.[16] Consistent with her general reading of Mark, she focuses on what she thinks the parable is saying about the condemnation of Israel. She first restricts the condemnation to Israel's leaders but on second thought suggests it "was intended as an indictment of Israel in general." She takes her thesis to the point of saying that the hints of restoration in Psalm 118 seem out of place "since the point of the parable is not the vindication and restoration of the wounded messengers, but the punishment of the tenants." She assumes that "the beloved son" was a messianic title and so concludes that the parable is about "the Jewish authorities rejecting their Messiah." Her commentary in fact does not title this passage "The Parable of the Vineyard" but "The Parable of Rejection." I think a very different reading can be found if one does not assume the polemical attitudes of a later Christian era but reads the parable instead in the context of biblical precedent, Early Jewish discourse, and Mark's own patterns of biblical allusion.

Rereading Mark 12:1–12 in a Jewish Context

The vineyard as a metaphor for Israel occurs in Isaiah, Hosea, Jeremiah, Ezekiel, and the Song of Songs. In Hosea, God recalls the unspoiled beauty of ancient Israel by comparing it to "grapes in the wilderness" and "the first fruit on the fig tree in its first season" (9:10) and "a luxuriant vine that yields its fruit" (10:1). In Jeremiah, God upbraids Israel from turning from "a choice vine" into a "a wild vine" (Jer. 2:21). In Ezekiel, the "vine" is a synonym for the "tree" of the righteous person of Psalm 1—"transplanted by the water, fruitful and full of branches" (Ezek. 19:10). In the Song of Songs the vineyard is the same as the garden that stands for God's beloved (compare Song 1:6, 6:11, 8:11). Seemingly linked with the Song of Songs, and certainly key to Mark's usage here, is Isaiah 5, where the prophet says he will sing for his "beloved" "a love song concerning his vineyard" (Isa. 5:1): how he "dug it and cleared it of stones, and planted it with choice vines" and "looked for it to yield grapes but it yielded wild grapes" (Isa. 5:2). In anger and disappointment at the lost harvest God says he will destroy the vineyard and "make it a waste" (Isa. 5:6). In deutero-Isaiah, when God proclaims "behold, I create new heavens and a new earth" (Isa. 65:17), he also promises new vineyards (Isa. 65:21). In short, in biblical usage, the vineyard—like the fig tree—has a seasonal, cyclical life that reflects the pattern of human innocence and failure and renewal and the corresponding pattern of God's delight, anger, and compassion. Throughout the seasons, the vineyard remains the object of God's love; the "song of the vineyard" is essentially a love song.

This rich tradition needs to be kept in mind when we read the Markan Jesus' parable of the Vineyard. The opening words—"A man planted a vineyard and placed a hedge around it and dug a trough for the juice and built a tower"—echo Isaiah, but the verse concludes on a significantly different note: "He leased it out to tenant farmers and went on a trip" (v. 1). This final action does not resemble any act of God's in biblical tradition; indeed, it does not sound like the action of anyone to whom the vineyard was "beloved." God as an absentee landlord is a different—and chilling—idea.[17]

As the narrative unfolds, moreover, it becomes clear that the vineyard does not disappoint the owner with a poor harvest. In fact, there is apparently a good harvest, which the owner would like to reap: it is for that purpose that he keeps sending servants and finally his son (vv. 2–6). The anger of the owner is not directed here at the vineyard itself but at the "tenants" who have conspired to keep him from the vineyard's fruit and who, in the process, have murdered his servants and son. What we have here, in other words, is not a replica of Isaiah 5 but a very different story.

Part of the difference is the fact that this narrative is clearly allegory: details are not submerged in metaphorical ambiguity but appear to be constructed as precise referents. The Temple priests, scribes, and elders (11:27) surmise Jesus is talking about them (12:12), and the reader as well perceives the murderous tenants as a thinly veiled reference to real people.

But who are these people? If we keep in mind that the "vineyard" is traditionally Israel, God's chosen and beloved, and that the vineyard here is bearing its expected fruit at the time of harvest—the owner sends the first servant "at the right season" (v. 2)—then we must realize that "the tenants" cannot stand for Jesus' fellow Israelites or the Jewish faith community. Indeed, further reflection suggests that the very term "tenant" indicates someone who has only a commercial attachment to the vineyard, not someone who is a member of the family. The scenario, then, is of Israel—God's vineyard—being placed in the charge of people who do not love it, who have only a tangential and venal attachment to it. There is a subtext here as well: How could God let this happen to his own, his beloved vineyard? It is as though God were an absentee landlord; as though God were away on a trip.

The actual, political situation to which this narrative corresponds is the situation in the Jerusalem Temple in the time of Jesus, when those in power were appointed by Rome. Even more than the despised tax-collectors, they were in league with the occupying government; they were not interested in the worship of God but in their own profit. They could well be described figuratively as "false shepherds" or as "money-changers" or as "thieves" in the Temple; or as venal leasers of the vineyard—hired hands, not rightful caretakers. These hired hands have no love for the vineyard or its owner, never mind his servants or his son. In telling this story, Jesus is repudiating not religious Jews but *irreligious* ones—those who were selling the Temple short for their own gain.[18]

After Jesus tells of their killing of the son, he asks, "What will the lord of the vineyards do? He will come and destroy the tenants and give the vineyard to others. Have you not read this scripture: 'The stone which the builders rejected has become the cornerstone'" (vv. 9–10). Later Christianity came to equate this "cornerstone" with Christ, and thus Christians living in a world separated from Judaism came to read Jesus' answer crudely, as a statement that God would take his vineyard from the Jews and give it to the Christians. What started out as an *interfamily* quarrel took on a different shape after the siblings not only parted but no longer recognized their kinship. Since all the parts of Mark are closely connected, one misreading feeds on another. Thus the anti-Jewish interpretation of the Vineyard parable has been bolstered by an anti-Jewish reading of the Temple-cleansing scene, the parable of the Fig Tree, and Jesus' prophecy of the Temple's destruction. All these readings seem to stem ultimately from a predisposition to distance Christianity from Judaism, as well as a lack of close familiarity with Jewish tradition.

If one is aware, however, of the Jewish habit of self-criticism and the scathing remarks the prophets addressed to their people in calling them to repentance, one will not confuse the criticism here with repudiation. More than once the prophets told the people that God would wipe them out for their wickedness, that he would allow their Temple to be a ruin and their city a shambles; yet in every instance the prophets also spoke of God's desire to restore his people, his kingdom, his Temple. Furthermore, it is important to be aware of the Jewish interpretation of Psalm 118: the "cornerstone" is conventionally identified with David—God's chosen one, who at first seemed an unlikely choice to Samuel, was hunted down by Saul, and was rejected by his own son, Absalom. Traditionally sung at Passover, the Psalm, moreover, celebrates the rejected stone because it also stands for Israel itself—the enslaved, rejected people who became the cornerstone of a nation covenanted to God.

Jesus' statement here can thus be read within the bounds of Judaism as an assertion typical of the prophets. If one does so, one finds that Jesus is saying that God will take the vineyard (his Temple *and his people*) away from the false leaders now in power in Jerusalem and give this vineyard to those who will truly care for it—those who are now rejected by those in power. These rejected ones will—like David, like the Israelites as a whole—through God's blessing become the foundation of his Covenant.

It is true, of course, that Mark is also using this traditonal imagery to identify Jesus as the rejected stone. But it is important to see that in the Markan context, Jesus is not being rejected by "the Jews" but by the false and venal people who have wrongfully grabbed the power in Jerusalem. It is those people—those who have sold out their Jewish heritage, who have murdered "the servants" (i.e., Moses and the prophets) before Jesus, who are in fact the betrayers of Israel—who are now plotting to murder him. In this context, Jesus is God's "beloved son" *as Israel is God's beloved son.* Jesus, in fact, may be said to *stand for* Israel here—not in the supersessionist way that later Christianity proposed but in the same pious way that Jacob and Joseph are seen to stand for Israel in Jewish exegetical tradition.[19]

That way of reading this last image is probably the most difficult for Christians to grasp, because they naturally tend to equate "son of God" with the the fourth-century creedal definition of the second person of the Trinity. Yet it is necessary to read Mark with fresh eyes in order to understand his discourse in its earliest sense. And in the context of the first century, "beloved son" was a Jewish topos, exegetically and midrashically understood to refer to Israel—God's "darling child" whom he taught to walk (Hosea 11:5)—and analogously to Isaac, to Jacob, to Joseph, and to David's promised descendant.[20] In this parable there is a particular echo of the Joseph story when the tenants say, "Come, let us kill him" (compare Mark 12:7 and Gen. 37:20). Joseph's story, we need to remember, is a narrative of hidden truths and ironic reversals: there the beloved son is plotted against but not actually killed; mourned as dead by his father, he in fact survives and reappears (although at first in disguise) as the one who saves his family—including those who plotted against him. The additional allusion to Joseph here is a significant clue to Mark's construction of a plot that will also turn on the dramatic reversal from apparent loss to restoration.

Finally, I think it is important to see that this is the third identification of Jesus as "the beloved son" and so must be considered in relation to the other two, especially the middle one, that generally functions in Markan triads to shed light on the others. In this case the middle use occurs in the transfiguration scene while Jesus is conversing with Moses and Elijah, and Peter suggests making three booths—one for each of them (9:4–5). The narrative of Jesus' congenial conversation with the two greatest prophets at the Feast of Booths indicates Mark's perception of Jesus' rapport with Torah tradition.

If one keeps this earlier use of "beloved son" in mind, one cannot read the usage here as indicating that Mark sees Jesus as somehow over and against Judaism.[21] On the contrary, the "son" here is associated with "the servants" (a conventional designation of the prophets), and opposed to those outside the family. The full mea-

sure of the tenants' alienation from the family is indicated by their
desire to kill the heir in order to gain the inheritance (12:7): this is
an illogical argument, as other commentators have pointed out; its
very absurdity suggests the tenants' unconnectedness to the vineyard's
owner. The threat to remove the wicked tenants from the vineyard
and give it to others is in line with many prophetic threats to purge
God's land or Temple of corruption. And the idea of rebuilding the
Temple from the rejected cornerstone is in keeping with Jewish
exegeses of Psalm 118 that find, in the stories of Jacob and Joseph and
David, a biblical paradigm for Israel's graced reversals. In seeing Jesus
as this rejected cornerstone, Mark is not, like later Christian exegetes,
coopting this tradition. Rather, he is placing Jesus firmly within the
tradition of Jewish hope for Jewish restoration.

It makes a difference to one's reading if one sees Mark's scriptural
references as a connected exegesis. Linking them, one sees that Mark
has constructed a midrashic lexicon of passages that give image to this
Jewish hope. He describes Jesus entering Jerusalem like Zechariah's
peacemaking king and cleansing the Temple like Simon Maccabeus.
He dramatizes Jesus reenacting the Genesis curse on the fig tree
and then telling his disciples that faith and prayer will reverse it. In
a later chapter he quotes Jesus promising that indeed, the fig tree
will bloom again. He complements the parable of the Vineyard in
which the landlord is away with the parable of the Householder who
comes home from his trip. From Scripture to Scripture, and from
image to image, Mark takes his readers on an exegetical journey that
reinterprets the recent disaster in Jerusalem in the light of the biblical experience of God's will to restore all things.

The Exegetical Debates in the Temple

After the Vineyard parable, what next follows in the Markan text are
four exchanges—questions asked and answers given—between Jesus
and various persons connected with the Temple. These exchanges
are labeled "controversies" or "debates" by most commentators and
treated as wholly antagonistic to Jesus. I would like to challenge that
perception, at least to some extent. The first question, it is true, is
presented by Mark as an attempt to trap Jesus. But the second one
has no such description attached to it, the third is spoken respectfully, and the fourth question is asked by Jesus himself. If one looks
at these discussions as another part of Mark's exegetical journey,
they do not appear to be all angry controversy but take on a different cast. In reading them it helps, I think, to bear in mind that
argument was (and is) a normal way for Jews to explore the meaning of Scripture. From what we know of the later *bet midrash* (the
house or school of Midrash), we find that it was customary for Jews
who were devoted to the Torah to gather in pairs or groups and

argue with each other over the meaning of the sacred text.[22] I plan to take up each exchange separately, but I would like to note at the outset that argument alone does not imply antagonism: the general setting that comes to mind here is that of Torah scholars engaged in lively but nonetheless tolerant debate.

The Exchange About the Tax to Caesar (12:13–17)

"Is it lawful to pay tax to Caesar or not?" (v. 14)

"Give back to Caesar what is of Caesar, and to God what is of God." (v. 17)

Tertullian's Reading (fl. c. 197–222 c.e.)

That means render the image of Caesar, which is on the coin, to Caesar, and the image of God, which is imprinted on the person, to God. You give to Caesar only money. But to God, give yourself. (*On Idolatry* 15 [ACC, 167])

Augustine's Reading (354–430 c.e.)

We are God's money. But we are like coins that have wandered away from the treasury. What was once stamped upon us has been worn down by our wandering. The One who restamps his image upon us is the One who first formed us. He himself seeks his own coin, as Caesar sought his coin. It is in this sense that he says, "Render to Caesar the things that are Caesar's, and to God the things that are God's," to Caesar his coins, to God your very selves. (*Tractates on John* 40.9 [ACC, 168])

Hooker's Reading

Jesus' answer is often interpreted as a clever evasion of the trap, but his reply is in fact unequivocal. However much the inhabitants of Judaea dislike it, they cannot escape the authority of Caesar and the obligations that entails. This reply is immediately balanced, however, by the command to "render to God what belongs to God." It has been suggested that there is here an allusion to Gen. 1.26f., and that the meaning is that those who bear the image of God belong to him and owe him all that they are. Although the saying is probably less subtle than this, it certainly suggests that man's duty to God is something much more important than his duty to Caesar. (p. 281)

Rereading Mark 12:13–17 in a Jewish Context

It is interesting to observe that both of the ancient commentators find a clear connection between Jesus' answer and the Genesis description of human beings made in the image of God, while Hooker dismisses this link as too subtle. To one familiar with the intricacies of Jewish exegetical argument, subtlety is not an unusual characteristic. And of course, if one thinks, as I do, that Scripture is Mark's primary orientation, one cannot easily dismiss this kind of allusion. Finally, the wordplay here connects so well with the historical situation surrounding the Temple that it seems hard to think of it as coincidence: it was, after all, the *image of Caesar* that stirred up the Maccabean revolt and is referred to by Daniel as "the abomination of desolation"—and that is the very phrase that Mark shows Jesus using in chapter 13 to designate the core evil of the time. To play off *the image of Caesar* against *the image of God* is not just to give a witty answer: it is a way of summing up the essence of the antagonism between religious Jews and Roman power.

Mark is making distinctions here, I think, between those Jews who truly had the interests of the Covenant at heart and those who were willing to sell out to Roman power: the linking of these Pharisees to "the Herodians" indicates that it is the latter group who were bent on entrapping Jesus. If one reflects on the usual diversity—including politicization—of any religious group, one realizes how normal such differences are. With respect to Judaism, differences of opinion and attitude seem to be the rule rather than the exception. Yet few Christian exegetes seem ready to make any distinctions between one Jew and another. In constructing the three debates that fill out the rest of chapter 12, Mark refines these differences.

The Exchange About the Resurrection (12:18–27)

And Sadducees came to him—those who say there is no resurrection—and they questioned him, saying, . . . "There were seven brothers. The first took a wife and dying, did not leave seed. And the second took her and dying, did not leave seed. And the third likewise. And the seven did not leave seed. Last of all, the wife died. In the resurrection, whose wife will she be? For the seven had her as wife." Then Jesus said to them, "Is it not in this that you are misled—in not knowing Scripture or the power of God? For when they rise from the dead they neither marry nor are given in marriage, but are like angels in heaven. Concerning the raising of the dead, have you not read about Moses at the bush, how God spoke to him saying, 'I am the God of Abraham, and the God of Isaac and the God of Jacob'? He is not God of the dead but of the living." (vv. 18–27)

Tertullian's Reading (fl. 197–222 C.E.)

The Sadducees indeed denied the resurrection, while the Lord affirmed it. In affirming it, he reproached them as being both ignorant of the Scriptures—which declare the resurrection—and disbelieving of the power of God as able to raise from the dead. He then spoke without ambiguity of the dead being raised. (*On the Resurrection of the Flesh* 36 [ACC, 169])

Hooker's Reading

The topic raised by the Sadducees' question was therefore one on which they were in fundamental disagreement with the Pharisees. If the incident goes back to Jesus' own lifetime, then it is interesting to note that Jesus sided with the Pharisees. . . . Jesus' answer falls into two parts. The first (v. 25) deals with the question by explaining that the manner of resurrection life is quite different from that which is presupposed in the problem. . . . The second answer "proves" the resurrection (in typical rabbinic manner) by means of a citation from the book of Moses—the one authority accepted by the Sadducees. . . . The argument is that since God describes himself as "the God of Abraham and the God of Isaac and the God of Jacob," these patriarchs must still exist. . . . It depends on the belief that God would not have described himself as the God of dead heroes, since "He is not the God of the dead, but of the living." (pp. 282–85)

Rereading Mark 12:18–27 in a Jewish Context

This time, both exegetes agree that the main thrust of Jesus' answer revolves around Scripture. For Tertullian, this is simply a matter of believing that Scripture "declares the resurrection." For Hooker, the significance is specifically exegetical: she is aware that argument by means of proof-text is known to be typical of the rabbis. She is also sensitive to the fact that Jesus' response shows him to be using the hermeneutical methods of the Pharisees. This is important because, according to Josephus, the Sadducees differed from Pharisees not only in respect to belief in the resurrection but in respect to the way they interpreted Scripture: the Sadducees maintained a literalist reading, while the Pharisees fostered the tradition of oral interpretation—the "Oral Torah."[23] I think this fact is important to note in order to see that Mark is placing Jesus in the hermeneutical tradition that is associated with the Rabbinic Midrash. Jesus' response here indicates that Mark sees him as not only the proclaimer of a living God but also the proclaimer of a *living word*.

The Exchange About the First Commandment (12:28–34)

And some of the scribes coming up [and] hearing them searching [that is, studying] together, [and] seeing that he answered them well, asked him, "Which commandment is the first of all?" Jesus answered that: "The first is, 'Hear, Israel, the Lord is your God; the Lord is one.' And you are to love the Lord your God with your whole heart and your whole soul and your whole mind and your whole strength.

The second is this: you are to love your neighbor as yourself. There is no other commandment greater than these." And the scribe said to him: "Right, teacher, you have spoken truly that 'He is one and there is no other beside Him.' And to love him with your whole heart and your whole understanding and your whole strength, and to love your neighbor as yourself, is beyond measure more than all whole-burnt offerings and sacrifices." And Jesus, seeing that he answered wisely, said to him: "You are not far from the kingdom of God." (vv. 28–34)

Bede's Reading (673–735 C.E.)

Neither of these two kinds of love is expressed with full maturity without the other, because God cannot be loved apart from our neighbor, nor our neighbor apart from God. (*Homilies on the Gospels* 2.22 [ACC, 173])

Hilary of Poitiers' Reading (c. 315–67 C.E.)

The answer of the scribe seems to accord with the words of the Lord, for he too acknowledges the inmost love of one God, and professes the love of one's neighbor as real as the love of self, and places love of God and love of one's neighbor above all the burnt offerings of sacrifices. (*On the Trinity* 9.24)

Hooker's Reading

Mark portrays the scribe as an honest questioner in search of truth. This is surprising in view of the hostile attitude of the previous questioners; it is even more surprising when we remember the antagonism shown to Jesus by the scribes elsewhere in Mark. . . . The question put to Jesus was one that was commonly discussed by the rabbis. . . . others beside Jesus quoted these passages in reply to similar questions. . . . The view that love is the one essential element of the Law is expressed by Paul in Rom. 13.8 when he says that the person "who loves his neighbour has fulfilled the Law." The comparative evaluation offered by the scribe in Mark 12.33, when he says that the principle of love is far more than all burnt offering and sacrifices, reflects a similar approach, though, of course, the words do not necessarily imply that the burnt offerings and sacrifices are unimportant: since the conversation is said to have taken place in the temple, where burnt offerings and sacrifices were offered up, the scribe himself has presumably come to worship there. The insistence that attitudes and behaviour are more important than religious observance echoes similar places in the Old Testament, e.g. Jer. 7. 22f., Hos. 6.6. But the fact that Mark has placed this incident in the temple, following Jesus' dramatic action there (11.12–17) and almost immediately before his prophecy of its destruction in 13.1f., suggests that for him the scribe's words would have been understood as an endorsement of Jesus' condemnation of the worship offered in the temple as inadequate. . . . Christians are inclined to assume that any teaching in the gospels which challenged current Jewish orthodoxy must derive directly from him, but it is worth noting that on this issue—and no other—Mark believes Jesus and his interlocutor to have been in agreement: the scribe fully endorses Jesus' reply. . . . The statement that the scribe is not far from the Kingdom of God is understood by some to mean that he does not have far to go to qualify, by others to be a promise that he will enter when the Kingdom arrives. (pp. 286–89)

Bede is concerned with exegeting the commandment itself, not with exegeting its place in the Gospel of Mark. Hooker, on the other hand, is deeply concerned about making sense of the scribe in terms of the whole Markan context. I think it is because of her consistent view of the Gospel as condemning Israel that she finds it "surprising" that Mark portrays this scribe as "an honest questioner" and "in agreement" with Jesus. Hilary of Poitiers, who also perceives the scribe to be in accord with Jesus, does not appear to have the same difficulty accepting this fact. Hooker needs to find an explanation because the very existence of this one righteous scribe challenges her basic interpretation. She accordingly looks at the incident from a variety of angles: she notes that not only was the question common to the rabbis, but so was the answer. She suggests that the scribe, in spite of his words, must be presumed to have come to the Temple to offer "burnt offerings and sacrifice." She finally suggests that Mark's placement indicates that the scribe endorses "Jesus' condemnation of the worship offered in the Temple as inadequate." She stresses that this is the only instance in which Mark shows Jesus to be in agreement with a scribe. She remains neutral on the question of what Jesus means when he praises the scribe.

Rereading Mark 12:28–34 in a Jewish Context

I think the incident fits coherently into Mark's narrative if one sees him as presenting Jesus as himself a righteous Jew, desirous not of destroying the Temple but of restoring it to its first principles. In this perspective, it makes sense that Mark shows Jesus reciting the Shema—"Hear, O Israel: the Lord our God, the Lord is one," the central creed of Jewish worship, and linking it to the first commandment of Deuteronomy, "You shall love the Lord your God with all your heart, and with all your soul, and with all your mind, and with all your strength" (Deut. 6:4), and the essential commandment of Leviticus—"You shall love your neightbor as yourself" (Lev. 19:6). As Hooker notes, there are parallels in other Jewish writings for the juxtaposition of the two passages from Scripture; the textual juxtaposition of these with the Shema, however, has no extant source.[24]

The whole composite is a typical midrashic lexicon, bringing to-gether the central tenets of Judaism.

When the scribe then approvingly repeats the words of Jesus (vv. 32–33), he contributes to the lexicon by adding an allusion to Psalm 40: "Sacrifice and offering you do not desire. . . . Burnt of-fering and sin offering you have not required. Then I said, 'Here I am . . . your will, O God, is my delight" (vv. 6–8). When Mark then shows Jesus assuring him of his place in the kingdom (v. 34), I think he is presenting an exchange of mutual admiration in order to make it clear on the one hand that Jesus' denunciation of corrupt Temple authorities was certainly not a condemnation of faithful Jews and on the other that not all faithful Jews were opposed to Jesus or his teachings.

I would interpret this incident, in other words, in a way that is almost opposite to that of Hooker. Considering Mark's placement of this exegetical exchange, I think it significant that in this key moment of Jesus' teaching in the Temple—after Mark has shown him citing Jeremiah about "the robbers in the Temple" and rewrit-ing Isaiah 5 so as to denounce the hired hands of the vineyard, refuting mercenary Pharisees in league with Herodians, and reject-ing the sterile interpretation of the Sadducees—Mark shows Jesus to be in perfect agreement with the righteous scholar of the Torah. I think Mark is making some careful distinctions here. I think that this agreement between Jesus and the scribe must be kept in mind as normative—the measure against which to regard any criticism Jesus utters against the scribes (or other Temple figures) before or after. I think Mark is presenting Jesus as a righteous Jew teaching in ac-cord with other righteous Jews.

The Exchange About the Meaning of the Messiah (12:35–37)

Teaching in the Temple [Jesus] said:

"How can the scribes say that the messiah is the son of David? David himself, in the holy spirit, declared, The Lord said to my lord, 'Sit at my right hand, until I have placed your enemies under your feet.' David himself says he is 'lord'; and how is he his son?" And the great crowd heard him gladly.

Augustine's Reading (354–430 C.E.)

For as he was [the son] of Mary, so, also, he was said to be the son of David; indeed the son of David precisely because the son of Mary. Hear the apostle speaking clearly: "who was born of the seed of David according to the flesh." Hear that he was also the Lord of David; and let David himself say this: "The Lord said to my Lord, Sit at my right hand." And Jesus proposed this to the Jews, and by it refuted them. (*Tractates on John* 8.9 [ACC, 175])

Hooker's Reading

Apart from John 7.42 there is no evidence that Jesus' Davidic descent was ever questioned. There is, then, little indication that this was an issue, either in Jewish-Christian debates, or within the Christian community. The quotation from Ps. 110.1, on the other hand, is not only used elsewhere . . . but is widely echoed in passages where Jesus is said to be seated at God's right hand. . . . If this psalm was widely used in Christian apologetic, it would have been natural to discuss how it was to be related to the traditional Jewish belief in a Davidic Messiah. This would provide an understandable Sitz im Leben for the argument developed in Mark 12.35–7; the pericope is likely to have been used, therefore, in christological debate in the Church concerning the best way of understanding Jesus' role and status.

It is much more difficult to suggest a possible setting in the life of Jesus himself. In his mouth, it could be understood only as a clear messianic claim, and this is totally out of character with the rest of the evidence. The argument that the Messiah is greater than David belongs to the theology of the Church, not the teaching of Jesus.

For Mark, the saying must have been understood as a statement about Jesus' messiahship: although Jesus' claim to be himself David's lord is only implicit, it is nevertheless plain. . . . The challenge to the Jewish authorities to accept Jesus as their Messiah is here made clear. . . . There is in Mark's view no excuse for those who fail to recognize Jesus as Lord.

What is less clear is the logic of the pericope itself. . . . The saying is put in the form of a question, almost a conundrum. It challenges its hearers to think about the position of the one who is now being proclaimed as Christ and to recognize that he is not simply "Son of David" but much more. (pp. 290–93)

Augustine's exegesis is not focused solely on the passage in Mark but has in mind the debate in John 7:42 and the beginning of Paul's letter to the Romans ("who was born of the seed of David according to the flesh," 1:3). Augustine, moreover, appears to assume as background a controversy between Jews and Christians over the idea of Jesus as Davidic Messiah. Hooker observes that there is no evidence that such controversies existed in the time of Mark; Augustine's assumptions would seem to be anachronistic. Hooker herself suggests that the citation from Psalm 110 might have been widely used in Christian apologetic and in christological debate within the church (although she does not give dates for any of this).

Hooker's overall view of the pericope is summed up in her observation that it "challenges its hearers" and is "almost a conundrum." On the one hand, she notes that for Jesus himself to have a messianic claim would have been "totally out of character." On the other hand, she asserts that "although Jesus' claim to be himself David's lord is only implicit, it is nevertheless plain. . . . There is in Mark's view no excuse for those who fail to recognize Jesus as Lord." At another point (not quoted here), she notes that the saying is challenging "because the unsolved riddle is left for us to work out."[25] I think that "conundrum" or "riddle" is precisely what Mark wanted to present and that it was an exegetical riddle typical of midrashic thought. In order to understand how the riddle works, I think we need to look closely at the scriptural passages contained in Jesus' "conundrum."

Rereading Mark 12:35–37 in a Jewish Context

Mark shows that to formulate his question, Jesus juxtaposes two scriptural traditions that appear to be contradictory: the tradition that the messiah is the son of David (a tradition based on 2 Sam. 7:12–14) and the phrasing of Psalm 110, where the speaker (assumed to be David) asserts, "The Lord said to my lord, 'Sit at my right hand.'" Parsing the words in a way that is typically Rabbinic, Jesus then asks, "David himself says he [i.e., the messiah] is lord, and how is he his son?" (v. 37) The midrashic question does not appear to have a neat answer. In constructing the passage, however, Mark has shown Jesus making an alteration in the original text that may provide a clue. In Psalm 110 the verse reads: "Sit at my right hand *until I make your enemies your footstool*" (v. 1). Here, Mark shows Jesus rewriting the end of the verse so that it echoes Psalm 8, where the psalmist speaks of God crowning human beings and putting *"all things under their feet"* (v. 6). The whole context of Psalm 110 speaks of God elevating a particular priest-king; the whole context of Psalm 8 speaks in wonder of how God has elevated every human being. I think the change implies a riddle within a riddle: could it be that God is so "mindful" of ordinary human beings (Ps. 8:4) that God's "anointed one" (messiah) is one of them? Although there was a wide range of messianic expectation in Early Judaism, the various messianic figures who appear (mostly in noncanonical writings) are either royal or priestly or both. The shift from Psalm 110 to Psalm 8 seems to suggest the perspective that God may elevate any human being, even one undistinguished by outer signs of power.

The effect of this riddle is to unsettle the various conventions associated with a messiah. Mark shows Jesus juxtaposing passages in a typically midrashic way that does not define certainties but raises questions and points to ambiguities. It opens up the possibility of alternative interpretations of Scripture by suggesting that the same word may be susceptible to multiple meanings.

In regard to this pericope, Daube observes that "if a question concerning the Messiah is placed in the scheme of typical Rabbinic discourse, then the answer implied is not that one notion is right and the other wrong, but that both are right in different contexts."[26] Daube also notes that all four questions have further significance as they relate to an ancient fourfold scheme of questioning typical of midrashic discourse: (1) a question of wisdom (*ḥokhma*) concerned with points of law (*halakha*); (2) a question of *haggadha*, concerned with apparent contradictions between verses of Scripture; (3) a question of *boruth*, or vulgarity—that is, a "mocking question, designed to ridicule a belief of the Rabbi . . . all directed against the same belief, namely, belief in resurrection"; (4) a question of *derekh 'eres*, that is, the right way, or "principles of a moral and successful life."[27]

Daube finds this scheme specifically applicable to Mark 12, although the questions obviously appear in a different order. Reflecting on this particular order, Daube finds a close parallel to the Midrash of the four sons preserved in the Passover Haggadah, the Mekhilta, and the Palestinian Talmud.[28] There, he observes, the first question is asked by "the wise son" (*ḥakham*) about "the statutes"; the second question is asked by "the wicked son" (*rasha'*), who "puts a scoffing question by which he rudely dissociates himself from the worshipping community"; the third question come from "the son of plain piety" (*tam*), who "puts a simple question about the meaning of the festival in general." Finally, the fourth son is one "who does not know how to ask" (*she'eno yodhe'a lish'ol*) and so compels his father to give instruction.

In applying this parallel, Daube finds that the Pharisees enact the role of the wise son, even though their question here is qualified by duplicity. The Sadducees accurately reflect the role of the wicked son and ask "the mocking question" designed to ridicule belief in resurrection. The scribe reflects the "son of plain piety" asking the most essential question. There is then a silence, which Daube sees as comparable to the reticence of the fourth son "who does not know how to ask"; Jesus' own question follows as a result—that is, he speaks like the father who is compelled to give instruction.[29]

I think that Daube's discussion here serves to confirm my observation that the four questioners who approach Jesus represent different kinds of Jewish believers. By showing Jesus' response to each one in turn, Mark makes some fine distinctions between those who find Jesus congenial and those who do not. It is also important, I think, to take note of what Mark describes as the reaction to each of Jesus' responses: the Pharisees are "utterly amazed" (v. 17); the Sadducees are silent; the scribe is praising (v. 32); the crowd "heard him gladly" (v. 37). The overall effect is not one of hostility but of appreciation. The setting suggested by the continual wrestling with texts and the delighted crowd is that of a school of Midrash where, in the words of Gerald Bruns (quoted earlier), "disputes are meant to go on, where there is always room for another interpretation, where interpretation is more a condition of being than an act of consciousness."[30]

This "condition of being" within Judaism—its innate diversity—must be kept in mind in reading the next and final section of this chapter, where Jesus contrasts the greedy scribes with the generous widow.

The Greedy Scribes and the Generous Widow (*12:38–44*)

And in his teaching he said: "Look at the scribes who like to walk about in robes of honor, and [who like] greetings in market-places, and the first seats in the synagogues, and the chief places at dinner; who eat up the houses of widows and pretend to pray for a long time. They will receive the severest judgment." And sitting down opposite the treasury, he watched the crowd throw money into the treasury. And many rich threw in much. And one impoverished widow came and threw in two copper coins—that is, about a penny. And calling his disciples to himself, he said to them: "Truly I say to you that this impoverished widow has thrown in more than all the contributors. For they contributed out of their abundance while she out of her deficiency has given everything she has, her whole livelihood." (vv. 38–44)

Hegemonius or Pseudo-Archelaus' Reading (*fl. c. 325–50* C.E.)

The Pharisees looked to the "tithing of anise and cummin and left undone the weightier matters of the law" [Matt. 23:23; Luke 11:42]. While devoting great care to the things which were external, they overlooked those which bore upon the salvation of the soul. For they also paid much attention to "greetings in the market-place," and to the "uppermosts seats at feasts." To them the Lord Jesus, knowing their perdition, made this declaration that they attended to things only which were external, and despised as strange those things which were within, and did not understand that he who made the body made the soul. (*The Disputation With Manes* 21 [ACC, 176])

Jerome's Reading (*347–420* C.E.)

The poor widow cast only two pennies into the treasury; yet because she gave all she had it is said of her that she surpassed all the rich in offering gifts to God. Such gifts are valued not by their weight but by the good will with which they are made. (*Letters* 118 *to Julian* 5 [ACC, 177])

I pass on to the widow in the Gospel who though she was but a poor widow was yet richer than all the people of Israel. She had but a grain of mustard seed, but she put her leaven in the measures of flour; and tempering her confession of the Father and the Son with the grace of the Holy Spirit, cast her two pennies into the treasury. (*Letters* 54 *to Furia* 17 [ACC, 177])

Hooker's Reading

The previous paragraph ["Beware of the scribes"] could be understood as an attack on the teaching of the scribes—of whom the one scribe in vv. 28–34 was not typical. . . . Not all scribes were guilty of the hypocrisy which is attacked here, as the story in vv. 28–34 demonstrates, but warnings about the behaviour of particular scribes tended to become sharpened into blanket condemnation of the whole party in the bitter conflict between the Church and the Jewish authorities. Those who are condemned here care nothing for true religion but are concerned only with their own position. . . . In contrast to men who exploit poor widows, we have the "poor widow" who sacrifices all she has. It is often assumed that this pericope has been linked to the preceding one in the oral tradition because they each contained the word "widow," and this is certainly one possibility. But it is also possible that they have been deliberately brought together (perhaps by Mark) because of their content. Certainly the illustration of true worship and generosity provided by the widow stands in sharp contrast . . . to the scribes condemned for their ostentatious piety. . . . The story's climax comes in the saying of Jesus, which brings out the contrast between the widow and the other visitors to the temple, whose piety costs them little. Her offering is acceptable because it arises out of the love for God and neighbour commended in vv. 30–3. (pp. 294–97)

Hegemonius lumps the Markan scribes together with "the Pharisees" in Matthew and Luke and suggests that Jesus damns them all to perdition. Hooker acknowledges that "not all scribes were guilty of the hypocrisy which is attacked here"; on the other hand, she asserts that the righteous scribe of verses 28–34 "was not typical." Her final judgment on the matter is that the "warnings about the behaviour of particular scribes tended to become sharpened into blanket condemnation of the whole party in the bitter conflict between the Church and the Jewish authorities." It is not clear if she finds this in the text of Mark or if she is speaking about conflict that took place at a later time.

In respect to the story of the widow, both Jerome and Hooker see a connection between the condemnation of the greedy scribes and the praise of the generous widow. Jerome, however, seems to see the scribes as Jews and the widow as a Christian: she is "richer than all the people of Israel" and her act somehow expresses a belief in the Trinity. Hooker, on the contrary, notices a connection between the widow's act of giving her whole livelihood and the texts approved by Jesus and the righteous scribe in verses 30–33. I would like to spell out the implications of this connection, because I see here an exegetical enactment of these sacred texts.

Rereading Mark 12:38–44 in a Jewish Context

From one point of view, money or venality is a unifying theme in this chapter, from the denouncing of the hired hands in charge of the vineyard, to the question about the poll tax, to this explicit criticism of those who use religion for their own profit. The denunciation of those religious authorities who "eat up widow's houses" is in the tradition of Jeremiah equating the oppression of the widow with idolatry (7:5) or Malachi placing oppression of the widow in the same list of sins as adultery and false oaths (3:5). What is important to see here, I think, is that to the prophets, true worship is never a matter of prayer alone but always includes the practical matter of how one uses money. The contrast between the greedy scribes and the generous widow is thus, first of all, a contrast in true worship.

Recognizing this tradition makes it easier to see, I think, that the contrast here is also an acting out of what the text does and does not mean when it declares that you should "love the Lord your God with all your heart, and with all your soul, and with all your mind, and with all your strength." The contrast between the socially honored scribes, who pretend to love God by offering long prayers, and the socially outcast widow, who acts to love God totally with her whole impoverished being, is part of the exegetical debate that characterizes this whole section of chapter 12.

Summary of Chapter 12

By means of parable and debate and enactments of Scripture, Mark makes the whole chapter work exegetically to discriminate between the righteous and the unrighteous within Judaism: the hired hands versus the true caretakers of the vineyard; the four types of "sons" of Israel; the good scribe and the greedy one. The righteous Jew is defined by Jesus' affirmation of the Shema, followed by the commandments to wholehearted love of God and neighbor. In this affirmation, Jesus is joined by two who represent the whole range of the Torah community—from scribe to widow.

As such, this chapter is an important bridge between the "Temple-cleansing" scene in chapter 11 and Jesus' "prophecy" about the Temple's destruction that follows in chapter 13. It is important precisely because it provides norms by which to measure Jesus' attitude toward Temple and Torah: this chapter in particular makes it clear that Jesus finds his center *within Judaism*, not outside of it, and that his negative acts and speeches are directed in a discriminating way only at those who, in one way or another, are "selling out" the faith.

From False Witness to Revelation in the Temple

The False Witness Against Jesus (14:57–58 and 15:29)

And some rose up who were bearing false witness against him, saying, "We heard him saying that 'I will destroy this sanctuary made with human hands, and after three days I will build another, not made with human hands.'" (14:57–58)

And the passers-by were blaspheming him, shaking their heads at him and saying, "Aha! the one destroying and building the sanctuary in three days!" (15:29)

Origen's Reading (fl. 200–254 C.E.)

The accusations they brought against our Lord Jesus Christ appear to have reference to this utterance of his, "Destroy this temple, and I will build it up in three days" [John 2:19]. Though he was speaking of the temple of his body, they supposed his words to refer to the temple of stone [John 2:21]. (*Commentary on John* 10:21 [ACC, 218])

Cyril of Jerusalem's Reading (315–86 C.E.)

Those who passed by wagged their heads. mocking the crucified, fulfilling the Scriptures: "When they see me, they shake their heads." (*Catechetical Lectures* 13:30 [ACC, 231])

Hooker's Reading

The statement that many gave false evidence against him [14:56] is reminiscent of Ps. 27.12. . . . A man could be condemned only on the evidence of two or more witnesses (Num. 35.30; Deut. 17.6): if two witnesses could not be found in agreement out of the many who came forward, then clearly their testimony was false. The specific charge brought against Jesus is that he threatened to destroy the sanctuary and build another. The accusation is repeated in 15.29. The terms for "sanctuary" used in both places and in 15.38 is naos, instead of Mark's more usual word for the temple, hieron. It is possible that the choice of term is deliberate and refers more specifically to the inner sanctuary containing the Holy Place and the Holy of Holies, so emphasizing the gravity of the charge brought against Jesus. . . . Since Mark regards it as false, he perhaps sees it as a misrepresentation of Jesus' saying in 13.2, which refers only to the temple's destruction and certainly does not suggest that Jesus threatened to destroy it himself. . . . This evidence [Acts 6.14 and John

2.19] (together with the incident in Mark 11) suggests a widespread tradition that Jesus did make some statement about the destruction of the temple (see 13.2). (pp. 358–59)

The derision of passers-by is probable enough, even though Mark's description of them shaking their heads (a gesture of contempt) echoes Lam. 2.15 and Ps. 22.7 (21.8). (p. 373)

The citation from Origen is a paraphrase of the Gospel of John where "the Jews" ask Jesus for a sign that he is justified in driving the money-changers out of the Temple. Jesus then gives the response "Destroy this temple, and in three days I will raise it up." In John, "the Jews" challenge this statement: "This temple has been under construction for forty-six years, and will you raise it up in three days?" John then explains: "But he was speaking of the temple of his body" (John 2:19–21). In relating this passage to Mark, Origen seems to assume that the theological perspective of one New Testament writer is the same as that of another.

Hooker seems to be making a similar assumption when, linking this passage in Mark both with John 2 and Acts 6, she speaks of "a widespread tradition that Jesus did make some statement about the destruction of the temple." Her assertion is puzzling in view of the fact that she also observes that Mark regards the accusation as "false." (Is she saying that a widespread Christian tradition grew out of false testimony?) Her explanations, in any case, are not consistent. On the one hand, she suggests that Mark may be presenting this testimony as false because he "sees it as a misrepresentation of 13.2"; on the other, she refers to 13:2 as part of "the evidence" that Jesus may have made a threat against the Temple.

If one reads Mark's narrative as one in which historical events reopen the meaning of Scripture, while at the same time they are themelves being intersected and interpreted by Scripture, then one has to pay particular attention to the framework of scriptural allusions. Hooker notes several ways the relevant Scripture converges in pointing to the falseness of Jesus' accusers. In Mark's statement that "many gave false evidence against him" (14:56) she hears an echo of Psalm 27: "false witnesses have risen against me, and they are breathing out violence" (v. 12). Mark's assertion that the false witnesses did not even agree with each other (14:56) causes her to recall the legislation of Numbers and Deuteronomy that "a man could be condemned only on the evidence of two or more witnesses."

Both Cyril of Jerusalem and Hooker are sensitive to the scriptural echoes of the passage that describes the passersby repeating the accusation of the false witnesses (15:29), although interestingly they have different echoes in mind: Cyril cites Psalm 109 while Hooker refers to Psalm 22 and Lamentations. Neither of them develops the implications of these allusions. I would like to suggest that these allusions are in fact the primary clue to meaning here, providing the interpretation Mark wants his readers to hear.

Rereading Mark 14:57–58 and 15:29 in a Jewish Context

The situation of the psalmist in Psalm 109 is that of having been falsely accused. The psalm establishes this setting in the very opening words: "Do not be silent, O God of my praise. For wicked and deceitful mouths are opened against me, speaking against me with lying tongues" (vv. 1–2). Near the end of the psalm he returns to his accusers' contempt: "I am an object of scorn to my accusers; when they see me, *they shake their heads*" (v. 25). In Psalm 22, the psalmist feels abandoned by God as well as human beings. Describing how he is scorned by others, he says: "All who see me mock at me; they make mouths at me, *they shake their heads*" (v. 7). In Lamentations, the psalmist weeps over the destruction of Jerusalem and the way it has become a laughingstock to its enemies. Describing that mockery, he says: "All who pass along the way clap their hands at you, they hiss and *wag their heads*" (2:15).

All three passages, in other words, use the same phrase to describe the righteous (either an individual Jew or the community of Israel) undergoing the experience of contempt. Lamentations is connected to the same historical situation Mark is confronting—the destruction of the Temple. Psalm 22 is connected to another place in Mark's rendition of Jesus' death: the moment when Jesus cries out the opening verse, "My God, my God, why have you abandoned me?" (15:34). Psalm 109 is connected to the specific circumstances described in Mark 14:55–58 of false witnesses making false accusations. It is appropriate to hear all three echoes here: indeed the similarity of situation and phrasing indicates a biblical pattern or rhetorical trope. Familiarity with that trope keeps one, I think, from reading the charge against Jesus in any way as true. Mark is interpreting the historical situation of Jesus by means of a biblical pattern in which the righteous one is invariably subject to false accusations. He states clearly that this particular accusation is "false testimony" (14:57), and he shows the same false testimony being repeated in mocking ways that echo the false accusers of Psalm 109 and the mockers of Psalm 22 and Lamentations. Mark places Jesus in the situation of these psalmists and, by filling in the gaps, extends the story.

Since Mark has set up this testimony as false in every way—first of all, a violation of Numbers and Deuteronomy combined, second, in the biblical tradition of false witnesses, and third, in the biblical tradition of unrighteous mockers—why have Christian scholars been so reluctant to accept these words as untrue? Raymond Brown's comprehensive summary of scholarly treatments of the statement cites only three scholars who label it as false and only one—D. Luhrmann—who thinks that "Mark wants his readers to think the statement in 14:58 was a total fabrication by the witnesses."[31] It is worth pausing to consider the causes and implications of this general resistance.

Perhaps the modern desire to discover the "real" truth of "the historical Jesus" has shifted the focus of analysis away from the theology of Mark. A more serious consideration is that an a priori judgment has taken over—namely, the presumption that Jesus either intended, or would have been pleased by, the destruction of the Temple. It sometimes appears that on the basis of this preconception, critics assume that the "real" Jesus *could* have said something similar to what the trial witnesses cite and thus probably did. Many scholars seem to take as factual "evidence" Mark's narrative account of those who deride Jesus on the cross. But it seems strange that this passage should be taken as reportorial even by those who are well aware of how directly it echoes Psalm 22.[32]

I would like to propose instead that Mark is constructing a scriptural lexicon here—in this instance, a lexicon of allusions to the betrayal of God's righteous one. Echoes of Psalms 27 and 109 establish the setting of false witnesses; echoes of Lamentations and Psalm 22 recall moments when the righteous felt totally abandoned by God. The echo of Lamentations is particularly relevant, I think, because it indicates a tone of grieving (not rejoicing) over the loss of the Temple. It is also suggestive of a subliminal equation noted between that destruction and the death of Jesus. In addition, the ridicule of the passersby here recalls what the "ungodly" say of the righteous man in the Wisdom of Solomon: "Let us see if his words are true, and let us test what will happen at the end of his life; for if the righteous man is God's son, he will help him, and will deliver him from the hand of his adversaries" (Wis 2:17–18). In this total perspective, the mockery of the passersby confirms the *falseness* of the original accusation; it is one more piece in Mark's web of allusions that places Jesus in the biblical tradition of God's holy ones being slandered.[33]

Revelation in the Temple (15:38)

The final "prooftext" for those who would argue that Jesus intended the destruction of the Temple is the one that describes the splitting of the sanctuary veil after Jesus' death:

> And the veil of the sanctuary was split in two from above to below.

Ephrem the Syrian's Reading (fl. 363–73 C.E.)

> The curtain was torn. [This was] to show that [the Lord] had the kingdom taken away from them and had given it to others who would

bear fruit. An alternative interpretation is: by the analogy of the torn curtain, the temple would be destroyed because his Spirit had gone away from it. Since the high priest had wrongfully torn his robe, the Spirit tore the curtain to proclaim the audacity of the pride [of the Jews], by means of an action on the level of created beings. Because [the high priest] had torn his priesthood and had cast it from him, [the Spirit] also split the curtain apart. Or [alternatively], just as the temple in which Judas had thrown down the gold was dissolved and rejected, so too [the Lord] pulled down and rent asunder the curtain of the door through which [Judas] had entered. Or [it was] because they had stripped him of his garments that he rent the curtain in two. For the heart of the rock was burst asunder, but their own hearts did not repent. (*Commentary on Tatian's Diatessaron* [ACC, 234–35])

Gregory Nazianzen's Reading (*fl. 372–89* C.E.)

He surrenders his life, yet he has power to take it up again. Yes, the veil was torn, for things of heaven are being revealed, rocks split, and dead men have an earlier awakening. (*Oration 29 On the Son* 20 [ACC, 235])

Hooker's Reading

> In view of 13.2, 14.58 and 15.29, it seems clear that Mark understands the symbolic rending to be a sign of the temple's future destruction.... For Mark, the rending of the curtain may well have a positive as well as a negative interpretation. With Jesus' death, the fate of Israel is sealed: she has rejected her Messiah, and her judgement is inevitable, since her condemnation has already been pronounced. But at the same time others are brought into the community of God's people.... Mark does not spell out the symbolism in terms of the ritual of the Day of Atonement, but he may well have in mind the idea of a removal of a barrier which kept men out of God's presence.... This is supported by the next verse where, astonishingly, the confession of faith is made by a Gentile. If barriers are broken down through the death of Jesus, even Gentiles can now enter. (pp. 378–79)

Because Ephrem is commenting on the Diatesseron, which was an attempt to harmonize all the Gospels, he feels free to interpret Mark's text by Matthew's (compare Matt. 21:43, 27:5, 25:51).[34] He also is trying to suggest, in his survey of alternative readings, that the Gospels provide a coherent view of Israel and the Temple, and, in his opinion, that view is a consistently damning one. Gregory of Nazianzen also seems to be looking at Matthew's text rather than Mark's because he speaks of rocks being split and the dead being raised (compare Matt. 27:51–52). He understands the tearing of the veil, however, in a radically different way from Ephrem, suggesting that it symbolizes revelation rather than condemnation. Hooker starts out sharing Ephrem's view that the rending of the sanctuary veil is "a sign of the temple's future destruction" and Israel's condemnation. She concludes, however, with an alternative reading that would bring her closer to Gregory: perhaps the symbolism here is that a barrier to God's presence has been removed. The brief incident appears to be a litmus test of one's general take on the theology of Mark. I would like to argue that even in this brief verse there is a scriptural echo that provides a key to its meaning.

Rereading Mark 15:38 in a Jewish Context

The verb here is *schizō*, an unusual term for "splitting open" that appears one other time in Mark—namely, when he speaks of the heavens being opened at the time of Jesus' baptism (1:10). It is an unusual word in that context and thus would seem to echo a comparable use in Isaiah when he prays that God might "rend the heavens and come down" and take back the sanctuary that Israel's enemies have trampled (Isa. 63:18–64:1).[35] Given the care with which Mark chooses his pattern of words, one is justified, I think, in assuming that he designed the last to echo the first. In both contexts, the meaning must then be seen as similar: Jesus' death, like Jesus' baptism, opens up the heavens, tearing open the veil covering the inmost place of God's dwelling and making God's presence felt. That understanding of the phrase would also make sense of the word change Hooker noted earlier: that Mark does not use the word for "Temple" here (*hieron*) but "sanctuary" (*naos*). The action here thus functions as the final refutation of the false accusation: by it Mark shows that far from destroying the sanctuary, Jesus opens it up. He does not replace the Temple but reveals its inner meaning. Precisely what that is, I will take up later. But if one recalls that the first splitting open of the heavens revealed God's spirit descending on the waters, one finds the echo here suggestive not of an ending but of a new beginning.

This reading of the verse is bolstered by one other small point. Other English translations say that the veil was torn "from top to bottom," which is certainly idiomatic. My translation of "from above to below" may seem less so, but it is an equally good translation of the Greek (*anōthen* and *katō*), and it is suggestive of God's act in Genesis when he divides the waters below the dome from those above (Gen. 1:7). Putting all these suggestive echoes together, one finds in this brief verse an indication of God in the act of creation.

Summary

If we consider the full sweep of Mark's references to the Temple, what we find here is an exegetical journey that reinterprets its meaning. I believe that the historical impetus for this reinterpretation was the Roman destruction of the Jewish Temple in 70 C.E., along with the many prior episodes of Roman desecration of the Temple precincts and attempts to stifle the Jewish faith, together with the Roman crucifixion of Jesus. This linking of Jesus' death with the death of the Temple does not set Jesus over and against the Temple but suggests something quite different: that Mark sees Jesus as embodying the values of the Temple—not as they are represented in the falsely appointed high priest but as they are expressed in the righteous scribe; that in Jesus' death Mark sees another instance of idolatrous power attempting to crush the core of Jewish faith; and that Mark sees the body of Jesus as an analogous dwelling place for the presence of God.[36] In a later time, when "Jewish faith" was set off from "Christian faith," these meanings were inevitably lost. But in the first century, I think these linked events are what "the reader" is meant to "understand" in chapter 13 when Mark speaks of "the desolating sacrilege" as the essential evil of his time. Around this historical core Mark shows Jesus, in chapter 13, giving a speech that reflects both on what has transpired in chapter 12 and on what will happen in chapters 14 and 15.

By weaving together various scriptural allusions in chapters 12 and 13, Mark constructs a lexicon that gives image to the Jewish hope for the Temple restored: Jesus cleansing the Temple of foreign desecration in the reformist tradition of Simon Maccabeus and in the manner of Zechariah's peacemaking king; Jesus telling three parables of hope: of God's vineyard taken away from "hired hands" and given back to the family; of God returning suddenly to his own house (as in Mal. 3:1); and of the primal fig tree—symbol of the primal sacred space—coming back into bloom. In those images of Temple renewed are also hints of Jesus raised.

In the second part of chapter 12, Mark constructs a series of exegetical debates in the Temple through which he shows Jesus debating scriptural matters in a setting suggestive of a school of midrash and in a manner typical of an ancient fourfold scheme of questioning. Through the exegetical debate, Mark makes distinctions between four types of sons of Israel and shows Jesus allied with the righteous—from the good scribe to the poor widow.

Chapter 13 then follows with its exegetical undermining of the apocalyptic perspective. While it warns clearly of many tribulations resulting from the loss of the Temple, it also speaks parabolically of God's homecoming, for which the disciples are exhorted, in the words of the Wisdom writings, to keep "watchful."

Chapters 14 and 15 dramatize many of the events warned about in chapter 13—among them, lying witnesses. Mark here constructs a scriptural lexicon that places Jesus in the tradition of God's righteous one who is falsely accused. In this instance, the false accusation is the most ironic one possible—that he intended to destroy the Temple. By using the word *schizō* to indicate the splitting open of the sanctuary veil at the time of Jesus' death, Mark recalls Isaiah's prayer to God to "tear the heavens and come down" and repossess the sanctuary. By the same word he links this moment to Jesus' baptism, itself described in terms that echo the first creation; by further describing the veil as splitting open "from above and below," Mark reinforces the image of the first acts of Genesis. By these rhetorical means, Mark takes the reader on an exegetical journey that moves from cleansing the Temple of its profanation to a reinterpretation of where God dwells: not in a majestic building but in human suffering, in human death, in a human being on the cross. What this implies about the identity of the Markan Jesus I will take up in the next chapter.

5

The Identity of the Markan Jesus: A *Mashal*

Jesus as "the Messiah"

For centuries Christian scholarship and piety have been based on the notion that there was a fixed concept of "*the* messiah" in ancient Judaism—promised to David, foretold by the prophets, fulfilled in Jesus. This clear-cut, linear view of biblical narrative made Jesus so obviously "the Messiah" that only the willfully blind could have missed his identity. Such a reading of the Bible—reflected as early as Justin Martyr's *Dialogue With Trypho*[1]—necessarily contributed to Christian feelings of superiority over the Jews. By the same token, ingrained Christian feelings of superiority have necessarily helped to maintain that reading of the Bible. Only in the present century has there been a turn in Christian humility and a sufficient openness to Judaism to work with Jewish scholars and to reconsider the terms and traditions. It is significant in itself that the pioneering reassessment has been achieved largely by the work of both a Christian scholar, James Charlesworth, and a Jewish scholar, Jacob Neusner. The result has been two anthologies compiled by Christian and Jewish scholars redefining messianism.[2] Both anthologies converge in the conclusion that there was no fixed idea of "the messiah" at the beginning of the Common Era.[3] A summary of what they do find is instructive.

Both books cover the biblical texts and the noncanonical writings of Early Judaism. Both break apart the various elements that Christianity has put together as an integrated concept of the expected messianic figure: "the Lord's anointed"; Davidic king; eschatological agent of salvation; final judge of the righteous and the wicked; victor over evil, death, and Satan; transcendent, preexistent, and resurrected heavenly figure sitting at God's right hand, one who will return at the end of time to establish God's kingdom.[4] Taken together, these studies show how these different elements occur in different ways in separate texts but never all at once; how they are sometimes combined with other elements—such as the traditions of the priesthood or Wisdom; how they appear in texts that have no mention whatsoever of *mashiah*.

Among contemporary scholars are those who perceive the chief function of the texts to be historical and sociological and those who see it to be poetic and liturgical; they nonetheless converge in appraising the leading figures of these texts as "tensive" symbols, pointing beyond themselves and susceptible of multiple meanings.[5] The difference from the way these texts have been assessed by scholars in the past can be related to changed preconceptions: in the past Christian scholars assumed an overall theological schema into which each text must logically fit; present scholarship presumes no such overarching system and thus focuses on each text as a separate entity. An analysis of some of these critical assessments helps to clarify how these two divergent principles of reading have achieved radically different results.

Seeking to break down the ideological approach, William Scott Green focuses on the precise uses of the word *mashiah* in the Hebrew Bible. He notes that it appears exactly 38 times, "where it applies twice to the patriarchs, six times to the high priest, once to Cyrus, and 29 times to the Israelite king, primarily to Saul and secondarily to David or an unnamed Davidic monarch" but "never an eschatological figure."[6] He notes further that there is no mention whatsoever of a messiah in many of the key (if noncanonical) texts of early Judaism—Maccabees, Jubilees, 1 Enoch 1–36 and 91–104,[7] 2 Enoch, the Assumption of Moses, the Sibylline Oracles, Josephus's description of Judaism, or Philo (2–3). Finally, he takes up those texts that contain some mixed or ambiguous references: Ben Sira—which does refer to an Israelite king as *mashiah* but makes the central figure a high priest; the Qumran scrolls—which posit two messiahs, a priest and a king; the Psalms of Solomon 17—which combines the image of "an idealized, future, Davidic king" with the traits of a sage and teacher; the Similitudes of Enoch—where the reference is not to a king but to a "transcendent, heavenly figure"; 4 Ezra—where the messiah dies before the eschaton, then returns to execute judgment; 2 Baruch—where the messiah is primarily a warrior, "the slayer of Israel's enemies"; and the Mishnah—where the reference is mainly to an anointed priest, "and the messiah as redeemer is negligible."[8] Green concludes: "In early Jewish literature, 'messiah' is all signifier with no signified; the term is notable primarily for its indeterminacy."[9]

John J. Collins supports Green's argument indirectly by pointing out the variety of images of *non-Davidic* "agents of salvation" that were current two centuries before the Common Era.[10] George Nickelsburg's treatment of the Enoch material demonstrates the transformations that can occur in the same material over several centuries.[11] In the Book of Parables, for example (Ch. 37–71), he shows the distinction between "the Lord's Anointed" and a Davidic king or Levitic priest. He finds the "Anointed" or "Chosen" one here to be "a transcendent heavenly figure with titles and functions drawn from several biblical (and non-Enochic) eschatological scenarios," an intertextual composite formed "to serve the judicial and salvific functions that the earlier Enochic traditions ascribed to men, angels, and God."[12]

Some Christian scholars, looking for a precedent for Jesus, make much of the Messiah in 4 Ezra (7:29), who dies and later returns to life as God's surrogate judge. But as Michael Stone points out, in this work "the Messiah" is only a judge and not a savior.[13]

Even closer in time to New Testament writing, the Qumran scrolls focus on the coming of *two* "messiahs." Shemaryahu Talmon analyzes the interrelationship between the shifting images in the scrolls and the changing circumstances of the authors, noting how in the beginning, the scriptural image gave birth to the community, and in the end, the community's situation reshaped the image.

Jacob Neusner's challenge to modern Christian scholars is to set aside the "Christian lens" through which all Jewish texts have been scanned for messianic types. Burton Mack's response is to set each text into two contexts—"the social history that provides the setting for a text's composition and address, and the literary-cultural traditon within which a text takes its place." His emphasis is on the function of each text in context. He outlines five kinds of ideal figures, arguing that the function of these ideal figures in the literature of Second Temple Judaism was to be symbols or "rationalizations" that anchored "essentially social anthropologies."[14]

Mack sums up his thesis with the succinct comment: "Texts and times belong together."[15] This view is also the perspective of Howard Clark Kee, who proposes that the word "messiah" should be seen to cover a range of conceptions "for depicting the agent of God" who is representative of "the self-understanding of the people of God and their place in the divine purpose."[16] He concludes: "What is evident, therefore, is that Messiah is not so much a title in this late prophetic and apocalyptic literature as an epithet used to designate someone in a range of roles whose function is seen to be essential for fulfillment of the divine purpose of the Covenant community."[17]

It can readily be seen that a persistent perception of contemporary scholars is the relationship of "the messiah" figure to the community to which it is addressed. Whether defined in political and social terms or in directly religious ones, that community, it is implied, provides both impetus and nexus for the idealization. Once that is recognized, a corollary follows: namely, that the figures and scenarios being evoked do not add up to a "belief system"—that is, to some logically ordered, static, and systematic perception of God's relationship to human beings; rather they represent a dynamic series of images that seek to find a center of balance in continually shifting circumstances, in order to convey what that relationship—at least in *this* moment—is *like.* Regarded as "a belief system," these images "slip, slide, crack, and perish" before our eyes; but regarded as a way of giving image to faith, they open up multiple layers of theological meaning. Understanding the writings of the Hebrew Bible and of Early Judaism as theological *metaphors* rather than as theological *concepts* results in a new perception of thematic variations, imaginative transformations, and counterpointing voices.

This way of understanding theological expression clearly also has consequences for understanding the language of the first followers of Jesus who were also Jews. If the meaning of "messiah" is perceived as a movable feast—variously imaged as king, priest, judge, sage, teacher, redeemer—but invariably symbolizing "the self-understanding of the people of God" in their relationship to God, then Mark's use of the term may be expected to be a reflection of the different perspectives of his time.

Peter's Understanding of "the Messiah" (8:28–33)

And Jesus and his disciples went into the villages of Caesarea Philippi, and on the way he questioned his disciples, saying to them, "Who do you say I am?" Then they replied, saying to him, "John the Baptist, and others [say] Elijah, others that you are one of the prophets." And he asked them, "Who do you say I am?" Peter answered and said to him, "You are the messiah." And he charged them lest they should speak about him. And he began to teach them that it is necessary for the son of man to suffer many things and be rejected by the elders and the chief priests and the scribes, and be killed, and after three days to stand up. And he spoke the word plainly. And Peter, taking him aside, began to rebuke him. Then turning around and seeing the disciples, he rebuked Peter and said, "Get behind me, Satan! For you are not God-minded but human-minded."

Bede's Reading (673–735 C.E.)

"Messiah" in the Hebrew language means "Christ" in Greek; in Latin it is interpreted as "the Anointed One." Hence "chrisma" in

Greek means "anointing" in Latin. The Lord is named Christ, that
is, the Anointed One, because, as Peter says, "God has anointed him
with the Holy Spirit and with power" [Acts 10:38]. Hence the
Psalmist also speaks in his praise, "God, your God, has anointed you
with the oil of gladness above your companions" [Ps. 45:7]. He calls
us his companions since we have also been fully anointed with visible chrism for the reception of the grace of the Holy Spirit in baptism, and we are called "Christians" from Christ's name. (*Homilies
on the Gospels* 1:16 [ACC, 110])

Hooker's Reading

Those who maintain that Jesus made no messianic claims and that
the identification was first made after the resurrection are bound to
conclude that the story has no historical basis. Yet it seems almost
inevitable that the question of messiahship would have been raised
during his lifetime, a probability which seems confirmed by the accusation brought against him at the crucifixion (15.26; cf. also
14.61; 15.2, 18), so that we cannot rule out the possibility that the
disciples believed him to be the Messiah. . . . But Mark's account tells
us nothing of the meaning of such an affirmation for Jesus himself,
and from the rest of his story it is clear that for Jesus it was the proclamation of God's Kingdom, not his own messianic status, that was
central.

Some scholars argue that the historical basis of the story was in fact
the rejection by Jesus of Peter's "confession," and that a vestige of this
rejection is to be found in Jesus' rebuke of Peter as "Satan." . . . It
seems hard to believe, however, that an indignant rejection by Jesus
could have been transformed by degrees into the enthusiastic acceptance that we have in Matthew's account of the scene. Another
suggestion is that Mark himself intends us to understand the story
as Jesus' rejection of Peter's affirmation: Peter's declaration sums up
the view of Jesus as theois anēr—a divine man, working miracles and
demonstrating divine power—but Jesus rejects this and substitutes
his own teaching about the suffering Son of man (T. Weeden,
Mark—Traditions in Conflict, pp. 64ff.). Although Jesus certainly
rejects Peter's understanding of what messiahship means, it is difficult to suppose that Mark intends to portray him as rejecting the
title: certainly Matthew did not understand his story that way.
Moreover, Mark himself has already used the term *Christos* of Jesus
in 1.1.

So at this half-way point in the story, we have a reiteration of the
truth about Jesus' identity. Peter's acclamation of Jesus as Messiah
is then endorsed by a scene in which the divine voice again affirms
that Jesus is the beloved Son. (p. 201)

Bede presses on the linguistic aspects of the word *messiah*, trying
to discover the depths of its meaning through verbal analysis. In the
process, he cites one instance of its use in Acts and another in the
Psalms. The citations remind him of the sacramental use of anoint-

ing in Christian baptism. It is interesting to observe that he never connects being anointed with the priests, prophets, or kings of Hebrew Scripture but rather with "the Holy Spirit" of Christian ritual. When he does associate it with a psalm, it is one that celebrates the anointing of a woman at a royal wedding.

Hooker, on the other hand, follows the primary concern of the twentieth century in worrying over the historical basis of the story. Just as she has done before, she regards Mark's narrative of accusation against Jesus as historical evidence. Trying to sort out Jesus' actual response to Peter from Mark's interpretive account, she notes that "some scholars argue that the historical basis of the story was *in fact* the rejection by Jesus of Peter's 'confession,'" while others suggest that "*Mark himself intends us to understand the story* as Jesus' rejection" (emphasis added). She proposes alternately that "it is clear that for Jesus it was the proclamation of God's Kingdom, not his own messianic status, that was central" and yet that "it seems hard to believe that an indignant rejection by Jesus" could have been transformed into Matthew's enthusiastic account. In the end she concludes that "although Jesus certainly rejects Peter's understanding of what messiahship means, it is difficult to suppose that Mark intends to portray him as rejecting the title." In short, her own analysis seems conflicted and uncertain. What does seem clear is her belief that "messiah" is not just a descriptive word but a *title*. Assuming that Mark is invoking that title in the opening verse of his Gospel, she feels justified in thinking it repeated "at this half-way point in the story." It is also clear that she further identifies "the messiah" with "the beloved Son"—which she reads as an alternative and nearly synonymous title.

In summary, Bede's approach seems to reflect a time when all Christians assumed that there was no ambiguity about the term "messiah" or its association with Jesus. Hooker's wrestling with possible meanings seems to reflect the arguments of the last age which posited a difference between "the Jesus of history" and "the Christ of faith." As a person of faith, Hooker seeks to arrive at the serene clarity that Bede possessed; as a scholar of her time, she is forced to struggle with the Gospel as a window on real events. I would like to suggest that both a smoother and a more comprehensive reading can be achieved by approaching the text midrashically.

Rereading Mark 8:28–33 in a Jewish Context

The midrashic approach finds the division between "the Jesus of history" and "the Christ of faith" to be a false dichotomy, based on a misguided assumption of two stages of reality: (1) the "real" Jesus and (2) myths created about him. The dichotomy dissolves if one approaches Mark's text as a midrashic composition in which, from the beginning, history and faith intersect. Reading Mark as midrash raises the expectation of multiple and varying scriptural perspectives intersecting with history and arranged into a poetic whole that provides neither a biography nor a "definition" of Jesus but rather engages its audience in reflecting on the mystery of his identity.

To become engaged in that reflection, we need to look carefully at the scriptural perspectives involved—not only that of "the messiah" and "the beloved son" but also the related traditions of the "suffering servant," the "son of David," and the "son of man." Finally, I will look at the relevance of the Wisdom traditions. In each case, I will explore the scriptural frame in general and then its particular function in Mark. At the end, I will try to sum up what I think Mark is about.

Most readers seem to agree that in the exchange between Jesus and Peter, Mark (unlike Matthew) represents Jesus as not accepting the designation "messiah" enthusiastically. At the very least, the fact that Mark shows Jesus immediately teaching about his coming suffering, rejection, and death suggests that Mark sees the necessity of including these elements in its meaning. Since even in the multiple images of the messiah that existed in Early Judaism, suffering and rejection are nowhere to be found, the paradoxical combination would have been startling.[18] Mark dramatizes how startling it is, I think, by having Peter rebuke Jesus for thinking this way. In Jesus' corresponding rebuke to Peter, Mark shows him labeling Peter's understanding of the messiah as "human-minded" and not "God-minded."

I think Mark is purposefully alerting his readers here to the fact that the same descriptive phrase can be applied with different intent. In so doing, he is reflecting, I think, the multiple uses of the word in Early Judaism. As a consequence, I do not think we can assume that every time the word *messiah* ("christ" or "anointed one") appears in Mark, it is used with the same referent. Indeed, I do not think we can casually assume that our own understanding of "messiah" reflects Mark's meaning: we need to probe each use that Mark makes of this term. The second crucial use of the term occurs in chapter 14 when Mark shows the high priest asking Jesus directly about his identity.

The High Priest's Understanding of "the Messiah" (*14:61–64*)

And the high priest questioned him and said to him: "Are you the anointed one, the son of the Blessed?" Then Jesus said, "I am. And you will see the son of man seated at the right hand of the power, and coming with the clouds of heaven." Then the high priest tore his clothes and said, "Why do we have need of any more witnesses? You have heard the blasphemy. What does it appear to you?" Then they all judged him to be deserving of death.

Hilary of Poitiers' Reading (315–67 C.E.)

If you will not learn who Christ is from those who received him, at least learn from those who rejected him. The ironic confession his adversaries were inadvertently forced to make stands as reproof of their very mockery. His accusers did not recognize Christ when he came bodily. Yet they had grasped firmly that the true Christ must be the Son of God. Thus, when the false witnesses whom they had hired against him did not score any blows, the priest interrogated him: "Are you the Christ, the Son of the most high God." . . . They did not question the assumption that Christ would be the Son of God. They only asked whether he indeed was the Christ, the Son of God. (*On the Trinity* 6.50 [ACC, 218])

Hooker's Reading

The form of the question suggests that it has been formulated by the Church and represents Christian confession rather than Jewish accusation. Nevertheless, the belief that Jesus was put to death as a messianic claimant is firmly established in the tradition, and if there was collusion between the religious and secular authorities, as the evangelists suggest, then the high priest's question may represent the substance of the accusation. . . . There is no clear evidence in the literature that has come down to us that "Son of God" was used by Jews as a synonym for Christ in the first century, though the idea that Israel, the king (and so the future king) and righteous individuals could be described this way was certainly known. But to use the phrase as a description that could be applied appropriately to various individuals is not the same thing as using it as a recognizable title for a particular individual. In the present passage, the phrase hovers between these two functions: it is not used on its own, as an independent title . . . but in order to fill out the meaning of the term "Christ." For Mark, however, the phrase "the Son of God" was itself a title—indeed, the title which best expressed Jesus' identity—and he uses it here as though it were equivalent to "Christ." (p. 360)

Hilary of Poitiers, writing in the fourth century, reads the language of Mark as the language of the Nicene Creed. Certain that his own terms of belief are identical to those of Mark, he assumes that Mark has placed an "ironic confession" in the mouth of Jesus' accusers. Hooker, on the other hand, is so imbued with twentieth-century awareness of "time-conditioned" words that she assumes the phrasing here represents the formula of the church rather than that of Jewish accusation. She is also aware of the historical research that has been done in recent times that shows "there is no clear evidence . . . that 'son of God' was used by Jews as a synonym for Christ [i.e., the messiah] in the first century." She acknowledges, moreover, that Jews used "son of God" as a descriptive phrase for a variety of individuals. (She does not seem to be equally aware that Jews used "messiah" as a descriptive phrase for different kinds of people.) In spite of her historical understanding, she comes to a conclusion not unlike Hilary's: namely, that Mark intended "son of God" and "Christ" to be understood as *titles*, and equivalent ones at that. I think we need to take Mark 8:29–33 as the baseline here and consider that perhaps Mark is once again showing different uses of the same words.

Rereading Mark 14:61–64 in a Jewish Context

Mark prefaces the high priest's question with two statements that indicate the high priest was trying to entrap Jesus: at the opening of the chapter he asserts that "the chief priests and scribes were seeking to catch him through deceit so that they might kill him" (14:1); later Mark observes that "the chief priests and the whole council sought testimony against Jesus to put him to death" (14:55). Thus when the high priest subsequently terms Jesus' assent to being both "messiah" and "son of God" a "*blasphemy*" (14:64), we need to consider what Mark is further showing us about the high priest. Calling oneself "God's anointed" or a "son of God" would not have constituted blasphemy according to Jewish law. Nor would either of these self-descriptions, taken in themselves, have warranted the Roman death penalty. Thus by having the high priest term these descriptions "blasphemy" and his council then label this "deserving of death," Mark seems to me to be dramatizing Jesus' condemners as those who either are ignorant of Jewish law or who willfully choose to misconstrue it. As I have argued before, it seems apparent that Mark does not present this hearing before the Sanhedrin as one in which the charges were *true* but rather one in which they were *trumped up*.

Mark interprets the proceedings through a network of scriptural allusions to God's righteous one betrayed by false accusers. In addition to the echoes of Psalms 27 and 109 (already looked at in the last chapter), Mark seems to have in mind the framework provided in the opening chapters of the Wisdom of Solomon. There "the ungodly" (1:16) express a philosophy of carpe diem that includes both sensual enjoyment and the seizure of power: "Let us crown ourselves with rosebuds before they wither" (2:8); "Let our might be our law of right" (2:11). In that context—and for no greater reason—they see "the righteous man" as their enemy:

> Let us lie in wait for the righteous man,
> because he is inconvenient to us and opposes our
>   actions;
> he reproaches us for sins against the law,
> and accuses us of sins against our training.
> He professes to have knowledge of God,
> and calls himself a servant of the Lord.

He became to us a reproof of our thoughts,
the very sight of him is a burden to us,
because his manner of life is unlike that of others,
and his ways are strange. . . .
He calls the last end of the righteous happy,
and boasts that God is his father. (2:12–16)

The unknown author of this work (presumably an Alexandrian Jew of the first century B.C.E.), fills in the pyschological gaps hinted at in many of the psalms: of a situation in which a good man is hated without cause—perversely, *because of his very goodness.* (Out of such pyschological insight, Shakespeare constructed Iago's hatred of Cassio: "He hath a daily beauty in his life that makes me ugly.") The opposition here, of course, is specifically in religious terms: the *ungodly* pit themelves against the righteous Jew, who "professes to have knowledge of God." The rest of the speech by the accusers in the Wisdom of Solomon is also germane to the events and language of Mark's passion narrative:

"Let us see if his words are true,
and let us test what will happen at the end of his life;
for if the righteous man is God's child, he will help him,
and will deliver him from the hand of his adversaries.
Let us test him with insult and torture,
so that we may find out how gentle he is, and make trial
    of his forbearance.
Let us condemn him to a shameful death, for, according to
    what
he says, he will be protected." (2:17–20)

The "shameful death" is not described. The author goes on to say that the plans of the wicked were thwarted because God "created us for incorruption, and made us in the image of his own eternity" (2:23). As one of the earliest references in Jewish writing to the idea of individual resurrection, it does not seem implausible to suppose that it was often quoted by the first followers of Jesus after his death. Familiarity with these passages, along with the desire to connect Jesus' death with a belief in his resurrection, would have lent themselves easily to placing Jesus in the same scenario.

And it does seem that, in large terms, Mark creates a similar scenario in his Gospel. Throughout, he shows the powerful and ungodly lying in wait to entrap the righteous: first, John the Baptist, because he was "inconvenient" and reproached them "for sins against the law"; here Jesus, because "he calls himself a servant of the Lord" and "boasts that God is his father." The high priest's question is suggestive of this context: the perspective of those who find the idea of someone being either servant or son of God to be threatening.

In the context of Jewish writing, "son of God" is not a title; every righteous Jew might make that boast.[19] I think that Mark, in showing Jesus' acceptance of the designation, is not giving him a title (which seems to enter Christian vocabulary much later) but rather establishing him as the righteous one whom God will raise up to immortality. What, then, did Mark have in mind in showing Jesus' assent to being "the messiah"?

The Markan narrative has in fact shown Jesus becoming "the anointed one," but in a special sense. At the beginning of chapter 14, in an episode inserted between the chief priests' plot to kill Jesus and the betrayal by Judas, Mark shows Jesus being anointed (vv. 3–9). But among all the messianic images in Early Judaism, there is none like this one. It is so removed from being elevating or glorious, it is almost a mockery: imagine being anointed by an anonymous woman in the house of a leper! What is more, the anointing is not for kingship or for power but for death. Yet Jesus accepts her gesture as the right one for his destiny: "She has anointed my body beforehand for burying"; and he commends his anointer in words that echo his praise of the generous widow: "She has done all she could" (14:8).

The connection between this incident and the high priest's question is obscured in the usual translations, which use the vernacular "anointed" in the first instance and the Greek title "the Christ" in the second. It would be clearer if the high priest's question were translated, "Are you the anointed one, the son of the Blessed?"[20] In such a rendering, "anointed" would more clearly function as a reminder of the scene in the house of Simon the leper, and Jesus' response would be seen to contain an ironic meaning: yes, he is "the anointed one" in respect to death. Here again Mark is not showing Jesus to be claiming a title but once again redefining "messiah" in uniquely inglorious terms.

Mark shows the high priest, on the other hand, to be using the term as one that lays claim to power. Mark dramatizes this further by constructing a parallel between Jesus before the Sanhedrin and Jesus before Pilate, so that when Jesus is sent to Pilate, the political question put to him—"Are you the King of the Jews?"—is clearly a match to the high priest's question. What Mark intends to imply here, I think, is an equation, in the minds of those who condemned Jesus, between "the Christ" and "the King of the Jews": to these people, both are equally titles of power. Mark is again making the distinction between a view of God's agent that is "human-minded" and one that is "God-minded."

Yet some may rightly note that while Jesus accepts his anointing for death, there is more to his answer: "You will see the son of man seated at the right hand of the power, and coming with the clouds of heaven" (14:62). How does this assertion fit with the argument I am making that Jesus lays no claim to power?

First of all, the matter is not helped, I think, by capitalizing "the son of man" and interpreting that as another messianic title. Later I will take up all the possible interpretations of this phrase, but here, at least, it is simplest to interpret it as the Aramaic form of self-reference and substitute "I": that is, "you will see *me* seated at the right hand of power." Taking the words at their simplest, the Markan Jesus is expressing a belief that beyond death, he will ascend to share God's glory.

Mark has shown Jesus making a similar assertion before. At the end of chapter 8, Mark shows Jesus saying to his disciples: "For whoever is ashamed of me and of my words in this adulterous and sinful generation, of him will the son of man also be ashamed, when he comes in the glory of his Father with the holy angels" (8:38). In context this statement takes its meaning from Jesus' plain speech about discipleship: "If anyone would come after me, let that person deny *self* and take up the cross and follow me" (8:34). Taking up the cross means accepting the shame of it; carrying the cross is not a heroic but a humiliating stance. Bearing public shame when one is innocent is the ultimate denial of self, of *who one is*, of one's very identity. By these words Mark suggests that the essence of the cross is the suffering of the falsely accused, falsely identified self.

The false identification of "the anointed one" involves not only the misunderstanding of who Jesus is but also the false application of the phrase to others or the false use of it as a title of worldly power: "Many will come in my name, saying, 'I am he!'" (13:6); "False messiahs and false prophets will arise and show signs and wonders" (13:22). This false understanding of the meaning of *christos*, the "anointed one," is exemplified not only by the high priest's identification of it with worldly aspiration but also by the final mockery of the priests and scribes when Jesus is hanging on the cross: "Let the messiah, the King of Israel, come down now from the cross, that we may see and believe" (15:32). Again, the words imply a false equation between *christos* and king; Mark has shown that for Jesus, it is the *ascent up* the cross, not the *descent down* from it, that marks him as *christos*, the anointed one of God.

Summary of Mark's Use of the Term "Messiah"

To sum up, although Mark identifies Jesus as "the anointed one" (*christos, messiah*), he nowhere equates this term with a purely victorious figure. In chapter 8, Mark shows Jesus denouncing Peter's understanding of God's anointed as one who would not undergo suffering. In chapter 14, Mark shows Jesus accepting the designation of God's anointed only after he has been anointed, in a far from glorious manner, for his death. In chapter 12 (as I discussed in the last chapter), Jesus poses the tradition of a kingly messiah as a kind of questioning riddle, in the process modifying the royal overtones of Psalm 110 with the words of Psalm 8, which suggest God's elevation of common humanity. In a typical Markan triad (which these three episodes form), the middle one always provides a key to the others. So, in this instance, the riddling nature of Jesus as "messiah" predominates. Until we have explored further, we can only say with certainty that Mark is presenting his hearers with a carefully nuanced and somewhat ironic image of what it means to be "God's anointed."

If Jesus came to be commonly referred to by his later followers as "the messiah," the phrase surely retained, at least initially, some overtones of Markan irony.[21] Indeed, Mark's consistent association between "the anointed one" and the cross sharply differentiates Jesus from the whole range of other conventionally glorious, messianic types of his day, none of whom undergo the humiliation of being unrecognized or wrongly identified, much less put to death. It links him instead, and most compellingly, to several other figures in Hebrew Scripture—the Prophets who suffered because of their speech on God's behalf, Isaiah's Suffering Servant, and the betrayed figures of the Psalms and the Wisdom of Solomon. Together they form a biblical tradition of those who bear witness to God and, because of that witness, are themselves misunderstood.

Jesus as "the Beloved Son"

While Mark shows some ambiguity about the term "messiah" in relation to Jesus, at the same time he shows Jesus clearly receiving the designation "beloved son." How do these designations relate to one another? In order to explore that question, I would like to look at the two places where Mark shows Jesus being addressed by the divine voice as "my beloved son": the baptism scene in chapter 1 and the transfiguration scene in chapter 9.

"The Beloved Son" in Mark 1:9–11, 9:6–7

And it came to be in those days, Jesus came from Nazareth of Galilee and was immersed by John in the Jordan. And straightway ascending from the water he saw the heavens splitting, and the spirit descending on him like a dove. And a voice came out of heaven: "You are my son, my one and only [my beloved], my chosen one."

And it came about a cloud overshadowed them and a voice came out of the cloud: "This is my beloved son. Listen to him."

Hippolytus's Reading (d. 235 C.E.)

For this reason did the Father send down the Holy Spirit from heaven upon the One who was baptized. . . . For what reason? That the faithfulness of the Father's voice might be made known. . . . Listen to the Father's voice: "This is my beloved Son, in whom I am well pleased."' This is he who is named the son of Joseph, who according to the divine essence is my only begotten. "This is my beloved Son," yes, none other than the one who himself becomes hungry, yet feeds countless numbers. He is my Son who himself becomes weary, yet gives rest to the weary. He has no place to lay his head, yet bears up all things in his hand. He suffers, yet heals sufferings. He is beaten, yet confers liberty upon the world. He is pierced in his side, yet repairs the side of Adam. (*The Discourse on the Holy Theophany* 7 [ACC, 15])

Ambrose's Reading (333–97 C.E.)

In his baptism he identified him, saying: "You are my beloved Son, in whom I am well pleased." He declared him on the mount, saying: "This is my beloved Son, hear him." He declared him in his passion, when the sun hid itself, and the earth trembled. He declared him in the centurion, who said: "Truly this was the Son of God." (*On the Holy Spirit* 2.6 [ACC, 120])

Origen's Reading (200–254 C.E.)

This is spoken to him by God, with whom all time is today. For there is no evening with God, as I see it, and there is no morning—nothing but time that stretches out, along with his unbeginning and unseen life. The day is today with him in which the Son was begotten. Thus the beginning of his birth is not to be found, as neither is the day of it. (*Commentary on John* 1:32 [ACC, 15])

Hooker's Reading

The words spoken from heaven are commonly traced to a combination of phrases from Ps. 2.7 and Isa. 42.1. . . . It is misleading to try to press the words in either quotation, however, since they are reminiscent of other Old Testament passages also. The idea of an individual as God's son is not a common one in Jewish thought. Occasionally—as in Pss. 2.7 and 89.27—the idea that the king is "adopted" as God's son appears; in the book of Wisdom we find the idea that the righteous man is the "child" of God (2.13–18; 5.5). The king is the representative of his nation, while the righteous man fulfils God's calling for the nation, and these passages reflect the more fundamental understanding of the whole nation as God's son which was one way in which the relationship between Yahweh and his chosen people was seen. (see Exod. 4.22; Deut. 1.31; Hos. 11.1)

It is certainly significant that Jesus is addressed in terms used in the Old Testament of the relationship which should exist between Israel and God. . . . Jesus is here revealed as the one man in whom that role of Israel's sonship is realized (p. 47). "This is my beloved Son" [9:7]. The first words of the divine voice echo those addressed to Jesus in 1.11. The command to the disciples—"listen to him"—is reminiscent of Moses' promise regarding a prophet like himself in Deut. 18.15, 18, but the authority exercised by Jesus is in fact far greater than that given to any other prophet (even Moses!) for it is the authority of one who is uniquely Son of God. (p. 47)

The comments of Hippolytus emphasize the humanity of Jesus. While he says that God sees Jesus as being his son "according to the divine essence," what he expands on are the paradoxes contained in the son who can heal the ills of humanity even while he shares them. For Hippolytus, the phrase "beloved Son" sets off theological speculation about how the divine essence can coexist with human vulnerability.

Ambrose, on the other hand, emphasizes Jesus' divinity. He finds God verifying Jesus as his son throughout the Gospel, and he clearly equates "my beloved Son" with "Son of God" in the Trinitarian sense.

Both Origen and Hooker press more on the text than theology and relate the phrase to Hebrew Scripture. Origen's comments show that he sees Psalm 2 as the prime referent here: "I will tell of the decree of the Lord: He said to me, 'You are my son; today I have begotten you'" (v. 7). His meditation is not on the meaning of "sonship" but on the meaning of "today" in respect to eternal time.

Hooker, on the other hand, seems unsure about the relevance of the scriptural texts. She seems hesitant to see a direct connection but finally concedes that it is "significant that Jesus is addressed in terms used in the Old Testament of the relationship which should exist between Israel and God." It appears that her initial hesitancy is caused by her overriding desire to see "Son of God" as a unique title bestowed on Jesus. I would like to pursue the scriptural references and how they have been understood in Jewish tradition.

Rereading Mark 1:9–11 and 9:6–7 in a Jewish Context

As Hooker notes, most of the references to "son of God" in Hebrew Scripture are not made of an individual but of the community of Israel. That fact, of course, is typical of all parts of the Jewish Bible: God has made a covenant with the *community*, and even when the first-person pronoun is used (as in the psalms), the "I" speaks with a communal voice. Even in Psalm 2, which speaks of an Israelite king under siege from the pagan nations, the plight of God's "anointed" is the situation of Israel as a whole. Thus when the psalmist recalls God's promise to him, "You are my son, today I have begotten

you," he is, in effect, recalling the Covenant. This underlying framework is explicit in Psalm 89, where the psalmist relates the father-
son relationship to God's "covenant" with David (vv. 3, 28). In
Exodus, God instructs Moses to say to Pharaoh: "Thus says the
Lord: Israel is my firstborn son. I said to you, 'Let my son go that
he may worship me'" (4:22–23). In this context, too, it is clear that
"my son" stands for all the Hebrews. In Deuteronomy, Moses expands on the metaphor when he reflects on the Exodus experience
and reminds the people that in the wilderness they saw "how the
Lord your God carried you, just as one carries a child" (1:31). In
Jeremiah, a turning point from God's anger to God's pity is expressed in the language of a tender father: "Is Ephraim my dear son?
Is he the child I delight in?" (31:20). In Hosea, this language is
extended: "When Israel was a child, I loved him, and out of Egypt
I called my son [11:1]. . . . Yet it was I who taught Ephraim to walk,
I took them up in my arms. . . . I led them with cords of kindness,
with bands of love. I was to them like those who lift infants to their
cheeks. I bent down to them and fed them" (11:3–4).

This tradition is so strong and so consistent that it is surely the
way a first-century, biblically literate audience would have heard the
words "You are my son," addressed by the divine voice to Jesus: not
as expressing a new and unique relationship between God and an
individual but as signaling an ancient relationship in which Jesus
stands for all God's people.

Calling Jesus the *beloved* son would have had even richer associations. It echoes one of the biblical stories most reflected upon in
ancient Jewish liturgy and midrash: the moment when God says to
Abraham "Take your son, *your only son* Isaac, *whom you love*" (Gen.
22:2). The multiple midrashic reinterpretations of the story of Isaac
shows this allusion to be by far the most significant.[22]

The oldest extant Targum (that of Job, discovered at Qumran and
dating from the first half of the first century) identifies Isaac with
Isaiah's Suffering Servant.[23] In general, the Targums view Isaac as
a young man rather than a child and present his sacrifice as a voluntary act that has atoning consequences for Israel. The Pseudo-
Jonathan Targum interpolates a dispute between Isaac and Ishmael
as to who is the rightful heir of Abraham. Ishmael claims he is more
righteous because he handed himself over to be circumcised at age
thirteen. Isaac replies that he is thirty-seven years old and "If the
Holy One, blessed be he, demanded all my members, I would not
hesitate." This statement prompts the Lord to make his extreme
request of Abraham, so here it appears that Isaac is the one who
actually initiates the sacrifice.[24]

At the moment of the Binding, Pseudo-Jonathan puts this liturgical speech into Isaac's mouth: "Bind me well that I may not
struggle at the anguish of my soul, and that a blemish may not be

found in your offering."[25] In effect, Isaac speaks of himself as the unblemished lamb of Exodus 12:42.

The Targum on Genesis 3 connects Isaac with Adam by suggesting that when God took Adam from the garden he placed him on Mount Moriah, the future site of Isaac's sacrifice. Pseudo-Jonathan completes this scenario by proposing that Adam built an altar on Mount Moriah which was destroyed by the Flood and restored by Isaac.[26] Both Targums add to Abraham's prayer of thanksgiving the notion that Isaac's sacrifice will have a propitiatory effect for Israel for generations to come. The Fragmentary Targum equates the mountain with the Temple and thus makes the Temple the place for the sacrifice:

> You may remember for their good
> the binding of Isaac their father,
> and absolve and forgive their transgressions,
> and rescue them from every trouble,
> that the generations which are yet to follow him
> may say: "In the mountain of the Temple
> Abraham offered Isaac his son.[27]

Talmudic passages confirm this tradition of perceiving Isaac's act as one of atoning sacrifice. The Mekhilta to Exodus 12:13 makes a connection between Isaac and Passover, suggesting that the reason the angel of death passed over the Israelites was because God beheld the blood of Isaac.[28] Another place in the Talmud connects it with the placing of the burnt ashes on the Ark: "it is as if the ashes of Isaac were gathered up upon the altar" (PT Ta'anit 2:1 [65a]).[29] The Sifre to Deuteronomy 6:5 ("And thou shalt love the Lord thy God with thy whole heart") connects the Binding with the first commandment: "R. Meir says . . . love Him with all your heart as Abraham did. . . . And with all your soul, like Isaac who bound himself upon the altar."[30]

The concept of Isaac's action as a model for faith is also expressed in both the Fragmentary Targum and the Neophiti by the addition of a voice from heaven that praises both father and son.[31] This liturgical, midrashic tradition is reflected in the pseudepigraphical Testament of Levi:

> Then shall the Lord raise up a new priest. . . .
> The heavens shall be opened,
> And from the temple of glory shall come upon him
>   holiness,
> With the Father's voice, as from Abraham to Isaac,
> And the glory of the Most High shall burst upon him,
> And the spirit of understanding and sanctification
> shall rest upon him. (v. 18)[32]

The parallels here to Mark's baptism scene are striking, and of course they increase in significance to the extent that one can assume a Jewish author who antedates Mark by a century.[33]

Jon Levenson has shown how the Isaac narrative is paradigmatic within the Bible, tracing it in the stories of Jacob and Joseph and observing how all three "adumbrate the great national epic in which the people of God, 'Israel . . . My first-born son' (Exod. 4:22) leaves the promised land in extremis, endures enslavement and attempted genocide in Egypt, and yet, because of the mysterious grace of God, marches out triumphantly."[34] He further suggests that it is the "foundational story of the people of Israel": "The story of the humiliation and exaltation of the beloved son reverberates throughout the Bible because it is the story of the people about whom and to whom it is told. It is the story of Israel the beloved son, the first-born of God."[35] He then delineates the development of the story in postbiblical Judaism, showing its role in the development of a sacrificial soteriology and its connections with the Passover liturgy.[36] He concludes:

> Never directly referred to within the Hebrew Bible, the aqedah [the Binding] had, by early in the second century B.C.E., emerged as a supreme moment in the life of Abraham. Soon thereafter it had already become a foundation story for the festival of Passover, with the near-sacrifice of Isaac foreshadowing the literal slaughter of the lamb. . . . At the same time Isaac's role in the drama was becoming increasingly active. He was reconceived as a willing participant, freely and gladly choosing, like a martyr, to give up his life in obedience to the heavenly decree, and again, like a martyr, his choice was seen as effecting atonement for many. This transformation, *already in evidence in the first century* C.E. [italics mine], gathered force in the rabbinic period.

He goes on to say that Isaac's death was imagined as having taken place—at least symbolically; he was then spoken of as having been "raised to life" again by God.[37] In a further chapter Levenson deals with the relevance of these midrashic developments to early Christianity: "Much early christology is thus best understood as a midrashic recombination of biblical verses associated with Isaac, the beloved son of Abraham, with the suffering servant in Isaiah who went, Isaac-like, unprotesting to his slaughter, and with another miraculous son, the son of David."[38]

Not only does the midrash about Isaac confirm a theological development within Judaism that emphasized the atoning nature of death for one's faith, it also indicates that the martyr's paradigm has implications for the way one *lives* one's faith. In the Sifre to Deuteronomy 32, for example, Rabbi Meir interprets: "You shall love the Lord your God with all your soul—like Isaac, who bound himself upon the altar." Levenson comments:

In Rabbi Meir's retelling, Abraham's binding of Isaac as a sacrificial offering is transformed into Isaac's binding of himself: child-sacrifice has been sublimated into self-sacrifice. And it is this note of self-sacrifice that God hears, according to Rabbi Abbahu in the third century, when Israel sounds the ram's horn in hopes of bringing the aqedah to God's remembrance (b. Ros. Has. 16a). The Jew is enjoined to imitate not only Abraham, but Isaac as well.[39]

Finally, a most significant aspect of the tradition's development is its link to the growing belief, within Judaism, in resurrection. Levenson quotes, for example:

> By the merit of Isaac who offered [*hiqrib*] himself upon the altar, the Holy One (blessed be He) will in the future resurrect the dead, as it is written: [For He looks down from His holy height; the Lord beholds the earth from heaven] to hear the groans of the prisoner, [to release those condemned to death] [Ps. 102:20–21]. (Pesikta de-Rab Kahana, zo't habberaka)

Several things are remarkable here: the link between Isaac, Psalm 102, and the servant of Isaiah 61:1 ("The Lord has anointed me . . . to proclaim liberty to captives and the opening of the prison to those who are bound"); the interpretation of the release of prisoners to mean *resurrection*; the fact that the passage implies an expansion from the early midrash, which simply indicated Isaac's personal survival, to the idea of general resurrection as one of the propitiary effects of Isaac's death.

To sum up, as Levenson construes the paradigm of "the death and resurrection of the beloved son," it delineates a rounded view of the theology of "chosenness." The "beloved son" is chosen by God for humiliation as well as exaltation; the son consciously and willingly accepts the humiliation and death or near-death because it is the will of the father; the physical or psychic or symbolic death of the son functions as a propitiary sacrifice that atones for the sins of others; the son is then exalted or raised up and shown in the sight of all to be truly God's "beloved"; the son's exaltation, being propitiary in an inclusive, universal way, brings with it the exaltation or raising up of others to the status of "beloved son."

Levenson shows how the narrative of Isaac is foundational to this paradigm; he also shows how the paradigm gives shape to the narratives of Israel's patriarchs Jacob and Joseph. He points out its relevance to the story of David as well—a younger son chosen to be king and then subjected to trials of persecution, attack, and exile before coming to his enthronement.[40]

What is also clear is how this paradigm undergirds the narratives of the suffering servants and witnesses of Hebrew Scripture: Isaiah's servant, Jeremiah, the speaker of Psalms 69 and 22, the unjustly executed man of the Wisdom of Solomon. Levenson does not show the use of the paradigmatic narrative in all these figures, but he does indicate, in his discussion of the shepherd-ruler image, how "the ancient image of the king as shepherd expresses the perennial idea that the ruler is to be the servant of his people."[41] Tracing the development of Joseph, Levenson finds: "That which legitimates Joseph's authority is . . . his service for those who would rule, his deliverance from dire affliction of those who do him obeisance."[42] The paradox of the ruler who must be servant is thus another aspect of what Levenson terms "the problematics of chosenness"[43]—the double edge of humiliation/exaltation that is the destiny of God's beloved. God's "chosen servant" and God's "beloved son" come close to being one and the same.

If we return to Mark's portrayal of Jesus, it becomes clear that he makes use of the full complexity of this paradigm to shape his narrative. In the first half of his narrative, Mark shows Jesus as God's "beloved son" in a graced and favored sense; in the second half, he reveals the dark side of chosenness. Both meanings are implicit in the baptism scene when the voice from heaven proclaims Jesus "my beloved son": the reverberations of the Isaac story make the designation both celebratory and ominous.

The overtones of the first creation here—the ascent out of the waters, the hovering spirit—also suggest God's first-begotten, *ha 'adam* ("the earthling"). This *'adam*, transposed to Adam, is linked (as I have just shown) to Isaac's foundational story by two Targums: one that suggests that when Adam was exiled from Eden, he was brought to Mount Moriah, the site both of Isaac's sacrifice and Solomon's Temple; another that proposes that Adam built an altar on Mount Moriah that was destroyed by the Flood and restored by Isaac. The Targums, in other words, fit Adam into the central paradigm by linking his exile to the near-death of Isaac and by hinting at a kind of ritual restoration or resurrection. In this opening scene, then, Mark's language would have presented Jesus as both Adam and Isaac, the first-begotten and the beloved son, whose destiny is fraught with ambiguity.

The closing words Mark uses for God's proclamation here confirm this two-edged chosenness: the phrase "with thee I am well pleased" is an Aramaic synonym for "chosen" and echoes both the Targum's rendition of Isaiah 42:1, "Behold my servant . . . my chosen, in whom my word is pleased," and Isaiah 43:10, "my servant, the anointed one, with whom I am well pleased." These renderings taken together reveal a convergence of meanings—that is, the coming together of *chosen*, *anointed*, and *servant*. This convergence again points to the paradox (or what Levenson terms "the problematics") of chosenness: the chosen one who is anointed not to rule but to serve. With these closing words Mark identifies Jesus as God's servant, with all the complexity Isaiah shows that role implies.

Mark develops both trajectories of Jesus as God's son and God's servant. Jesus is recognized as God's son by the unclean spirits (3:11, 5:7). He acts as God's son in his miraculous powers. Most significantly, he speaks of himself as God's son in certain particular ways. First of all, the Markan Jesus distinguishes himself from the Father: he will come "in the glory of his Father" (8:38) but he is not himself the source of that glory; he notes that not he "but only the Father" knows the day and hour of the End Time (13:32). Second, he defines relationship to God not in terms of entitlement but of deed. This is most apparent when the crowd tells him that his family is asking for him and he replies: "Who are my mother and my brothers? . . . Whoever does the will of God is my brother, and sister, and mother" (3:31–35). The implication is that being God's child means conformity to God's will; sonship does not mean privilege but obedience. This implication is dramatized in the scene in Gethsemane where Jesus, addressing God as "Abba," begs him to remove his suffering and then submits to it: "yet not what I will, but what thou wilt" (14:36). In the Markan framework, to be God's son means to be obedient even unto death.

The same obedience unto death, Mark shows, also characterizes Jesus as God's servant. Mark develops the image of Jesus as Isaiah's servant-figure in the second part of the Gospel where, by the juxtaposition of speeches and allusions, Mark indicates that Isaiah's image of servanthood applies both to Jesus' way of life and to his way of death. Being God's chosen servant—like being God's beloved son—means being chosen for humiliation.

The two trajectories come together in Mark's wordplay on Jesus as God's "anointed." The word "anointed" (*mashiah*) is used in the Hebrew Bible and the Targums as a synonym for both "beloved" and "chosen." In the angel's second speech to Abraham he refers to Isaac as "your chosen one" (Gen. 22:16); in Isaiah, God's servant is interchangeably spoken of as God's "chosen" (Isa. 42:1) and God's "anointed" (Isa. 61:1). As such, "anointed" carries with it the same double edge: God's anointed, like God's son and God's servant, is chosen for humiliation before exaltation. God's anointed is *anointed for death*. Mark dramatizes this meaning of anointedness when he shows Jesus being anointed by a woman in the house of a leper and quotes Jesus saying, "she has anointed my body beforehand for burying" (14:8). This episode, as I have shown, brings irony to the high priest's question "Are you the anointed one, the son of the Blessed?" (14:61) With full grasp of the biblical traditions of God's son, God's servant, God's chosen, we can see that indeed it is as God's son that Jesus is also God's anointed, but that does not mean anointed for power: it means *anointed for death*.

Humiliation and death, however, are not the end of the story: Isaac either does not die or (according to the Midrash) is resurrected; Jacob returns to the land of blessing; Joseph is recognized and esteemed by his family; Isaiah's servant is given "a portion with the great." So here, Mark's use of the first part of the paradigm implies the second. This moment of ultimate restoration or resurrection is implied in the second scene in which God calls Jesus his "beloved son"—the scene of transfiguration. In that scene Jesus is not only portrayed in the company of Moses and Elijah but also depicted in such a way that he resembles them: like Moses, he ascends a high mountain to encounter God; like the Elijah figure in Malachi 3, his garments become gleaming white (9:2–3). Peter's desire to build a booth or tent for each of them (9:5), moreover, implies a certain parity between them. The overall effect is to identify Jesus as not only God's "beloved son" but also as God's servant-prophet, Torah-obedient son. This episode, as the middle of a Markan triad, sheds light on the other two instances when Jesus is referred to as the "beloved son," indicating that Jesus fits the Torah paradigm of sonship in all its dimensions. It is important, I think, to see that the implication of resurrection here is not for Jesus alone but for Moses and Elijah as well—indeed the implication seems to be that the latter two have preceded Jesus in their ascent to glory.

In presenting Jesus both as God's "beloved son" and God's chosen and anointed servant, Mark presents him, I think, as Israel itself. I do not, of course, mean to suggest that Mark is proposing Jesus as the *replacement* of Israel. I do not think one should read into Mark either the perspective of Paul or the polemics of a later time.[44] The clashes between the Markan Jesus and the Pharisees, scribes, priests, and Sadducees do not reflect the antitheses of two rival faiths but rather an ongoing, interfamily debate. Not only have these clashes typically been read by scholars in the light of later Jewish–Christian antagonisms, but they have also been analyzed literally and piecemeal as arguments for or against specific legislation. But if one considers them in the whole Markan context, one perceives that while Jesus sometime appears more strict than the Pharisees (e.g., in respect to divorce) and sometimes more liberal (e.g., in respect to fasting), he is consistently shown to be delineating the ideal configuration of values that pertain to the End Time/new Genesis. Thus, for example, he does not denounce fasting but simply suggests it is unnecessary as long as "the bridegroom" is present (2:19); he does not repudiate Moses' teaching but simply uses "the beginning of creation" as his point of reference (10:6).

It is also crucial, I think, to see that in the Markan Gospel Jesus' primary enemies are the forces of desecration and dehumanization, wherever they exist. This is a broad moral stance rather than a narrowly political one; yet in the historical context of Jesus' time and of Mark's, these negative forces are chiefly represented by the Roman oppression and corruption of Israel's faith.[45] Thus Mark shows that the plot against Jesus begins with the Pharisees *in league with the Herodians* (3:6), and the terrifyingly destructive spirits within the Gerasene demoniac are given the name (with a certain satiric wit) of "*Legion*"—a unit in the Roman army (5:9). Mark interpolates his long narrative of Herod into the midst of the mission of Jesus' disciples, so that *Herod's murder of the prophet* functions as a forewarning; at the same time he arranges it so that *Herod's banquet of death* stands in stark contrast to Jesus' abundant feeding of the crowd in the desert. This sense of Herod's poisonous food carries over to Jesus' subsequent warning of his disciples against "the leaven of the Pharisees and *the leaven of Herod*" (8:15). In his third prediction of his death, the Markan Jesus says that the priests and scribes will "*deliver him to the Gentiles*" (10:33–34). The Markan Jesus' anger against "robbers" in the Temple (11:17) resembles Jeremiah's diatribe against the corruption of Jewish worship; in terms of historical setting, the corrupters and "money-changers" in the Jerusalem Temple of the first century c.e. are *Roman appointees.* In the same vein, "the desolating sacrilege set up where it ought not to be" (13:14) is a clear reference to the idolatrous act of *the tyrannical Jew-hater, Antiochus Epiphanes* (and perhaps the later act of *Caligula*). The narrative line suggests that it is the priests *who are in league with Rome* who conspire to arrest Jesus and who turn him over to *the Roman governor*, Pilate. Pilate's questioning of Jesus secures his death on the grounds of the false accusation that he claimed to be *a rival to Caesar* (15:2).

"*The Beloved Son*" *in Mark 12:16*

All this needs to be kept in mind, I think, as further background to the reading of the third reference to "the beloved son" in the parable of the Vineyard. Who does Mark intend as the ones who "perceived that he [Jesus] had told the parable against them" (12:12)? As I have argued before, it does not make any sense to say that they represent *all Jews* or *all Israel*. Just before the parable Jesus is questioned about his authority by a group of chief priests, scribes, and elders who were not supporters of the prophet John (11:31); right after the parable, Mark says, "And they sent to him some of the Pharisees and *some of the Herodians* to entrap him in his talk" (12:13). It is this mixed group of Jewish leaders *in league with Roman ones* who proceed to ask Jesus about *the lawfulness of Caesar's poll tax* (12:14). In other words, the parable is framed by references to *Roman authority*. The Jewish leaders who had no use for John the Baptist were presumably those who sided with Herod; if one recalls that John's quarrel with Herod was over his incestuous marriage, these leaders are not just those who had a difference of opinion with Jesus—they are leaders indifferent to the observance of the Torah.

It is in this framework—where Jesus is being challenged by *nonobservant, Roman collaborators*—that Mark shows Jesus telling the parable of the Vineyard. And in his telling, it will be recalled, he deviates strikingly from Isaiah's "song of the vineyard" (Isa. 5) by projecting God's "beloved" vineyard in the possession of cruel and mercenary tenants. What more apt and more obvious way of allegorizing the takeover of the Temple by Roman mercenaries and mercenary priests? The killing of the "servants" is a barely veiled reference to Herod's killing of John. Given the whole context, the killing of "the beloved son" indicates not only the rigged murder of Jesus but the attempted destruction of Judaism itself—from the genocidal laws of Antiochus to the selling out of Judaism by greedy leaders, to the physical destruction of the Temple. Given the whole of Mark's perspective, Jesus does not stand over and against Israel: rather, Jesus *is* Israel, God's beloved son. Mark sees Jesus, like Isaac and Jacob and Joseph, Jeremiah and Isaiah's servant, as paradigmatic for Israel's story.

Jesus as "the Son of Man"

Jesus refers to himself as "the son of man" fourteen times in the Gospel of Mark, sufficiently often to set commentators worrying about whether this is a variant title and, if so, what it means. A sampling follows of the phrase in Mark and of various interpretations of it.

Jesus' Self-References as "Son of Man"

When Jesus saw their faith, he said to the paralytic, "My child, your sins are released." There were some scribes sitting there and arguing in their hearts, "Why does this man speak thus? He blasphemes. Who is capable of forgiving sins except God alone?" And straightway Jesus, perceiving in his spirit that they were questioning thus within themselves, said to them: "Why do you wonder thus in your hearts? Which is easier to say to the paralytic, Your sins are forgiven, or to say, Rise up, and take up your stretcher, and walk? But in order that you may perceive that the son of man has the power to forgive sins upon the earth"—he said to the paralytic, "Rise up, take up your stretcher and go home." (2:5–11)

And he said to them, "The Sabbath was made for human beings, not human beings for the Sabbath. Therefore the son of man is lord even of the Sabbath." (2:27–28)

And he began to teach them that it was necessary for the son of man to suffer many things and be rejected by the elders and the chief priests and the scribes, and be killed, and after three days to stand up. (8:31)

"But in that day, after that suffering, the sun will be darkened and the moon will not give its light, and the stars will be falling from heaven, and the power in the heavens will be shaken. And then they will see the son of man coming in clouds with great power and glory. And he will send the angels to gather the chosen from the four winds, from the ends of the earth to the ends of heaven." (13:24–27)

"For whoever is ashamed of me and my words in this unfaithful and sinful generation, the son of man will be ashamed of him, when he comes in the glory of his Father with the holy angels." (8:38)

Again the high priest questioned him and said to him, "Are you the anointed one, the son of the Blessed?" Then Jesus said, "I am, and you will see the son of man sitting at the right hand of the Power and coming with the clouds of heaven." (15:61–62)

Novatian of Rome's Reading (*fl.* 235–58 C.E.)

In the same manner that he, according to his humanity, is like Abraham, even so, according to his divinity, he is before Abraham. As he is, according to his humanity, the Son of David, so he is also, as God, the Lord of David. As he is, according to his humanity, born under the law, so is he as God, the Lord of the sabbath. (*The Trinity* 11 [ACC, 36])

Bede's Reading (673–735 C.E.)

We note that the Lord called himself "Son of man," while Nathanael proclaimed him "Son of God" [John 1:49]. Similarly is the account in the Gospels where Jesus himself asks the disciples who people say the Son of man is, and Peter answers, "You are the Christ, Son of the living God" [Matt. 6:16]. This was done under the guidance of the economy of righteousness. It shows that the two natures of the one mediator are affirmed: his divinity and his humanity, are attested both by our Lord himself and by human mouths. By this means the God-man declared the weakness of the humanity assumed by him. Those purely human would themselves declare the power of eternal divinity in him. (*Homilies on the Gospels* 1.17 [ACC, 110])

Hooker's Reading

Beginning from the evangelists' clear belief that Jesus was referring to himself when he spoke of "the Son of man," the phrase has often been understood as a messianic claim on his part.... Others have taken the opposite view, suggesting that the term had little significance in itself and that Jesus saw his vocation primarily in terms of the Suffering Servant of Isaiah (so Dodd, *The Founder of Christianity*, pp. 110–13); but why, in this case, did he refer to himself as "the Son of man" rather than as "Servant of the Lord"? Since there are frequent echoes of Daniel 7 in the Synoptic sayings, there is perhaps more to be said for the view that Jesus was deliberately referring to Daniel's vision, and that he believed himself to be fulfilling the role of the one like a Son of man—or rather, the role of those who are symbolized by this figure. In other words, he accepted the calling of the saints of the Most High, who suffer at the hands of God's enemies, but who are promised final vindication. . . . The phrase was used, not as a title, but as an allusion to this role. Moreover, it may well have been used by Jesus with a corporate significance (as in Daniel 7); Jesus is the nucleus of the righteous and elect community in Israel. . . . A fresh approach has been opened up by scholars working on the Aramaic background who have found new evidence to support an old suggestion that the phrase is little more than an Aramaic idiom meaning "I." . . . Maurice Casey has defined the idiom more precisely when he says that a speaker could use it in a general statement in order to say something about himself. . . . Building on the work of [Geza] Vermes and Casey, Barnabas Lindars has suggested that the phrase refers, not to men in general, nor to "I" in particular, but to someone in the particular circumstance in which the speaker finds himself (*Jesus—Son of Man*, pp. 17–28). . . . The phrase is thus used by Jesus as a way of referring to his vocation, rather than as a claim to personal authority. . . . It seems unlikely that Jesus could have used the phrase to refer to his own mission without reminding his readers of its use in Daniel and Ezekiel. . . . The phrase was by no means a colourless way of referring to oneself: it conjured up all kinds of associations: the prophetic calling; the mission of God's obedient people; the possibility of suffering for those who were faithful to his will; the promise of final vindication. Jesus used the phrase, we suggest, not as a title, not because he was claiming to "be" the messianic Son of man, but because he accepted for himself the role of obedient faith which the term evokes, and because he called others to share that calling with him. (pp. 89–93)

For the ancient commentators, the phrase seems to have generated less puzzlement than for the modern ones. Novatian and Bede both relate it to the Christian belief that Jesus contained two natures in one person. Interestingly enough, however, Novatian thinks the phrase "son of man" refers to Jesus' divinity (hence its relationship to Jesus being "the Lord of the sabbath"), while Bede perceives the phrase as Jesus' acknowledgment of his humanity.

Hooker, on the other hand, does not deal with the phrase in christological terms but rather focuses on its meanings in Jewish tradition. In a passage not cited she observes that its Hebrew equivalent is *ben 'adam,* and she takes particular note of its appearance in Psalm 8, Ezekiel, and Daniel.[46] Although she reads "beloved Son" as a unique and messianic title, she sees "son of man" as an allusion to the corporate role of God's saints. In this context, she sees Jesus as "the nucleus of the righteous and elect community in Israel." This perception brings her back to its use in Daniel and Ezekiel.

I would like to follow up on her insistence that Jewish tradition is the key to meaning here. Yet, as Hooker's survey of conflicting opinions shows, the phrase "the son of man" has generated so much controversy that it would be foolish to rush boldly into the fray. F. H. Borsch has pointed out that the meaning of the term "seems open to different understandings by the best trained scholars" and that different approaches seem to yield totally contrary results:

> What for one group is early and Aramaic is for another late and formed in a Greek-speaking milieu, and vice versa. For some it is eschatology and then reflection on the resurrection and exaltation of Jesus which gave birth to the Son of Man tradition. For others this stage came relatively late in the development.[47]

Rather than argue right away for one particular interpretation of the term, it seems wiser, first, to expand on its use in scriptural tradition and, second, to try to determine, from internal evidence, which meaning seems to be operative in each Markan passage.

Rereading "Son of Man" in a Jewish Context

As Hooker notes, the phrase *ben 'adam* first appears—without the definite article—in the Psalms and in Ezekiel, where it simply and clearly means "human being." In these writings it is generally used to emphasize the distance between the human being and God. The speaker of Psalm 8 asks, "What is man [*'enosh*] that you are mindful of him, And *ben 'adam* that you care for him?" (v. 4) Ezekiel stresses that in seeing "a likeness, as it were, of a human form," (1:26), he is perceiving but "the appearance of the likeness" of God's glory (1:28); later, when he himself is addressed by God as "son of man," the phrase functions as an indication of how far removed he is from the deity. The phrasing in Psalm 80 also seems particularly relevant to its usage in the Gospel because it sounds like a reference to a chosen individual: "But let thy hand be upon the man of thy right hand, the son of man whom thou hast made strong for thyself!" (v. 17). Read in context, however, it is clear that this chosen "son of man" is Israel, and I agree here with Hooker that this collective use is perhaps the most helpful analogy for reading the phrase in Mark.

Although Daniel is often spoken of as the origin of the titular use of the phrase, he in fact seems to use it in the same way as Ezekiel. The mysterious figure who is presented to "the Ancient of Days" and given dominion in chapter 7 appears in a vision and is described in Ezekiel's terms as "one *like* a son of man" (Dan. 7:13)—a phrase that suggests analogy, not title. Here, as in Ezekiel, the author seems to be speaking of an angelic figure in human form rather than some kind of "heavenly man." This interpretation seems to be confirmed by Daniel's description of Gabriel in the next chapter as "one having the appearance of a man" (Dan. 8:15). Gabriel's function here is to serve as an intermediary between God and Daniel in explaining the meaning of his visions; he addresses Daniel himself (as God addressed Ezekiel) as "son of man" (Dan. 8:17).[48]

The Similitudes of 1 Enoch rework Daniel's vision.[49] In this rewriting, the Ancient of Days—here described as "the Beginning of Days"—is accompanied by a figure whose face is both "like that of a human being" and "full of grace like that among the angels" (46:1). Whereas Ezekiel and Daniel seem to indicate an angel in human form, Enoch seems to invert the emphasis and suggest a human being who has angelic status.[50] This figure is also perceived as existing before Time: Enoch calls him "the prototype of the Before-Time" (46:2) and "the Antecedent of Time" (47:3). In a key passage Enoch is told: "This is the son of human beings" (46:3).[51]

In 4 Ezra (a document considered Jewish in origin and dating around 100 C.E., yet available only in a Latin text and after known Christian interpolations),[52] there is a vision of a mysterious "man from the sea," who is both God's agent for delivering his people and God's surrogate judge whom God refers to as "my son" (13:21). Although this man is sometimes referred to by scholars as a "son of man" figure, the phrase is in fact not applied to him.

We are left, then, with the New Testament as the only extant literature that seemingly uses the phrase as a title. Yet even there, its use as a *title* is far from proven. Although it seems more like a title in Matthew and Luke than in Mark, Borsch points out that if it were truly a familiar title for Jesus, it ought to appear in Paul.[53] The matter is further complicated by the fact that the phrase in Aramaic can simply function as an idiomatic circumlocution for "I."[54] Borsch queries: "Is it because it is solely a self-reference of Jesus in the tradition that he [Paul] makes no mention of it?" [55]

Borsch himself offers the interesting possibilty that the second article in the Greek phrase *ho huios tou anthrōpou* is significant; if translated "the son of *the* man," it might indicate a reference to Adam "as the first man, as a kind of representative humanity."[56] Unfortunately, the linguistic evidence here is ambiguous, because Greek syntax uses the definite article to bind together several words that form a unified concept; elsewhere Mark clearly refers to generic human beings with the phrase *tois huiois tōn anthrōpōn* (3:28). Yet Borsch's suggestion might be taken up another way: if one assumes a Hebrew thought-process underlying Mark's awkward Greek, then one might take note that the underlying Hebrew here is *ben 'adam*, a generic reference to humanity that is also suggestive of the first human name. If *ho huios tou anthrōpou* is understood as *ben 'adam*, the phrase would not be seen to function as a title but as a description that links Jesus to the first human creature. Such a reading would certainly fit with the other passages in Mark that project the End Time as a new Genesis. Yet it is important not to make any a priori assumptions but to look at each use of the phrase in turn.

The first use of the phrase in Mark occurs in chapter 2 in the scene where Jesus upsets the scribes by saying to the paralytic, "My son, your sins are forgiven" (2:5). The scribes begin "questioning in their hearts, 'Why does this man speak thus? It is blasphemy! Who can forgive sins but God alone?'" and Jesus responds in a riddling way, "Which is easier to say . . . 'Your sins are forgiven' or to say, 'Rise, take up your stretcher and walk?' But that you may know that the son of man has authority on earth to forgive sins . . ." (2:6–10). "The son of man" could be interpreted here as the Aramaic mode of self-reference. In that case Jesus might simply be making a special claim for himself—that is, "But that you may know that *I* have authority," and so on. On the other hand, if it is interpreted to mean a generic human being (as Casey suggests), then the meaning is almost the opposite—that is, Jesus would then be saying that all human beings have the authority on earth to forgive. If we take up Borsch's suggestion and interpret the phrase as suggesting that Jesus as *ben 'adam* has authority to forgive, then we have a combination of meanings—that is, forgiveness is said to be special to Jesus but special because of his role as representative humanity. *Ben 'adam* would stand for all humanity in its state of original or restored innocence—that is, the Endtime or resurrected human being restored to its primal beauty. In that original and/or final state of wholeness, the human being reflects "the image and likeness of God"; thus human forgiveness on earth reflects God's forgiveness in heaven.

This last interpretation seems most compatible with what Mark shows Jesus saying about forgiveness in chapter 3. There he asserts that "All sins will be forgiven *the sons of men*, and whatever blasphemies they utter, except whoever blasphemes against the holy spirit never has forgiveness, but is guilty of an eternal sin" (3:28–29). First, it is worth noting that this speech itself uses the phrase "the sons of men" in a clearly generic way. More important, in the context of persons being healed of possession by an "unclean spirit," possession by "the holy spirit" appears to represent a direct antithesis; thus "blaspheming against the holy spirit" would seem to mean denying the reality of God's spirit within the human person. Jesus' speech here is linked to his speech in chapter 2; like the earlier episode, this one involves the issues of blasphemy and forgiveness. Mark seems to be suggesting that Jesus' belief in the essential reality of the holy spirit in each person is what allows him to treat demonic possession as a pathological state; the scribes' view, on the contrary, seems to divide people into either holy or demonic camps. Thus the scribes in the first episode consider it "blasphemous" that Jesus tells the paralytic his sins are forgiven; here Jesus asserts that *all* sins will be forgiven and implies that the only blasphemy is to deny that possibility.

The Markan Jesus' second use of "the son of man" phrase is less ambiguous than the first: "And he said to them, 'The Sabbath was made for man, not man for the Sabbath; so the son of man is lord even of the Sabbath'" (2:27–28). If we translate "man" in the first two instances here as "human beings" (which in fact is the implication of the Greek), it is hard to see the justification for not doing so in the final instance. Thus the statement would read straightforwardly: "The Sabbath was made for human beings, not human beings for the Sabbath; so the human being is lord even of the Sabbath." Such a reading is compatible with the Rabbinic saying (Mekhilta 109b on Exod. 31:14) that points out that in the Genesis order of creation, since the Sabbath was created *after* human beings, it was created *for* them.

The Sabbath-Genesis context also lends support to the idea that "the son of the man" here should be interpreted as a reference to *ha 'adam*. Read that way, Jesus would be saying generic humanity in its state of primal wholeness is lord of the Sabbath. Such a state characterizes the Beginning and the End Time, or the End Time as a new Beginning. In this reading, Mark would again be seen portraying Jesus as a new *'adam*, representing humanity in its restored or resurrected being. Such an understanding does in fact fit the context of the whole chapter, which shows Jesus referring to himself as the Endtime "bridegroom" (2:19) and allowing his disciples to nourish themselves with the End-time harvest (2:23–26).

The phrase does not occur again until chapter 8, when the immediate context is the discussion of Jesus' identity. After Jesus has asked his disciples, "Who do men say that I am?" Mark says: "And he began to teach them that the son of man must suffer" (8:31). In this context, an equation between Jesus and a new Adam may seem problematic. It is easiest, certainly, to read this as a simple self-reference ("he began to teach them that he must suffer"). It is interesting to substitute "human beings": "And he began to teach them that human beings must suffer many things." This substitution, however, seems to lose its sense in the remainder of the sentence, which speaks specifically about being "rejected by the elders and the chief priests and the scribes." Nonetheless, the full context here is Jesus' teaching that "[i]f anyone would come after me, let that person deny self and take up the cross and follow me" (8:34), so in a real sense Jesus is indicating that his pattern of suffering and death and rising again, is—or could be—paradigmatic for every human being. In that sense Jesus as *ben 'adam* remains the representative of humanity restored, only now it is clear that this identification includes bearing the human lot of suffering and death before being returned or raised up to a state of divine radiance.

This sense of the phrase continues in Jesus' next use of it: "For whoever is ashamed of me and of my words in this adulterous and sinful generation, of him will the son of the man also be ashamed, when he comes in the glory of his Father with the holy angels" (8:38). One can substitute "I" here but not generic "human being." One can, however, interpret the phrase as *ben 'adam*, indicating the restored or Endtime Adam, and make both symbolic and grammatical sense: "For whoever is ashamed of me . . . of him will the son of Adam also be ashamed when he comes in the glory of his Father." That reading of the phrase makes Jesus' statement a fuller wording of the basic paradigm in which humiliation is the necessary prelude to exaltation.

One can see how this representation of Jesus as a second Adam dovetails with the portrayal of Jesus as "the beloved son." Jesus as the beloved son stands for Israel, the chosen one, the anointed servant—anointed for death before being raised and exalted; Jesus as a second Adam stands for everyone, for all human beings who must undergo the process of death as the way to life. The first image is particular and historical; the second is universal and mythic. The images are not exactly the same, yet the paradigms overlap.

Both representations of Jesus are brought together at the beginning of chapter 9. In the moment of transfiguration Jesus is shown exalted. The scene fits the transformation scenes Martha Himmelfarb describes in her study of heavenly ascents, and the details here are similar to those she defines in cultic terms. The white garment, in particular, is a recurring phenomenon; Himmelfarb sees it as the plain linen robe the high priest wore to enter the holy of holies on the Day of Atonement (see Lev. 16:4).[57] The context of Temple worship is supported here by the ascent up the mountain—an icon of the Temple; Peter's idea of setting up booths suggests the Feast of Succoth. Taken together, the details suggest the New Year rituals, from atonement to harvest. It is perhaps worth noting that through these feasts the paradigm of humiliation-exaltation is realized on a ritual level. In any event, Himmelfarb suggests that the "ascension" literature of the time developed the idea of human transformation implicit in these rituals and merged it with the idea of resurrection.[58]

In every way the scene is a confirmation of Jesus as one who is raised up after being put down: he is like the priest who must put off his splendid garments in order to enter the sanctuary; or like the observant Jew who must reckon with atonement before celebrating the harvest; or like the righteous in Daniel and Enoch who undergo death before ascending to angelic glory. In this context Jesus is called both "my beloved son" (9:7) and "son of man" (9:9). I have already shown how the idea of resurrection fits the pattern of the beloved son; here it is linked specifically with "the son of man" as well.

The immediate context is the disciples' descent from the mountain after their vision: "And as they were coming down the mountain, he [Jesus] charged them to tell no one what they had seen, until the son of man should have risen from the dead" (9:9). The phrase once again could simply be replaced by "I," but the passage that follows seems to indicate more specific identification. The disciples, Mark says, "kept the matter to themselves, questioning what the rising from the dead meant. And they asked him, 'Why do the scribes say that first Elijah must come?'" (9:10–11). This elliptical question implies a link between resurrection and the End Time— that is, the disciples seems to be connecting the idea of universal transformation in the End Time with the idea of individual resurrection, and querying how Jesus could be raised up before the establishment of the Kingdom. Jesus' response here has many parts worth analyzing:

> And he said to them, "Elijah does come first to restore all things. And how is it written of the son of man, that he should suffer many things and be treated with contempt? But I tell you that Elijah has come, and they did to him whatever they pleased, as it is written of him." (9:12–13)

In this reply Jesus clearly makes a distinction between "the son of man" and Elijah, yet he implies that Elijah's return exhibits a pattern of suffering that will prove precedent for "the son of man." This pattern of suffering is further linked here to Elijah's mission to "restore all things." Since Mark has connected John the Baptist consistently with Elijah, Jesus' comment here serves to confirm the similarities and dissimilarities Mark has dramatized between John and Jesus. Elijah is the prophet whom Malachi identifies as the one sent by God to "turn hearts" before a day of final judgment. Jesus is here distinguishing "the son of man" from that eschatological agent, just as the Markan narrative distinguishes Jesus from John. At the same time Jesus indicates that both Elijah and the "son of man" exhibit the same written (i.e., biblical) paradigm of suffering, just as the Markan narrative shows John's death as precedent for that of Jesus. In terms of the transfiguration scene, there seems to be the further implication that Jesus will be exalted (transformed, raised) just as Elijah ascended to a heavenly state.

Thus Jesus' statement here about "the son of man" is complex, on the one hand placing "the son of man" into a paradigm that includes resurrection and on the other hand distinguishing him from the prophet of eschatological judgment. The phrase is clearly not being used by Mark as a title for a divine agent. On the contrary, it seems to function here as a description that emphasizes Jesus' experience of being regarded with contempt: in that respect, the "son of man" blends into "the beloved son."

Summary of Mark's Use of the Term "Son of Man"

It is clarifying to substitute *ben 'adam* in all these contexts. For example, when Peter calls Jesus "the anointed one"—with apparent implications of royalty and special favor—Jesus replies by teaching that the "*ben 'adam* must suffer many things." By calling himself *ben 'adam*, Jesus is stressing that he shares the common lot of humanity. He then indicates a paradox by which, through this very suffering, *ben 'adam* will ascend to the glory of the Father. By calling himself *ben 'adam*, Jesus does not project this exaltation as peculiar just to him but rather implicates all humanity in this glorious destiny. The inclusion of all humanity in the paradigm is supported by his unrestricted invitation to "any one who would come after me." Jesus then appears before his disciples in his ascended and transformed state and is identified by God as "my beloved son." Such a radiant appearance and designation might seem to be unique to Jesus except for the fact that he still calls himself *ben 'adam* (9:9). By implication, every human being contains the potential for such transformed radiance; every human being is identified as God's beloved. The riddle of combining Psalm 110 with Psalm 8 (12:36) becomes clearer. Yet to God's "beloved," as I have shown, also belongs the paradigm of humiliation before exaltation. The Markan Jesus brings both ideas together when he asks, "how is it written of *ben 'adam* that he should suffer many things and be treated with contempt?" (9:13).

This double meaning of the phrase functions throughout the rest of Mark's narrative and, with hindsight, appears to have been implicit before. It is worth noting that it appears in every instance in which Jesus foretells his death; to understand the double entendre is to perceive the tension inherent in each prediction. "The son of Adam [the beloved son] must suffer many things and be rejected by the elders and the chief priests and the scribes, and be killed, and after three days rise again" (8:31). "The son of Adam [the beloved son] will be delivered into the hands of men, and they will kill him, and when he is killed, after three days he will rise" (9:31). "Behold, we are going up to Jerusalem and the son of Adam [the beloved son] will be delivered to the chief priests and scribes, and they will condemn him to death and deliver him to the Gentiles, and they will mock him, and spit upon him, and scourge him, and kill him, and after three days he will rise" (10:33). In each instance Jesus refers to himself as "son of Adam" and describes the paradigm of "the beloved son." The paradigm of Jesus' dying and rising is thus projected as both universal and particular; his death and resurrection is special to the beloved son and at the same time normative.

In the five remaining uses of the term, three stress the suffering aspect of the paradigm and two the aspect of glory. In respect to suffering, the Markan Jesus particularly relates his betrayal to a biblical pattern. Speaking of betrayal by one of his own, Jesus says: "For the son of Adam [the beloved son] goes as it is written of him, but woe to that man by whom the son of Adam [the beloved son] is betrayed!" (14:21). The statement follows the explicit prediction that the betrayer is "one of the twelve, one who is dipping bread into the dish with me" (14:20). It has often been noted that the gesture and the language serve specifically to recall Psalm 41—"Even my bosom friend in whom I trusted, who ate of my bread, has lifted his heel against me" (v. 9); beyond this specific text, of course, is the whole body of literature in which God's faithful one is betrayed as part of God's overall scheme of redemption. It is that sense of a total scheme or pattern or drama being worked out that gives meaning or purpose to the particular moments within it. Thus while Jesus prays to his Father to remove his suffering, he also accepts it as having a certain inevitability: "The hour has come: the son of Adam [the beloved son] is betrayed into the hands of sinners" (14:41). The implication that Jesus is about to act out a previously written script should not be understood as Jesus uniquely fulfilling a unique prediction; rather it is a clear indication that the suffering of "the son of Adam" fits into an ancient biblical pattern. It is not a new pattern but a repeated pattern to be newly realized (that is, *reactualized*)—the pattern of "the beloved son."

The merging of "the son of Adam" with "the beloved son" is most apparent in the scene where Jesus remonstrates James and John for wanting to sit on thrones in heaven and then teaches all his disciples: "Whoever would be first among you must be the slave of all. For the son of Adam [the beloved son] also came not to be served but to serve, and to give his life as a ransom for many" (10:44–45). Through referring to himself both as "son of Adam" and as Isaiah's servant figure, the Markan Jesus indicates they are one and the same. He decidedly does not use the phrase "the son of man" as a title aligned with divine prerogatives, victory, power, or judgment. Rather he indicates the exact opposite: as "son of Adam" he is also God's beloved son and chosen servant, chosen "to give his life" for others. This context indicates further that one meaning of dying for others is to live for them and that the ultimate meaning of self-giving, in both senses, is that of "ransom."

All these dimensions of the phrase must be kept in mind in reading the two instances in which it is used in the context of glory. At the end of chapter 13, after Jesus has described the "tribulation such as has not been from the beginning of creation until now" (13:19), he promises they will see "the son of Adam coming in clouds with great power and glory. And then he will send out the angels, and gather his chosen from the four winds, from the ends of the earth to the ends of heaven" (13:26). If this passage were the only one in which Jesus referred to "the son of man," we might be justified in reading it as the title of an eschatological agent. But we cannot read this passage in isolation from all the others, and in the others, as I have shown, this "son of Adam" is servant and ransom. We must therefore read this passage in the light of the whole biblical paradigm of exaltation after humiliation and resurrection after atoning death.

We must read it, too, in the light of those passages where Jesus has said he has come to serve, not to rule. I, along with others, have observed before that what is striking here, in fact, is the absence of any word of judgment: Jesus speaks of an "elect" but not a "damned," of an ingathering but not a sorting out.[59] The omission does not suit the role of a doomsday agent; it does not fit "the son of man" as some have defined him. It is appropriate, however, to a figure who represents humanity restored, a new or second Adam. This reading is further supported by the preceding reference to "the beginning of creation" (13:19) and by the subsequent reference to a new blooming of the fig tree (13:28). It is appropriate to the chosen servant and/or "beloved son" whose way of death gives life to others.

All these meanings must finally be brought to bear on the key scene in which the high priest asks, "Are you the anointed one, the son of the Blessed?" and Jesus responds, "I am. And you will see the son of Adam seated at the right hand of power, and coming with the clouds of heaven" (14:61–62). Here Jesus uses various terms for himself interchangeably—"the anointed one," "the son of the Blessed," and "the son of Adam." This is another passage in which all Jesus' forms of self-reference have been read as triumphant titles—that is, as claims that he is the "Messiah," the "Son of God," and the "Son of Man" (understood as a title of victory and power). But close and honest reading shows that the Markan Jesus uses all of these terms in a different way: he is anointed in respect to death; he is God's son in respect to obedience. He is ordinary *ben 'adam* who by undergoing death in the manner of God's "beloved son" is raised up to God's glory. Jesus' relationship to God's first-begotten is confirmed when he is crucified on Golgotha—the place of not just any skull but, according to the Midrash, specifically of Adam's.

Jesus as "Son of David" and "Son of Mary"

In a phrase linguistically parallel to *ben 'adam*, the Markan Jesus is also called both "son of David" and "son of Mary." At first glance these references seem incidental, but they are of particular interest because of the pattern of sonship.

Jesus as "Son of David" (10:46)

Jesus is addressed as "son of David" only by Bartimaeus—the blind beggar whose own name means "son of the unclean." As a blind "son of the unclean," this figure seems to incorporate all the religious outcasts of the Markan Jesus' outreach—the leper, the menstruating woman, the dead child, the Gentile, the demoniac. Bartimaeus appears by the roadside just after Jesus has defined his mission in the words of the Isaian servant ("For the son of man came not to be served but to serve, and to give his life as a ransom for many"). In that context this corporate figure of uncleanness both recognizes Jesus as his healer and identifies him as "son of David." The messianic designation "son of David" is thus applied to Jesus in a context that makes it ironic: Jesus appears to be a "messiah" only to one who is poor, blind, and "unclean."

Mark also shows Bartimaeus redefining the meaning of the term "son of David" as he uses it, because he implies that it is one who "has mercy." He thus identifies the Davidic heritage not with power but with compassion. This meaning is close to what Mark has shown to be Jesus' own self-definition as one who has come "not to be served but to serve." Mark thus shows Bartimaeus's understanding of Jesus to be more to the point than that of anyone else in the Gospel—more than those who see him as Elijah returned or John the Baptist raised up, more even than those who see him as teacher or prophet, and certainly more than Peter, who sees him as a non-suffering, triumphant messiah.

As I have discussed before, in chapter 12 Mark shows Jesus himself posing a riddle that points to different ways in which one might understand the messiah as David's son (12:35–37). Implicitly it raises the questions *What is meant by the messiah? What is meant by the son of David?* Earlier Mark shows Jesus placing himself in the tradition of David when he uses David as precedent for placing human need over human law (2:25–26); here the blind man similarly associates the "son of David" with mercy.

Jesus as "Son of Mary" (6:3)

While the references to Jesus as "son of David" (*ben David*) point to an unconventional way of understanding a conventional term, the reference to Jesus as "son of Mary" (*ben Miriam*) runs counter to convention. The reference occurs only once—in the scene where Jesus returns to "his own country" and is rejected (6:3). Mark constructs the scene as a parallel to the first teaching of Jesus' ministry. In both instances he teaches in a synagogue, and both times, we are told, those listening were "astonished" at his teaching (see 1:22 and 6:2). In the first instance, however, the congregation is astonished because "he taught them as one possessing power, and not as the scribes" (1:22) and "commands even the unclean spirits" (1:27), while in the second instance, they reject him out of hand because he is too familiar: "Where [comes] all this, and why all the wisdom and the mighty works, and all the powerful things that have come about through his hands? Is not he the carpenter, the son of Mary and brother of James and Joses and Judas and Simon? And are not his sisters here with us?" (6:2–3)

The implication of these questions, of course, is that they do not expect to learn God's wisdom from someone who is too much like themselves; they look for someone other and superior, someone who can show some "mighty works." It is easy to dismiss this incident as simply an example of Mark's insight into human nature, but it is important to see its function in Mark's theological design. The convention of the day would have been to identify Jesus by his father; this designation startles because it takes note of the feminine side of Jesus' lineage. This unconventional appellation has several effects. First of all, it places him outside the kingly line and emphasizes his very ordinariness,[60] in that way confirming him as the representative of common humanity, the *ben 'adam* of Psalm 8. Second, and equally important, it functions as a corrective to the tendency to interpret *ben 'adam* as an exclusively male term; it indicates instead that the Markan Jesus represents all humanity, female as well as male.

A digression is needed here to clarify what is meant by these distinctions. The term *ha 'adam*, as it first appears in Genesis, is related to *ha 'adamah*, the Hebrew word for "the dust of the earth" (Gen. 2:7) and thus, as Phyllis Trible has compellingly argued, simply means "the earth creature." When God casts *ha 'adam* into a deep trance (Gen. 2:21), God makes two creatures out of one; in effect, Trible suggests, God creates sexuality. After that, the male member of the species is given the specific designation of *ish*, or "man," and the female is given the comparable designation of *isha*, or "woman." At that point—and only at that point—the term *ha 'adam* becomes used as a proper name. It is at this point, in short, that the sexes are linguistically distinguished in the Hebrew Bible and *ha 'adam* becomes a reference solely to the first male.[61] The translation of these words into Greek obscured these meanings because the clearly related terms *ha 'adam* and *ha 'adamah* became *anthrōpos* and *choun apo tēs gēs*, and the clearly parallel terms *ish* and *isha* turned into *anēr* and *gynē*. Thus anyone who knew only the Septuagint would have had little reason to suspect the nuances of the narrative,[62] and it is easy to see how *adam* soon became regarded as simply the name of the first male. It is important for us today, however, to recognize that in the original Hebrew *ha 'adam* and *ben 'adam* are terms that inclusively comprehend all humanity. In that context Jesus as *ben 'adam* represents the primal earth creature, holistically containing both male and female. Mark, by calling attention to the fact that Jesus is *ben Miriam*, confirms the idea of this inclusiveness.

This way of identifying Jesus links him, in turn, to the Wisdom traditions with their particular consciousness of feminine images of the divine. In terms of the large patterns I have looked at earlier, Jesus as *ben David* is linked to the covenantal traditions of Israel as God's beloved son; Jesus as *ben Miriam* is linked to the Wisdom traditions with their focus on ordinary humanity, inclusively understood as created "male and female" to reflect God's image.[63] Accordingly, I next turn to the way Mark presents Jesus as God's Wisdom.

Jesus as "Wisdom"

The ancient commentators frequently identify Jesus as "the Word of God" or as God's "Wisdom." Morna Hooker does not take up this tradition, but some feminist critics have. Here are some examples of these readings.

Commentaries That Identify Jesus as Wisdom

Clement of Alexandria's Reading of Mark 2:9 (190–215 C.E.)

The physician's art, according to Democritus, heals the diseases of the body; wisdom frees the soul from its obsessions. But the good instructor, Wisdom, who is the Word of the Father who assumed human flesh, cares for the whole nature of his creature. (*On the healing of the paralytic in Mark 2: The Instructor* 1.4 [ACC, 28])

Origen's Reading of Mark 13:6 (fl. 200–254 C.E.)

Christ is truth. Antichrist falsifies truth. Christ is wisdom. Antichrist deftly simulates wisdom. (*Commentary on Matthew* 32 [ACC, 181])

Athanasius's Reading of Mark 13:32a (fl. 325–73 C.E.)

When his disciples asked him about the end, he said with precision: Of that day or that hour no one knows, not even he himself. . . . He said this to show that, viewed as an ordinary man, he does not know the future, for ignorance of the future is characteristic of the human condition. . . . Viewed according to his divinity as the Word and Wisdom of the Father, he knows, and there is nothing which he does not know. (*Four Discourses Against the Arians* 3–46 [ACC, 191–92])

Elisabeth Schüssler Fiorenza's Reading of the Gospels

Some of the earliest traditions of the Jesus movement understood the mission of Jesus as that of a prophet of Sophia sent to proclaim that the Sophia-G*d of Jesus is the G*d of the poor, the outcasts, and all those suffering from injustice. It is likely that these early Jesus traditions interpreted the Galilean mission of Jesus as that of Divine Sophia because Jesus of Nazareth understood himself as messenger and child of Sophia. The G*d of Jesus is Israel's G*d in the Gestalt and the figure of Divine Woman Wisdom." (*Jesus: Miriam's Child, Sophia's Prophet* [New York: Continuum, 1994], 140)

Although all three ancient commentators speak in reference to a particular passage, it is clear that they bring to the gospel text a preconceived belief that Jesus is "the Word" or "the Wisdom" of God. Their focus, it appears, is not aimed at deriving theological understanding *from* the text but in making the text fit their theological understanding. Thus Clement does not pause to consider if there is any ambiguity in what Mark is saying about Jesus' power to forgive sins but simply assumes that the episode is an illustration of divine power—a power Clement can sum up neatly and abstractly. Similarly Origen does not look to the text to distinguish between Christ and Antichrist but relies on his own abstract reasoning. Athanasius seems to wrestle somewhat more with the text, but in the end he interprets it according to his creedal understanding of Jesus' two natures. Elisabeth Schüssler Fiorenza, writing in and for a different age, does not speak in creedal terms. Instead, she sums up "early Jewish Wisdom theology" and "early Christian Wisdom theologies" and then applies her findings to the Gospels of Matthew and John with the same broad brush the church fathers used to interpret the texts in the light of church doctrine.[64] If one rereads Mark in the context of specific Jewish Wisdom writings, one finds confirmation both of the church fathers' view that Jesus in the gospels is presented as the Wisdom of God and of Schüssler Fiorenza's emphasis on Wisdom as a womanly figure. Yet one also finds a depth and richness in Mark's presentation that exceeds the claims of either. I will first explore closely the wide range of Jewish Wisdom writings and then relate them concretely to Mark's text.

The Jewish Wisdom Traditions

Whereas covenantal theology makes use of a large canvas that depicts the drama of Israel as a chosen people among the nations of the world, Wisdom theology inheres within the small frame of domesticity and the diurnal round of human relationships, together with the inner frame of individual well-being. "The good wife" of Proverbs 31 is representative of this everyday framework, which is found in the sayings and instructions of Proberbs 2–4, the maxims of Ecclesiastes (chs. 4–7), the moral precepts of Sirach (chs. 24–43), and some of the Psalms. These precepts express a confidence in rational order: as in Psalm 1, the one who follows God's law is "happy" or "blessed," while the one who does not is subject to "woe." The moral perspective that emerges from such repeated antitheses might be summed up as the conventional wisdom that virtue guarantees happiness. Job's suffering and Qoheleth's experience that "all is vanity" present a challenge to this popular piety, making it appear smug and reductive. In different ways both these works arrive at a different kind of wisdom, one that discovers the extent of human limitations and the vastness of God's mystery. One side of this new wisdom, painfully earned, is the acknowledgment that human beings cannot calculate their happiness or control God. The other side is a letting go of the need for security (both material and metaphysical) and a consequent abandonment to, and trust in, the purposes of God.

Proverbs is a collection of teaching materials compiled in the postexilic period from different times and places. Job, at least in its extant form, is clearly postexilic and roughly dated in the sixth century B.C.E. Ecclesiastes is considerably later (third century B.C.E.) and may have consciously used as a starting point the questions raised by Job and/or the dialogue in Proverbs 30 between the skeptic and the believer. Sirach, a century later still, eschews the radical wisdom of Job and Qoheleth and returns to the more comfortable recommendations of Proverbs. In its concluding praise of "famous men" (ch. 44–50) Sirach in fact outdoes Proverbs in its support for cultic piety, suggesting directly that wisdom resides in the keeping of the Covenant: wisdom is placed in the tabernacle in chapter 24 and in the high priest of the tabernacle in chapter 50. In this work covenantal theology and Wisdom theology merge.

All these works are tied together by the prevailing theme that "fear of the Lord is the beginning of Wisdom." Each one, however, implicitly defines "fear of the Lord" in a different way. For Proverbs and many of the psalms, "fear of the Lord" means respect for God's law in daily relationships; Sirach and some other psalms add respect for the obligations of the cultic community. For Job, however, "fear of the Lord" means respect for God's transcendence—an awe that brings with it both a new humility and a new willingness to risk. Job's humility is explicit—"I have uttered what I did not understand, things too wonderful for me" (42:3); his new attitude of abandon is implied in the way he treats his daughters—giving them the decidedly nontraditional names of "Dove," "Cinnamon," and "Horn of Eye-Shadow" (42:14) and leaving them an inheritance along with their brothers (42:15).[65] Qoheleth does not experience God's greatness directly but rather works backward through many observations of human weakness and failure to assert that fear of God is the only thing that matters (12:13). He also comes to find wisdom in a certain generous abandonment to life, advising others to "cast your bread upon the waters" (11:1) and to "sow your seed without calculation" (11:4–6).

The Wisdom of Solomon—written in Greek by an Alexandrian Jew in the first century B.C.E.—is different again, combining and shifting many elements from other sapiential works and yet being innovative in its point of view. Part of the work sounds like the Book of Proverbs, setting up antitheses of beatitudes and curses (chs. 3–5) or teaching prudence and self-control, even while, like Sirach, it deals with the role of Wisdom in Israel's history (chs. 10–19). Yet the opening dramatizes the unpopular wisdom of Job: that virtue is not a shield against suffering and that indeed God's perspective on suffering may be radically different from the usual human one (chs. 1–2). The chief difference of the work lies in its direct treatment of Wisdom: Wisdom here is not commonly accessible but seeks those who are "worthy of her" (6:16); Wisdom is in fact praised for being "undefiled" instead of ordinary; the reward of Wisdom is not in life here and now but in immortality (6:18). Wisdom does not inhere either in the order of household and cultic duties or in accepting the mystery of disorder but takes on a still different aspect, being described both as "the image" (7:26) and "holy spirit" (9:17) of God. It is undoubtedly a clue to this difference in perspective that the "beginning of Wisdom" in this work is not "fear of the Lord" but "a sincere desire for instruction" (6:17). The very nature of wisdom seems to have shifted here from a human virtue to a divine attribute.

Clearly Wisdom is treated differently in each work. Nonethless one can find a common denominator in the way that Creation rather than Covenant is the prevailing frame. In their different ways all the works of the Hebrew Wisdom literature give image to God as one who not only brought about all life, but who continues to care for it and sustain it, to heal and restore, to oppose death in all its forms, to recyle and re-create. Significantly, the Wisdom writings give image to God's nurturing presence in female terms, in contrast to other biblical images of God as male judge, king, and covenant-maker. Thus, although their particular understandings of wisdom vary widely, the Wisdom traditions as a whole provide a feminine image of the divine that functions as a corrective and balance to the male metaphors for God.

In Proverbs, Woman Wisdom is linked to the primordial Garden—"She is a tree of life to those who lay hold of her" (3:18). She is linked as well as to the creating energy of God—"The Lord by wisdom created the earth" (3:19). Wisdom speaks as the personification of this divine energy—"The Lord created me the beginning of his way" (8:22)—and articulates the opposition between life and death that implicitly animates all the patterns of antitheses: "Happy is the one who listens to me, watching daily at my gates, waiting beside my doors. / For whoever finds me finds life and obtains favor from the Lord; / but those who miss me injure themselves; all who hate me love death" (8:34–36).

What happens next is more complex. Wisdom is described as a woman who has built a house and set a table for "whoever is simple" (9:4); here God's nurturing intent is extended to include human understanding, and God's outreach is made specifically to those who do not understand. Wisdom, as God's nurturing aspect, seeks out those who are not wise. The author, clearly playing on the Genesis tradition in which God creates by means of word, makes God's word (wisdom) also the substance of God's Creation. Or to put it another way, God is here both the creator of physical life and of the life-giving words that sustain Creation.

This sophisticated imagery has many trajectories. Later in Proverbs the importance of physically sustaining all human life is expressed in the exhortations to care for the poor (25–29) and even to feed your enemy when he is hungry (25:21). "The good wife" whose portrait concludes the book of Proverbs embodies the life-sustaining energies of God's wisdom as they are actualized in ordinary human relationships: that is, in a wife who is trustworthy, provident, fruitful, strong; ceaseless in active concern and generous in outreach; attentive to the details of human need.

Sirach opens with Wisdom as God's created and creating presence: "created before all things" (1:4), Wisdom functions as the divine life-force, "poured out upon all God's works" (1:9) and "dwell[ing] with all flesh according to God's gift" (1:10). Yet Wisdom is also the human recognition of God's presence in Creation—a profound knowing of God that is on the one hand "created with the faithful in the womb" (1:14) and on the other has to be pursued "like a hunter" (14:22)—or rather, like a lover who "peers through her windows," "listen[s] at her doors," and "pitches his tent" nearby (14:23–25). So sought after, Wisdom becomes for the searcher "a sheltering tree" (14:26–2) and a "nurturing mother and wife" (15:1–8). The image of sheltering boughs is suggestive of Wisdom as "the tree of life" in Proverbs 3:18, itself evocative of Genesis 2. The imagery of "peering" and "listening" evokes the language of the Song of Songs (2:9), itself another reflection of the primal Garden. The portrait of the mother and wife is similar to that of the good wife in Proverbs 31 but not exactly the same: here the food and drink which the wife provides are "the bread *of understanding*" and "the water *of wisdom*" (15:3). The shift is from a symbolic representation to an allegorical one, and in the process there is a shift from Wisdom as a physical life-force to a metaphysical one.

In part 2 (24–43) personified Wisdom articulates her dual role: on the one hand, she is the word of God that formed the natural Creation—"I came forth from the mouth of the Most High, and covered the earth like a mist" (24:3); on the other hand, she is the word of God that formed the faith-community of Israel—"In the holy tabernacle I ministered before God, and so I was established in

Zion" (24:10). In her latter role she evokes the garden imagery of the Song of Songs: there are similarities between the imagery here of the "plane tree," "fragrance," "vine," "blossoms," and "fruit" (Sir. 24:14–17) and the lover's description there of the maiden "stately as a palm tree" with breasts "like clusters of the vine," along with the maiden's invitation to the lover to go with her to the vineyards to see "whether the grape blossoms have opened," to smell the fragrance of the mandrakes, and to observe the "choice fruits" (Song 7:6–13). Wisdom also addresses the one who has been searching for her as her lover: "Come to me," she says, "you who desire me" (Sir. 24:19), much as the maiden in the Song of Songs says, "I am my beloved's, and his desire is for me. / Come, my beloved" (Song 7:10–11). In the Song of Songs the woman invites her lover to "come to his garden and eat its choicest fruits" (Song 4:16), and the lover responds, "I come to my garden, my sister, my bride. . . . I eat my honeycomb with my honey" (Song 5:1). In similar language the woman here invites the one who desires her to "eat your fill of my produce. For the remembrance of me is sweeter than honey, and my inheritance sweeter than the honeycomb" (Sir. 24:19–20). As the Song of Songs revisualizes the Genesis garden as a place of love-making, so the author of Sirach transposes the imagery of a love affair to the allure and satisfactions of Wisdom.

The sensuous language makes the experience of possessing Wisdom a holistic one. When Wisdom goes on to say, "Those who eat me will hunger for more, and those who drink me will thirst for more" (Sir. 24:21), the meaning embraces both physical and spiritual realities. The work thus unites the goodness of the natural creation with the goodness of the cultic creation. These parallel creations are implicit in the great paean to nature that concludes part 2 (ch. 43). In part 3 (chs. 44–50) the search is explicitly for cultic wisdom—"I sought Wisdom openly in my prayer. Before the temple I asked for her" (51:13–14). Wisdom's reply suggests that it can be found in a temple school (51:23) and "the yoke" of the Torah (51:26). But this seemingly intellectual pursuit of Wisdom is informed by the earlier images of a holistic and passionate experience of God's presence in a creation that is "very, very good."

Job also searches for wisdom but does not find it: "Where shall wisdom be found? And where is the place of understanding? Man does not know the way to it, and it is not found in the land of the living" (28:12–13). To Job it is hidden from creation itself (28:20–21). Yet even before God challenges him with reminders of his Creation, Job reasons that only the one who ordered the universe into existence could have the wisdom to understand it: "God understands the way to it, and he knows its place. For he looks to the ends of the earth, and sees everything under the heavens. When he gave to the wind its weight, and meted out the waters by measure . . .

then he saw it and declared it; he established it and searched it out"
(28:23–27). At this point, however, it is noteworthy that Job is
equating "wisdom" with a manageable, human idea of "order."
When God speaks to him out of the whirlwind, it is not the rational aspects of Creation that God points to but the *ir*rational and
*non*rational ones: the joy of the morning stars singing together
(38:7), the power of the sea bursting forth from its womb (38:8),
the unseen depths of both the sea and death (38:16–18). Unlike the
serene ordering of Genesis 1, God's creating acts are rewritten here
to suggest God's mighty and ceaseless struggle to give direction to
powerful and chaotic, nearly uncontainable forces: "Who has cleft a
channel for torrents of rain?" (38:25). "Can you send forth light-
nings, that they may go and say to you, 'Here we are'?" (38:35). It
is the untamed creatures that God highlights: the lions crouching for
prey (38:39), the mountains goats (39:1), the wild ass (39:5) and
the wild ox (39:9), the cruel ostrich (39:16), the battle-loving horse
(39:19), the blood-sucking hawk (39:30), Behemoth (40:15), and
Leviathan (41:1). It is not just the grandeur but the vast incompre-
hensibility of the natural Creation that effects a dramatic change in
Job's perspective and brings him to the wisdom of knowing that he
cannot know (ch. 38–42). For Job, Creation as a theological frame
confirms his experience of incomprehensible suffering and brings
him to wisdom through a *via negativa*.

Qoheleth also comes to wisdom through a negative process, but
he moves from a state of total negativity to qualified affirmation of
life. Beginning in a state of total cynicism—saying "All is vanity"(1:2) and "there is nothing new under the sun" (1:9)—he first
considers even the search for wisdom to be a folly (1:16–18). Gradually, however, he comes to the limited wisdom that "[f]or everything
there is a season" (3:1), so there may be some, albeit transitory,
value to certain activities. Yet cynicism remains, making him consider
how wickedness exists even in the place of justice (3:16), how the
fate of human beings is no different from that of beasts (3:19), and
how afterlife is uncertain (3:21). Later in the book he nonetheless
begins an earnest search for wisdom (7:23) and reflects on wisdom's
transforming effect: "A man's wisdom makes his face shine, and the
hardness of his countenance is changed" (8:1).

The wisdom he eventually attains is similiar to that of Job: "then
I saw all the work of God, that man cannot find out the work that
is done under the sun" (8:17). He returns to saying that "all is
vanity" (9:1), but the words have a different meaning from what
they had at first, being now informed by his search. Like Job he has
come to see that acknowledgment of not-knowing is itself a kind of
knowing. Almost like a modern existentialist, Qoheleth then moves
from this moment of recognizing emptiness to a zest for living: "Go
eat your bread with enjoyment, and drink your wine with a merry

heart; for God has already approved what you do" (9:7). . . . Enjoy life with the wife whom you love, all the days of your vain life which he has given you under the sun, because that is your portion in life" (9:9). Qoheleth's own countenance has clearly been changed by the wisdom he has acquired. In the end he counsels abandonment to whatever life brings, based on a trust that God's providence is at work in Creation: "Whoever observes the wind will not sow; and whoever regards the clouds will not reap. Just as you do not know how the breath comes to the bones in the mother's womb, so you do not know the work of God, who makes everything. In the morning sow your seed, and at evening do not let your hands be idle; for you do not know which will prosper, this or that, or whether both alike will be good" (11:4–6).

It is this trust in the life-giving purposes of God that seems to underlie Qoheleth's final exhortation to "remember also your Creator" (12:1), even in, and in spite of, the time of one's dying. Strikingly, the process of the human person dying is described here in language used in other works for the undoing of Creation— Qoheleth speaks of death as a time when "the sun and light and the moon and the stars are darkened and the clouds return after the rain" (12:2). Thus the total effect is to suggest a parallel between the fate of the cosmos and the fate of the individual human. It is a parallel that underscores the realization that in spite of all appearances, one must trust what one can neither calculate nor control— namely, that God's life-giving intent is at work in all instances. When Qoheleth repeats for the third time that "all is vanity" (12:8), its final meaning cannot be taken as cynicism: it is now simply a realistic appraisal of human limitation, coupled with abandonment to God's will. Qoheleth's last admonition to "Fear God" is not the voice of one who is fearful but of one who is accepting. The other side of "fear of the Lord" is trust.

In the Wisdom of Solomon, as I have already noted, Wisdom is described as a divine attribute as well as a human virtue. The opening, on the one hand, calls Wisdom "a holy and disciplined spirit" within the soul (1:5) and, on the other, implicitly links it with "the Spirit of the Lord" that "has filled the whole world" (1:7). The essence of this spirit is that it "holds all things together" (1:7), both morally and physically. It is thus that aspect of God that creates and sustains life. It is of the essence of God "because God did not make death, and he does not delight in the death of the living" (1:13). This description is prologue to the narrative of the wicked who lie in wait for the righteous one and put him to death for no cause, while God justifies him and raises him up again to immortality (ch. 2). Here immortality is presented as an extension of God's creation: being made in God's image means being made "in the image of God's eternity" (2:23). Having thus established eternal life as

God's purpose for human creation, chapters 3 to 5 proceed to describe the afterlife of the righteous and the unrighteous. Here, as in Psalm 1, the unrighteous disappear from life—they are "like chaff carried by the wind" (5:14), while the righteous do not merely prosper but "live forever" (5:15). Through linking phrases, the righteous person is identified with the wise one (e.g., 4:17), and being wise is described as imaging the divine life that never ceases to exist. "Lawlessness" destroys and self-destructs (5:22) while "Wisdom is radiant and unfading" (6:12).

In chapters 6 and 7 Wisdom is once more personified as a woman but her description is different again from the personifications in either Proverbs or Sirach. In Proverbs Wisdom notes that whoever watches daily at her gates will be happy (8:34), while here Wisdom reverses roles and sits at the gates of the one who seeks her (6:14). In Proverbs Wisdom inclusively offers her banquet to all who are not wise (9:3–6), while here Wisdom "goes about seeking those who are worthy of her" (6:16). In Sirach Wisdom is sensuously described as a woman desired and beloved; here, in the Wisdom of Solomon, she is also spoken of as a woman he seeks, but she is described as pure spirit. The terms Solomon uses in fact suggest something simultaneously divine and human: both God's breath and and the image of God's breath, both outside the human realm—"a pure emanation of the glory of the Almighty" (7:25)—yet something that "passes into holy souls and makes them friends of God" (7:27). The author seems to have reflected on Genesis 1:26 and perceived Wisdom as the particular form in which human beings were created to reflect the deity: "For she is a reflection of eternal light, a spotless mirror of the working of God, and an image of his goodness" (7:26). At the end of his prayer in chapter 9, Solomon asks questions similar to those of Job—"For what person can learn the counsel of God?" (9:13)—but comes to a different conclusion: he does not accept the state of not-knowing but prays instead for God's spirit to dwell within him—"Who has learned thy counsel, unless thou hast given wisdom and sent thy holy spirit from on high?" (9:17).

It is clear that Wisdom here is much more of a philosophical idea or mystical experience than elsewhere in the sapiential writings of Judaism. Yet all the works are linked in taking God's life-giving purposes as their theological premise and in presenting Wisdom as God's life-force made visible.[66] In the final chapters here (10–19), the author retells the book of Exodus as a story of judgment that sorts out—not only historical peoples, the Israelites from the Egyptians, but also the righteous from the unrighteous, the wise from the foolish. In this retelling, idolatry is seen as a foolish and rival Creation, and the climax of the exodus is a new and wise Creation (19:6, 18).[67]

Rereading Mark in the Context of the Jewish Wisdom Traditions

Clearly one cannot equate Jewish "Wisdom" with a system of thought. As usual when one explores any body of writings in Early Judaism, what one finds is not logical, organized theology but multiple, shifting images that convey different angles of truth. Showing the relationship of the Markan Jesus to the Wisdom traditions, therefore, can be done only after one acknowledges that one is dealing not with a static, monolithic concept but with a living organism of chameleon metaphors. There is no question, moreover, but that Mark makes use of the Wisdom writings in a nonsystematic way, borrowing one image from one place and the next from another, allowing them to function as still one more scriptural lens through which to view the identity of Jesus. When one explores all the echoes, allusions, and influences, it appears that the Wisdom literature in fact provides the prevailing perspective.

Creation/Wisdom Theology as the Frame of the Gospel

I suggested in chapter 2 that an audience in Early Judaism would have recognized multiple resonances in Mark's opening, hearing it as: "Beginning [*first Creation/Wisdom*] of the [*bringing of*] good news, of Jesus, anointed son of God." To such an audience the opening words would have signaled that Creation/Wisdom theology is the frame for what is to come. The essence of that frame, as I have just shown, is the belief that in spite of the appearances of evil, God's life-giving energy is ceaselessly at work, transforming chaotic forces and completing God's creation. This perspective is deepened in Mark's first chapter by the scene of Jesus' baptism, with its image of God's spirit hovering over the water, and of Jesus, like the first human being, receiving God's blessing. The scene is echoed in the turning point of chapter 9 when Jesus' radiant transfiguration in the face of death seems to anticipate another ending beyond it. The perspective of primal wholeness prevails in chapter 10 when Jesus recalls the original unity of man and wife (1–12), holds up the child as the model member of God's Kingdom (13–16), and counsels the rich young man to return to a state of primal simplicity (17–31). In chapter 13 the images of a new Creation—the "birth pangs" (8), the "good news" (10), and the summer of the fig tree (28)—counterpoint the disasters. In chapters 14 and 15 the chronology of Jesus' death (as I will show later) is worked out to suggest the reversal of God's creating acts in Genesis 1, while in chapter 16 this reversal is itself reversed with the images of transformation and a new beginning. The repeated references to Jesus as *ben 'adam* also suggest, as I have just shown, that Jesus functions in some way as a second

Adam. Creation theology clearly provides the frame for the structure of Mark's Gospel and for its overriding perspectives. It remains to show how these perspectives are also informed by Wisdom.

Emphasis on Wisdom's Inclusiveness

When Jesus returns to teach in his own synagogue, his fellow townsfolk say: "Where [comes] all this, and why all the wisdom? . . . Is he not the carpenter, the son of Mary?" (6:2–3). Among the many ironies here is the fact that these folk identify "wisdom" with something out of the ordinary, while the Wisdom traditions themselves locate it in everyday relationships and events. I have already noted that the identity of Jesus as *ben Miriam* reinforces the image of him as the representative of common humanity and, in connection with the Wisdom traditions, that is particularly a reminder of the feminine consciousness that imbues personified Wisdom.[68] Although Mark remains focused on Jesus as a concrete person and never turns him into an allegorized abstraction, there are many ways that his characterization of Jesus evokes the figure of female Wisdom.[69]

Jesus Described Like Proverbs' Wisdom

Seeing Jesus in the context of Proverbs' Wisdom gives a fresh and deeper meaning to many of his actions. Jesus' invitation to unlearned fishermen, for example, takes on a different dimension if viewed in the context of personified Wisdom inviting "the simple" to "leave simpleness, and live, and walk in the way of insight" (Prov. 9:6). Jesus' further insistence on calling sinners seems like an extension of Wisdom's logic that Wisdom must seek out those who need her— that is, those who are *un*wise. The sapiential perspective is confirmed by the fact that Jesus' explanation for his actions here takes the form of folk aphorism: "Those who are well have no need of a physician, but those who are sick" (2:17).

Jesus' sitting at table with tax collectors and sinners (2:15) also takes on heightened meaning as it echoes Wisdom's inclusive banquet (Prov. 9:3–6). I have noted before that by imaging Jesus' table fellowship as a "wedding feast" (2:19), Mark connects it with Isaiah's future feast "for all peoples" (Isa. 25:6); at the same time it is a reminder of Wisdom's invitation to those "without sense" (Prov. 9:4) to come to a banquet that is here and now. Strikingly, this banquet is made up of simple fare: the invitation is to bread and wine (Prov. 9:5). Thus the echoes of Wisdom's feast, initiated here, continue in Mark through the miraculous feedings of chapters 6 and 8 and touch the Passover meal of chapter 14.

Repeatedly Mark emphasizes the nurturing aspects of Jesus. In one of his first arguments over the meaning of Torah, Jesus invokes the example of David to support his view that feeding the hungry takes precedence over Sabbath restrictions (2:23–27). His concern for nourishing the needy runs like a refrain throughout the Gospel: in the same phrase he expresses his desire to give "something to eat" to Jairus's young daughter (5:43), to the crowd in "a lonely place" (6:35), and to the crowd with him three days "in the desert" (8:4). The Syrophoenician woman wins him over by jokingly begging for the crumbs under the table (7:28). Jesus' two miracles of abundant food enclose Herod's birthday slaughter (6:21–28): a banquet of death is bracketed by two banquets of life. In the climactic moment of this theme of food, Jesus becomes himself the meal (14:22–24). All this emphasis on nurture can be related to Proverbs' figure of Wisdom as a generous hostess setting her table and to "the good wife" who will not see her household go hungry but "brings her bread from afar" (Prov. 31).

Jesus Described Like Wisdom in Creation

The nurturing aspect of Wisdom is part of her self-articulation as the divine life-force. In the typical antithetical pattern of Proverbs, Wisdom suggests that choosing her is opting for life versus death (8:34–36). Here Jesus offers a similar pair of stark choices—"Is it lawful on the Sabbath to do good or to do harm, to save or to kill?" (3:4). Indeed if one considers Jesus' chief sayings and actions throughout the Gospel—his continual exorcising and healing and "raising up," together with his repeated concern for feeding the hungry—one finds him making a consistent choice for whatever is life-giving. Mark highlights this choice by showing it as a contrast to some prevailing conventions. Thus, for example, the Markan Jesus, unlike John the Baptist, thinks it more appropriate for his disciples to feast than to fast (2:18) and, unlike the Pharisees, to satisfy their hunger than to observe the Sabbath rules (2:23). Jesus' attitude toward those possessed by demons is shown from the outset as surprising: he does not attack the demon but transforms the demoniac (chs. 2, 5, 9). He does not refer to demons by that name but as "unclean spirits." In his discussion about exorcism in chapter 3 he counters the idea of an "unclean spirit" with the idea of a "holy spirit" (3:29). There as well as in chapter 2 he suggests that exorcism and healing are signs that point to forgiveness as the essential activity of God (2:8–11 and 3:28). Forgiveness is part of the general pattern in which Jesus seeks not to reject or condemn but to accept and restore "the unclean." In these attitudes and actions he reflects, as Wisdom does, the Creator God acting to regenerate all parts of Creation.

The language of resurrection that runs throughout the Gospel is part of this thematic insistence—which is also in the Wisdom literature—that the perspective of the Creator transforms the meaning of death. In Ecclesiastes death is only one in a round of seasons; in the Wisdom of Solomon, Wisdom as God's breath brings immortality. So here, the Markan Jesus may be angered that the fig tree is out of season (12:13), but he also imagines the summer of its reblooming (13:28). So, too, Jesus' own death is consistently coupled with his resurrection, and that, in turn, is envisioned not as some final state but as a recycling of his ongoing activity (16:7).

Jesus and Wisdom Eschatology

Many works in Early Judaism envisioned the End Time as a return to the Garden of Genesis. In the sapiential literature, imagery of the Garden forms part of the description of Wisdom herself: in Proverbs Wisdom is a "tree of life," in Sirach a "sheltering bough." Similar imagery appears in Mark in Jesus' parable of the Mustard Seed—a parable (as I have already shown) that offers a contrasting perspective to the opening parable. This contrast takes on even richer meaning when seen in the context of the Wisdom traditions. Notably, all three parables in chapter 4 use the imagery of Creation—God as the sower of seed and the seed as representative of human destiny. One might characterize the opening parable as expressing a rigid interpretation of covenantal theology—that is, one of quid pro quo, an eschatology of strict retribution. Only the second and third parables, however, are introduced by Jesus as analogies for God's kingdom, and they counter this strict view with perspectives taken from Wisdom. The seed that grows by itself expresses the abandonment of Qoheleth; the seed that becomes the sheltering bough is suggestive of Sirach's Wisdom. This suggestion is enhanced by the commonness of the mustard seed and the humbleness of its final stature: like the Wisdom traditions as a whole, the Mustard Seed parable points to God's presence in the ordinary and the everyday.

Jesus as a Teacher of Wisdom

The perspectives of the Wisdom traditions in fact serve to clarify much of Jesus' teaching in chapter 4. Jesus, teacher of Wisdom, follows the style of the *bet midrash* and juxtaposes counterpointing scriptural views. The first parable presents the most familiar and the most widely accepted—the idea of the Covenant as a simple dividing point between good and evil. If the exegesis that follows is authentically Mark's, then he shows Jesus explaining it in the plain and conventional terms of a moral allegory. At the same time he tells them that they confront a "mystery" here (4:11). Later he remarks that "nothing is secret, except to come to light" (4:22) and then tells two parables about seeds that grow mysteriously—one into a harvest (4:29) and the other, in effect, into the tree of life. The language of both parables suggest that the seed, as well as the harvest and the sheltering branch, is Wisdom itself. This suggestion is confirmed by Jesus' paradoxical insistence that the purpose of hiding the mystery is to bring it to light, together with his admonition to "heed what you hear; the measure you give will be the measure you get" (4:24). The paradox expresses the midrashic view that hidden in Scripture is the mystery of God, yet it is hidden only to be disclosed. It implies that the one most attuned to understanding Scripture (that is, attuned to Wisdom) will uncover the greatest meaning. There is clearly an analogy being made between the seed hidden only to be brought to light and the process of God's revelation. The divine mystery resides not only in *what* is revealed but in the process itself—in God's creative word ceaselessly yielding new meanings, continually regenerating itself. The affirmation of this generative process in the last two parables is an oblique critique of the finality and sterility of the first parable with its rigid explanation. Jesus as Wisdom's teacher does not teach certainty but "watchfulness."

Jesus and Wisdom's Time-Frame of "Watchfulness"

"Happy is the one who listens to me, watching daily at my gates, waiting beside my doors," Wisdom says in Proverbs (8:34). In Sirach the seeker of Wisdom acts like a lover listening at her doors (14:24). In the Wisdom of Solomon, she is found by the one who "rises early" to seek her (6:12). In a similar way Jesus admonishes his disciples to be "watchful": first, when he tells the parable of the absent master (13:32–37) and, second, when he seeks their company in the garden of Gethsemane (14:32–38). In each instance the imperative "watch" is repeated three times like a refrain. The episodes, moreover, are linked: the parable merges into a direct warning to watch for the master lest he come at cockcrow and find them asleep (13:35–36); in the events that follow, they do fall asleep and cannot keep watch with him (14:37–41), while Peter denies him precisely at "cockcrow" (14:72). The Wisdom frame gives the thematic concern with "watching" a larger context, suggesting that Jesus, like Wisdom, is also calling his disciples to an ongoing state of wakefulness.

Covenantal theology tends to be linear, looking to the past and future. Creation theology tends to be circular, aware of repeating patterns. Wisdom theology, springing from the latter, is focused on the present. The urgency of Wisdom's watchfulness, therefore, is not to be confused with the urgency of eschatological hope. The alternating time-frames in Mark permit both kinds of expectation, but the prevailing emphasis is on Wisdom's *here and now*. Jesus' uncertainty about the day or hour of the End Time (13:32) is crucial, signifying an "unknowing" wisdom like that of Job. It is a wisdom linked to an acceptance of the vastness of the divine mystery. Jesus as a teacher of Wisdom does not impart knowledge or "secrets" of the future but calls his disciples to a profound "wakefulness" to the mystery of the present moment.

Jesus and Wisdom's Via Negativa

Jesus' suffering and death take on a different dimension when seen in the context of Wisdom's negative way. Jesus' vulnerability, like that of Job, serves to challenge the ever popular idea that suffering is somehow punishment for sin or that virtue will somehow make one immune from suffering. Jesus' suffering, like Job's, dramatizes that suffering is the common lot of all humanity; what matters is the meaning one gives to it. In the Markan text meaning is specifically given, as I have shown, through allusions to the innocent righteous one in Isaiah, the Psalms, and the Wisdom of Solomon. In the last work, the death of the righteous one is obliterated by immortality: "for God created humanity for incorruption, and made human beings in the image of God's own eternity" (2:23). In this context, not only does Jesus' death show his common humanity, but his being raised shows it as well. Jesus' resurrection is part of a pattern in which Mark dramatizes how Jesus, like Solomon's Wisdom, is a "mirror of the working of God, and an image of his goodness" (7:26).

Jesus Described Like Woman Wisdom

In the Wisdom writings, Wisdom is personified as a woman—inclusively nurturing, attractive and elusive, ceaselessly restoring order and attentive to whatever is life-giving. Mark portrays Jesus as a person with these very qualities of being. In so doing, he also portrays him as the opposite of the typical male hero of ancient writings—who is conventionally royal, rational, and powerful.

Mark portrays Jesus as a teacher of wisdom but not a philosopher. What Mark conveys of Jesus' sayings do not add up to a rational system of thought. On the contrary, his teachings, according to Mark, frequently "astound" his audiences because they seem to defy what is conventionally considered to be reasonable. It does not fit conventional wisdom for a religious teacher to eat with sinners or to encourage his followers to feast instead of fast (2:16–20), to preach total forgiveness (3:28), or to dismiss death as a kind of sleep (5:39). It is something other than pure reason that lies behind the proposal to "sell what you have and give to the poor" (10:21) or the command to "be the slave of all" (10:44). Above all, the central teaching of Jesus—that "whoever would save his life will lose it; and whoever loses it for my sake and the gospel's, will save it" (8:35)—turns conventional rationality inside out. The cross is a key to mystical, not rational thought. Mark emphasizes this aspect of Jesus early in his narrative when he says that Jesus' family thought him "out of his mind" or "beside himself" (3:21)—the word is *exestē*, related to *ecstasy*.

Mark not only attributes to Jesus the strong feminine aspects of Hebrew Wisdom but the very qualities that the contemporary Gentile culture ascribed pejoratively to women—irrationality; vulnerability; susceptibility to suffering and shame; lifestyle of lowly service. In short, while Mark speaks about Jesus as a historical male, he characterizes him in female terms. These dual aspects taken together present Jesus as an undivided, androgynous human being—suggestively like the first human made "in the image and likeness of God."

Jesus Described Like Wisdom as God's "Image and Likeness"

"Whose likeness is this?" Jesus asks of the Roman coin (12:16). The other side of that coin is humanity formed by God "in our image and likeness." In Jewish tradition, the implications of Genesis 1:26 were obvious matter for theological pondering and midrashic interpretation. In one midrashic exegesis the angels are shown so dazzled by the reflection of God in the first human being that they bend in worship.[70] This perception of humanity made in God's image seems to underlie the literature that dramatized humanity restored to an original state of radiance—the literature of ascent and transformation, the imagery of the End Time as a return to Genesis. And, significantly, the Wisdom of Solomon, as I have shown, plays imaginatively with the idea that Wisdom is God's breath dwelling both in his Creation and in human beings as "an image of his goodness" (7:26). Mark is working with the intersection of all these traditions when he shows Jesus to be, at one and the same time, *ben 'adam*—common humanity—and the very likeness of God.

In almost every chapter, Mark uses scriptural echoes and allusions to work this out. At the beginning of his ministry Jesus is shown calling disciples and saying to them: "Follow me and I will make you fishers of human beings" (1:17). This unusual image seems to be an echo of Jeremiah 16 where God, having just promised to restore his people to their promised land, also indicates how he will pursue his people until they turn back to him: "Behold, I am sending for many fishers, says the Lord, and they shall catch them; and afterwards I will send for many hunters, and they shall hunt them from every mountain and every hill, and out of the clefts of the rocks." In context, these "fishers" and "hunters" are the Babylonians, and the image is harsh. Yet the passage also suggests God's relentless pursuit of his own. In echoing it here, Mark reworks this image in a different mode, on the one hand relating it to Wisdom's calling of the simple and on the other placing Jesus in a role parallel to God's.

Two similar uses of Scripture occur in chapter 3. First of all, Mark cites Jesus formulating a choice that resembles, as I have already noted, Wisdom's anititheses of life and death. It also echoes Deuteronomy 30 where God confronts his people with the fundamental moral option: "I set before you this day life and good, death and evil. . . . I have set before you life and death, blessing and curse; therefore choose life, that you and your descendants may live" (Deut. 30:15–19). Jesus frames the question of a particular healing in similar terms—"Is it lawful on the Sabbath to do good or to do evil, to save life or to destroy?" (3:4)—then commands the man with the withered arm in words that echo God commanding Moses to stretch forth his arm over the sea (Exodus 15:26).

This scene also speaks of Jesus looking at those who would prevent the healing "with anger, grieved at their hardness of heart" (3:5). These mixed emotions of anger and grief are suggestive of the mixed feelings God is shown to have in Exodus and Hosea and throughout Hebrew Scripture; the "hardness of heart" that draws out these emotions (a phrase used by Jesus twice again—6:52, 10:5) is both an echo of Pharaoh's recalcitrance and a reminder of the constant warning of the prophets against human resistance to grace.[71] These feelings placed in the context of the fundamental choice between life and death again suggest that Jesus resembles God.

The same kind of echo occurs in chapter 6 when Jesus feeds the people in the wilderness. The nurturing theme, I have noted, is an aspect of Wisdom. At the same time the scene in itself recalls Exodus, a reminder that is bolstered by Jesus' invitation to "come apart . . . and rest awhile"—a phrase suggestive of the Sabbath, which was instituted in Exodus at the same time as the miraculous manna. Because of the Sabbath framework, the multiplication of loaves also places Jesus in the role of God.

The second feeding in the wilderness confirms the first impression: whereas the first time we are told that Jesus "had compassion on them [the crowd] because they were like sheep without a shepherd" (6:34), here we see him saying firsthand, "*I* have compassion on the crowd" (8:2)—thus reflecting directly the primary attribute of God described in Exodus 3:7.

The dramatization of Jesus as God's image is encapsulated by Mark when he depicts Jesus having power over the sea by walking on it—like God in Job and Sirach (Job 9:8 and 38:16; Sir. 24:5–6). This scene is prepared for by the close of chapter 4. In the concluding passage a great storm arises, and Mark says that Jesus "rebuked the wind and said to the sea, 'Peace! Be still'" (v. 39), and the disciples, "filled with awe," say to one another, "Who then is this, that even wind and sea obey him?" (v. 41). The words function as an allusion to Psalm 89, itself a midrashic reflection on Genesis: "O Lord, God of hosts, who is mighty like you, O Lord? Your faithfulness surrounds you; you rule the swelling of the sea, when its waves surge, you still them" (vv. 9–10). The disciples' echo of this psalm is suggestive, pointing to Jesus as particularly the image of God in the act of Creation.

In the Markan narrative, in other words, Jesus is shown to function in the same way as Wisdom in the Wisdom of Solomon: he acts as the divine life-force; he is "an image of his goodness." The full significance of this imaging takes its meaning from the question of Jesus: "With what can we compare the kingdom of God or what parable shall we use for it?" (4:30). Jesus poses the conventional introduction to the *mashal* (*What is God like?*) and replies with parables that point to God's creating energy as both a power beyond human control and a shelter for all of Creation. When Mark then shows Jesus reenacting the scene of God the Creator, he implies that Jesus himself is parable as well. He is Wisdom in parabolic form. The theological framework of Creation/Wisdom is embodied in the Markan Jesus.

Theological Implications

Saying that Mark presents Jesus in the mode of Wisdom parable is not to suggest that his account of the life and death of Jesus is a total invention. Rather it is to acknowledge that Mark is working within an exegetical tradition in which both person and event are rendered not in terms of realistic detail but in terms of scriptural significance. It is to perceive Mark's link to the imaginative theology of Early Judaism. It is to see Mark's connection with the sages who tried to concretize their idea of Wisdom by personifying it. It is to see his relation to the prophets who not only spoke their message but frequently described themselves as acting it out. Mark is, on the one hand, making use of prophetic literature in presenting Jesus' actions as acts that are also *signs*. At the same time he is making use of the Wisdom traditions in showing how Jesus as *ben 'adam* (that is, "son of man," or common humanity) reflects the deity. The writings of the Prophets and the Wisdom traditions converge in Mark's presentation of Jesus as a living image of the living God.

It is important to know that the question of how humanity images God was of great concern to the Jewish exegetes of the first century (and later). Rabbi Simeon ben Azzai deemed belief in the human likeness to God to be "the great *kelal*" (midrashic condensation).[72] Neusner calls the matter "the central question of midrash."[73] Let us put these thoughts together with the fact that the prototypical form of midrash was the compact, exegetical narrative called the *mashal*, and the *mashal* typically opened with the question, "To what is this like?"—the *this* usually referring either to God's kingdom or to some aspect of God's relationship with humanity. Describing its theological function, Stern asserts: "The *mashal* is a mimesis of God."[74] Let us consider further that Neusner speaks of the midrashic way of constructing faith through Scripture as a way of exploring the "meaning of humanity viewed as image and likeness of something else, of life lived like a metaphor . . . a way of seeing life 'as if.'"[75] These Jewish perspectives provide a context in which to understand how Mark presents Jesus theologically and rhetorically as a living exegesis of what God is like. On the one hand he presents the story of Jesus to us through varied lenses of Scripture; on the other hand he suggests that the narrative of Jesus in some way reinterprets the meaning of that Scripture. The narrative functions as "a mimesis of God," or as "a way of seeing life 'as if'" humanity were indeed God's image and likeness.

Other Christian scholars have tried to suggest this idea in various ways. John Donahue speaks of the "native power of parable to point beyond itself" so that "the medium is the message." Thus, he concludes, "Jesus himself is parable; so also the Gospel presentations of him."[76] In a more elaborate argument, W. D. Davies has suggested that in a period when the Jewish canon was in transition and Oral Torah was evolving in multiple ways, Paul came to view Jesus—that is, "the totality of his ministry and person, his cross and resurrection"—as "a kind of equivalent of . . . the oral tradition in Judaism as the clue to the scriptures."[77] What Davies perceives in Paul, and Donahue in all the Gospels, I find particularly apparent in Mark: namely, that the narrative of Jesus is not presented in the terms of an ordinary biography but rather is carefully put together as a sophisticated, rhetorical-theological construct, expressing "the great *kelal*" and suggesting imaginatively "what God is like."

We trivialize this imaginative theology if we excerpt from the total and identify Jesus with particular words or actions. It is "the totality of his ministry and person, his cross and resurrection" (to borrow Davies's words), interwoven with scriptural passages, allusions, and interpretations, that turns the narrative of Jesus into a living *mashal*. As a *mashal*, this narrative is exegetical: Jesus' story is presented as a living text shedding light on Jewish Scriptures. That means that every presentation of Jesus (Pauline, Markan, or whatever) represents a *different* exegesis of those Scriptures, and so we cannot simply equate one with another. That means, further, that each presentation must itself be exegeted as a living text. Thus who Jesus is cannot be readily assumed or easily defined or summarily transposed from one generation to the next; each presentation is rich with ambiguous possibility. The task of the Christian exegete is to continually reopen this text in the light both of new understandings of the Jewish and Christian Scriptures and of the changing context of the times. It is that task I now approach, acknowledging that at best I can do no more than approach it.

The God Whom Jesus Images

By repeatedly dramatizing Jesus' actions as a reflection of God's, Mark provides a context in which to view Jesus' attitudes toward sinners and forgiveness, toward what is clean and unclean, toward religious rules and human need. If Jesus is shown to reflect God through scriptural likeness, then he must be inferred to be reflecting God in his searching out of sinners, in his equation between forgiveness and healing, in his insistence that "all sins will be forgiven," in his outreach to "the unclean," in his restoration of the possessed, in his raising up of women, in his placing of need over rule.

Most radically, Mark suggests that Jesus particularly images God in his suffering and death. In the first half of the Gospel (aside from that uncertain opening verse) Jesus is called "son of God" only by demons or unclean spirits (3:11, 5:7), while in the second half of the Gospel he twice refers to himself as "son of God" (13:32, 14:62), clearly addresses God as "Abba" (14:36), and, after his death, is proclaimed "son of God" by a Roman centurion (15:39). Mark structures his Gospel, in other words, so that Jesus' reflection of God is stated with increasing clarity even while the drama of his vulnerability grows. As the narrative shifts from miracle to suffering, we need to keep in mind that Mark consistently implies that Jesus in pain, as well as in power, is a likeness of God. God so envisioned is not remote, perfect, and static but ceaselessly engaged in the labor of creation.[78] God is seen in feminine terms.

The Humanity That Gives Image to God

As the external references to Jesus as "son of God" increase, so too do his self-references as *ben 'adam*. In the first part of the Gospel, Jesus uses the term only twice; in the second part (beginning with the close of chapter 8) he refers to himself in this fashion twelve times. The first two uses both occur in chapter 2, and in contexts that imply that *ben 'adam* resembles God: "*ben 'adam* has authority on earth to forgive sins" (2:10); "*ben 'adam* is lord even of the Sabbath" (2:28). I have noted before that *ben 'adam* in these contexts suggests primal humanity and/or resurrected humanity—both states in which the human likeness to God shines through unimpaired. In the next twelve uses of the term, *ben 'adam* is used in the contexts of suffering and service—both borrowing from scriptural narratives of "the beloved son."

If we look at how Mark structures his whole narrative, we can see how he negotiates a convergence and exchange of meanings. In Jesus' first, unimpaired, exalted state, *ben 'adam* as ruler of creation, only the devils recognize his relationship to God; in his suffering

state—*ben 'adam* as sacrificing servant—his kinship to God is perceived by his greatest foe. The narrative structure brings together
Jesus as *ben 'adam* and "son of God"; they converge in the portrayal
of Jesus as God's living image and likeness.

It is important to see that here again Mark uses feminine as well as
masculine images. Although masculine terminology seems to predomi-
nate, a key aspect of Mark's presentation of Jesus is the way he links
him to the feminine attributes of Wisdom in her acts of creating and
sustaining life. These connections serve an important function, making Jesus a holistic image in respect both to God and to humanity.

The Convergence of Images

The total convergence of images is not easily summed up. It involves
the whole rich complexity of the various scriptural allusions Mark is
weaving together. To say that he presents Jesus as a living parable
does not mean that he portrays the life and death of Jesus as a simple
illustration of any one thing. Again the Wisdom traditions and the
Hebrew meaning of *mashal*—a story that is both riddle and enlight-
enment—must be kept in mind. It is in this tradition that Mark
shows how Jesus enfleshes in his person a dialectic of biblical images.
The image of God's suffering witness is counterpointed to that of
"God's anointed," while both come together in the paradigm of
"the beloved son." The paradigm of "the beloved son" connects
Jesus to Israel, as indeed does the image of Jesus as a living temple
of God's spirit. Yet both can also be read as part of the paradigm of
Jesus as *ben 'adam* or second Adam, representative of common
humanity. Both paradigms coalesce in the image of Jesus as the
dwelling place of God. The image of Jesus as "son" is qualified by
Jesus as feminine Wisdom; the image of Jesus' power is qualified by
the image of Jesus' vulnerability; yet the image of Jesus as powerless before death is countered by the image of Jesus as Wisdom,
God's life in Creation.

By showing Jesus' likeness to God, Mark gives image to a God
who is not remote from human suffering but is one with human
pain. At the same time Mark gives image to the human person as not
an outsider to God's radiance but susceptible to being raised up and
transformed to holiness. By connecting Jesus to Wisdom, Mark
brings together the divine and the human life-force. The imaging
works all ways at once, suggesting above all the mystery of the
divine-human exchange.

Mark's Theological Language

The simultaneity of meaning is more readily held in balance when
the theological language is understood as metaphor and riddle. Not

so understood, the meaning tends to splinter into conflicting parts. This phenomenon may explain why early Christianity was divided between those who saw Jesus as a kind of "divine man" and those who saw him as God made human—a conflict repeated, in a different way, in the twentieth-century division between "the Jesus of history" and "the Christ of faith." It may also explain the division acutely felt in our time between Jesus as historical male and Jesus as representative of all humanity. Grasping the metaphor as a whole, one sees that the Markan Jesus is above all an image of the ongoing (nonstatic) relationship (exchange and convergence) between God and the human beings holistically made in God's image, "male and female." The Markan Jesus is an image in which God is both hidden and disclosed. As an image and not a definition, a parable and not a concept, his identity invites ongoing dialogue and reflection. Mark does not portray the person of Jesus as something fixed and closed but rather as a midrashic riddle that continues to disclose new meanings.[79]

Understanding Mark's theology as one formed by the biblical, midrashic habits of image and allusion, contradiction and coalescence, makes sense out of his narrative as an integrated whole. It also makes sense of what Mark does *not* say. John Donahue sees the parables' use of metaphor and paradox as a bulwark against what he terms "the idolatry of language": "God cannot be captured in a verbal image any more than by a plastic one. . . . Religious language is limit language, not in the sense of imposing limits but in the sense of pushing toward the limits of intelligibility where one stands at the threshhold of mystery."[80]

The acknowledgment of the limits of language in respect to the divine mystery is evident in the very structure of the Hebrew *mashal*, which refuses to define God's kingdom in direct terms. It is evident in the Rabbinic restraint from naming God. It is evident in biblical Judaism—from the indirect answer given to Moses' question as to who God is to Ezekiel's stammering vision of what God is *like*. To the Jew of ancient as well as modern times, the human attempt to define God outright is a form of hubris.

Mark is thus composing within the norms of Jewish theology when he uses imagery that suggests not that Jesus *is* but that he is *like* God.[81] He is reflecting midrashically on the creation of human beings in God's image—on the son as the image of the Father and on the Father reflected in the anguish of the son; on Jesus as Woman Wisdom embodying God's provident concern and on God's feminine nurturance reflected in Jesus' life-affirming acts. Through Jesus as image, Mark reflects on who God is in relation to humanity and who human beings are in relation to God. He is making a proposal not to the mind's logic but to its imagination So understood, the allusive, riddling quality of the Markan Jesus is a hedge against idola-

try, forcing his followers to acknowledge the limits of human understanding and inviting them to ponder the mystery of the divine
creation. Here is the crux of the difference between the early Jewish followers of Jesus and the later Gentile church.

Monika Hellwig has lucidly outlined the differences in theological understanding that come from a shift in the use of language:
"This is where the serious and apparently intractable difficulties on
Christology begin—in a simplification in gentile context and language of the elusive and allusive Hebrew way of speaking about the
mystery of God."[82] She observes that "a divinity claim for a human
individual has a very wide variety of meanings for people according
to the cultural and religious—and in some cases philosophical—background they bring to it."[83] She takes note of the Eastern Church tradition that interprets the divinity of Jesus as confirmation of the
divine image in every human person.[84] She concludes:

> The biblical and intertestamentary heritage common to Christians
> and Jews involved a respect for mystery—and an intellectual humil-
> ity before it—which was largely implicit. The judicious use of narra-
> tive, symbolism, discreet allusion, paradox, and so forth, was an
> implicit acknowledgment of the nature and limitations of religious
> language and its assertions. The Christian option for Greek philo-
> sophical categories in patristic times and for intensively philosophi-
> cal systemization of the religious heritage in medieval times did much
> to weaken that acknowledgment.[85]

Finally she suggests that modern philosophy, by taking "relentless
(one might say merciless) note of the nature and limitation of all
language," including "the relation of religious language to truth
claims" and "the role of symbol in human understanding and expression," has opened a new window for the reconsideration of traditional doctrinal formulations.[86]

In such a reconsideration, the recognition of Mark's presentation
of Jesus as a midrashic Wisdom parable, an elusive image of what
God is like—an image centered simultaneously in the divine mystery
and the human one—may prove important as the bridge to deeper
Christian understanding of its origins in Judaism, and that deeper
self-understanding may in turn prove to be a fertile stimulus to
theological renewal.

6

The Discipleship of Wisdom:
A Process of Transformation

Mark's use of the Creation/Wisdom traditions to frame his Gospel cannot be understood as a systematic, philosophical schema. Mark is not making a dogmatic argument but creating a theological landscape, a scriptural, intertextual environment that abounds with poetic allusions and artful transposition of themes. Mark does not simply borrow from other writings or repeat them but, in keeping with midrashic methods, he creatively reappropriates them. Mark relates Jesus to Wisdom by echoing various literary images of Wisdom and reconfiguring them. They form a constant, subliminal presence—one that a modern audience may have to work to uncover but a first-century audience would have instantly known.

This subliminal frame constitutes the very setting of the Gospel. As I noted in the last chapter, the covenantal theology of Exodus and the Prophets is concerned with Israel among the nations of the world and thus makes use of the large and panoramic screen of history. In contrast, the Wisdom writings—that is, Proverbs, the Psalms, Job, Ecclesiastes, Sirach, the Song of Songs, and the Wisdom of Solomon—are largely focused on family and psychic struggles and thus function within the smaller framework of everyday domestic scenes and interior monologues. It is clearly the latter that make up the gospel scene. In chapters 1 through 8 Jesus moves chiefly between the sea of Galilee, the synagogue, and various homes; in the second half of the Gospel Jesus' actions take place within the circumscribed scope of table and Temple. The events of the Gospel, in short, are not linked to the biblical literature of God's mighty deeds in history but rather to the images of Wisdom strolling the market-place, building a house, setting a table, feeding her household.

The Foolish Disciples

Awareness of this background has implications for understanding Mark's portrayal of Jesus' community. The depiction of the disciples in Mark's Gospel has generally caused much dismay because the portrait is so unflattering. But the source of this dismay seems to stem from reading the Gospel as either literal biography or straight kerygma. Either way Mark's characterization of these disciples as obtuse and faithless offends the Christian believer's desire to revere the twelve apostles as the founders of the church and to hold them up as models of faith. This "problem" in Mark has been handled in different ways over the centuries. I cite here two ways it has been addressed.

Eusebius's Reading (fl. c. 315–40 C.E.)

Mark writes these things, and through him Peter bears witness, for the whole of Mark is said to be a record of Peter's teaching. Note how scrupulously the disciples refused to record these things that might have given the impression of their fame. Note how they handed down in writing numerous charges against themselves to unforgetting ages, and accusations of sins, which no one in later years would ever have known about unless hearing it from their own voice. By thus honestly reporting their own faults, it is reasonable to view them as relatively void of false-speaking and egoism. This habit gives plain and clear proof of their truth-loving disposition. . . . If it was their aim to deceive, and to adorn their master with false words, they would never have written these demeaning accounts of his pain and agony and that he was disturbed in spirit, that they themselves forsook him and fled, or that Peter the apostle and disciple who was chief of the apostles denied him three times, unless they had an extraordinarily high standard of truth-telling. (*Proof of the Gospel* 3–5 [ACC, 220])

Hooker's Reading

Much of the teaching in the second part of the gospel concerns the meaning of discipleship . . . and the story, when it is not the story of Jesus, is the story of the disciples' failure—of their misunderstanding and lack of faith . . . and of their final collapse . . . Judas' betrayal . . . and Peter's denial. Their failure is so great that it is sometimes suggested that Mark is launching a deliberate attack on the Twelve, who perhaps represent a group in his own community. It is more likely, however, that Mark's emphasis on the inability of the Twelve to comprehend the truth about Jesus is due to his insistence that this truth is revealed through the Cross and resurrection. The disciples thus act as a foil to Mark's own readers who are able to recognize the good news for what it is. (pp. 20–21)

For Eusebius, who reads Mark's Gospel as biography, the portrait of the first disciples must have been particularly distressing; he deftly turns the source of his distress into a virtue by using it as a proof of authenticity. Hooker is aware of modern readers who similarly read the Gospel for biographical verisimilitude and who seek an explanation for the disciples' failure by positing that Mark is writing about his own community rather than that of Jesus. She herself follows a more theological reading in suggesting that Mark has chosen to describe those who lived prior to Jesus' death and resurrection as a foil to those who live afterward.

Rereading Mark's Presentation of the Disciples in the Context of Jewish Wisdom Traditions

I find that reading Mark as midrashic discourse resolves the problem by shifting the reader's expectation from biographical similitude or moral exemplum to theological metaphor. If one further places that metaphor into the context of the Wisdom traditions, one sees that the failures of the disciples serve an important theological function. As Wisdom invites those who are *unwise*, so Jesus invites those who are furthest from his company.

The Disciples as "Those Outside" Wisdom

In chapters 3 and 4 Mark makes a significant analogy between Jesus' family and his disciples. Those "close to" Jesus (usually interpreted as family) appear in chapter 3 as persons who think him mad and try to stop him (3:21).[1] Subsequently we are told that "his mother and brothers came, and *standing outside* they sent to him" (v. 31). The crowd notices and repeats the words: "Your mother and your brothers are *outside*, asking for you" (v. 32). The scene is a prelude to the one in chapter 4; it is useful to read these scenes as a Markan doublet and to note who is "outside" in each instance. In the first episode Mark shows Jesus responding: "Who are my mother and brothers? . . . Whoever does the will of God is my brother, and sister, and mother" (3:33–35). Notably the statement does not restrict the familial bond to blood relationship or to those who do God's will in a particular way or according to a set of particular beliefs and practices. The statement as it stands is open-ended and inclusive. The conventional family appears to be "outside"; the "insiders" are neither predestined nor predictable. We should not be surprised to find the disciples implicitly defined by Mark in an analogous way.

It can be argued, in fact, that the existential nature of discipleship underlies the statement Mark shows Jesus making in chapter 4—"To you is given the mystery of the kingdom, while *for those outside*, everything happens in parables." The key word here is usually taken to be "mystery," but the more striking word is *ginetai*—"happens." Because *ta panta ginetai* is a strange expression to describe "teaching,"[2] many manuscripts replaced the verb with various forms of "speaking," and some translations have simply replaced it with "is."[3] But the very strangeness of the word *ginetai* makes a point: namely, that the "mystery" Mark has in mind is not a body of knowledge but a *happening*. As the Wisdom writings show that Wisdom is best known through experience rather than books, so Mark shows Jesus' teachings to be more enacted than spoken. The words here imply that Mark sees Jesus containing the mystery of the kingdom *in himself*; those who are his disciples in some way experience the mystery directly. Implicitly Mark is indicating that Jesus' disciples encounter God's kingdom primarily through the way Jesus is living and acting.

This interpretation does not imply a contrast between a fixed "elect" and a predetermined crowd of outsiders. On the contrary, it confirms the idea that Jesus' disciples constitute a community that is formed existentially. They are or are not his disciples, not by virtue of being preordained or even by virtue of being called (in fact, he has called all sinners) but by virtue of their response to the mystery contained in his being. Mark is not only suggesting that Jesus is teaching midrashic wisdom but that, in effect, he is midrashic Wisdom: "Truly, the mystery of the kingdom of God has been given to you, but to those outside everything takes place in parables." If those called to be his disciples cannot see or hear the mystery given to them directly in his person, they remain among "those outside."[4]

Christian believers have always wanted to see the disciples as "insiders," a chosen "elect." But an honest reading of Mark reveals that he is intent on showing something both more subtle and more rich. In different ways and in different contexts the Wisdom writings show that being called to follow Wisdom does not make one wise; the wise are those who find her. In a similar way Mark shows that being called to be a disciple of Jesus does not automatically make one a member of his community; the call only changes those who understand the invitation and respond to it. *Understanding* is the first step in the response, and Mark shows that understanding Jesus, like understanding Wisdom, is not a matter of the intellect but of the heart. This characteristic is implicit in the way Mark describes both resistant intellectuals and confused fishermen as persons with "hardened hearts"; it is evident in the way he dramatizes the repeated failures of the would-be disciples to "see" or to "hear" what Jesus is saying and doing.

Throughout most of the Gospel, in fact, Mark shows Jesus to be a living sign that his nominal disciples fail to read. At the end of chapter 4, for example, Mark's allusive language suggests that Jesus' action reflects God's own, but the disciples do not understand his parabolic action any more than they understood his spoken parable. It is telling that Jesus rebukes them at that point for their lack of *faith* (v. 40). As Mark presents Jesus as a living parable, so he suggests that those who encounter him must enter into the dimensions of the metaphor or remain outsiders to his meaning. Mark develops his narrative to show how continually those called to be disciples remain literal-minded and obtuse.

In chapter 5 the disciples remain outsiders to the deeper meaning of the healing miracles—the restoration of the demoniac out of the tombs, the saving of the woman with the twelve-year menstrual flow, the raising up of Jairus's daughter. The disciples are entirely absent from the episode with the demoniac. In the incident involving the "unclean" woman, Mark shows both the woman and Jesus speaking of "touch" in a figurative, sacramental way while the disciples understand Jesus' question only on the most literal level: "And his disciples said to him, 'You see the crowd pressing around you and you say, Who touched me?'" (v. 31).[5] In the final episode, the raising up of the child from death, Jesus takes along the very disciples who will be witnesses to his transfiguration—Peter, James, and John (v. 37)—yet they make no connections. At the same time that Mark uses language that signals to his audience that these miracles presage resurrection, he also shows that the disciples are blind to these implications.

In chapter 6 Mark creates an experience of déjà vu. Once again the disciples are in a boat and the wind comes up against them (v. 48); once again Jesus seems indifferent to their plight ("he intended to pass them by"). Once again Jesus' speech and actions mirror those of God in Hebrew Scripture: like God in Job and Sirach, he walks upon the sea (see Job 9:8 and 38:16; Sir. 24:5–6). Once again the reaction of the disciples to this divine echo is fright (v. 50), and Mark suggests it is their closed minds that is the underlying cause: "they had not understood about the loaves but their hearts were hardened" (v. 52).

In chapter 7, when the Pharisees and scribes question the ways of Jesus' disciples—"Why do your disciples not walk according to the traditions of the elders, but eat bread with defiled hands?" (v. 5)— Jesus' response specifically challenges them in respect to their exegeting of scriptural texts (vv. 10–13).[6] Ironically, the disciples also fail to get Jesus' meaning and, in an echo of chapter 4, "began to question him about the parable," so that Jesus is driven to exclaim, "Are you in the same way without insight?" (vv. 17–18). When Mark concludes the chapter with Jesus' healing of the deaf-mute, the healing functions as a sign-act that implies that Jesus wills to transform all who are deaf to God's word—Pharisees and disciples alike.[7]

Two episodes follow that underscore the similarity between unseeing disciple and resistant Pharisee. After the Pharisees come to test Jesus one more time, ironically "seeking a sign from heaven" (v. 11), the disciples are also portrayed as literal-minded: when Jesus instructs them to "take heed against the leaven of the Pharisees and the leaven of Herod" (v. 15), the disciples confuse the symbolic leaven of his speech with the literal loaf in the boat and reply in some bewilderment, "We have no bread" (v. 16).[8]

Jesus' response to their confusion is a reminder of all the previous moments in which the disciples have missed the point. He says, "Do you not yet understand?" (v. 17)—a question that echoes both chapter 4 (v. 13) and chapter 7 (v. 18). He asks, "Have your hearts been hardened?" (v. 17), a question reminiscent of chapter 6. Finally, he echoes the passage from Isaiah that speaks of Isaiah's unseeing and unhearing audience: "Having eyes do you not see and having ears do you not hear?" (v. 18). The question repeats Jesus' description in chapter 4 of those "outside" the kingdom of God (v. 11) as well as his response to the disciples' obtuseness in chapter 7 (v. 18). In Mark it is not just the hostile Pharisees who misunderstand Jesus; his own disciples are equally obtuse. Through his parallel structures of miracle and misunderstanding, Mark indicates that there is a certain universality in the dullness of those called by God.

The Disciples' Dullness

In chapter 9 the disciples seem temporarily transfigured along with Jesus, but within the immediate narrative the moment does not last. On the way down from the mountain Jesus commands them "not to tell anyone what they had seen until the son of man had risen from the dead" (v. 9). The command seems to be superfluous; the disciples have already returned to their uncomprehending state.

They appear to have already forgotten the vision, and not linking the idea of resurrection with their most recent experience, they are "seeking together what it is to be risen from the dead" (v. 10).

The whole incident dramatizes on a larger scale what Mark has repeatedly shown in more subtle ways: namely, that the disciples repeatedly see and do not "see" who Jesus is; they hear and do not "hear" what he is saying. In this condition, the disciples are unable to exorcise a demon, and Jesus relates their inadequacy to lack of faith (9:19). Jesus then repeats, in almost identical words, the teaching he gave his disciples just before the transfiguration scene in 8:31: "The son of man will be handed over into the hands of human beings and they will kill him, and having been killed, after three days he will rise up." He omits any reference here, however, to being rejected by the elders, chief priests, and scribes—the immediate associates of his historical lifetime. Instead, the role of rejecting Jesus is taken over by his own disciples in their failure to understand him: "But they did not understand the saying and they were afraid to ask him" (v. 32). On the one hand, the phrase echoes all the previous instances in which the disciples failed to understand Jesus: the parables (4:13); the loaves (5:52 and 8:21); the "riddle" about what makes a person unclean (7:17); the meaning of rising from the dead (9:10). On the other hand, the absence of the elders, chief priests, and scribes seems to project some other, timeless, framework; in that context it is the misunderstandings of all disciples—past, present, and future—that function analogously as the agency of his rejection.

The content of chapter 13 suggests that Mark composed his narrative almost immediately after the fall of the Temple. This might be inferred, in any case, from the tradition of ex eventu prophecy but, more pointedly, it is indicated here by the predictions Jesus makes to his disciples that they must expect both to be "beaten in synagogues" and to "stand before governors and kings" (13:9), not because they belong to a formal *ekklēsia* (this word in fact does not appear in Mark) but *for his sake* and *in his name* (13:6, 9, 13). The phrasing seems to indicate a time when the followers of Jesus still considered themselves within the structures of Judaism and yet were subject to persecution both by Rome and by some of their fellow Jews. It suggests, in other words, that Mark writes before "the parting of the ways," yet on the cusp of the separation.

The references to suffering *in Jesus' name* further suggest that when Mark speaks of "the disciples" he is using a double lens, blending the disciples of Jesus' lifetime with those of his own time. Understanding this double focus also enriches the meaning of Mark's emphasis on the disciples' weakness and failures: he is, we may infer, portraying himself and his community, with all the confusion, doubt, and vulnerability they were currently experiencing. By merging time-frames, he universalizes the experience, turning the weak disciples into timeless symbols of a community of "outsiders"—that is, into an inclusive community of sinners.

The persistent obtuseness of the Markan disciples works still further to involve even his future readers. The disciples are stand-ins for the audience, and their "slowness to understand" functions as a device that stimulates the response of the hearer; when they fail to hear or see, the listener is moved to fill in the blanks. Finally, the very weakness of the disciples serves the theological purpose of highlighting God's inclusiveness. Their glaring faults indicate that they are decidedly not a special elite. Through his images of the noncomprehending disciples Mark excludes no one but invites all who listen to identify.

The Disciples as Metaphors for Folly

In dramatizing the disciples as consistently failing to understand, Mark effectively turns them into metaphors, timeless types of those who are outsiders to Wisdom. He demonstrates their folly by showing how they reverse the instructions—and example—of their teacher in Wisdom. In particular, he shows them acting as symbolic fools in respect to their self-aggrandizement, their greed, and their failure to "watch" for God's kingdom.

After all the different ways Mark has shown Jesus indicating that the way of the Kingdom is the way of dispossession—the instruction to be the servant of all (9:35), the holding up of the child as model (10:14), the injunction to the rich young man to sell all he has (10:21), the declaration to Peter that the "last will be first" (10:31), the three plain predictions of his own death (8:31, 9:31, 10:32–34)—after all that, the request of James and John "that we might sit on your right and your left in your glory" (v. 37) is climactic irony. The irony is intensified with hindsight: in the Passion Narrative, the ones on the right and left of Jesus will be the two thieves who are crucified with him (15:27). But even greater irony resides in the way their request suggests that these two especially chosen, especially instructed disciples have totally missed the point. It is also part of the irony that James and John order Jesus about as though he were their servant—"We want that you should do what we ask you" (v. 35).

The disciples are similarly uncomprehending about Jesus' teaching on generosity. When Jesus is depicted "reclining at table" at the house of Simon the leper (ch. 14), the disciples are pitted against the woman who anoints him. Mark shows them to be excessively rational and pinched in spirit in contrast to the woman's lavish giving: "But there were some angry within themselves, [saying] 'To what end has the oil been wasted? For this oil could have been sold for more than 300 denarii and given to the poor.' And they reproved her" (vv. 4–5). Mark creates several ironies here: those who could not imagine selling their own possessions to give money to the poor (ch. 10) are quick to give away the possessions of others; those who have called Jesus "the messiah" or "the anointed one" (i.e., *christos*) are slow to see the point of actually anointing him.

There are various kinds of wisdom in the Wisdom writings, but there is unity in the insistence that Wisdom is not found through texts but through some kind of daily "watching" at Wisdom's gates. The phrase is again suggestive of experiential understanding and of openness to God's presence. This tradition gives particular significance to the disciples' repeated failure to "watch" as Jesus requests. In the parable of the man on a journey Jesus indicates that *watchfulness* is a key to discipleship. Mark then dramatizes the significance

of being "watchful" in the scene in Gethsemane. The scene is constructed by Mark as the reverse of the scene of transfiguration. Jesus
takes the same three disciples and changes again before their eyes,
only in precisely opposite ways. Whereas earlier Jesus ascends a high
mountain, here he is seen "falling on the ground" (v. 35); whereas
there he appears to be "glistening" and glorious in a way that the
disciples have never seen him, here he appears for the first time to
be "distressed and anguished" (v. 33); whereas there a voice from
a cloud calls Jesus "my beloved Son," here Jesus addresses God as
"Abba," begging him to change his will (v. 36). In both episodes the
disciples do not know what to say (9:6 and 14:40), yet otherwise
their responses are markedly different: when Jesus appears glorious,
Peter understands his relationship to Moses and Elijah (9:5), and the
disciples connect his transfigured state with Elijah and the End Time
(9:11); when Jesus appears "sorrowful even to death" (14:34), the
disciples close their eyes and fall asleep.

Once again Mark constructs his narrative in triadic form: Jesus admonishes his disciples to stay awake and "watch," and then he comes
three times to find them asleep. The first time, Jesus merely charges
his disciples to "remain here and watch" (v. 34). The second time
Jesus links the "watching" to prayer: "Watch and pray that you may
not enter into temptation" (v. 38). The third time he finds them
sleeping, he ironically shifts his injunction to "Sleep and cease."

Mark thus dramatizes the total failure of the disciples to act as
disciples: far from being *watchful*, in the most critical moment of
Jesus' betrayal, "their eyes were heavy" (v. 40). He has in fact constructed a scene that shows the disciples acting the part of the dull
audience that frustrated Isaiah: a people whose ears are "heavy" and
who "shut their eyes" (Isa. 6:10). By means of this pointed dramatization Mark suggests that the very ones Jesus called to be his disciples act like "outsiders" to the Kingdom—indeed like those whom
Jesus earlier compared to Isaiah's resistant audience (4:11).

Jesus concludes his address to his disciples with the statement
"Behold the son of man is handed over into the hands of sinners"
(v. 41b). The assertion stands as a hinge between the failed "watch"
in the garden and the coming of Judas, suggesting an equation
between them: the external drama of Jesus' betrayal has been anticipated by the less visible betrayal of the disciples' somnolence.

The Disciples' Forms of Betrayal

Mark's description of Jesus' betrayal by Judas continues in an ironic
mode. To begin with, Mark describes Judas's arrival with the thematic word *euthus*, "straightway" ("And straightway, while he was
speaking, Judas came," v. 43). The word *euthus* is a keyword attached to Jesus in Mark's prologue (v. 10), where it tallies with

eutheias in the summons of Isaiah to "make straight the ways" of the Lord (v. 3).[9] Mark connects the word with Jesus eighteen times in the Gospel. It is striking here because its application to Judas's act of betrayal is so clearly an ironic reversal of the "straight way" of Isaiah and of Jesus. Mark's deliberate irony is confirmed by his repetition of it when Judas kisses Jesus (v. 45). Next Mark tells us that "the betrayer had given them a *sign*"—certainly another irony, if one considers how repeatedly the disciples have missed the signs of the Kingdom that Jesus has given them. There is further irony in the fact that Judas is seeking to point Jesus out, while Peter is about to deny knowing him. And finally, of course, there is irony in the very fact that the sign itself is the reverse of what it stands for—a kiss in order to betray (vv. 44b-45). Most ironic of all, Judas is perversely the watcher and the witness the other disciples fail to be.

Mark adds to the irony by structuring his narrative so that the very trials and disasters Jesus warns of in chapter 13 are realized in chapters 14 and 15. In Judas's betrayal we see a fulfillment of the prediction of deception and betrayal by a brother. In the response of the other disciples to this moment of betrayal, there is also a perverse echo of what Jesus instructed them to do. On the one hand, instead of exhibiting lack of anxiety and trust in the holy spirit (see 13:11-13), one of them responds with violence and cuts off the ear of the high priest's servant (14:47).[10] On the other hand, when they flee from the scene, one of them might be said to be following Jesus' advice to "not turn back for his mantle" (see 13:16 and 14:51-52).[11]

However one looks at it, Mark structures his narrative of the handing over of Jesus to show that Judas's betrayal does not stand alone. The other disciples exhibit a range of responses that are also forms of betrayal, from violence to flight. The climactic moment in this narrative of betrayal is Peter's total refusal to witness.

Mark's narrative of Peter forms a frame around his narrative of Jesus' trial before the high priests. As usual with Markan structures, this fact is not random but suggestive of the way the two episodes interlock in meaning. In this case, the interlocking motif is that of *false witness*—another evil against which Jesus warned in chapter 13 (v. 22). While the high priests judge Jesus on the basis of false witnesses (14:56—58), Peter, who is called to bear true witness (13:9), refuses to be a witness at all.

The first part of the frame is contained in verse 54. There Mark depicts Peter still following Jesus, even though "from afar." After the narrative of false witnesses before the high priests and Jesus' condemnation, Mark returns to the scene of Peter in the courtyard. He then constructs a triadic narrative—similar to Peter's three denials of his forthcoming betrayal and his three failures to watch in Gethsemane—in which Peter is given three opportunities to acknowledge his relationship with Jesus, and three times he refuses. There is, moreover, an escalation in the exchange. The first time Mark couches Peter's answer in language that typifies his general obtuseness to Jesus' message—"I do not know or understand what you are saying" (v. 68). The second time, Mark uses a word that means repeated, habitual denial (*ērneito*). In the third instance, Peter not only denies but begins "to curse and swear" (v. 71).

It is worth pausing here to note Mark's thematic use of the verb "deny" (*aparneomai*). Its use here echoes chapter 8 where Jesus makes it the key virtue of discipleship: "If any one would come after me, let him *deny* himself and take up his cross and follow me" (8:34). Through the verbal echo Mark makes the point that *denying Jesus* instead of *denying oneself* is the antithesis of true discipleship.

Mark concludes the episode and the chapter with Peter's repentance. Mark's choice of words underline this moment as a significant turning point. First Mark notes that "*straightway* the cock crowed" (v. 72). Second, he says that "Peter *remembered* the word Jesus had spoken to him." The phrase is symbolic of that *remembering* of God's word that effects human repentance; in this instance, the particular word remembered is the "cockcrow" that figured not only in Jesus' specific warning to Peter but also in the warning parable of chapter 13. Finally Mark describes Peter's repentance with an unusual word, *epiballō*. Literally, this word means "to throw oneself or beat upon," and no one is quite sure how to translate it here,[12] but it is worth noting that it is clearly kin to the word for the *thrusting out* of unclean spirits—*ekballō*—that Mark has used throughout his Gospel. It does not seem far-fetched to say that by using it, Mark intends to suggest a cleansing of Peter's spirit. Last of all, Mark tells us that Peter "began to weep." In this final detail Mark suggests that Peter finally loses his "hard-heartedness" and comes to share and mirror the anguish and sorrow of Jesus in the garden.

Looking at the whole sequence of Mark's narrative of Peter, one might note that Peter's boastful claims of invincibility do not prepare him for the reality of Jesus' suffering, while his ability to accept his own sinfulness, his ability to weep at himself, is what ultimately changes him into a reflection of Jesus—who is, like Isaiah's servant, "a man of sorrows and acquainted with grief" (Isa. 53:3). Mark has constructed a narrative in which Peter's identity is bound to that of Jesus: that is to say, Mark has worked it out so that Peter, in denying Jesus, is simultaneously denying who he is himself—that is, not "with the Nazarene"(v. 67), not "one of them" (v. 69), not "a Galilean" (v. 70). Peter's act of weeping involves recognition of Jesus and self-recognition at the same time.

The Theological Function of the Disciples in Mark

If one places Mark's characterization of Jesus' disciples into the context of the Wisdom traditions, one finds that their weaknesses function as metaphors for folly. As Proverbs' Wisdom invites the unwise to her banquet, so the Markan Jesus calls not the righteous but sinners. As a community of sinners, these disciples are simultaneously a community of fools (of "outsiders" to Wisdom) failing to grasp the basic instructions of their teacher, Wisdom/Jesus—the instructions to serve others, to become dispossessed of themselves, to be awake to God's presence. In Mark's symbolic narrative the foolish disciples seek to make themselves great, are dumbfounded at the idea of voluntary poverty, and fall asleep at the critical hour. In a final ironic moment Peter denies Jesus rather than risk himself, while Judas the betrayer is the only watcher and witness to Jesus' identity.

The disciples are not mentioned again in the Passion Narrative of Mark. The role of discipleship, of following Jesus, is picked up by the women who watch his death, who observe where he is laid, and who come to the tomb. The only indication, in fact, Mark gives that the disciples eventually returned to being Jesus' followers is in the message that is entrusted to the women: "Go, tell his disciples and Peter that he is going before you into Galilee" (16:7). By this final message Mark implies that the disciples are also changed and transformed—but beyond the boundaries of his immediate narrative.

The Disciples' Potential for Transformation

In the Wisdom writings it is common to pose an antithesis between the wise and the foolish. Yet this antithesis is usually cut-and-dried: a person is either one or the other, and accordingly either cursed or blessed. Mark, however, adapts these traditions creatively to suggest the human potential for moving from one state to the other. He does this in two distinctive ways, linking each to his theology of transformation: first, he hints at some future change in the foolish disciples; second, he describes disciples who are wise.

The Scriptural Allusions

Midrashic commentary was not concerned with keeping chronological time-frames but rather synchronized them, juxtaposing events and allusions in an ahistorical manner. Mark has incorporated this aspect of midrashic structure into his narrative. The result, especially in respect to his portrayal of the disciples, is a double lens, so that we are constantly seeing the disciples in two time-frames simultaneously: the present of Jesus' (or Mark's) lifetime is juxtaposed to events of a biblical past or to a projected and ideal future. The disciples of the present are portrayed as weak, vulnerable, and faithless. Yet biblical allusion links them to a rich tradition of faithful people and to images of future transformation.

When Jesus first calls his disciples, they respond "straightway" (1:18, 20)—that is, with the sense of moral urgency implicit in Isaiah; singleheartedly, they detach themselves from all other things, even livelihood and family. At the beginning of the Gospel they are thus model disciples, responding with the wholehearted commitment that the rich young man subsequently cannot muster (ch. 10). While Jesus stresses, moreover, in chapter 2 that he has come for sinners, the scriptural references project the disciples into the context of the biblical End Time: they are described as friends of the bridegroom who have no need to fast (2:19–20); they are shown satisfying their ordinary needs with the Endtime harvest (2:23–24). Mark thus compresses two time-frames and dramatizes the disciples' capacity to change: called as sinners, they are yet called to a transformed state.

In the second calling of the disciples (3:13–19), they are termed "the Twelve," indicating the tribes of Israel.[13] The other words in this calling scene also bear biblical weight. Mark tells us first that Jesus "ascends the mountain and calls to himself those whom he wanted, and they went to him" (v. 13). The "mountain" is suggestive of Sinai and places Jesus in the role of Moses. The word "ascent" here confirms this identification with Moses and also echoes Jesus' first rising out of the waters (another Mosaic motif) at the start of his ministry. In short, in two brief verses Mark constructs a scene in which Jesus' calling of his disciples is made to resemble Moses' ascent to God at Sinai and his subsequent calling of the people according to the Lord's command—when he designated them "a kingdom of priests, a holy nation" (Exod. 19:3–6).

Mark constructs the transfiguration scene (9:1–13) as the middle one of a triad, on the one hand repeating elements of Jesus' baptism and on the other pointing toward Jesus' resurrection. This episode also functions as the middle of a triad regarding the disciples. Jesus chooses the same three disciples to witness his metamorphosis here that he chose to witness the resurrection of Jairus's daughter (5:37); they are the same three he also chooses to "watch" with him in Gethsemane (14:33). In chapter 5 they are silent; in chapter 14 they are described as unable to stay awake (14:37, 40, 41). Here their response is markedly different. Peter's desire to build a tent or "booth" (as in the Feast of Booths) for Jesus, Moses, and Elijah, together with his proclamation "It is good for us to be here" (v. 5), suggests that he has been transported into an Endtime vision. The vision, in effect, is of an Endtime conversation between Jesus and the two greatest prophets of Jewish tradition—one might call it a midrashic dialectic of persons. At the same time we are told that both Peter and the two other disciples do not know what to say "for they had become *ekphoboi*"—that is, "filled with awe."[14] The overshadowing cloud and the voice identifying "my beloved son" speak to them out of this context of reverential faith (v. 7). The disciples are momentarily metamorphosed as well as Jesus; the scene that anticipates his resurrection also anticipates their transformation.

The Liturgical Language

The potential for the disciples' transformed existence is also hinted at by Mark through his use of liturgical language. The vocabulary he uses is of particular interest because it bridges both Jewish and Christian worship. To modern Christians it is heard as sacramental vocabulary: "baptism," "anointing," "eucharist," and "cup." Yet each of these terms had a meaning within Early Judaism as well: "baptism" was ritual purification; "anointing" meant consecration; "eucharist" was the Greek translation of the Hebrew thanksgiving before meals; "cup" was associated with the wine of Passover. When Mark uses these words, we cannot restrict them to either an ancient Jewish sense or a modern Christian one: their very usage here suggests a time when the liturgy of the Jesus community was beginning to evolve out of Jewish roots. Either way it is the language of grace.

"Baptizing" appears at the beginning of the Gospel as the ritual by which John called his disciples to repentance. When "baptism" appears again, it is linked with "cup" in a context that suggests redemptive death: "Are you able to drink the cup that I drink, or be baptized with the baptism with which I am baptized? . . . The cup that I drink you will drink; and the baptism with which I am baptized you will be baptized, but to sit at my right hand or at my left is not mine to grant" (9:38–39). When Jesus speaks of "cup" a final time, he relates it to his blood, to the Covenant, and to the new wine of the Kingdom (14:23–25). He thus links his own life's blood with the sacrificial blood of Abraham's Covenant—and both with the Passover wine that symbolizes God's Genesis/Endtime bounty. When, therefore, he calls his disciples to "baptism" and "cup," he is calling them to a full relationship with God, with all the richness of these various meanings.

In the same way Mark's use of the language of "eucharist" makes it apply both to the bread of Passover and the meal of Christian communion. The double meanings infuse the description of the two parallel miracles of feeding. The narrative of the feeding of the four thousand in chapter 8 (vv. 1–10) is striking both in its likeness and in its unlikeness to the miraculous feeding of the five thousand in chapter 6. In the first feeding scene, Jesus' compassion is caused by his perception that the people "were like sheep without a shepherd" (6:34); in the later scene he states that his compassion is drawn forth by his recognition that the people "have remained with me now three days and have nothing to eat" (v. 2). The first image is an allusion to God's compassion in Ezekiel 34:5, while the second reference to "three days" is suggestive of the time between Jesus' death and his resurrection. The second miracle, in other words, seems to project a postresurrection time. This idea is also supported by the shift from *eulogeō* (Jesus' blessing over the bread) to *eucharistēsas* (Jesus' giving of thanks)—a shift that seems to reflect the eucharistic liturgy evolving out of the prayers of Passover and Jewish blessing.

Yet in other respects the two scenes are identical: in each instance a hungry crowd is gathered around Jesus in the desert (vv. 1 and 4); Jesus wants to feed them out of "compassion" (v. 2), while the disciples consider the feeding of such a large crowd impossible (v. 4). The dialogue that ensues between Jesus and his disciples is nearly the same, with Jesus asking them in each case "How many loaves have you?" (6:38, 8:5). Both times Jesus orders the crowd to "recline"— a Passover word (6:39 and 8:6)—offers a blessing over the bread (6:41 and 8:6), and breaks it and gives it to the disciples to distribute (6:41 and 8:6). Afterward, in both narratives, the crowd is said to be "satisfied" (6:42 and 8:8), and an abundance of leftovers is gathered up (6:43 and 8:8). However one regards the meal, it is linked, like the "cup," to Endtime abundance, and the ministerial role of the disciples remains the same. However one sees it, Jesus' feeding of the hungry here functions like Wisdom's banquet, and the disciples are called to act as Wisdom's ministers in distributing the divine nourishment.

Last but not least, the disciples are sent forth for the purposes of preaching and anointing (6:13). The latter gesture is not described here as the consecration of kings or priests but as a way of exorcism and healing—acts that Mark has shown to be most characteristic of Jesus, who, again like Wisdom, reflects God's ceaseless concern with generation and regeneration. The disciples are thus not only called to be transformed themselves; they are sent forth to transform others in an ongoing chain of healing and transformation. It is in the context of being nurturers themselves—and only that context—that Mark refers to them by the term "apostles" (6:30). It is their life-sustaining activities that signal their transformation into a Wisdom community.

Women Transformed: The Ending of Mark Is the Beginning of Wisdom

Mark also describes disciples who are wise, and his choice of metaphor here is apparently so surprising to most readers that they have missed it: for while he shows all the foolish disciples to be men, he depicts all the wise as women. In the Wisdom writings, as I have shown, life-sustaining activities are given image though the personification of Wisdom as a female figure: the faithful, provident wife of Proverbs, the female Wisdom "poured out" in Sirach as a divine lifeforce upon Creation, and the radiant feminine Wisdom who mirrors God in the Wisdom of Solomon. It is in keeping with these traditions that Mark dramatizes women as the foil to the foolish disciples, symbols of the wise. Mark works out this metaphorical antithesis in three distinct, although overlapping, ways. In the first part of the Gospel he shows Jesus' healing miracles to be acts in which women are "raised up" to a new status; in the second part of the Gospel, he shows women acting out the roles the male disciples have failed to perform; at the end of his Gospel, he uses language that suggests the women are so transformed by Jesus' resurrection that they become both bearers and symbols of God's renewed Creation.

The "Raising Up" of Women (Mark 1–7)

Changing the Status of Simon's Mother-in-Law (1:29–31)

It cannot be fortuitous that Mark, in portraying the beginning of Jesus' ministry, describes three healings: of a demoniac, a mother-in-law, and a leper. The first and last make clear that he is depicting Jesus' outreach to the most reviled of the community; situated between a demoniac and a leper, "the mother-in-law," we assume, is an ancient joke. But there are serious implications here as well: before the time of Hillel and Jesus, women, like lepers, were relegated to the outer courts of the Temple, and women received social status only through their relationship to males—usually their fathers or husbands; for a woman to be known through her son-in-law is so extreme as to suggest that Mark is making a special point of her social anonymity. In that context, Mark's way of describing Jesus' miracle is reflective of the new attitude toward women that was emerging in Early Judaism:[15] the miracle has a historical base as well as a theological purpose.

In different ways Jesus acts to restore each person he heals to the center of communal life: he distinguishes between the man possessed and "the unclean spirit" and restores him through purgation; similarly, he cures the "unclean" flesh of the leper and returns him to the priests and the Mosaic ritual. The center of this triad (always a key placement for Mark) is the healing of the woman.

The word used to describe woman's condition—"lying down" (*katekeito*, imperfect middle *katakeimai*)—is frequently used to describe someone already dead;[16] the word used to describe her cure—"raised up" (*ēgeiren*, imperfect *ēgeirō*)—is the word Mark uses repeatedly to describe Jesus' resurrection. The words combine to sound out the motif of death and resurrection. A similar configuration of words is repeated in chapter 5 when Jesus raises the daughter of Jairus from death (5:40–41). In both places Jesus' gestures of healing are described in the exact same words as though to indicate a ritual: "taking her hand" (*kratēsas tēs cheiros*), he raises [her] up (1:31 and 5:41). In the first chapter this "raising up" is mentioned so briefly as to be easily missed;[17] in the fifth chapter it is called attention to by the addition of the Aramaic word "arise" (*cumi*).

The words describing the woman's healing are also significant: literally, "the fever released her" (*aphēken*, aorist *aphiēmi*). It is a word Jesus subsequently uses as a synonym for "forgive" ("Your sins are *released*," 2:5, and "All sins will be *released*," 3:28) and for the opening of the deaf man's ears ("Be *released*" 7:34). The repeated use of this word in Mark indicates a theological perspective in which evil *binds*, while the healing acts of Jesus are consistently directed toward releasing, opening up, and setting free.

Most important is the word describing the cured woman's immediate response: "and she began to *serve*" (*diēkonei*, imperfect inceptive of *diakoneō*). The word is a leitmotif in Mark's Gospel. It is used first in chapter 1 to describe the angels ministering to Jesus in the desert (1:13). What is more significant, it is used by Jesus to describe the essence of discipleship: "If anyone wants to be first, he will be the last of all and the servant [*diakonos*] of all (9:35). . . . Whoever wants to be great among you will become your servant [*diakonos*]. . . . For the son of man did not come to be served but to serve [*diakoneō*]" (10:43–45). It is the way of life that is clearly modeled on Jesus' own. As such it is not surprising that *diakonos* eventually came to designate the first ministers of the Jesus community.[18] It is thus to be remarked that the only person in the entire Gospel to be described as *diakonos* is a *woman*. In terms of the Markan narrative, she is the first to act like Jesus himself.

In summary, this first healing of a woman is fraught with theological significance: although she is *lying down as one dead*, Jesus *takes her by the hand, raises her up*, and *releases* her from fever; she immediately begins to minister to him. Her transformation is significantly preceded by the purging of "the man with the unclean spirit": as Jesus distinguishes there between the man and his uncleanness, so his transformation of the woman distinguishes between the marginalized status of the woman and her capacity for a ministerial role. Her healing is also significantly echoed by the cure of the leper: through the action of Jesus, the leper is not only restored to his religious community but also changed from being one who was prohibited from normal converse into the first preacher of the gospel. Those on the religious fringe—the woman and the leper—are changed into the first ministers of food and word.

The transformation of the woman, placed in the middle here by Mark, is a hinge episode. Before her cure, she is not exactly called "unclean," but she is described as lying ill; she is not entirely anonymous, but she is identified only by her relation to a male. Her healing involves a ritual gesture on the part of Jesus—a taking by the hand and a raising up. The effect of this healing is twofold: she is released from her illness, and she begins to act as one of Jesus' followers and imitators. The transformation of this semianonymous woman from "mother-in-law" to *diakonos* is a paradigmatic *sign-act* in the Gospel of Mark.

Healing the Menstruating Woman; Raising Up the Dead Girl (5:21–43)

Like chapter 1, chapter 5 is also organized around three healings of those considered "unclean"—a Gentile possessed by unclean spirits (vv. 2–13), a woman suffering because of menstrual blood (vv. 25–34), and a child presumed to be a corpse (vv. 35–43) The central story is again that of a woman—this time of a woman whose menstrual flow has gone on for twelve years (v. 25). The very fact that this female condition is presented sympathetically indicates an emerging attitude toward women that might be characterized as special to both Early Judaism and Early Christianity. Within both later Christian and Rabbinic law, a menstruating woman was considered "unclean."[19] In ancient Judaism the prophets use the image of a menstruating woman as a metaphor for Israel defiled by idolatry. Thus Jesus' cure of a menstruating woman has implications far beyond that of a simple miracle: on one level, it may symbolize the healing of idolatry; on another, it seems to indicates a shift in consciousness in respect to women. On both counts, Jesus' healing of this woman expresses an attitude of outreach to the "unclean" rather than one of judgment and exclusion.

The cure of this woman is further remarkable because of the way Mark tells the story, combining both folk and liturgical language. When Mark first describes the woman, he shifts from the use of past tense to a series of present participles, which gives the effect of folk idiom:

> And a woman being there with blood flowing for twelve years, and she suffering much from many doctors, and spending freely all that she had, and had not profited, but had become much worse, hearing about Jesus, and coming into the crowd [and] following after him, she touched his garment. (vv. 25–27)

The shift to aorist in the last verb—"touched"—underscores that gesture as a decisive turning point. After that point, Mark couches the story in theological and liturgical language; the narrative ceases to sound like a folk tale and becomes a story of faith. Mark's very use of language here dramatizes God's power to transform the ordinary.

While the woman in the first chapter is the passive recipient of healing, the woman here takes the initiative, even "following after" (*opisthen*) Jesus to effect her cure. She also consciously reflects: "If I should touch even his garments, I will be saved (*sōthēsomai,* v. 28). Mark further emphasizes the theological nature of this healing by his repeated use of "straightway" (*euthus*)—"And straightway the source of blood dried up. . . . And straightway Jesus recognizing . . . power had gone forth" (vv. 29–30). The verbal link underscores the theological link: the healing of the woman is not just a physical cure but a moral one, affecting her very identity. The woman's reaction of "fear and trembling" (*phobētheisa* and *tremousa,* v. 33) is an expression of awe,[20] and it is followed by a gesture of faith: "[she] came and fell down before him and told him the whole truth" (v. 33). Jesus' reply is couched in the vocabulary of liturgical formula: "Daughter, your faith has saved [*sesōken*] you. Go in peace" (v. 34). The formula of "faith" that "saves" suggests early Christian preaching, while the formula "Go in peace" suggests a familar Jewish blessing, *Lekh(i) l'shalom.*[21] Together they reinforce the idea that this is an episode of theological and liturgical significance.

An important aspect of this significance is the emphasis on faith: at the end of chapter 4, Jesus reproaches his disciples for their lack of faith (v. 40); here he commends the woman for having faith. In fact, as I have shown, the woman, although not called to be a disciple, *acts like one,* following after Jesus and trusting him to save her. The woman is a model of the faith the disciples lack. This disparity foreshadows the Passion Narrative, where the male disciples all flee while the women remain faithful followers of Jesus. This foreshadowing needs to be kept in mind in reading the very end of the Gospel, where the women are again described as experiencing "fear and trembling"; we need to note the echo of this earlier episode where such emotions are unmistakably the mark of a saving faith.

The theological term "salvation" frames the incident: the woman says: "If I should touch even his garments I will be *saved*" (v. 28); he tells her: "Daughter, your faith has saved you" (v. 34). The power going forth from Jesus without his explicitly willing it is reminiscent of the seed of the kingdom that grows without the farmer's conscious attention. On one side of this incident is healing in a pagan and foreign territory (the Gerasene demoniac); on the other side is healing in a synagogue and home (the healing of Jairus's daughter). The interlocking structure makes a parallel between the last two: the seeking of the unclean woman and the seeking of the synagogue leader; the menstruating woman and the girl of menstrual age; the twelve years of hemorrhage and the age of the little girl; the restoration of the woman and the raising up of the little girl. The whole triad suggests a parallel between all three forms of uncleanness and all three seekers of healing—the Gentile demoniac, the woman outcast, the synagogue leader. It further suggests that none of them represents a fixed or permanent condition: not demon-possession or female "uncleanness" or even death. Placing the story of the healing of the menstruating woman in the center suggests that this illness is like the ones on either side, and this healing is the key to the other two. Ending with the raising up of the little girl hints that all three episodes are forms of resurrection. There is a strong implication that Jesus, in allowing a woman to touch him in a time of "uncleanness," is virtually raising her from the dead.

This implication is bolstered by Jesus' touching of the child presumed dead; it is a parallel instance of outreach to someone considered ritually unclean. In the third episode the theme of resurrection is more explicit than in the first; Jesus' command to "rise up" is given directly and given twice—first in Aramaic and then in Greek. The idea of resurrection is also implicit in Jesus' first observation to the mourners: "The child is not dead but sleeping" (v. 39). The word for "sleeping" here is *katheudō* (as in 4:27 and 4:38), which can mean either death or sleep, so that the verbal effect is one of mirror images. The importance of the scene is underlined by the presence of the same three disciples who will be witnesses to the transfiguration.

The raising up of the little girl thus echoes the raising up of the mother-in-law and anticipates the raising up of Jesus. At the same time, the renewed life of the twelve-year-old girl is linked structurally to the healing of the "unclean" woman. In this way Mark suggests that the transformations of all three women are related theologically, not only to each other but also to the transformed life that the disciples witness in Jesus.

The Exorcism of the Gentile Woman's Daughter (7:24–30)

Chapter 7 brings to a climax Jesus' relation to conventional ideas of the "unclean." In the context of these views, the Syrophoenician woman is "unclean" on three counts: as a woman; as a Gentile; as one who has a daughter possessed by a demon. Her condition combines different forms of "uncleanness" that Mark has portrayed earlier—women in general, the Gentile demoniac, the daughter of Jairus. Just as the chapter as a whole summarizes Jesus' earlier encounters with "unclean" persons, so his encounter with this Gentile woman functions as a summary of his previous relationship to women.

Strikingly different here, however, is Mark's description of Jesus' reluctance to become involved with this woman and her persistence in seeking him out. Mark says that Jesus entered a house "he did not want anyone to know" (v. 24), "but straightway a woman hearing of him—having a little daughter with an unclean spirit—came and fell down before his feet" (v. 25). The application here of the key term, "straightway," coincides with the woman's hearing of Jesus. Earlier in this chapter, Jesus emphasizes the importance of hearing God's word, even repeating the phrase of chapter 4, "He who has ears to hear, let him hear!" (v. 16) and also rebuking his disciples for their slowness (as usual) to understand (v. 18). In this context, the quickness with which this Gentile woman "hears" of him is a significant contrast. The recurrence of "straightway" signals an action of theological import. [22] Finally, the woman's immediate response—her gesture of reverence in kneeling before him—echoes the menstruating woman's gesture of faith.

This Gentile woman is thus presented as being similar in many ways to the Jewish woman who sought Jesus out and whom Jesus commended for her faith. Yet the initial dialogue that follows between Jesus and this woman reflects the typical wariness of a pious Jew toward a non-Jew. Jesus' first reply to her symbolizes the customary attitude: "Allow the children to be fed first, for it is not fitting to take the bread of the children and throw it to the little dogs" (v. 27). To grasp the full weight of this response, it is important to know that contemporary Jewish writers did in fact often refer to Gentiles as "dogs"; Jesus' reply is in keeping with this harshness and exclusivity.[23] Knowing this fact makes it clear that Mark is indicating here how normative Judaism was for Jesus. In that context, the dialogue that ensues in which the woman eventually persuades Jesus to provide her with the "bread" she asks for, seems symbolic of the reluctant turning of the early Jesus community to Gentile converts. Mark thus uses the witty exchange between Jesus and the woman to express the slowly evolving process by which the gathering in the name of Jesus was shifting from a totally Jewish community to a Jewish-Gentile one. It acts out, on a playful level, a growing inclusiveness as to who is fit to receive God's word (the "bread") and God's healing.

The details of the concluding miracle also have to be read symbolically. The woman, trusting in Jesus' power even without physical contact, goes home to find the demon gone and her daughter whole; Jesus cures the child without touching her—a fact that symbolizes the action of faith in a later time-frame. There are echoes of earlier narratives: as Jesus earlier cast a demon out of the synagogue, so here he has cast a demon out of a child; as earlier he raised up a little girl to renewed life, so here he has brought a little girl back to a healthy existence; as earlier he responded to the request of a synagogue leader to heal his daughter, so here he responds to the request of a Gentile woman. As his earlier miracles implied more than physical healing, so does this one. Mark suggests that what happens here is the same as in every previous instance in which Jesus has responded to a woman: there is a transformation of the person that corresponds with a shift in perception as to that person's worth. "The mother-in-law" becomes a *diakonos*; the "unclean" woman becomes a model of faith; the "dead" child is shown to be merely sleeping. So here, the Gentile woman comes to trust in God's desire and power to heal, and a Gentile child is purged of her demons. To sum up, Mark indicates, through his recounting of Jesus' actions, that Jesus' outreach is not excluding but inclusive and his presence is not condemning but transformative. Through his transforming energy Gentiles are brought into the blessings of the Covenant and women are given the dignity of faith and ministry.

The Wise Women as Foils to the Foolish Disciples (Mark 14–15)

Women reappear to play an active role in the final chapters of Mark's narrative (chs. 14–16), where they stand in marked contrast to the betraying, sleeping, denying, and fleeing disciples.

The Woman Who Anoints Jesus (14:3–9)

In the whole of chapter 14, a woman's anointing of Jesus is the only gesture of faith. The incident is framed by the betrayal of Judas. Just before it, we hear the chief priests and scribes plotting to murder Jesus (vv. 1–2); just after, we hear of Judas seeking out the high priests in order to "hand him over" (vv. 10–11). Structurally, the anointing at Bethany is thus interpolated into the key narrative of Jesus' betrayal. The rest of the chapter is taken up with multiple betrayals: Jesus' prediction of betrayal (vv. 18–21), the failure of the three disciples to watch (vv. 32–42), the actual moment of Judas's betrayal (vv. 43–49), the flight of the disciples (vv. 50–51), the condemnation based on false witnesses (vv. 55–65), and the denial of Peter (vv. 66–72). It is no small matter that in the midst of these betrayals of Jesus, a woman performs a gesture of honor, a ritual of anointing.

The incident has meaning on several levels. First of all, it is important to notice the setting: the location in Bethany is a reminder of Jesus' glorious entry into Jerusalem at the beginning of chapter 11. Paired there with Bethphage, which means "house of figs," it is suggestive of Endtime abundance. It thus provides a setting conducive to the coming of God's chosen, the *anointed one*.

The conjunction of the woman with the leper here is a reminder of Jesus' first miracles, which transformed those two persons into ministers of food and word. The reappearance of the woman and the leper here is also suggestive of an Endtime community in which these two once-marginalized figures are now the ones who preside. The fact that the leper is no longer anonymous but now has a name is also significant—particularly, of course, the name "Simon." As Jesus entered the house of Simon the disciple in the first chapter (1:29), so here he enters the house of "Simon the leper." The echo underscores the irony of the betrayal to come: while Simon the disciple denies his master, Simon the leper welcomes him into his home. The irony will be repeated when still a third Simon helps carry the cross. In emphasizing three "Simons," Mark seems to be playing with the name and identity of Simon-Peter, underscoring the constant potential for human change. The parallel here points up the transformation of the original leper from outcast to host.

The new dignity of the leper goes along with the new dignity of the woman. The gesture of anointing with oil links the woman to the ministry of the disciples in chapter 6 (6:13). Significantly, as I have shown, this particular ministry of the disciples—along with that of bearing "witness"—is added to their initial calling in chapter 3 where they are designated *apostles* for the first time (6:7). When the woman here anoints with oil, she thus fulfills an apostolic role.

The precise description of the oil is also important. The woman brings the oil in an "alabaster vase" (v. 3)—a costly container that indicates this is no ordinary oil. The oil is "sweetsmelling" (v. 3), anticipating the "spices" that the women will later bring to Jesus' tomb (16:1). Mark further describes it as *pistikos* and *poluteles* (v. 3): the second word means "pure" and "of great price"; the first has no known referent other than *pistis*, the word for faith.[24] The healed woman of chapter 5 is the only person commended for having *pistis*; *pistikos* links the two women, suggesting that this is the *oil of faith*. This interpretation is supported by the context of the whole incident, in which Jesus commmends this woman as he did the earlier one.

The gestures of the woman are also significant: "having shattered the alabaster vase, she began to pour the oil on his head" (v. 3). The word used for the breaking of the vase, *suntribō*, connotes total destruction—similar to the word Jesus uses earlier in Mark to connote the loss of the Temple.[25] The word for "pour" here, *katacheō*, is kin to the word used by Jesus when he speaks of his blood being "poured out for many" (14:24)—a word that in turn echoes the anguished speaker of Psalm 22, "I am poured out like water."[26] The two words together suggest a totality of action; they connote a sense of total giving that applies both to the woman's gesture and to Jesus' words about his death.

In a poetic way these linking words serve to anticipate the Passion Narrative to come. There is a graphic link between the woman's breaking of the alabaster vase and Jesus' breaking of the bread that stands for his body, between the woman's action of "pouring out" the oil and Jesus' reference to the wine as his blood "poured out for many" (vv. 3, 22–24). The woman's gestures also appear to take place at a Passover meal, for the incident is set on the eve of Passover (v. 1), and Jesus is "reclining at table" (v. 3). Jesus himself says the woman has anticipated his burial (v. 8). Thus this *breaking* and *pouring out* in the house of Simon the leper is linked to the *breaking* and *pouring out* of the Passover meal—actions that, in turn, are linked to the narrative of Jesus' death. The woman's gestures here anticipate both Jesus' death and Jesus' own gestures in symbolizing his death—the gestures of bread broken and wine poured out.

Jesus' own comments on the woman's actions indicate their theological and liturgical significance. When those around complain in mundane terms that this effusion of oil is a "waste" because it "could have been sold for more than 300 denarii and given to the poor" (vv. 4–5), Jesus replies in liturgical terms: "She has worked a fitting work on me. . . . She has done what she could beforehand to have anointed my body in preparation for burial" (v. 8). The word for "work" here—*ergon*—may refer to practical action but is also used in Scripture to characterize the deeds of God.[27] The comment "she has done what she could" echoes Jesus' praise for the poor widow who contributed to the Temple "everything she had" (12:44). The assertion that she was anointing Jesus' body for burial confirms her gesture as a liturgical act.[28]

Most significant of all, Jesus applies to the woman the liturgical idea of "remembering": "Truly I say to you, whenever the good news is preached in the whole world, then what she has done will be told in memory of her" (v. 9). The Greek word for "memory" here, *mnēmosunon*, must be understood in relation to the Jewish word *zikkaron*—a word used for a liturgical reenactment that reactualizes, it is believed, the moment of God's saving grace. Within Jewish tradition this word is used in reference to Passover, expressing the belief that through the liturgy, God frees his people again each year; the celebration is not just of the past but of the present. The same belief was carrried over to the Christian celebration of the Eucharist. The word used here is thus rich in meaning: it suggests that since these acts of a woman at a Passover meal anticipate the final acts of Jesus, in some future time she will be remembered as Jesus' death is remembered, for the reenactment of his death will be a reenactment of her acts of breaking and pouring. Time is not linear here but synchronic: her gestures anticipate the liturgical remembering of Jesus' death; her gestures enact the eucharistic remembrance. She is the presider at a eucharistic liturgy.[29]

The Women Who Follow and "Watch" (15:40–41, 47)

As "remembrance" is a key to Jewish liturgy, so "watchfulness" is a key to Jewish Wisdom. At the end of the crucifixion scene Mark indicates that while the male disciples have fled the pain of Jesus' death, the women have been watching: "And there were women seeing from a distance, among them Mary Magdalene, and Mary mother of James the younger and Joses, and Salome, who, when in Galilee, followed him and served him, and many others who went up together with him into Jerusalem" (vv. 40–41). Brief though the assertion is, it is remarkable for the contrast it presents to the behavior of everyone else: the high priests and scribes who plot against Jesus, Pilate who condemns him, the Roman soldiers who scourge, mock, and crucify him, the mere passersby who ridicule him, and above all, his disciples, who betray, deny, and flee him.

The vocabulary of these two verses, moreover, indicates that this is more than a casual statement. The word for "seeing" here—*theōrousai*—is a word that means "notice" or "perceive" and can also imply "spiritual perception." This deeper understanding of the word is warranted because the contrast here points up the fact that the women have been the only ones faithfully watching Jesus' death. They have been faithful while the disciples have fled; they have done the "watching" Jesus asked his disciples to do; they are the "witnesses" Jesus called his apostles to be. While those called to be "disciples" have failed, these women are in fact acting the part. This function of the women is borne out even further by Mark's use of the words "follow" (*akoloutheō*) and "serve" (*diakoneō*) to describe their relationship to Jesus—words I have already shown to be keywords of discipleship.

Significantly, there are three women named here, so they serve as a balance and counterpoint to the three male disciples whom Jesus chose to be his special witnesses in the garden and who fell asleep instead. The naming of the three is itself worth noticing: instead of the anonymous women we have encountered before in the narrative, these women have achieved a new status.

Finally, the names themselves are meaningful: there are two *Marys*—"Mary Magdalene" and "Mary, the mother of James the younger and Joses." Of the first we know nothing in Mark; the latter echoes the scene where Jesus' hometown folks reject his miracles because they know him as "the son of Mary and brother of James and Joses" (6:3). The clear implication, then, is that this second Mary is Jesus' mother. Mark's focus here is not on biographical information but theological irony. Jesus' miracles are rejected earlier because he is too common, too ordinary; yet those very miracles, as we have repeatedly seen, are aimed at making the common and ordinary holy. So here his mother, a common woman the homefolks think could not possibly be the mother of a prophet, is shown to be acting with uncommon faithfulness. It is very much to the point that Mark describes Jesus' mother Mary as neither more nor less than "Mary of Magdala." What is remarkable about these ordinary women is not *who they are* but *what they do*. And in terms of the

Markan narrative, what they do is to act like faithful followers (i.e., *disciples*), like servants (i.e., *ministers*), and like unfailing witnesses and anointers (i.e., *apostles*). Their role is reinforced by the final verse of chapter 15—"Now Mary Magdalen and Mary of Joses were perceiving where he had been laid" (v. 47): Mark repeats the verb for spiritual perception (*theōreo*) and indicates that these women were the only ones who were witnesses of Jesus' tomb.[30]

Women as Witnesses and Signs of a New Creation (16:1–8)

Mark describes the same three women who witnessed the crucifixion as the ones who come first to the tomb. Again the two *Marys* reappear like a refrain. The third name, *Salome*, is striking because it reminds us of the other Salome who danced for John the Baptist's head.[31] The effect is similar to the pairing of Simon Peter with Simon the leper or Simon of Cyrene: while Simon Peter denies Jesus, Simon the leper welcomes him and Simon of Cyrene carries his cross; while Herod's Salome danced for death, this Salome brings spices for life. The repetition of names conveys a sense of alter egos, or the possibility of transformation: "Simon" may deny Jesus, or receive him, or share the burden of his cross; "Salome" may be a shallow woman who becomes an accomplice to murder or a strong and faithful woman who is among the first to hear the news of resurrection.

The scene of the three women here reverberates with echoes. These women, like the first woman whom Jesus healed, had *ministered* to him (15:40–41), and like the "unclean" woman, had *followed after* him. They have come to anoint Jesus like the woman in Bethany. In fact, *the anointing of Jesus by women* forms an inclusio around the whole narrative of his passion and death. While the narrative of Jesus seems to be moving him toward total defeat, the ritual action of the women continues to claim him as God's *anointed*.

This second anointing is inevitably a reminder of the first, with its sacrificial gestures of breaking and outpouring. But there are differences that are also significant. The first woman anointed Jesus "for his burial," while these women, coming to the tomb, find his body is not there. Thus these spices cannot be used to perform the ritual of sealing the body in death; they are only appropriate to a liturgy of life. These women coming to the tomb, moreover, are in a different time-frame: they are, Mark tells us, in a time beyond the Sabbath (16:1). In that context, the reference to spices is suggestive of the closing of the Sabbath liturgy where the distribution of spices accompanies a prayer that the Sabbath-time will continue to hallow and sweeten the "ordinary time" of the week.[32] The liturgy for death has become a liturgy for hallowing ordinary life. In both instances, it is women who perform it.

Symbolic of a new creation, the women come "very early in the morning on the first day of the week . . . on the rising of the sun" (v. 2). In this context, the entry of the women into the tomb also bears symbolic import: "And they were saying to each other, 'Who will roll away for us the stone outside the door of the tomb?' And looking up they see that the stone had been rolled back" (vv. 3–4). There is an echo here of the crazed demoniac who "lived among the tombs" (5:3) and "was bruising himself with stones" (5:5) before Jesus healed him. Even the word for "door" (*thuran*) is a reminder of the "doorkeeper" in the parable whom the master told to be "on the watch" (13:34). Both echoes may be subliminal, but they work to raise our expectations. These expectations are then confirmed by the appearance of a "young man sitting on the right clothed in a white robe" (16:5). He is suggestive of three transformations: the transformed demoniac "sitting clothed and in his right mind" (5:15); the white clothing of the transfigured Jesus (9:3); and the rehabilitation of the frightened youth who fled naked from the scene of Jesus' arrest (14:51). The women's entry into the tomb is thus placed in a context of transformation, and their fleeing from the tomb (16:8) must be seen not as an act of fear but of new life.

The message the "young man" or angel subsequently gives the women is one of new life in more than one sense. There is first the news that Jesus has been raised. Beyond that, the word of the angel also suggests that *they themselves, the women,* are to leave the tomb and take on a new existence. In a total reversal of ancient conventions (both religious and social) the women are "sent forth"—that is, as *apostles*—and given the ministry of preaching the word to the male disciples. In a narrative that has repeatedly stressed Jesus' "raising up" of women, it is fitting that the first effects of his resurrection should be reflected in their transformed state.

This transformation of the women has been seriously undermined by translations. It is therefore important to look carefully at the vocabulary Mark uses. The women's immediate response is one of being utterly astounded: *exethambēthēsan,* a word peculiar to Mark among New Testament writers,[33] is one he has used to indicate the response of the crowd to Jesus' first exorcism (1:27) and the reaction of the crowd upon seeing Jesus after the scene of transfiguration (9:15). Their further responses—*tromos, ekstasis,* and *ephobounto* (16:8)—are words whose meaning is also linked to other contexts. As I have shown, *tromos*—"trembling"—is used earlier by Mark to describe the awed faith of the woman healed of her twelve-year hemorrhage (5:33); it is coupled there with *phobētheisa,* a pairing that is customary in the Septuagint to express the kind of dread one has before a superior being.[34] Here the "trembling" is paired with *ekstasis,* which conveys an even stronger sense of religious awe.[35]

In Jewish Scripture, "ecstasy" is a word associated with a form of prophecy induced by the powerful overtaking of God's spirit.[36] In the Septuagint the word is used twice in Genesis, both times to indicate a deep trance imposed by God in order to bring about a new order of being—the "deep sleep" of Abraham at the making of the Covenant (Gen. 15:12) and the deep sleep of *'adam* at the making of sexual beings.[37] Both allusions are relevant, but the reference to Genesis seems most pertinent, indicating that Mark is deliberately choosing a word that suggests God in the process of a new creation.

Within Mark's Gospel itself the same word has appeared before to express the feelings of those who have just seen Jesus raising up Jairus's daughter (5:42). In addition, a related term appears in 3:21 where Jesus himself is thought by those close to him to be "beside himself" or "out of his mind" (*exestē*, aorist *existēmi*). The two words come together at the end of chapter 5 where Mark describes the response of the crowd witnessing the child's resurrection from presumed death: *"exestēsan ekstasei"*—that is, they were out of their minds with ecstasy. The convergence underlines the fact that the word meaning "madness" and the word meaning "ecstasy" are related both in idea and in etymology: they both indicate a state of being that is other than the purely rational. The linguistic closeness is suggestive of how that state may appear simultaneously to be irrational to the onlooker and visionary to the one experiencing it. Here, then, is another Markan triad: Jesus, near the beginning of the Gospel, and the women at the end are described in parallel and balancing terms; at the center stands the crowd overwhelmed by the experience of witnessing an unexpected restoration of life. *Ekstasis*, therefore, is far more than mere "astonishment": it indicates a transformed state of consciousness.

The final word—*ephobounto*—also has a range of possible meanings: while its first and simplest meaning is "to be afraid," it also bears the sense of *reverence*, as for God. In Mark, this word is twice applied to the male disciples: first, after Jesus has stilled the storm (4:41) and second, after Jesus has been transfigured (9:6). The first instance is translated by the NRSV as "filled with great awe," the second as "terrified." In short, this is a clear case where translation is tantamount to interpretation. The singular use of *ekstasis* here, however, lends weight to the meaning of "awe."

"Fear" as holy awe seems to be remote from the minds of those translators and commentators who consider all experiences of fear to be negative and unhealthy. Yet the Hebrew Bible contains many instances in which human beings express a feeling of deep reverence in the presence of the numinous. From Moses at Sinai to Job before the whirlwind, the Bible speaks repeatedly of the human experience of *mysterium tremendum* as the beginning of wisdom. "Fear of the

Lord," in these contexts, is not to be equated with fright or terror but rather with the profound recognition of how little one understands of the divine mystery. In keeping with the Wisdom traditions, it is this kind of holy fear that Mark makes his theme, and he uses the same word to express this holy fear as an appropriate response to Jesus' stilling of the seas, to the vision of Jesus in a transformed state, and to the news of Jesus' resurrection.

Among the commentators who do interpret the women's response as reverence rather than timidity, are D. E. Nineham, who speaks of their "holy awe";[38] John Donahue, who refers to their "numinous fear";[39] Gerard Sloyan, who relates the verb here to Mark 9:14;[40] Donald Senior, who speaks of their being "gripped by the same wondrous awe that had stunned biblical witnesses from Moses to Paul";[41] and Robert H. Gundry, who relates the description of their feelings here to several other instances in Mark:

> Fear is a healthy sort elsewhere in Mark . . . as are trembling (5:33) and astonishment (2:12, 5:42, 6:51). . . . Therefore Mark is not criticizing the women for their trembling, astonishment, or fear. Rather, he is using these reactions to highlight the supernaturalness of Jesus' resurrection.[42]

All the episodes that Gundry singles out as using similar vocabulary to the ending are instances of miracle, and the words in every case clearly indicate a human being not only overwhelmed but gladdened and changed by divine power. The woman who realizes that just touching Jesus' hem has healed her kneels down in "fear and trembling" (*phobētheisa kai tremousa*, 5:33), and Jesus commends her for her faith (5:34). Those who see the paralytic take up his bed and walk experience an ecstatic joy that makes them glorify God (*hoste existasthai pantas kai doxazein ton theon*, 2:12); those who witness the raising up of the little girl go out of their minds with ecstasy (*kai exestēsan ekstasei megale*, 5:42); the disciples who watch Jesus walk on the water and then quiet the wind are "utterly [and beyond measure] beside themselves" (*kai liav [ek perissou] ev heautois existanto*, 6:51). Jesus himself is thought to be "beside himself" (*exestē*) by those who do not understand him (3:21). If we add to these examples the moment when the disciples, seeing Jesus still the sea, are "filled with great awe" (4:41) and the moment when Peter, upon seeing Jesus transfigured, feels moved to build places of worship (9:6), we see that there is precedent, indeed a pattern in Mark, of expressing religious experience through words of fear and ecstasy. If we are aware of this pattern, then we will perceive that verse 8, which combines these feelings, is not letdown but climax: the meaning of the women's "fear" is contextualized not only by the precedents of the disciples' awe but also by their "trembling and ecstasy" (*tromos kai ekstasis*)—which are, in Mark, the feelings that accompany a breakthrough in human perception.

The connecting *eichen* here literally means "had," but usage suggests the sense of *being possessed* by something. The same construction appears in 9:17 when the father tells Jesus about his son "having a dumb spirit." The fact that the phrase here is similar calls attention to its inverse meaning: the child was possessed by a demon that kept him from speaking; the women are possessed by a God-induced ecstasy and are thus silent for opposite reasons.

Putting these meanings together, this final verse of Mark's Gospel should read:

> And going out they fled the tomb, for trembling [*mysterium tremendum*] and ecstasy possessed them, and they said nothing to anyone, for they were filled with awe.

So translated, this verse represents a climax in the motif of *transformation*. Each part of it, in fact, bears symbolic weight. The women's fleeing from the tomb not only mirrors the change in the healed demoniac but also Jesus' own release from the tomb. Their sense of being possessed by holy ecstasy is the reverse of possession by the devil. The word *ekstasis* points to the trance-like state of a new creation. Their silence is not a dumb or fearful silence; their speechlessness comes from being "filled with awe."

Mark's assertion that "they said nothing to anyone" must be taken as the final Markan irony. The statement echoes Jesus' first charge to the cured leper "not to say anything to anyone" (1:44); as one hears the echo, one must also remember that the leper immediately "went out and began to talk freely" (1:45). The leper became a preacher; so here the very fact of Mark's Gospel is testimony to the eloquence of the women.

The women's significance becomes clearest when they are compared with the male disciples. The disciples are called to *follow* Jesus (ch. 1), to follow after *his cross* (ch. 8), to follow him in being *the servant of all* (ch. 9). They are called to be *prepared* for his death, and to *watch* with him in his distress (chs. 13–14). They are called to *bear witness* to God's kingdom and to heal through *anointing with oil* (ch. 6). Within the boundaries of the Markan narrative the male disciples of Jesus fail to do any of these things, while the women in fact fulfill them: they *follow and serve* (chs. 1, 5, 15); they *follow Jesus to the cross and the tomb* (chs. 15, 16); they *watch faithfully* to the very end and even beyond the end (chs. 15, 16); they *prepare for his death,* they *anoint with oil* (chs. 14, 16); they are the first to be sent forth as *witnesses* of the resurrection. While Jesus repeatedly reproaches the male disciples for their lack of understanding, he commends women (both a Jewish and a Gentile woman) for their *faith* (chs. 5, 7). In his dying, while the male disciples betray, deny, and flee from Jesus, a woman gives "everything she has" to anoint him (ch. 14).

Through the role of the women, Mark's Gospel ends as a new beginning: "very early in the morning on the first day of the week . . . on the rising of the sun" the women are cast into a trance-like state—such as that which accompanied the first making of the Covenant (Gen. 15:12) or the making of male and female (Gen. 2:21)—God's very "image and likeness" (Gen. 1:26). The End Time is a return to Genesis. The women as the first transformed disciples exemplify the return to God's *Beginning*—the codeword for Wisdom.

The Theological Implications

Mark's representation of Jesus' disciples—both male and female—has significant implications for the inclusive nature of the Jesus community, both then and now. Comparison with contemporaneous first-century theology makes clear the significance of the Markan perspective. In the Qumran documents, for example, we find a community oriented toward preparation for a final war between good and evil. To be considered for the community, one had to be examined and judged worthy; a period of initiation followed after which one was "set apart as holy" and allowed to share in "secret" teachings. By this separation "from the habitation of ungodly men" one could "prepare the way of the Lord" (1QSVIII). In the *War Scroll*, the standards exclude anyone "who is lame, or blind, or crippled, or afflicted with a lasting bodily blemish, or smitten with bodily impurity," while women are treated like "young boys" (1QMVII). This extreme example points up the antithesis of the Markan Gospel: the Markan Jesus reaches out to touch and transform the very ones whom the Qumran community excludes.

The inclusiveness of the Markan community also stands in contrast to the community of the book of Revelation, where we find images of a predestined elect, esoteric knowledge, a fixed separation between the righteous and the wicked, and an exclusion of women from the ranks of the saints (14:4). In Mark, the Wisdom community is an open community because it springs from the acknowledgment that God's ways are not subject to human calculation. In Mark, we find Jesus calling all sinners as his disciples and discipleship validated existentially. The most striking image of this existential authentication lies in the dramatic example of the women.

The use of women to exemplify holiness draws out meanings implicit in the Wisdom writings. It is in keeping with the theology that frames these traditions that the women in Mark are repeatedly "raised up" and brought to a moment of renewed creation. It is in the context of these traditions that the conclusion of Mark's Gospel finds its full significance, for it dramatizes ordinary women coming to a new understanding of God's mystery through watchfulness, through not-knowing ("Who will roll away for us the door to the tomb?"), and through profound reverence (*tromos kai ekstasis*). Mark in effect ends his Gospel by dramatizing the unifying theme of the Wisdom writings: that *"Fear of the Lord is the beginning of Wisdom."*

The idea of an inclusive religious community is congenial, moreover, not only with Wisdom perspectives but in general with midrashic theology, which perceives God's word to be a dynamic, unending source of new disclosures, a timeless word that is relevant to changing times, an open-ended, ongoing revelation. In Mark's theological narrative, Jesus' life, death, and resurrection are constructed as midrashic commentary on Hebrew Scripture; his very person is shown to reflect the dynamism of divine Wisdom whose meaning is continually unfolding. It is consistent with this midrashic openness that Mark shows Jesus forming his followers as an open, existentially defined community. It is consistent with the perspective offered by midrashic Wisdom that membership in this community is exemplified by women.

Within the Markan Gospel it is the transformation of the women in particular—from being excluded and semianonymous to being disciples and deacons and models of faith, to being anointer of the anointed one and celebrator of his liturgy of death, to being visionary prophets entrusted with preaching the word of ongoing resurrection—it is this transformation above all which functions as a sign of God's kingdom. The women point to an Endtime community that is inclusive and ongoing; they are a sign of God's new Creation.

Contrary to this view, many readers of Mark have found his ending abrupt, concluding as it does with Jesus unseen, the male disciples absent, the women silent. Even the syntax of the final verse supports the sense of things unfinished, ending (in a way that is permissible in Greek) on *gar*, the preposition "for." It was undoubtedly as an attempt to tidy matters up that some later hand added the verses 9–20. Unfortunately, their sharp antithesis, both to Mark's theology and to his theological method, suggest that this later author badly misunderstood what Mark was about. An audience familiar with midrashic strategies would not have been put off by the lack of closure. It would have understood that the absence of an ending was part of the meaning, allowing for God's continuing revelation and their own part in receiving it. From this perspective Mark's open-endedness is purposeful, inviting each faith-community to complete the meaning for themselves. To respond to that invitation is to acknowledge that Mark's Gospel has implications for our own time.

To consider these implications, it is important, first, to observe what Mark is *not* saying. To note that Mark concludes his Gospel with new symbols of Covenant and Creation is not to suggest that

Mark renders obsolete their primary value. On the contrary, the power of the symbols here derives precisely from their significance in Jewish tradition. Midrashic theology, as has been shown, does not limit the times God's word can be fulfilled, but allows for infinite repetitions of the divine being. Thus the consciousness of a new way of being expressed through the image of the women's prophetic trance does not negate God's promise to the entranced Abraham but fulfills it in a different way. Similarly, the echo of the transformative sleep of *'adam*, which concluded in paired creatures created to image God through their relationship, infuses and enriches the symbolic drama here of women as the first witnesses to men of the resurrected life.

The metaphorical level must not be dismissed. Mark is not making the argument that women always replace men in religious leadership any more than he is asserting that Christianity is the replacement of Judaism. Such a reading, in either case, is literalist and reductive. Rather, the images work, in both instances, to suggest that God's will and word are fufilled in ceaselessly new and surprising ways. Taken as imaginative theology, the images do not enclose us in definitions but open us up to new possibilities.

As the earliest formulation of apostolic witness, Mark's Gospel ought to have a special claim on the Christian conscience. As such, it provides not only a witness to the riddling person of Jesus but also a creative way of witnessing that we might do well to reappropriate. Understood as part of the theological discourse of its time, it offers us a model for doing theology that is imaginative and open-ended, dialogical and participatory. Through its imaging it projects God's kingdom as a state of transformed consciousness that it inclusively invites all hearers to enter. If we accept that invitation to dialogue with the text and complete its meaning for our own time, we will need to ponder its image of women as followers and reflectors of Wisdom/Jesus who is image of God. Beyond that, we will need to reflect on how the Jesus movement grew out of Early Judaism with its imaginative language and its humble refusal to limit the fulfillment of God's word. If we can do that, we will also be faithful, on both counts, to Augustine's "rule of faith," which is the measure of love.

7

The Unending Revelation: Mark 16:8 as a Theological Choice

Although there is a unanimous scholarly consensus that Mark ended his Gospel at verse 8, modern Bibles persist in printing verses known to have been added at least a century later by another hand, generally with the most nonchalant recognition that these words are not part of the original Gospel. What is worse, this spurious text has not been reserved for scholars but has been made part of the Christian lectionary and has thus reached generations of pious believers as the authentic words of "Saint Mark."[1] To grasp the full dimensions of this change, one needs to look at the ending from four angles: (1) the textual evidence, both external and internal; (2) the canonical argument; (3) the literary shape—that is, the relationship of ending to genre; (4) the theological implications—that is, the significance of one ending versus another for the community of believers. It is the last issue—the theological differences between one ending and another—that seems to have been particularly obscured by editors and downplayed by most commentators.[2] Yet, as I hope to show, the attachment of verses 9–20 to Mark's Gospel is no mere textual matter: it constitutes the very undermining of Mark's theology.

The Spurious Ending

9 Now when he rose early on the first day of the week, he appeared first to Mary Magdalene, from whom he had cast out seven demons. 10 She went and told those who had been with him, as they mourned and wept. 11 But when they heard that he was alive and

had been seen by her, they would not believe it. *12* After this he appeared in another form to two of them, as they were walking into the country. *13* And they went back and told the rest, but they did not believe them. *14* Afterward he appeared to the eleven themselves as they sat at table; and he upbraided them for their unbelief and hardness of heart, because they had not believed those who saw him after he had risen.

15 And he said to them, "Go into all the world and preach the gospel to the whole creation. *16* He who believes and is baptized will be saved; but he who does not believe will be condemned. *17* And these signs will accompany those who believe: in my name they will cast out demons; they will speak in new tongues; *18* they will pick up serpents, and if they drink any deadly thing, it will not hurt them; they will lay their hands on the sick, and they will recover." *19* So then the Lord Jesus, after he had spoken to them, was taken up into heaven, and sat down at the right hand of God. *20* And they went forth and preached everywhere, while the Lord worked with them and confirmed the message by the signs that attended it. Amen.[3]

The Textual Evidence for Mark 16:8

Burton Throckmorton, in his thorough analysis of gospel manuscripts, begins by noting that

> None of the original manuscripts of the New Testament have survived nor, presumably, any direct copies of the original manuscripts. What we have are copies of copies. Into these copies crept errors; moreover, additions and "corrections" were sometimes made by the copyists, for the only Bible of the early church was the Old Testament, and it was not imperative to copy the gospels and epistles— still uncanonized—exactly word for word.[4]

Throckmorton goes on to explain that New Testament manuscripts are classified into "families" according to the religious center from which they were derived, and that the best text—because it is considered "uncontaminated"—comes from Alexandria. The oldest texts, written in capital letters, are known as "uncials"; much later manuscripts (actually after the ninth century) appear in small cursive letters and are known as "minuscules." The two best codices (dating from the fourth century) are Sinaiticus (S) and Vaticanus (B), both of which contain the Alexandrine text in uncials. Unfortunately for the English-speaking world, Erasmus's printed edition of the Greek New Testament (1516) and the Authorized King James Version, which is based on it, descend from an inferior family of manuscripts—the Byzantine text (also known as the Syrian, Antiochene, Koinē, or Textus Receptus). Throckmorton observes that this text "is characterized by conflations (combinations of readings from other manuscripts) and revisions in the interests of smoothness and intelligibility."[5]

The Markan manuscripts that end at 16:8 come from the two best and oldest codices, S and B. Of the manuscripts that contain the longer ending, none (with the exception of a palimpsest)[6] are from the Alexandrian family of texts. One is from the Washington Codex (W), which uses both the Caesarean and Western texts. The Western text refers to "Graeco-Latin manuscripts of western Europe, the Old Latin version, and quotations from western Church Fathers such as Cyprian," and Throckmorton characterizes it as "marked by omissions and insertions sometimes the length of several verses, and by eccentric readings."[7] He describes the Caesarean text as something "between the Alexandrian and the Western," being "as early as the Alexandrian type" but lacking "the extravagant readings of the Western."[8] In respect to Mark, the W manuscript is particularly unreliable: one of its "omissions" is Mark 15:13–38 (i.e., the crucifixion!), and one of its "extravagant readings" is still another addition to the ending known as "the Freer Gloss."[9] Of the remaining texts that give the longer ending, D uses the Western text entirely; *Phi* comes from minuscules that date from the twelfth through fifteenth centuries and appear to be Caesarean in character; *Lambda* is a collection of minuscules whose origin is unknown; *Theta* uses a Caesarean text for Mark; A and *Koinē* use the Byzantine text entirely. In short, the manuscript evidence is hardly controversial: only corrupt manuscripts give the longer ending; the best manuscripts show the ending of Mark to be 16:8. This ending is also attested to by Clement and Origen.

All this external evidence notwithstanding, modern editors continue to print this second ending to Mark as though there were little difference between manuscripts. The King James prints the longer ending without a break or comment, as though it were in fact part of the original. The scholarly Aland edition ("8th corrected edition 1987") places the longer spurious ending (as well as a shorter spurious ending)[10] on a separate page but with only the bland comment: "Some of the most ancient authorities bring the book to a close at the end of verse 8. . . . In most authorities verses 9–20 follow immediately after verse 8; a few authorities insert additional material after verse 14."[11]

It is remarkable that there is no discussion whatsoever in the Aland edition of types of manuscripts or the criteria for assessing their varying reliability. Similarly, The New Oxford Annotated Bible (1977) says ingenuously: "Nothing is certainly known about how this Gospel originally ended or about the origin of vv. 9–20, which cannot have been part of the original text of Mark."[12] The latest edition (1994) uses similar language. A footnote starts out declaring that "[n]othing is certainly known either about how this Gospel originally ended or about the origins of vv. 9–20, which because of the textual evidence as well as stylistic differences from the rest

of the Gospel, cannot have been part of the original text of Mark."
Later in the same paragraph, however, the editors continue misleadingly: "Many important witnesses, some ancient, end the Gospel
with vv. 9–20, thus showing that from early Christian times these
verses have been accepted traditionally and generally as part of the
canonical Gospel of Mark." (There is no acknowledgment that the
"many witnesses" come from corrupt texts, while the texts unanimously conceded to be the best do not contain these verses.
Furthermore, one has to wonder about the implications of labeling
contaminated text "traditional": are errors acceptable as long as they
are repeated?) Finally, the editors speculate that these verses were
"compiled early in the second century as a didactic summary of
grounds for belief in Jesus' resurrection" and then "appended to the
Gospel by the middle of the second century."[13] The only second-
century witnesses to this appendage, however, appear to be Tatian
in his heretical harmonization the *Diatesseron* and Justin, who quotes
him. Tellingly, Clement and Origen, a century later, show no awareness of these verses. Vincent Taylor, in his monumental commentary
on Mark's Gospel, cites the finding of F. J. A. Hort: "In the whole
Greek Ante-Nicene literature, there are at most two traces of verses
9–20, and in the extant writings of Clement and Origen they are
entirely wanting."[14] Finally, one must note that by indicating that
the longer ending of Mark is acceptable, the editors violate their own
standards (as they define them in their introduction to the New
Testament) for choosing among variant readings—that is, a preference for the readings that are the older, or the shorter, or the less
harmonious with others.[15] Since the editors say forthrightly in their
introduction to Mark that "in the earliest Greek manuscripts and
versions (Latin, Syrian, Coptic, Armenian) the author's account
breaks off suddenly with the words 'for they were afraid' (16.8),"[16]
why is it that they do not also express a clear preference for the
earlier ending? Since the editors acknowledge, moreover, that "harmonization of divergent accounts" was a "scribal tendency," why do
they not also acknowledge that verses 9–20 could well have been
simply the work of a scribe?[17]

Taylor goes on to analyze the internal evidence—that is, the
vocabulary and style of the verses—in a way that proves conclusively
that whatever their origin, verses 9–20 certainly were not written by
the author of Mark. His findings fall into three categories: (1) vocabulary that is not in Mark; (2) vocabulary that is used differently
in Mark; (3) vocabulary that could be Markan but that is used here
to express a different theology from Mark's.

There are nine instances of wording that Taylor finds to be unlike
Mark.[18] First of all, the word for "appeared" (*ephanē*)—which occurs
in verses 9, 12, and 14—is nowhere in Mark. In verse 10, Taylor
labels the phrase "those who had been with him" (*tois met'autou*

genomenois), as flatly "not Markan." The word for "see" or behold"
(*etheathē*) in verse 11 is "frequently found in John," never in Mark.
In the same verse, the verb for "disbelieve" (*apisteō*) Taylor finds to
be "common in classical Greek" and frequent in Luke, Acts, Romans, Timothy, and the letters of Peter but not characteristic of
Mark. (It appears just once [11:31] in a passage where it forms part
of the speculation of the Pharisees.) The transitional phrase "after
this" (*meta de tauta*) in verse 12 is one Taylor also finds to be "common in John, never used by Mark." And the description of Jesus
appearing "in another form" (*en hetera morphē*) leads Taylor to
comment that "[o]nce more, as in 9–11, the writer is a compiler
whose methods and outlook are different from those of Mark." The
verses that speak of "the signs" that will accompany the believers
(vv. 17–19) are particularly fraught with un-Markan vocabulary. For
instance, the word for "deadly poison" (*thanasimon*), Taylor observes, "is a classical word not found in biblical Greek." The phrase
"it will not harm him" (*ou mē autous blapsē*), is not like Mark but
"recalls Luke 4:35 which recounts that after Jesus had rebuked a
demon, it came out of the man 'having done him no harm.'" Most
telling, the phrase for "being well" (*kalōs exousin*) is also a classical
one that is found nowhere else in the whole New Testament. Finally
and of most significance, the reference to Jesus as "the Lord"
(vv. 19–20) is "used several times in Acts and occasionally by St. Paul,
but is not found elsewhere in the Gospels." The plain use of "the
Lord" as a way of referring to Jesus appears in Mark only once—in
the incident in which the disciples are sent to find a colt (11:3)—and
in that context the usage is ambiguous, more probably being a simple
term of respect according to ordinary social convention rather than a
term for divinity.[19] As for the whole description of Jesus' ascension
into heaven, Taylor comments crisply: "Manifestly a summary passage, the section both in vocabulary and ideas is post-Markan."[20] In
respect to the concluding statement that "they went forth and
preached everywhere" (v. 20), Taylor observes: "The writer follows
the Jerusalem tradition of the Appearances"[21]—that is, the writer is
not concerned with Jesus' ongoing ministry in Galilee.

In short, what Taylor's analysis shows is that this longer ending
is a patchwork of phrases and ideas taken from other New Testament
writings—partly Matthew but particularly Luke and John. Such a
melding of texts can be acceptable only to those who do not perceive the evangelists as theologians—that is, as *individual* theologians, not mere compilers of creedal documents—and who therefore
assume that the distinctiveness of their voices does not matter. It is
not surprising that Tatian incorporated the longer ending into his
harmonization of the Gospels, but it is somewhat perverse that the
church that rejected the *Diatesseron* in the second century[22] has
nonetheless allowed this blurring of theological perspectives to con-

tinue for two thousand years. To grasp the full implications of this blurring, we must consider the place and function of the original Markan ending in relation to the canon.

The Canonical Argument for Mark 16:8

The formation of the New Testament canon is a controversial matter. There is no consensus on the key issues regarding it: on when or what or why. In the first century, "the Scriptures" always refers to the Bible of the Jews. Christian writings are not explicitly given equal status until Irenaeus in the second century makes a statement that suggests that the Gospels are parallel to the Prophets.[23] The reference to a "canon"—in the sense of a list, rather than a measure, of sacred writings—does not appear until Athanasius in the fourth century.[24] Even then, while Athanasius gives the now conventional list of twenty-seven New Testament books, he simultaneously notes that "there are also other books apart from these that are not indeed in the above list, but were produced by our ancestors to be read by those who are just coming forward to receive oral instruction in the word of true religion."[25] This secondary list is an interesting combination of specifically Christian writings (the "Teaching of the Apostles" and "the Shepherd") and specifically Jewish ones (the Wisdom of Solomon, Sirach, Esther, Judith, and Tobias). A study of the history of the canon shows little unanimity among the church fathers who listed sacred writings and (aside from Marcion)[26] not much rigidity about them before the fourth century. Indeed another comment of Athanasius is suggestive of documentary practices that contributed to the imprecise boundaries of sacred writings: he rejects "the secret writings (the apocrypha)" as "a device of heretics, who write them when they will, furnishing them with dates and adding to them, in order that by bringing them forth as ancient books they may thus have an excuse for deceiving the undefiled."[27]

In assessing the second Markan ending, it is important to recognize the commonness of these misleading devices and to realize that before the fourth century, there is evidence of great fluidity not only with regard to the way sacred documents were listed but also to the way individual documents (and parts of them) were dated and assigned authorship. There were no copyright laws protecting the integrity of either author or manuscript—indeed, pride of authorship was apparently unimportant to those who felt they were presenting "the Word of the Lord"—and the use of pseudonyms, revisions, and interpolations was common practice. Thus the idea of a later hand adding ten verses to the end of Mark was not unthinkable in the early centuries of the church. It is telling that these verses do not seem to have been used in the church until the fourth century, because that was the time when the church moved toward uniformity.

The formation of the canon, as Bruce Metzger has delineated at some length, was a long and unwieldy process, involving many factors—defense against heresy, the burning of sacred books in time of persecution, and the development of the codex.[28] The specific act of drawing up a list of books in the fourth century, however, seems to have been largely motivated by political forces. The merging of church with state brought with it a pressure to codify and absolutize, and it was in the context of this political pressure that the church began to definitively separate "orthodoxy" from "heresy."[29] Constantine's desire for his empire's unity, moreover, is apparently what caused him to ask Eusebius for fifty copies of a list of sacred books. Although the believer would like to allow for the action of grace, it is clear that Eusebius's response did not involve much theological judgment: he arrived at his list by simply counting the number of times a particular writing was attested to in the various churches.[30] Perhaps it was in the context of this drive for unanimity and majority rule that the longer ending of Mark's Gospel was confirmed.

Certainly the very construction of this later ending, with its clear echoes of Matthew, Luke, and John, suggests a deliberate attempt to create a single, homogenous text. Although some modern Christians may be tempted to think that biblical homogeneity would be a desirable goal, it is well to consider what might have been the church's reasoning in rejecting the homogenous text of Tatian. It is worth reflecting on what can be deduced about the canon as "rule" from the fact that in almost every instance, canon as "list" includes *four* Gospels, not just one.[31] As James Dunn has astutely observed, by keeping four gospels, the church in effect "canonized diversity."[32] This canonization of diversity implies that the earliest "rule of faith" allowed for plural ways of perceiving the same reality. More pointedly, it offers further confirmation that the evangelists functioned within the midrashic tradition, with its habits of multiple and even contrasting voices speaking about the same thing. Within the midrashic framework, this plurality of voices acknowledges both the dynamic nature of God's ongoing revelation and the time-conditioned limits of human experience, perception, and language. The insistence on keeping four Gospels is of a piece both with the Rabbinic practice of preserving a range of biblical commentaries on the same page and with the preservation within the Bible itself of two accounts of creation, two renditions of the conquest of Canaan, different rewritings of the Ten Commandments, and the multiple versions of the exodus.

If we consider the ending of Mark in terms of the criteria that have been conventionally applied to determining canonical status— antiquity and apostolic witness, usage, inspiration, and orthodoxy[33]—we find that they all point to this midrashic mindset. The oldest evidence points to four distinct Gospels, variously used according to the shifting exigencies of the church. By implication, the earliest idea of "inspiration" was fluid, applying to more than one revelation or to more than one way of understanding it. "Orthodoxy," when it finally occurred, in fact canonized diversity. "Apostolicity" is thus represented by different voices in conversation: it is no single voice but *a dialogue of voices* that constitutes the apostolic witness.[34] Thus to blunt the distinctiveness of Mark's voice—to write over it with words taken from the other Gospels—is to undermine not only Mark's theology but the very balance that forms the apostolic testimony. It remains to consider in what ways the ending at 16:8 is a truly fitting climax to Mark's narrative and why his particular theological voice is crucial to the apostolic witness as a whole.[35]

How Mark 16:8 Fits the Literary Shape of Mark's Gospel

Whether or not one finds the ending at 16:8 to be satisfying depends on the literary as well as the theological expectations one brings to the text. If one believes the genre of Mark's Gospel to be *history*, then one is surprised by the historical issues left unresolved; if one thinks of his Gospel as *creed*, then one finds it difficult to explain the doctrinal gaps; if one assumes his Gospel to be *apocalyptic*, then one is stymied by an ending of silent women; if one considers his Gospel to be pure *narrative*, then one finds the ending anticlimactic. Most commentators fall into one camp or another and allow their preconceptions to dictate their assessment. My findings may seem no different in this regard, yet there is a great difference in results because the expected genre is one to which the ending *fits*. Indeed the riddling ending of 16:8 confirms the argument that the genre of Mark's Gospel is not pure history or creedal statement or artistic narrative—and particularly not as those terms are understood in modern Western culture—but rather exhibits the characteristics of Near Eastern Wisdom parable and midrashic Jewish discourse.

Although it is difficult to disentangle the literary issues entirely from the theological ones, it is possible to focus on three specifically literary questions raised by the commentators: of vocabulary, of tone, and of structure. Would any author have ended his work with the preposition *for*? Is it thematically consistent for Mark to end on a tone of "fear"? Does it make any structural sense for Mark to end abruptly and ambiguously?

In respect to vocabulary, the first word that needs to be considered is the very last one—*gar*. Ending a sentence with the conjunction "for" is not out of place, of course, in Greek, as it would be in English or some other languages: Greek syntax in fact fosters this kind of arrangement, as is attested to in the numerous examples of sudden endings in ancient literature culled by J. L. Magness[36] and the many Greek sentences ending specifically in *gar* that have been compiled by R. H. Lightfoot.[37] Robert H. Gundry has listed six other instances in Mark's Gospel itself in which *gar* appears near the end of a pericope as a word expressing purpose.[38]

Gundry concludes that the *gar* of 16:8 was intended to introduce a new pericope that is now lost.[39] T. E. Boomershine, however, does not find it necessary to project a further passage but sees it as a characteristic purpose of Mark to leave his readers with an "unanswered question."[40] Hooker takes this idea even further, suggesting that since the angel's message demands a response, the urgent but uncertain ending shifts this demand to us, the readers: thus the Gospel ending becomes the readers' starting point.[41]

The reader's response to *gar* is conditioned by the other words in these last verses that are suggestive of some kind of "fear." Here the commentators run the whole gamut of possible theories. A. Stock relates the ending to an Aristotelian catharsis of tragic fear.[42] T. W. Manson and Schüssler Fiorenza, on the other hand, both give practical explanations for the women's fear: Manson asserts that "the women's silence grew out of fear for their own safety,"[43] while Schüssler Fiorenza explains the political risk the women faced if found at the tomb of one who had been executed.[44] Many commentators simply lump together the women's fear with that of the male disciples and find all instances to be equally negative. A. T. Lincoln, for example, makes no distinctions between the disciples experiencing "fear" at Jesus' transfiguration (9:5–6), the crowd who followed Jesus to Jerusalem being "afraid" (10:32), and the leaders who were plotting to kill Jesus "fearing" the multitude (12:12).[45] W. H. Kelber terms all instances of fear "dysfunctional" and suggests that the fearful disciples are "representative of a false theology attacked by Mark."[46] Frank Kermode, looking at the ending from the perspective of narrative art, finds it deliberately anticlimactic: "Mark's book began with a trumpet call. . . . It ends with this faint whisper of timid women."[47] Juel, who is also concerned with reading Mark as art (as well as theology), is compelled by Kermode's argument that artful narrative, in order to be faithful to life, often gives us unsatisfying endings. He thus interprets the women's final silence as indicative of fright and concludes that Mark intends his readers to experience disappointment at the end.[48]

It is striking how few commentators bother to take note of nuances in the experience of "fear"—both within and without the Gospel—and the shifting vocabulary that reflects these differences.[49] Hooker is one of those who does focus on Mark's vocabulary. She begins by noting the uniqueness of one of Mark's words for being afraid: "The verb translated *astounded* in v. 5 and *alarmed* in v. 6 (*ekthambeomai*) is used by Mark alone among New Testament writers. He used it in 9:15 of the crowd's astonishment at seeing Jesus on his descent from the mountain, and in 14:33 of Jesus' own emotion in Gethsemane." The conclusion she draws from this fact, however, reverts to the usual assumptions that the women were scared: "Clearly Mark means that the women were terrified, rather than simply amazed."[50] It seems a difficult conclusion to justify: the crowd in 9:15 are so far from being "terrified" of Jesus that they "ran up to him and greeted him." And Jesus' emotion in Gethsemane is surely one of extreme stress rather than "terror." Hooker does not mention the fact, moreover, that Mark also uses *ekthambeomai* to describe the reaction of the crowd to Jesus' first exorcism—a response that leads them to exclaim, "What is this? A new teaching!" (1:27) The sense in all these instances seems to be one of shock rather than fright. "Shocked," or "state of shock," in fact, might be the best translation in each case, suggesting both abnormal stress and heightened perception.

Such an understanding of *ekthambeomai* is also more congenial with translating *ekstasis* as it sounds—as "ecstasy." Hooker translates *ekstasis* as "terror"[51]—which again seems hard to justify. Gundry points out the distinctions in Mark's words for fear, translating *ekthambeomai* as "extreme amazement" and *tromos kai ekstasis* as "trembling astonishment." He then translates the final word, *ephobounto*, as plain "fear," commenting that what we have here is "not redundancy, but progression: from extreme amazement through trembling astonishment to fear, each with a different outcome (explanation, flight, and silence, respectively.)"[52] Given Gundry's careful observations, it seems strange that he does not notice that *ephobounto* is also used in 4:41 to describe the disciples' response to Jesus' stilling of the sea and that there, it is usually translated "filled with great awe."[53] It is also the very word used to describe the disciples' response to Jesus' transfiguration (9:6)—a context that surely suggests that holy awe is what is meant.[54] As I noted in chapter 6, Mark's Gospel contains a pattern of expressing religious experience through words of fear and ecstasy. If we are aware of this pattern, then we will perceive that verse 8, which combines these feelings, is not letdown but climax: the meaning of the women's "fear" is contextualized not only by the precedents of the disciples' awe but also by their "trembling and ecstasy" (*tromos kai ekstasis*)—which are, in Mark, the feelings that accompany a breakthrough in human perception.[55]

From a tonal or emotional point of view, this breakthrough—the sense of being suddenly transported beyond or out of oneself—is intensified by the abrupt silence of the ending. It remains to consider how the ending also relates to the structural patterns of the Gospel as a whole. As I have noted before, Mark's structure is typified by various forms of repetition—doublets, triads, inclusios, and circularity. The ending at verse 8 provides a fitting climax to these patterns: the women's "trembling" response is doublet to the gesture of faith made by the woman in chapter 5 (5:33); their fleeing from the tomb is an echo of the healed demoniac's escape (5:3–16); their holy awe is the last of a triad connected to Jesus' reflection of God's glory (4:41, 9:6, 16:8); their holy ecstasy is the fifth occurrence of persons (including Jesus himself) seemingly possessed by joy ("out of their minds" or "beside themselves") as the result of witnessing God in the act of restoring life. The scene constructed here bears an inverse relationship to the triad of miracles with which Mark's Gospel opens: the women are "possessed"—but by God's spirit rather than a demonic one; the women are not lying down anonymous or ill but come, fully named, with the spices that hallow both death and life; the women, bid to preach, do not babble like the leper but are stunned into speechlessness—a silence that is not less but more than words. There is a circularity of phrases and meanings that underscores the doublet of Jesus' promise—"I am going before you into Galilee" (14:28 and 16:7). The repetition of this promise points us back to the beginning of the Gospel, to the start of Jesus' ministry. The final *gar* does not undermine but rather underscores its purposeful thrust. This circular, teasing, poetically packed ending is a fitting climax to Mark's work, understood as a Wisdom riddle or *mashal*.

16:8: Mark's Theological Voice

Understanding the Gospel's literary shape is the first step in hearing Mark's particular theological voice. Grasping his genre as one that is unfamiliar to modern Christians may open the way to fresh understanding of his content. In the past, most commentators have struggled over what to make of four aspects of the Markan ending: that there is no scene of Jesus' resurrection; that one cannot clearly say that Jesus' promise reached "fulfillment"; that the male disciples are in hiding and the only witnesses are women; that the work ends in uncertainty and silence. Looked at carefully, however, each of these "problems" seems to arise out of certain preconceptions of what Mark *ought* to have said. Most commentators, for example, read Mark through the lens of the other Gospels[56] and speak of Mark "omitting" a resurrection appearance, although logically, since Mark comes first, they should speak of the other Gospels *adding* one. Similarly, many critics look for Matthew's "fulfillment" formulas in Mark's text. The downplaying, in the other Gospels, of the women as witnesses seems to lie behind the perplexity of many readers concerning the role of the women here. The presentation elsewhere of Jesus' certain identity is what seems to make readers uneasy with Mark's ambiguity. Different perceptions, however, arise out of granting Mark his own voice: distinct from Matthew, Luke, and John, it is one still speaking within the framework of Early Judaism in respect to historical context, literary modes, and theological purposes. It is helpful to compare Mark's ending with those of the other Gospels not by blending his voice with that of the others but by listening for his distinctive tones.[57]

In Matthew, Jesus' resurrection is signaled by two earthquakes. The first, occuring at the same moment as Jesus' death, anticipates his resurrection:

> [T]he earth shook, and the rocks were split; the tombs also were opened, and many bodies of the saints who had fallen asleep were raised, and coming out of the tombs after his resurrection they went into the holy city and appeared to many. (Matt 27:52–53)

Matthew speaks of both the earthquake and these resurrection appearances as having a converting effect on those who witnessed them: "When the centurion and those who were with him, keeping watch over Jesus, saw the earthquake and what took place, they were filled with awe,[58] and said, 'Truly this was the Son of God!'" (Matt. 27:54) A second earthquake immediately precedes the women's discovery of the empty tomb:

> And behold there was a great earthquake; for an angel of the Lord descended from heaven and came and rolled back the stone, and sat upon it. His appearance was lightning, and his raiment white as snow. And for fear of him the guards trembled and became like dead men. (Matt. 28:2–4)

Seeing how clearly Matthew has made the scene a dramatically supernatural one throws into relief Mark's ambiguous rendering of the divine presence in the ordinary: in place of Mark's "young man dressed in a white robe"—an image that hovers suggestively between a human and angelic figure—is Matthew's explicit "angel of the Lord"; in place of the women's open question, "Who will roll away the stone for us?" is an unequivocal assertion. The earthquakes suggest "the day of the Lord" in the Prophets (Ezek. 38:19–20; Joel 3:16; Zech. 14:5). Certain elements appear to have been taken from Mark and transposed: the "raiment white as snow" has been moved from Mark's transfiguration scene; the "trembling" has been shifted from the women to the guards and defined by the additional phrase "like dead men." The angel's message, moreover, explicitly validates Jesus' promise: "He is not here; for he has risen, as he said" (Matt. 28:6). In addition, Matthew narrates a unique story about the priests and elders paying the guards to lie about the empty tomb and say that Jesus' disciples came in the night and stole his body, concluding: "So they took the money and did as they were directed; and this story has been spread among the Jews to this day" (Matt. 28:11–15). Whether that particular story is fact or metaphor is beside the point; what matters is that Matthew uses every device he can to indicate that Jesus' resurrection cannot be explained away in ordinary human terms but must be recognized as an extraordinary act of God. His emphasis is consistent with his explicit attempts to present Jesus as a new Moses. Thus, while he acknowledges the witness of the women and even shows them meeting Jesus directly (Matt. 28:9–10), he places the final scene on the mountain, with Jesus commanding his disciples to spread his teaching (Matt. 28:16–20).

It is almost as though Matthew had heard the questions modern commentators ask about the Markan ending and answered them: yes, God did raise Jesus from death (just as God has raised others); yes, Jesus' promise was fulfilled "as he said"; no, the women were not scared but departed from the tomb "with fear *and great joy*"; far from being speechless with fright, they "ran to tell his disciples" and upon meeting Jesus expressed their reverence (Matt. 28:8–9); yes, the male disciples saw Jesus for themselves and received their commissioning directly from him; yes, he said explicitly that they were to "[g]o forth and make disciples of all nations" and that he would be with them always (Matt. 28:19–20). Matthew sounds, in fact, as though he were at least partly on the defensive, responding to any insinuations that the empty tomb was a hoax or that there were no male witnesses or that Jesus was a false prophet. In the process he organizes his Gospel to show—from genealogy to Sermon on the Mount to the final commandments on the mountain—that Jesus is a new Moses sent by God and, as such, the "fulfillment" of Mosaic teaching.

To a large extent, of course, Matthew is in accord with midrashic practice in reinterpreting the material in Mark. But he may also be simply clarifying what had come to be misunderstood. In that sense, the fact that Matthew transposes the white raiment from Mark's transfiguration scene to the resurrection scene may suggest that he understood Mark to have intended the first to anticipate the second; it certainly underscores how he developed the parallel, implicit in Mark's transfiguration scene, between Jesus and Moses. In the same way, the fact that he shows the women's "fear" mingled both with "great joy" and reverence may suggest that he understood this spiritual state to be the meaning of Mark's *tromos kai ekstasis*; the fact that he shows them running to tell the male disciples may be his way of indicating that Mark did not mean they were tongue-tied.

Some of the differences between Mark and Matthew might be accounted for by the fact that the latter was confronting a Jewish orthodoxy that, devastated and decimated by the Romans, had begun to retrench, to argue over "Who is a Jew," and to throw the followers of Jesus out of the synagogues. In that climate, Matthew is driven both to fierce polemic against "the Pharisees"—his immediate hostile critics—and to a defensive clarifying of certain issues. In any event, whether or not he was responding to questions or to a different situation in the emerging Christian community, Matthew clearly had his own theological focus that was different from Mark's. His explicitness has generally seemed more satisfying to more readers, over the centuries, than Mark's hints and ambiguities. Yet it is a thinner, weaker faith that loses sight of Mark's values: that God's revelation is ongoing; that what is open-ended allows for new kinds of fulfillment; that watchfulness rather than certainty is the way of wisdom; that God makes his presence felt in the ordinary and the common more than in spectacles of power; that every human being, male and female, is made in God's image and is thus capable of reflecting it.

In some ways Luke's ending serves as a corrective to Matthew's thrust toward finality because it concludes on a note of suspense, with the disciples sent back to Jerusalem to await "power from on high" (Luke 24:49). In this case, however, the attitude of waiting is not a permanent mode of spirituality—as it is in Mark—but rather a temporary posture allowing for a time of transition before the coming of the Spirit and the establishing of the church. In other ways Luke's ending is even more carefully explicit than Matthew's and carefully orchestrated to suggest the Christian liturgy. The women are confronted at the tomb by two dazzling figures (not just one)—a phenomenon that suggests the iconography of the Christian tomb.[59] This chorus of angels offers a ritual, hymn-like question— "Why do you seek the living among the dead?" (24:5)—and provides a creed-like answer, spelling out the details concerning Jesus' prophecy of his crucifixion and resurrrection (24:6–8). Luke narrates that the women relayed all this to the apostles without any undue trauma but mutes their witness by saying that to the apostles "these words seemed an idle tale, and they did not believe them" (24:11). He later verifies the women's story (24:24) but also sets the stage for the male disciples to hear the message directly and become the real bearers of it. He next interpolates a narrative that disarmingly dramatizes the disciples' doubts. Uncertainty here is equated with lack of recognition of Jesus: they had thought he was a prophet who would redeem Israel; they do not recognize him walking beside them now. The women's story, they say, left them "beside themselves" (*exestēsan*, 24:22): here the verb Mark uses to describe various experiences of divine presence (3:21; 5:42; 6:51) is transferred to the effect the women's witness has on the men. The male disciples proceed to verify the women's story for themselves but remain unconvinced (24:24). In Luke's narrative, faith is a process; it is a journey finally brought to completion through the liturgical elements of Scripture (24:27, 44–45) and the breaking of the bread (24:30–35).

In speaking of Scripture, the Lukan Jesus is both more general in his reference than in the other Gospels and more insistent about its explicit relevance: he first reproaches his disciples for being "slow of heart to believe all that the prophets have spoken" (24:25) and later asserts: "These are my words which I spoke to you, while I was still with you, that everything written about me in the law of Moses and the prophets and the psalms must be fulfilled" (24:44). We see here a shift in the meaning of "fulfillment": Mark and Matthew use specific passages from Scripture as a lens or frame for certain episodes in their narrative that they see as a "reactualization" of the events of the Pentateuch or the teachings of the Prophets; they do not speak as Luke does, as though the Hebrew Bible contained a hidden code foretelling specific events in the future (24:26–27; 44–47). Luke's use of the word "fulfilled" signals a radical shift in biblical theology: the ancient midrashic understanding (which Mark and Matthew share) was that God continues to disclose new meanings in Scripture, that Scripture intersects with history, and that each faith community has both the opportunity and the task to search out this mutual relevance. Luke to the contrary suggests not an ongoing revelation but a fixed one.

In addition, Luke's narrative takes pains to describe Jesus' resurrection as an event of the *body*, not of the soul. Luke conveys the resurrection as a physical experience through his narrative of Jesus offering his hands and feet for touching (24:39) and then eating a piece of broiled fish (24:42–43). As Matthew's story of the bribed guards seems to be responding to a rumor that the empty tomb was a hoax concocted by Jesus' disciples, so Luke's story here seems to be responding to questions and controversies about the reality of the resurrection. Luke disarms those who might have expressed skepticism by dramatizing the disciples undergoing a process of belief: initially frightened because they supposed Jesus to be a ghost (24:37),[60] the disciples come to a point where they "still disbelieved for joy, and wondered" (24:41); next, their minds are opened to understand the Scriptures (24:45), and finally, they are promised still one more phase in which they will be "clothed with power from on high" and so enabled to be witnesses (24:49). Again, through the last two phases, Luke seems to be describing a transformation that occurs through a *liturgical* process—here, Scripture and baptism. In terms of his full context, his emphasis on the bodily nature of Jesus' resurrection seems to be part of his emphasis on sacramentality. Luke's conclusion—which pictures Jesus ascending into heaven and the disciples returning to Jerusalem to wait in joy and prayer for the coming of divine power (24:50–53)—is suspenseful but not open-ended; rather it leads the reader forward to the establishment of the church.

In his focus on the emerging Christian church, Luke moves away from Judaism. His view here is almost opposite to that of Matthew. The Matthean Jesus says he has not come to abolish the Law and the

Prophets but to fulfill them (Matt. 5:17)—that is, the Matthean Jesus suggests that the Law and the Prophets give meaning to his actions. The Lukan Jesus teaches that the Law and the Prophets are fulfilled *in him* (Luke 24:44)—that is, he suggests that it is he who gives meaning to the Law and the Prophets. Matthew is engaged in a fierce inner-family debate; thus forced into an apologetic posture, he shapes his resurrection narrative as proclamation. He uses Scripture as a proof-text for the authenticity of Jesus' Judaism. Drawn into battle with the orthodox Jews of the postseventy era, he downplays the resurrection witness of the women and rehabilitates that of the men. Luke's attention is focused on a newly Gentile church desirous of simultaneously following Jesus and separating itself from Jewish culture; he accordingly suggests how God's grace comes directly through Jesus and Christian ritual. Where Matthew shows Jesus revitalizing Scripture, Luke shows Scripture pointing to Jesus. Intent on accommodating Greek and Roman custom, he also bolsters the idea of male leadership. Different from either is the voice of Mark, which is simply *at home* with the Law and the Prophets, instinctively using them to frame his narratives and express his values. Scripture for him is neither argument nor ritual but integral to his very mode of thinking. His resurrection narrative is open-ended because he perceives revelation to be open-ended. Intent upon dramatizing God's surprising ways of re-creation, and working within a Judaism flexible enough to permit an emerging role for women, he makes the witness of the women the chief sign of God's new creation.

Mark and Matthew, in different ways, both focus on the End Time, but for Mark that means Genesis whereas for Matthew it means Judgment. Luke's concern is for the future of the Church, and for him that means a focus on the Spirit. John develops this focus but shifts the angle from the faith-life of the community to the personal, charismatic spirituality of the individual. His concluding narrative accordingly presents multiple resurrection stories and individual experiences: there are two episodes involving Mary Magdalene (20:1–2; 20:11–18) and two involving John and Peter (20:2–10; 21:1–24); there is one resurrection appearance for a gathering of most of the disciples (20:19–23) and a special one for the absent Thomas (20:24–29). Different from the other three Gospels, John's account contains no mediating angel: although there are angels mentioned (20:12), each person encounters the risen Jesus directly. Unlike Mark, there is no ambiguity about the resurrection, yet unlike Matthew, there are no eschatological signs of it, and unlike Luke, there is no suggestion that faith comes through ritual. Yet at the same time, John's narrative dramatizes Jesus' appearance in a complex way that combines elements of all the Gospels.

Matthew's empty tomb story is repeated in a different form. Here it is Mary Magdalene who assumes that an anonymous "they" have stolen Jesus' body; devastated, she repeats the suggestion in a refrain-like way: "They have taken the Lord out of the tomb, and we do not know where they have laid him" (20:2); "they have taken away my Lord, and I do not know where they have laid him" (20:13); "if you have carried him away, tell me where you have laid him, and I will take him away" (20:15). The lyric repetition forms a poetic lament; Mary's weeping words have a cathartic effect. At the same time Mary's emotion is counterpointed by the precise observations of Peter and John: entering the tomb, John takes note of "the linen cloths lying, and the napkin, which had been on his head, not lying with the linen cloths but rolled up in a place by itself" (20:6–7). John thereby suggests that these two chief disciples come to believe in Jesus' resurrection through a process of rational deduction. John's narrative is as effective as Matthew's in disarming those who might suggest that the disciples themselves stole Jesus' body, but his tone here is not polemical and his focus is elsewhere—namely, on the different ways in which different persons came to believe in the risen Jesus.

John is like Luke in indicating that belief is a process. In John's narrative, a rational experience comes first for John and Peter—John even indicates that this took precedence over their knowledge of Scripture (20:8–9). Mary, on the other hand, is dramatized as undergoing an intensely emotional experience: of seeing the stone rolled away and assuming the worst (20:1–2); of lamenting her loss three times—to the disciples, to the angels, and then to Jesus himself (20:11–15); and then of recognizing Jesus when he speaks her name (20:16). Mary is given the commission of witnessing to the other disciples and she carries out the task (20:17–18), yet John's narrative does not indicate that she is instrumental in their coming to believe: first Peter and John make their own deductions and then they and the other disciples are confronted by the appearance of Jesus coming through locked doors and showing them his hands and his side (20:19–20). This experience—which is simultaneously supernatural and physical—is repeated and intensified in the appearance to Thomas, who is presented as one who needs experiential proof before he can shift from radical doubt to radical faith (20:24–28). The faith of all future believers—whose experience may be different again—is included in Jesus' blessing (20:29).

What is meant by the resurrection of Jesus is also a complex matter in John. As in Luke, Jesus is shown to be bodily present and yet not always recognizable (20:15). As in Matthew, there are supernatural aspects to the resurrection, but in John these are not external to Jesus but integral to his person: his mysterious words to Mary that he cannot be "clung to" because he has "not yet ascended to the Father" (20:17); his ability to pass through doors (20:19; 26). And, if chapter 21 is accepted as a valid ending, then John, like Mark, is dramatizing the resurrected life of Jesus as a return to his ministry in Galilee.

Unlike Mark, however, John does not simply indicate a return to what went before but uses the setting in Galilee as a device for clarifying the future roles of John and Peter. Here particularly the role of Peter as chief pastor is made explicit, but in a way that again seems personal and charismatic rather than institutional (21:15–19). Overall, in fact, the emphasis in these last two chapters is on the personal bond of love between Jesus and his followers: John speaks of himself as "the one whom Jesus loved" (20:2; 21:20) and recounts Jesus' final exchange with Peter as the thrice-repeated question "Do you love me?" (21:15–17). And Mary's experience is clearly phrased as that of one who loves and is loved.

John is like Matthew in showing the disciples receiving a final commission from Jesus, but again, the words of the Johannine Jesus are more charismatic: "'Peace be with you. As the Father has sent me, even so I send you.' And when he had said this, he breathed on them, and said to them, 'Receive the Holy Spirit. If you forgive the sins of any, they are forgiven; if you retain the sins of any, they are retained'" (John 20:21–23). Although this final phrase has been used to explain and justify the role of clergy in sacramental confession, in itself it is open to wider interpretations: it can be construed, for example, to suggest that Christians are *obliged* to forgive others because that is the freeing (redeeming) way of the Spirit; to refuse to forgive—to "retain the sins" of others—is to negate redemption.

Unlike Matthew, this commissioning does not involve authority, teaching, and ritual; unlike Mark and Luke, it does not involve waiting for the Spirit and future transformation. Instead, John shows the disciples both commissioned and receiving the Spirit at the same time. In chapter 21, John shows the disciples already living a transformed life with Jesus—a life that, like Jesus' resurrected body, both is and is not familiar.

The way that Jesus passes on the Spirit to the disciples by "breathing" on them echoes the way God breathes life into the first human being in Genesis 2:7. It is an action that completes the suggestion in John's prologue that Jesus functions as God's creating Word. Through this inclusio, John is like Mark in using Creation theology as his ultimate framework and projecting the End Time as a return to the Beginning.[61] Through his projection of Jesus' ongoing life in Galilee, through his assertions that there is more to know than his work contains (20:30; 21:25), and through his ambiguous description of the effect of the Spirit, John is also like Mark in being openended. It is interesting to observe that while the second Gospel stresses judgment and authority, and the third Gospel emphasizes church and ritual, the first and fourth Gospels are alike in indicating God's unpredictable and ceaseless work of Creation.

John and Mark are mirror images. John works with Creation theology as it was adapted by Philo, with all his Platonic overtones; Mark works with Creation theology as it was formed in the Wisdom traditions of Proverbs and Psalms. In both Gospels Jesus functions as the Word of God. John's perspective, however, colored by Philo's philosophical Logos, dramatizes Jesus in a series of ideal roles: as "the true light" (1:9); "living water" (4:10 and 7:37); "the bread of life" (6:35, 48); "the light of the world" (8:12); "the good shepherd" (10:14); "the resurrection and the life" (11:25); "the true vine" (15:1). In this framework Jesus as "the Son of God" also functions as an ideal figure, a perfect copy of God the Father. It is in this sense that he replies to Philip: "He who has seen me has seen the Father" (14:9), even while he points to the Father as a separate and greater identity (14:28). The effect is to elevate and idealize the person of Jesus.

In contrast, Mark follows the Wisdom traditions in dramatizing the way God's Wisdom inheres in ordinary human situations and ordinary humanity. Like Proverbs' Wisdom, Jesus seeks out the simple and invites them to a banquet; like Proverbs' "good wife," Jesus is a nurturing figure. Like Solomon's Wisdom, the Markan Jesus is a "mirror of the working of God, and an image of his goodness" (Wis Sol. 7:26). Yet for Mark that does not mean a perfect, static form but *ben 'adam*, ordinary humanity, which reflects a dynamic God who both suffers and transcends suffering and whose way of creation is not by way of mental cloning but by way of transforming energy constantly engaged in the labor of giving birth. The effect is to suggest the divine inhering in the humanity of Jesus, and to present a figure with whom every human being—male and female—can identify.

Conclusion

In this way, as in others, Mark offers a valuable balance to the theological perspectives of the other Gospels. Turning again to the four aspects of the Markan ending that have troubled many commentators, I can now summarize his distinctive contribution. Matthew ends his Gospel with the eleven disciples being given a definitive prescription for salvation; Mark leaves the meaning of the resurrection open, allowing God room to make new disclosures. Luke ends his Gospel with specially elected disciples waiting for the Spirit within the structures of the church; Mark concludes with surprisingly ordinary witnesses already possessed by holy ecstasy and holy awe. John ends his Gospel by focusing on the faith and ministry of particular individuals; Mark's open-endedness in effect extends the meaning of the Gospel to all his readers.

Mark accomplishes a similar function in respect to "fulfillment." Matthew uses Scripture to show that Jesus is a "fulfillment" of the teachings of Moses. Luke shifts the meaning to suggest that Hebrew Scripture predicted specific events that have come true in Jesus. John makes the words of Jesus a kind of scripture in itself and uses it as a prooftext of Jesus' divine qualities. All these uses of "fulfillment" limit Scripture to a specified purpose. Only Mark gives voice to a more fertile view of Scripture by concluding with the ancient midrashic understanding of the scriptural word as revelation that can be reactualized—that is, "fulfilled"—again and again. Thus while Matthew ends with Jesus like a new Moses giving commandments on the mountaintop, and Luke concludes with Jesus as an exegete explaining the Scriptures in terms of himself, and John ends with Jesus making predictions about the fate of Peter, Mark's unresolved ending invites his readers to respond for themselves.

In preserving this view of the ongoing function of Scripture, Mark also preserves the Jewish theological context of Jesus more clearly than any of the other Gospels. This context is gradually blemished in the others by a growing separation from Judaism: what begins as a protesting polemic in Matthew against those Jews who were hostile to the followers of Jesus turns in Luke into growing alienation from Jewish ways and concludes in the estrangement from Judaism evident in the abusive insults of John. Mark's voice is thus our clearest link to the theological milieu of Jesus himself.

It is that theological milieu, moreover, that enables Mark to give prominence to the role of women. All the other Gospels show women as key witnesses to the resurrection, but in various ways and for various reasons, they mute their significance: Matthew, intent on proving Jesus to be the authentic successor to Moses, wants to compare the disciples to the male heads of the twelve tribes of Israel; Luke, intent on delineating a Gentile church, looks to the Gentile world for models where at most women were chiefly rulers of households; John, striving to be detached from the pagan culture around him, focuses on the charismatic gifts of individuals. John does place certain key women in witnessing roles—the Samaritan woman (4:39); Martha (11:27); and Mary Magdalene (19:25; 20:1–2, 11–18)—but their witness is ultimately made less significant than the testimony of Peter and John. In the same way John gives a prominent place to Jesus' mother (2:3–5; 19: 25–27) but also shows her role to be subordinate—first to the instructions of Jesus (2:5) and then to the protection of John (19:26). In Mark, being "son of God" means being *ben 'adam,* and vice versa—being an ordinary human being means also and profoundly being God's child. This emphasis on the divine image in common humanity, which Mark takes right from Genesis, is what gives force to Mark's depiction of women as theological witnesses. In addition, Mark's use of the Jewish Wisdom traditions is what provides the imagery of Wisdom as a woman, and women who are wise.

It appears to be ignorance of the Jewish theological context—both its imagery and its mode of interpretation—that has particularly underlain the Christian failure to grasp the import of Mark's verse 8. Once that verse is placed in its Jewish context and translated properly, one sees that Mark's Gospel does not end in dumb fright but in a stunning silence that is beyond words. Only Mark's voice, rightly heard, preserves this vision in which God's revelation is beyond the limits of human articulation.

To add or substitute verses 9–20 to Mark's authentic ending at verse 8 is to blunt the voice that can reopen God's word for us today: to the lost Jewish contexts of the Christian Scripture; to lost traditions about women; to lost emphases on the inclusiveness of the divine image in humanity; to lost ways of doing theology. It is particularly our age that needs to hear the balancing voice of Mark again.

Notes

Preface

1. Attributed to Rabbi Ben Bagbag (M. Avot V 22).

2. For a lengthy and compelling argument that it is "a major historical anachronism" to use the terms Judaism and Christianity "as the denominators for two separate religions" in the first century, see Anthony Saldarini, *Matthew's Christian-Jewish Community* (Chicago: University of Chicago Press, 1994), 2. Saldarini's whole book is devoted to showing that "the believers-in-Jesus began as a Jewish sect before growing into a varied religious movement of its own" (9). For two other valuable discussions of the idea of Christianity as a religious movement that evolved *simultaneously* with rabbinic Judaism, see James Charlesworth's introduction to *The Old Testament Pseudepigrapha* (Garden City, N.Y.: Doubleday, 1983, 1985) and Alan Segal, *Rebecca's Children* (Cambridge: Harvard University Press, 1986). Segal speaks of Early Judaism and Early Christianity as "twin siblings" that emerged from the same womb (179).

Early Judaism is a term recently coined by scholars as a way of indicating the time-frame of the Second Temple period. Shaye Cohen discusses the ramifications of the terminology referring to this period, warning that "periodization derived from religious or cultural achievements is not bias-free" and taking note of the disparaging intentions of Christian scholars to call this time *late* or *intertestamental* Judaism: "After the birth of Christianity 'late Judaism' lost all importance and could be ignored by scholars and Christians alike. The fact that Judaism continued to flourish and develop for millennia after the period of 'late Judaism' did not affect the currency of the term, because the term derived not from historical analysis but from theological belief." See *From the Maccabees to the Mishnah* (Philadelphia: Westminster Press, 1989), 18. Cohen finds the term "early Judaism" to be at least "bias-free" but "chronically vague" (20). He prefers "second temple Judaism," which he describes as follows: "Second temple Judaism is a 'book religion.' At its heart lies the Bible, the book which Jews call 'Tanak' and Christians call 'the Old Testament.' Pre-exilic Israel produced the raw materials out of which most of the Bible was constructed, but it was second temple Judaism that created 'the Bible' . . . and devoted enormous energies to its interpretation" (24). I have chosen to stay with "Early Judaism" because I am deliberately trying to indicate a time of fluidity.

3. See Bruce Chilton, trans. and ed., *The Isaiah Targum* (Wilmington: Michael Glazier, 1987), xxviii. Also relevant to this book is his earlier work *A Galilean Rabbi and His Bible: Jesus' Use of the Interpreted Scripture of His Time* (Wilmington: Michael Glazier, 1984). Of related interest are a number of studies he has coauthored with Jacob Neusner: *God in the World* (Harrisburg, Pa.: Trinity Press International, 1997); *Revelation: The Torah and the Bible* (Valley Forge, Pa.: Trinity Press International, 1995); *Judaism in the New Testament: Practices and Beliefs* (London: Routledge, 1995).

4. See Jacob Neusner's preface to *Introduction to the Talmud and Midrash*, edited by H. L. Strack and G. Stemberger (Minneapolis: Fortress Press, 1992), viii–ix.

5. San Francisco: Harper and Row, 1980, 1983, 1988.

6. *According to the Scriptures: The Origins of the Gospel and of the Church's Old Testament* (Grand Rapids, Mich.: Eerdmans, 1998) was published posthumously. In it van Buren argued that what Christians designate the "Old Testament" represents the Christian interpretation of the Hebrew Bible. Thus he sees modern Judaism and modern Christianity as both linked and divided by their respective readings of the ancient Scriptures. I share his argument that the Hebrew Bible was sacred to the writers of the New Testament (130). I disagree, however, with his conclusion that from the start, the Christian reading somehow produced an intrinsically different Scripture: what I see instead is an intrinsically Jewish reading that is later changed by the understandings of an increasingly Gentile church.

7. See *From Sacred Story to Sacred Text* (Philadelphia: Fortress Press, 1987), 20.

8. See "Old Testament Theology, Tanakh Theology, or Biblical Theology? Reflections in an Ecumenical Context," *Biblica*, 73, 3 (1992): 441–51.

More and more current scholars are in fact following that line of thought and reflecting afresh on the New Testament use of the Jewish Scripture. Earle E. Ellis has written on the hermeneutic of the Hebrew Bible as a model for early Christianity. See *The Old Testament in Early Christianity. Canon and Interpretation in the Light of Modern Research* (Tubingen: J. C. B. Mohr, 1991). His research has illuminated many valuable connections, yet I differ with him in two key ways: first of all, he understands inner-biblical exegesis to be a process of typological correspondence, while I see it as an intertextual dialectic; second, and even more important, he invokes the principle of progress in interpretation, suggesting that later is better and "the new surpasses the old" (47). The latter strikes me as another form of Christian triumphalism. In any case, I do not agree that such a notion can be found in Jewish theologizing—indeed I hope to show a very different principle at work.

More faithful to the essence of Jewish exegesis, I think, is William Stegner's *Narrative Theology in Early Christianity* (Louisville, Ky.: Westminster Press,

1989), which asks this helpful question: "What knowledge of the Scriptures would the hearers of Mark's Gospel bring to the story?" (59). It is the purpose of this study to explore not only *what* Mark's hearers knew of the Jewish Scriptures but *in what way* they knew it—that is, what hermeneutic framed their theological understanding.

Also relevant to my work is the monumental scholarship of James Charlesworth, who has done so much to aid modern understanding of Jesus' theological contexts. See *The Old Testament Pseudepigrapha*, vols. 1 and 2 (Garden City, N.Y.: Doubleday, 1983, 1985), and *The Messiah: Developments in Earliest Judaism and Christianity*, The First Princeton Symposium on Judaism and Christian Origins (Minneapolis: Fortress Press, 1992), and the anthology *Jesus' Jewishness: Exploring the Place of Jesus in Early Judaism* (New York: Crossroad, 1991). Also see *Jesus Within Judaism: New Light From Existing Archaeological Discoveries* (New York: Doubleday, 1988).

I must also mention the work of James Dunn, who has placed New Testament writings within the four pillars of Second Temple Judaism. See *The Partings of the Ways Between Christianity and Judaism and Their Significance for the Character of Christianity* (Philadelphia: Trinity Press International, 1991). Dunn stresses the fact that there was no single or uniform Judaism at this time, but nevertheless believes one can speak of certain core elements, which he names as monotheism, election, covenant (centered on the Torah) and land (connected to the Temple). See his second chapter, "The Four Pillars of Second Temple Judaism," 18–36.

Finally, although I have chosen to study the Gospel of Mark, I must acknowledge how many have paved the way for me in their study of the Jewish contexts of other gospels, especially those of Matthew: first of all, the classic studies of W. D. Davies—*The Setting of the Sermon on the Mount* (Cambridge, England: Cambridge University Press, 1963), and Krister Stendahl, *The School of St. Matthew* (Philadelphia: Fortress Press, 1968). I have also benefited from Celia Deutsch, *Lady Wisdom, Jesus, and the Sages* (Valley Forge, Pa.: Trinity Press International, 1996), and Dale Allison's study of Matthew's use of Moses typology, *The New Moses: A Matthean Typology* (Minneapolis: Fortress Press, 1993). Allison makes a particularly strong case for the need to know the Jewish Scriptures in order to understand the New Testament. He asserts: "No man is an island. Neither is Matthew. At every juncture the book presupposes that the reader is bringing to its ubiquity of allusions an intimate knowledge of Judaica, knowledge without which one is reading commentary without text" (270). In his final chapter he discusses the modern phenomenon of the "criterion of dissimilarity" (by which the teachings of the "real" Jesus are held to be those that are dissimilar either from Jewish teaching or Christian church teaching) and argues that while the modern age seeks originality and uniqueness over imitation, "Matthew thought otherwise. For him imitation was not an act of inferior repetition but an inspired act of fresh interpretation" (272). From a different vantage point but in a similar vein, Anthony Saldarini gives a sophisticated argument for the Jewishness of Matthew's community; see *Matthew's Christian-Jewish Community*. My study of Mark is based on the same assumptions as these two recent studies. In addition, I have found Calum Carmichael's illuminating analysis of Philo's relationship to the fourth gospel a helpful measure of the distance between the Jewish contexts of John and Mark. See *The Story of Creation: Its Origin and Its Interpretation in Philo and the Fourth Gospel* (Ithaca, N.Y.: Cornell University Press,

1996). Carmichael makes a compelling case for Philo's Logos as John's source and model for Jesus, the preexistent Word "who, acting at the original creation, enters the historical realm of existence as the Word becomes flesh" (37). He shows how the Johannine Jesus functions like Philo's Logos because he contains the power both to create and to remedy creation—that is, to re-create. I see Mark also working with Creation theology as his frame but finding his sources in the Wisdom writings rather than Philo.

9. See *Of Christian Instruction* 1.36.4: "If it seems to anyone that he has understood the divine scriptures or any part of them, in such a way that by that understanding he does not build up that double love of God and neighbor, he has not yet understood." Later he refers to this "double love of God and neigh-bor" as *praescriptio fidei* (*Of Christian Instruction* 3.5). As a principle for Christian hermeneutic it seems irrefutable, and one can only wonder how Christians have, for so many centuries, allowed interpretations that foster hatred and prejudice toward others—particularly, of course, the Jews.

Chapter 1

1. *An Introduction to the New Testament* (New York: Doubleday, 1997), 7.

2. Dom Donatien de Bruyne argued that this prologue, which exists in Old Latin, and similar prologues to the other Gospels date from 160–80 C.E. See "Les plus anciens prologues latine des Evangiles," in *Revue Benedictine*, 40 (July 1928): 193–214.

3. Thomas C. Oden and Christopher A. Hall, eds., *Mark, II, Ancient Christian Commentary on Scripture* (Downers Grove, Ill.: InterVarsity Press, 1998), suggest in their introduction that Jerome might have thought Philo's description of the Theraputae at Alexandria were Christian communities and then linked Mark with them (xxvii–xxviii).

4. See *The Theology of the Gospel of Mark* (Cambridge, England: Cambridge University Press, 1999), 10–12.

5. *The Gospel According to Saint Mark* (London: Macmillan, 1963), vii.

6. See Martin Hengel, *Studies in the Gospel of Mark*, translated by John Bowden (Philadelphia: Fortress Press, 1985), 3–4.

7. *Mark*, 55.

8. *Studies in Mark*, 9.

9. Translation taken from Taylor, *Mark*, 2.

10. *The Theology of the Gospel of Mark*, 11.

11. The Greek name appears to have no special significance, but looked at as the translation of a Hebrew word, it is rich in connotations. The Hebrew word for "mark" is *taw*, which stands both for "signature" and for the last letter of the Hebrew alphabet. David Daube observes that this last letter probably acquired the meaning of signature because in ancient script it looked like an *x*, that is, "more or less like an oblique cross." Daube further notes that the *taw* was a sign of God's protection for both David (1 Sam. 21:14) and Ezekiel (9:2), and he speculates that these various associations were still operative in the first century. *The New Testament and Rabbinic Judaism* (1956; reprint, Peabody, Mass.: Hendrickson, 1994), 401–02. Add to these suggestive facts some further observations: first, that the Gospels were used for at least fifty years without reference to an author; second, that it was customary among Jews of the first century either to write anonymously (certainly if they were writing bibli-

cal exegesis) or to use a name other than their own; third, that the names of the biblical Prophets are symbolic—e.g., Isaiah means "Yahweh gives salvation," Jeremiah means "Yahweh lifts up," Ezekiel means "God strengthens"; and fourth, that Mark's theology is centered on the cross. Is it not possible that the earliest gospel manuscript was simply marked with a Hebrew *taw*—that is, the sign of the cross, which was subsequently translated into the Greek name *markos?*

12. *The Theology of the Gospel of Mark*, 15.

13. *Mark*, 30.

14. *Mark*, 55.

15. *Studies in Mark*, 46.

16. *The Theology of Mark*, 11.

17. All translations from the Gospel of Mark are my own. Other biblical translations are taken from *The New Oxford Annotated Bible*, NRSV, edited by Bruce M. Metzger and Roland E. Murphy (New York: Oxford University Press, 1991).

18. See Taylor, *Mark*, 335, for a summary of different theories.

19. Taylor is one who thinks that v. 2b (the explanation of "defiled hands") is a later addition (*Mark*, 335).

20. Taylor notes the rareness of this connotation in classical Greek. He does also note, however, that it is found in this sense in the papyri as an agricultural term (as in letting a field lie fallow) and in connection with death (*Mark*, 319). Both of those meanings would be congenial with the idea of Sabbath "rest."

21. The posture is not incidental but an intrinsic part of the liturgy which calls attention to the fact that "On this night we recline because it is the position of freed people." Some scholars have suggested that the "meal-eating groups" allude to a Greek symposium, but that would link Jesus' miraculous feeding with intellectual debate—a context that seems totally unwarranted.

22. See Taylor, *Mark*, 60 and 323.

23. Even those critics who have demonstrated Mark's craftmanship—e.g., David Rhoads and Donald Michie, *Mark as Story* (Philadelphia: Fortress Press, 1982)—do not seem to have been struck by this discrepancy between language and design.

24. *Mark*, 2–3.

25. *What Are the Gospels? A Comparison With Graeco-Roman Biography* (Cambridge, England: Cambridge University Press, 1992).

26. *What Are the Gospels?* 1–15.

27. *What Are the Gospels?* 26–32.

28. *Validity in Interpretation* (New Haven: Yale University Press, 1967), 83 and 73.

29. *What Are the Gospels?* 36.

30. *Kinds of Literature: An Introduction to the Theory of Genres and Modes* (New York: Oxford University Press, 1982), 22.

31. *What Are the Gospels?* 48.

32. *Kinds of Literature*, 37.

33. *What Are the Gospels?* 47.

34. Geoffrey Hartman and Sanford Budick, in their introduction to *Midrash and Literature* (New Haven: Yale University Press, 1986), comment that it is "a mode of interpretation that has been lost to literary study, though the impulse behind it surfaced, historically, in many different ways. The important thing to recognize is that at this point [1986], by and large, even students of Judaica

had cut themselves off from this vast body of interpretive materials, centered on the Hebrew Bible, yet permeable to the epochs through which it passed, and displaying a high degree of imaginative consistency" (xii). Daniel Boyarin makes a similar comment in his introduction to *Intertextuality and the Reading of Midrash* (Bloomington: University of Indiana Press, 1990).

35. This is especially true of the form-critics who, in seeking the Sitz im Leben of the Gospels, assumed the kind of Christian catechesis with which they were familiar in modern times. It is similarly true of Philip Carrington, who tried to establish that the Gospel of Mark was written as a Christian lectionary adapting Jewish feasts to the Christian calendar. See *The Primitive Christian Calendar: A Study in the Making of the Marcan Gospel* (Cambridge, England: Cambridge University Press, 1952). W. D. Davies criticized the rigid systematization of the latter in his article "Reflections on Archbishop Carrington's 'The Primitive Christian Calendar,'" in *Christian Origins and Judaism* (Philadelphia: Westminster Press, 1962), 67–97.

36. *Midrash and Literature*, ix.

37. "Inner-Biblical Exegesis: Types and Strategies of Interpretation in Ancient Israel," in Hartman and Budick, *Midrash and Literature*, 19. Also see Michael Fishbone, ed., *The Midrashic Imagination: Jewish Exegesis, Thought, and History* (New York: SUNY Press, 1993).

38. Again see Fishbane, "Inner-Biblical Exegesis," 19, and *Biblical Interpretation in Ancient Israel* (Oxford: Oxford University Press, 1985), 14.

39. Burridge, for example, says he has investigated "three main areas of Judaism: . . . Old Testament literature, midrash, and Rabbinic biography." He then discusses possible "models" or parallels for parts of Mark in the Old Testament literature without recognizing that if such parallels exist, they are, ipso facto, *midrashic.* He confines his discussion of midrash to Michael Goulder's work *Midrash and Lection in Matthew* (London: SPCK, 1974), which builds on ideas found in Philip Carrington's *Primitive Christian Calendar*, and he uses the criticism made of these limited studies as reasons for dismissing the whole midrashic genre. *What Are the Gospels?* 19–20. Similarly, Mary Ann Tolbert limits the meaning of midrash to "midrashic lectionary" or "apocalyptic drama." *Sowing the Gospel* (Minneapolis: Fortress Press, 1989), 58.

40. *Biblical Interpretation*, 1. Fishbane is speaking of the relation between Hinduism, Buddhism, and Confucianism as well as that between Judaism, Christianity, and Islam.

41. His perceptions dovetail with those of Robert Alter, who both describes and demonstrates the "internally allusive" character of the Bible. *The Literary Guide to the Bible*, edited by R. Alter and F. Kermode (Cambridge: Harvard University Press, 1987), 13. For Fishbane's full remarks, see *Biblical Interpretation*. Noting that "the content of tradition, the *traditum*, was not at all monolithic but rather the result of a long and varied process of transmission, or *traditio*" (7), he goes on to argue that different texts within the Bible represent a deliberate reworking or interpretation of other texts so that "the Hebrew Bible has an exegetical dimension in its own right" (14). In *The Garments of Torah* (Bloomington: University of Indiana Press, 1989) he explicitly applies the term "intertextuality" to this hermeneutical process: "What I have in mind is the well-known structuralist concept of intertextualité, which is concerned with the relationship of any one text to others. Or, in the words of Julia Kristeva, 'Every text is the absorption and transformation of other texts'" (127). Daniel Boyarin sub-

sequently developed an extensive analysis of midrash around this principle in *Intertextuality and the Reading of Midrash*. More recently, Ithamar Gruenwald has concurred in this evaluation: "Scholars and literary critics have gradually realized that Midrash as a literary genre and form of interpretative expression is present in almost all forms of literary creation." "Midrash and the 'Midrashic Condition': Preliminary Considerations," in Fishbane, *The Midrashic Imagination*, 6.

42. The full text reads: "The textual sanctity of Scripture is signalled by its status not only as the preserved verbal traces of an older divine communication, but—for the Pharisees at least—as the source of ever-new revelations and guidance *through living interpretations of it* . . . for the role of interpretation is neither aesthetic illumination nor aesthetic judgment, but rather the religious duty to expound and extend, and so to *reactualize* the ancient word of God for the present hour." *The Garments of Torah*, 38.

43. It is more customary to speak of making the word relevant to the present situation, but that way of putting it appears to make the word the subordinate factor, whereas in fact it is primary not only in time but in weight. I take my phrasing from a discussion of "relevance" in D. Ritschl, "A Plea for the Maxim: Scripture and Tradition," in *Interpretation* 25 (1971): 126: "It is not the ancient words that are artificially transported into the present in order to become relevant, but it is the present occasion, the situation, which becomes transparent and relevant both to the ancient message and to the hope which permits the interest and concern for ancient texts." The passage is cited by John Goldingay, *Models for Scripture* (Grand Rapids, Mich.: Eerdmans, 1994), 364.

44. "Inner-Biblical Exegesis," 20. This article was also reprinted as the opening chapter of Fishbane, *The Garments of Torah*.

45. See Moshe Idel, "Midrashic Versus Other Forms of Jewish Hermeneutics: Some Comparative Reflections" in *The Midrashic Imagination*, ed. Fishbane, 50.

46. This last example, and many others, are given by the Pontifical Biblical Commission in the pamphlet *The Interpretation of the Bible in the Church* (Rome: Librera Editrice Vatican, 1993) 86–87.

47. "Inner-Biblical Exegesis," 27.

48. "Inner-Biblical Exegesis," 32.

49. "Inner-Biblical Exegesis," 32.

50. "Inner-Biblical Exegesis," 33. For a sensitive analysis of how allusive echoes function exegetically in Paul, see Richard B. Hays, *Echoes of Scripture in the Letters of Paul* (New Haven: Yale University Press, 1989). Hays makes use of literary criticism, especially John Hollander, *The Figure of Echo: A Mode of Allusion in Milton and After* (Berkeley: University of California Press, 1981). Hays writes: "Allusive echo can often function as a diachronic trope to which Hollander applies the name of *transumption* or *metalepsis*. . . . Allusive echo functions to suggest to the reader that text B should be understood in light of a broad interplay with text A, encompassing aspects of A beyond those explicitly echoed" (20).

51. *Intertextuality*, 47.

52. *Intertextuality*, 60.

53. *Intertextuality*, 77.

54. *Intertextuality*, 78.

55. See Birger Gerhardsson, *Memory and Manuscript: Oral Tradition and Written Transmission in Rabbinic Judaism and Early Christianity* (Uppsala: C. W. K. Gleerup-Lund, 1961), 143.

56. For an analysis of this example and others, see Daniel Patte, *Early Jewish Hermeneutic in Palestine*. Society of Biblical Literature Dissertation Series, 22 (Missoula, Mont.: Scholars Press, 1975), 41–45. Also see Ben Zion Wacholder's preface to Jacob Mann, *The Bible as Read and Preached in the Old Synagogue* (New York: Ktav, 1971), xxxi.

57. For a discussion of this technique, see Boyarin, *Intertextuality*, 16, and John Bowker, *The Targums and Rabbinic Literature* (Cambridge, England: Cambridge University Press, 1969), 50.

58. These descriptive terms come from David Stern, "Midrash and the Langage of Exegesis: A Study of Vayikra Rabbah, Chapter 1," in Hartman and Budick, *Midrash and Literature*, 113.

59. Some modern readers may question whether an ordinary audience would readily pick up multiple and slight biblical allusions, but they need to remember that those trained to be listeners rather than readers have different skills. Dale Allison, in his study of Matthew, offers an interesting analogy: "There are in fact contests—I have heard them—which require people to name a musical piece after hearing only a slight excerpt from it, one lasting no more than a second or two, and consisting of no more than two or three notes or chords. The uninitiated will discern only noise. But to those with the requisite musical knowledge (gained, be it noted, not through arduous study but through effortless listening), the briefest extract can conjure up a world; a song, an album, a musical group. Was it not maybe similar with those Jews who first heard the Gospel of Matthew?" *The New Moses: A Matthean Typology* (Minneapolis: Fortress Press, 1993), 18.

60. One is reminded not only of Marshall MacLuhan's dictum that "the medium is the message" but also of his analysis of "hot" versus "cool" media: the latter, he suggested, resulted in a passive audience, the former in an interactive one. Jacob Neusner relates this aspect of midrash to contemporary reader-response theory. See *A Midrash Reader* (Minneapolis: Fortress Press, 1990), 1. David Stern relates it to the "language of *havivut*" (i.e., the love-language between the divine and human): "Just as havivut represents an attempt through literary discourse to recover God as a speaking presence, so the literary homily must be seen as an attempt on the part of the redactor to capture in writing those qualities of intimacy and familiarity that would have been associated by a reader with the oral sermon, like the petihta and the parable, in the literary homily. Moreover, just as the language of havivut attempts to restore the fullness of divine presence by attributing to God a special way of speaking rather than a particular message with a specific content, so the literary homily presents the interpretation of Torah as process and activity rather than as a fully grasped understanding of the world." See "Midrash and the Language of Exegesis," 122.

61. David Stern makes a distinction between the function of "parable" in Greek rhetoric and the function of the *mashal* in the Hebrew Bible and in midrash. He notes that, for Aristotle, a parable was an "illustrative parallel," that is, an example, either fictitious or historically factual, that serves as a form of proof in argument, and he asserts that because the Hebrew word *mashal* is translated *parabolē* in Greek, scholars have mistakenly identified the functions of Greek rhetoric with Jesus' parables and the Rabbinic *meshalim*. He distinguishes the *mashal* from the Greek *parabolē* because he sees it not as an "illustrative parallel" but as an "allusive tale." See "Rhetoric and Midrash: The Case of the Mashal," *Prooftexts* 1 (1981): 261–91.

62. I am indebted again to David Stern, *Parables in Midrash: Narrative and Exegesis in Rabbinic Literature* (Cambridge: Harvard University Press, 1991). For this example and Stern's analysis, which has a different purpose from mine, see p. 91.

63. See Charles Perrot, "The Reading of the Bible in the Ancient Synagogue," in *Mikra: Text, Translation, Reading and Interpretation of the Hebrew Bible in Ancient Judaism and Early Christianity*, edited by M. J. Mullder (Minneapolis: Fortress Press, 1988), 153. Perrot cites the Aramaic word used to introduce the Prophets in the Palestinian Cycle—*ashlemata*. Perrot notes that "[t]he ordinary term, *haftara*, first meant rather 'the conclusion' of the reading or 'the word of farewell,'" and he suggests that *ashlemata* indicates that the text from Prophets was perceived as "the fulfillment of Moses." Jacob Mann makes a stronger case: "The meaning of this term is clear, viz., that the Prophetic lection is 'the completion' of the Torah reading." See *The Bible as Read and Preached* (vol. 1, 155). Fishbane notes the antecedent for this practice when he lists the various words for "completed" that appear in the Psalms, seeing them as a scribal convention that indicates the conclusion of a literary unit. See *Biblical Interpretation*, 28.

64. "Two Introductions to Midrash," in Hartman and Budick, *Midrash and Literature*.

65. "The Hermeneutics of Midrash," in *The Book and the Text*, edited by Regina Schwartz (Cambridge, England: Blackwell, 1990), 200.

66. "Hermeneutics," 190.

67. See Heinemann, "The Nature of Aggadah," in *Midrash and Literature*, 42. The Second Temple period is dated from 520 B.C.E. to 70 C.E.

68. "Two Introductions to Midrash," 80.

69. *The New Testament and Rabbinic Judaism* (London: University of London Press, 1956; reprint, Peabody, Mass.: Hendrickson, 1991).

70. *Jewish Sources in Early Christianity* [translation of Yahadut u-mekorot ha-Natsrut] (New York: Adama Books, 1987), 150–209.

71. See *Parables in Midrash*, 188–205.

72. *The Bible as It Was* (Cambridge: Harvard University Press, 1997), 41.

73. See Bruce Chilton and Jacob Neusner, *Judaism in the New Testament* (London: Routledge, 1995), 175–88.

74. Of course, Philo's attempt to turn the Hebrew Bible into a form of Platonic philosophy was maverick at best and hardly represents the mainstream of Jewish exegesis.

75. *The Jewish Heroes of Christian History: Hebrews 11 in Literary Context* (Atlanta: Scholars Press, 1998).

76. In addition, Trypho himself offers such foolishly weak arguments that one can only assume he is fictitious—a Socratic "straw man" conveniently devised to bolster Justin's arguments.

77. For an exposition of this Valentinian view, see Ptolemy, *Letter to Flora* 7.1.

78. Translation of Irenaeus taken from Karlfried Froelich, *Biblical Interpretation in the Early Church* (Philadelphia: Fortress Press, 1984), 44.

79. Thomas C. Oden and Christopher A. Hall, editors of *Mark, II, Ancient Christian Commentary*, single this trait out as one that distinguishes the ancient Christian exegete from modern ones (xxx).

80. Translation of this passage from Origen taken from Robert M. Grant, *A Short History of the Interpretation of the Bible* (Minneapolis: Fortress Press, 1984),

57. All subsequent translations of Origen taken from Froelich, *Biblical Interpretation*, 48–75.

81. Translation of Diodore taken from Froelich, *Biblical Interpretation*, 85–93.

82. Translation of Tyconius taken from Froelich, *Biblical Interpretation*, 115–129.

83. It is worth noting in passing that this hermeneutical posture is directed toward the retrieval of *meaning*, not the retrieval of an earlier *text*.

84. See his essay "Theological Interpretation of the Scriptures in the Church: Prospect and Retrospect," in Robert M. Grant with David Tracy, *A Short History of Interpretation of the Bible* (Minneapolis: Fortress Press, 1984), 185.

85. "Theological Interpretation," 159, 170.

86. "Theological Interpretation," 170.

87. "Theological Interpretation," 170.

88. "Theological Interpretation," 170.

89. "Theological Interpretation," 165.

90. In citing the church fathers, I have made use of *Mark, II, Ancient Christian Commentary on Scripture* (hereafter referred to throughout the book as ACC). The editors note that "there are no complete commentaries of Mark that have survived the patristic period" and that hence they had to reconstruct what the early Christian writers had to say about Mark from "various references found scattered in homilies, letters and treatises." They have made use of computer searches to uncover these and discovered that "some of the most important commentary on Mark was found embedded in Origen's, Chrysostom's or Augustine's commentaries or homilies on Matthew or John, not just on Mark" (xxxi). Morna Hooker's commentary, *The Gospel According to Saint Mark*, is part of A and C Black's New Testament Commentary series (Peabody, Mass.: Hendrickson, 1991).

91. It is interesting to note that the Biblical Pontifical Commission also argues for the necessity of "a certain pluralism" in interpretation. It says: "Granted that tensions can exist in the relationship between various texts of Sacred Scripture, interpretation must necessarily show a certain pluralism. No single interpretation can exhaust the meaning of the whole, which is a symphony of many voices." The commission further acknowledges the need for a dialogue between different generations of interpreters: "Dialogue with Scripture in its entirety, which means dialogue with the undertaking of the faith prevailing in earlier times, must be matched by a dialogue with the generation of today.... Hence the interpretation of Scripture involves a work of sifting and setting aside; it stands in continuity with earlier exegetical traditions, many elements of which it preserves and makes its own; but in other matters it will go its own way, seeking to make further progress." *The Interpretation of the Bible in the Church*, 91–92.

Chapter 2

1. For a discussion of this phenomenon, see James Kugel, *The Bible as It Was* (Cambridge: Harvard University Press, 1997), 53–57. For the idea of Wisdom as a cocreator of humanity, Kugel cites 2 Enoch 30:8: "And on the sixth day I commanded my wisdom to create man."

2. These examples (and others) are given both in Kugel, in the pages just cited, and in John Bowker, *The Targums and Rabbinic Literature* (Cambridge, England: Cambridge University Press, 1969), 100.

3. Boyarin translates the passage from *Bereshit Rabbah*, edited by Theodor-Albeck, vol. 1, 3: "Rabbi Yehuda the son of Simon opened: 'And he revealed deep and hidden things' [Dan. 2:22]. In the beginning of the creation of the World, 'He revealed deep things, etc.' For it says, 'In the beginning God created the heavens,' and He did not interpret. Where did He interpret it? Later on, 'He spreads out the heaven like gossamer' [Isa. 40:22]. 'And the earth,' and He did not interpret. Where did He interpret it? Later on, 'To the snow He said, be earth' [Job 37:6]. 'And God said, let there be light,' and He did not interpret. Where did He interpret it? Later on, 'He wraps Himself in light like a cloak' [Psalms 104.2]." *Intertextuality and the Reading of Midrash* (Bloomington: Indiana University Press, 1990), 17.

4. As I have noted before, Vincent Taylor calls attention to Mark's "translation Greek" and numerous "semitisms." *The Gospel According to Saint Mark* (London: Macmillan, 1963), 55.

5. See his article "From Crucified Messiah to Risen Christ," in *Jews and Christians Speak of Jesus*, edited by Arthur E. Zannoni (Minneapolis: Fortress Press, 1994), 103.

6. See *The Death of the Messiah*, vol. 1 (Garden City, N.Y.: Doubleday, 1994), 473–80.

7. See *The Messiah: Developments in Earliest Judaism and Christianity*, The First Princeton Symposium on Judaism and Christian Origins, edited by James H. Charlesworth et al. (Minneapolis: Fortress Press, 1992), xv. Also see Marinus De Jonge, *Jesus, the Servant-Messiah* (New Haven: Yale University Press, 1991), who notes that the appositions "Christ" or "Son of God" should not be taken as "fixed concepts" or titles, but "rather stand for different combinations of traditionlal concepts (often connected with certain texts from Scripture) adapted to the specific situations of the authors or readers" (67). He further observes that "the term *anointed one* occurs surprisingly seldom in Jewish sources around the beginning of the Common Era" (68).

8. Taylor notes that "the reasons which suggest that iv.13–20 is secondary tradition are: (1) the un-Hebraic character of style; (2) the vocabulary, which includes several words found only in the Epistles; (3) the impression conveyed of an existing Christian community; (4) the concentration of the interpretation on important details rather than the main point of the parable." *The Gospel According to Saint Mark*, 258.

9. Translations of Ezra are taken from J. H. Charlesworth, ed., *The Old Testament Pseudepigrapha* (Garden City, N.Y.: Doubleday, 1983), vol. 1, 525–29.

10. Charlesworth discusses the reasons for dating Ezra around 100 C.E. in *The Old Testament Pseudepigrapha*, vol. 1, 520.

11. The translation here of "secret" for *mystērion* is gravely misleading. The word is clearly used in the Pauline letters (e.g., Eph. 5) to indicate the transcendence of God's plan for human beings, not esoteric knowledge. The word "secret" misleadingly connotes not only the latter but also secret rites or an elite group, as at Qumran. See Raymond E. Brown, *The Semitic Background of the Term "Mystery" in the New Testament* (Philadelphia: Fortress Press, 1968). Also Taylor, *Mark*, 255. Perhaps the popularity of Wrede's thesis was a factor in the translator's choice (See William Wrede, *The Messianic Secret*, translated by J. C. Grieg [Greenwood, S.C.: Attic Press, 1971]), but it misrepresents Mark's theology. More recently, David Stern has also commented on Mark 4: "Jesus used the parable . . . in essentially the same way as the Rabbis employed the mashal"—

i.e., not as medium for doctrinal instruction or as a literary device "for conceal-ing true teaching from unwanted outsiders . . . its key lies in the word 'mystery,' *mystērion*, which is not a secret or concealed truth but rather something which can be well-known, but only to those whom God chooses to give that knowl-edge." *Parables in Midrash* (Cambridge: Harvard University Press, 1991), 200–205. With the exception of that final qualifying phrase—which strikes me as still too exclusionary—I find Stern's description of the Hebrew *mashal* particularly helpful in establishing the function of Jesus' parables in Mark.

12. Consider Ps. 119:105, "Thy word is a lamp to my feet," or Proverbs 6:23, "the commandment is a lamp and the teaching a light."

13. From the introduction to the Song of Songs Rabbah. For a discussion of its implications, see Boyarin, *Intertextuality*, 87.

14. Remarkably similar words appear in the Talmud: "Not as with man is the method of God. With man a full vessel receives no more; an empty vessel gets filled. With God, the full is filled, the empty is not filled. If you have heard, you will continue to hear; if you have not heard, you will not hear [subse-quently]. If you have heard the old, you will also hear the new; if you have turned your heart away, you will hear no more (*Berakhot* 40a). Translation from C. G. Montefiore and H. Loewe, *A Rabbinic Anthology* (New York: Schocken Books, 1974), 223.

Chapter 3

1. *Jesus-Christ et les croyances messianiques de son temps* (Strasbourg: Treuttel and Wurtz, 1864), 201. George Beasley-Murray comments that "Colani had in fact so mutilated the Gospels that his Jesus could not have shared these views" (i.e., the views of Jewish eschatology). See *Jesus and the Last Days: The Interpre-tation of the Olivet Discourse* (Peabody, Mass.: Hendrikson, 1993), 17.

2. *The History of the Synoptic Tradition,* translated by John Marsh (New York: Harper and Row, 1963), 125.

3. See G. R. Beasley-Murray, *A Commentary on Mark Thirteen* (London: Macmillan, 1957), and "Second Thoughts on the Composition of Mark 13," *NTS* 29 (1983): 414–20. In *Jesus and the Last Days* he considers all the argu-ments of scholars both pro and con and concludes that the consistency of Mark's style throughout compels him to see chapter 13 as integrally part of the Gospel. He adds, however, that by this he does not mean that Mark did not redact ma-terial from other sources. He particularly points out the connections between chapter 13 and the parables of chapter 4 (363).

4. See Lars Hartman, *Prophecy Interpreted* (Uppsala: Almqvist and Wiksells, 1966).

5. See Lloyd Gaston, *No Stone on Another: Studies in the Significance of the Fall of Jerusalem in the Synoptic Gospels* (Leiden: Brill, 1970). Earlier critics who also argue for this relationship include: J. Munck, "Discours d'adieu dans le Nouveau Testament et dans la litterature biblique," in *Aux Sources de la Tradi-tion Chretienne,* Festschrift M. Goguel (Paris: Neuchâtel, Delachaux, and Niestlé, 1950), 155; E. Lohmeyer, *Das Evangelium des Markus,* 2nd ed. (Gottingen: Vandenhoeck and Ruprecht, 1951), 286; W. Grundmann, *Das Evangelium nach Markus,* edited by E. Fascher (Berlin: Evangelische Verlagsanstalt *TKNT* 2, 1959), 259; N. Walter, "Tempelzerstorung und synoptische Apokalypse," *ZNW* 57 (1966): 40, n. 2.

6. See "The Phenomenon of Early Christian Apocalypse: Some Reflections on Method," in *Apocalypticism in the Mediterranean World and the Near East,* edited by David Hellholm (Tubingen: J. C. B. Mohr, 1983): 295–325.

7. *Visions of Hope: Apocalyptic Themes From Biblical Times* (Minneapolis: Augsburg, 1978), 105.

8. See "A Future for Apocalyptic?" in *Biblical Studies in Honour of William Barclay,* edited by Johnston R. McKay and James F. Miller (London: Collins, 1976): 56–72.

9. See *Documents of the Primitive Church* (New York: Harper, 1941): 14–15.

10. *Jesus and the Last Days,* 366.

11. See 2 Macc. 4:39–41.

12. See the note to *Josephus,* translated by William Whiston (1736; Peabody, Mass.: Hendrickson, 1987), *Jewish Antiquities* 13.10.7 (Loeb, 299). "Here ends the high priesthood, and the life of this excellent person Hyrcanus: and together with him the holy theocracy, or divine government of the Jewish nation." The editor then cites Strabo 16.761–62: "Alexander was the first that set himself up for a king instead of a priest; and his sons were Hyrcanus and Aristobulus."

13. For this view of the Essenes, see Richard A. Horsley and John S. Hanson, *Bandits, Prophets, and Messiahs* (San Francisco: Harper and Row, 1985): 24.

14. See *Jewish Antiquities* 13.13.5 (Loeb, 372). In this instance, the crowd doubly resented his unpriestly lineage: Josephus says "they reviled him as derived from a captive, and so unworthy of his dignity and sacrificing."

15. Horsley and Hanson discuss the irony of the Hasmoneans, who, having struggled for Jewish freedom, then established a regime "much like any other petty, semi-Hellenized oriental state" (*Bandits,* 23). They also discuss the Herods as "Roman client kings" (30) and "Herodians" as collaborators with Rome (205). Finally, they observe that some leading Pharisees—e.g., Josephus—at certain times also tried to reach an accommodation with the Romans (216). All of this political background is important to recognizing that the Jews designated as enemies of Jesus in Mark's Gospel are not representatives of the Jewish religion but of secular power.

16. See *Jewish Wars* 2.169–74. Josephus relates that indignant throngs came to Pilate, not only from the city but from the country, to ask him to remove Tiberius's ensigns from Jerusalem. Pilate's response was to surround them with Roman soldiers and say "they should be cut in pieces unless they would admit of Caesar's images." Nonetheless, Josephus recounts, the Jews refused to submit: "Hereupon the Jews, as it were at one signal, fell down in vast numbers together, and exposed their necks bare, and cried out that they were sooner ready to be slain, than that their law should be transgressed." Josephus continues: "Hereupon Pilate was greatly surprised at their prodigious superstition, and gave order that the ensigns [images] should be presently carried out of Jerusalem." It appears that their fierce courage caused Pilate to give in to their demand. Even more dramatic is the story Josephus tells of Gaius Caesar (Caligula) sending Petronius with an army to Jerusalem in order to place statues of himself in the Temple. The Jews again resist en masse, and when Petronius exclaims, "Will you then make war against Caesar?" they reply: "We offer sacrifice twice every day for Caesar, and for the Roman people, but if he would place images among them, he must first sacrifice the whole Jewish nation." Again the insistence of the Jews forces the Roman to back down. In this instance, the Roman Petronius seems genuinely moved by the people; Josephus says: "Petronius was astonished and

pitied them on account of the inexpressible sense of religion the men were under, and that courage of theirs which made them ready to die for it" (*Jewish Wars* 2.198). He further takes pity on them because it was "about seed-time that the multitude continued for fifty days together idle" (*Jewish Wars* 2.200) and gallantly decides to risk his own life by giving in to their demands (*Jewish Wars* 2.202).

17. In Isaiah, the imagery of "birth pangs" is associated with the "Day of the Lord," which is a localized and temporary day of judgment on Babylon (Isa. 13:8; 21:3). In Jeremiah, it functions in various ways: one time as a richly ambivalent description of Israel in a state of crisis, caught between death and birth (4:31); another time as a straightforward judgment on Jehoiakim (22:23). In some of the Pseudepigrapha—1 Enoch, the Assumption of Moses, the Syriac Book of Baruch, 4 Ezra—the phrase is extended to include "the messiah" and is suggestive of a new age being born out of the old. For similar uses of the phrase in the Midrash, see Hermann Strack and Paul Billerbeck, *Kommentar zum Neuen Testament aus Talmud und Midrasch* (Munich: Beck, 1961), vol. 1, 950.

18. Beasley-Murray is a notable exception here. He comments: "It may be noted in passing that the so-called apocalyptic cipher of Mark 13:14, 'the abomination of desolation,' was no cipher to the Jews of our Lord's day. The memory of Antiochus Epiphanus and the deliverance from his blasphemous oppression were kept fresh in the people's mind through the annual celebration of the Festival of Dedication" (*Jesus and the Last Days*, 367).

Later he gives a detailed commentary on the verse (408–16) in which he sums up the classic interpretations: (1) that the abomination refers to an idol in the Temple (414); that it represents the destructive Roman forces (415); (3) that it represents "the Antichrist" (413) or an anti-Christian commander (415). He is cautious in his conclusions, saying that one can only say generally that it indicates "something or someone or even action that is detestable to God and produces horror and destruction among humankind" (416). While I find most of his analysis congenial, I am distressed by his easy switch from an "idol in the Temple" to an "antichrist"; the first, after all, pertains to first-century Jewish rhetoric, while the second—an antichrist as "idol"—would only make sense in the context of much later Christian thought. The switch seems to ignore the fact that Jesus and Mark belonged to the earlier context.

Daube gives the most exhaustive textual analysis, noting that the phrase in Mark has a grammatical irregularity that is probably intended—as in Rabbinic writing—as a deliberate signal. In this case, the irregularity is the use of a masculine participle—*estēkota* ("who will stand")—in reference to the neuter noun *bdelygma* ("abomination"). (See *The New Testament and Rabbinic Judaism* [1956; reprint, Peabody, Mass.: Hendrickson, 1994], 418.) Daube thinks the irregular masculine participle is intended to point to a particular man as the "abomination." He suggests "the Antichrist, a heathen god, the Emperor or his statue" (420). For the same reasons I have already given, I think "the Emperor or his statue" is what is meant.

19. A. Yarbro Collins expresses this kind of puzzlement. See her chapter on Mark 13 in *The Beginning of the Gospel: Probings of Mark in Context* (Minneapolis: Fortress Press, 1992). Beasley-Murray, however, notes that most commentators have observed that Jesus' purpose here is clearly to bring salvation and not judgment. In particular he cites the thesis of Lohmeyer that "the chief

theme of Mark 13, unlike that of apocalypses generally, is the coming of the Son of Man, not in judgment on the world but for the gathering of the saints, i.e., for the formation of the eschatological community." See *Jesus and the Last Days*, 430, n. 160.

20. Richard H. Hiers suggests that a possible rendering of Mark's Greek might even be: "may no one eat of your fruit again *until* the coming age." See "Not the Season for Figs," *JBL* 87 (1968): 394–400.

21. See Michael Fishbane, *Text and Texture* (New York: Schocken Books, 1979), ch. 9, "The 'Eden' Motif/The Language of Spatial Renewal," especially 111–19. N. T. Wright, in *Christian Origins and the Question of God*, vol. 1 (Minneapolis: Fortress Press, 1993), argues for the importance of "the Land" in first-century Judaism as "the new Eden, the garden of YHWH" (226), but he does not connect it with the Temple. If he had, he might not have argued, as he does elsewhere, that Jesus "had staked his reputation upon the claim that the Temple would be destroyed" (459).

Chapter 4

1. See my discussion of Maccabean history in chapter 3, pp. 58–66.

2. The picture I have painted here reflects the generally accepted view among scholars up until the last few years. It is probably too simplistic in view of recent studies that question the extent to which the Pharisees actually led communal prayer and study in the first century. See, for example, Shaye J. D. Cohen, "Were Pharisees and Rabbis the Leaders of Communal Prayer and Torah Study in Antiquity? The Evidence of the New Testament, Josephus, and the Early Church Fathers," in *Evolution of the Synagogue*, edited by Howard Clark Kee and Lynn H. Cohick (Harrisburg, Pa.: Trinity Press International, 1999), 89–105. Popular Christian homilies still persist, however, in labeling the Pharisees and their scribes as rigid legalists, so it is important to realize that in fact they were moderate realists and creative interpreters of Scripture. Because of this very creativity, they are less susceptible than any other group of the time to stereotyping: among those we know was Gamiliel, who argued against taking violent action and for trusting God's will to prevail; Josephus, who fought against the Romans and then wrote history as their friend; and Rabbi Akiba, who perceived martyrdom by Rome as the fulfillment of the first commandment—a way to "love God with all one's heart."

3. Perhaps the description here of Simon "cleansing" the citadel is what influenced later editors of Mark to use this language to describe Jesus' action in the Temple. Mark, after all, nowhere uses the verb "cleanse" for what Jesus does and, on the contrary, repeatedly shows him reaching out to "the unclean."

4. See Vincent Taylor, *The Gospel According to St. Mark* (London: Macmillan, 1963), 456.

5. See *Logoi kata Ioudaion* [Homilies against the Jews], translated by Paul W. Harkins as *Discourses Against Judaizing Christians*, vol. 68 of *The Fathers of the Church* (Washington, D.C.: Catholic University Press, 1979).

6. I am aware that some commentators take these actions to be historical fact, but from my perspective, they are clearly rhetorical ploys. I do not believe that Jeremiah actually wore either a yoke (Jer. 27:2) or a loincloth (Jer. 13:1–11) in the manner described but rather that these descriptions are brilliant metaphors for the condition of Israel. I think that the allegorical names of Hosea's chil-

dren—"God sows," "Not pitied," "Not my people" (Hos. 1:4–11)—are an obvious clue to the fact that the narrative is to be taken rhetorically, not literally.

7. E. P. Sanders also notes the emphasis in Mark on restoration. There is one important difference between us: he thinks the Markan Jesus actually wanted the destruction of the Temple, while I see Jesus as only observing the destruction and acting to restore. See *Jesus and Judaism* (Philadelphia: Fortress Press, 1985), 75.

8. *Saint Mark*, 320.

9. For additional examples, see D. E. Nineham, *The Gospel of Saint Mark* (New York: Penguin Books Ltd., 1963), who finds the cursing out of character for Jesus (299); Larry W. Hurtado, *Mark* (Peabody, Mass.: Hendrickson, 1983), who sees it as an act of violence (181); Mary Ann Tolbert, *Sowing the Gospel* (Minneapolis: Fortress Press, 1989), who calls it "a miracle of destruction and death, the symbolic cursing of all unfruitfulness" (231); and Raymond Brown, *An Introduction to the New Testament*, who assumes it symbolizes the future punishment of the chief priests and scribes (143).

10. As I have noted before (chapter 3, n. 20), Richard H. Hiers suggests that a possible rendering of Mark's Greek might even be: "may no one eat of your fruit again *until* the coming age." See "Not the Season for Figs," *JBL*, 87 (1968): 394–400.

11. A notable exception is W. R. Telford, *The Barren Temple and the Withered Tree* (Sheffield, England: Sheffield Academic Press, 1980), who comments: "Here, then [in Mark 11 and 13] Mark may perhaps be seen reflecting the two different sides of the fig-tree's eschatological symbolism" (195). Unfortunately, he sees the negative side as Jewish and the good side as Christian(!): "that is, its withering as a sign of judgement, its blossoming as a sign of blessing (at least for Christians)" (195). George Beasley-Murray, who reads Mark 13 with exhaustive scholarship and extreme sensitivity, also sees the blooming of the fig tree as a hopeful sign but connects it solely with Jesus' parousia. He does not connect this episode with the withered fig tree of chapter 11. (See *Jesus and the Last Days* (Peabody, Mass.: Hendrickson, 1993), 374–75). Indeed, he comments elsewhere: "Mark has placed the account of the temple cleansing within his narrative of the withering of the fig tree (11:12–14, 20), which he clearly wishes to be understood as as an act of prophetic symbolism, setting forth the impending judgment of God on the 'fruitless' nation (cf. Hos. 9:10–10:2)" (381). He cites W. R. Telford in support of this view (*Barren Temple*, 216–17). It is striking that in alluding to Hosea he does not take note of the fact that in the final chapter God says: "I will be as dew to Israel; he shall blossom as the lily . . . his shoots shall spread out. . . . They shall return and dwell beneath my shadow, they shall flourish as a garden" (Hos. 14:5–7). The pattern in Hosea—as in the prophets generally—is dynamic, moving from judgment to renewal. It is this Jewish pattern I find in Mark—and I find it signaling Mark's hope for *Jewish* renewal.

12. It may be a small point, but I think to translate the *'ek* here as "*away from*" instead of just "from" (as Hooker does) makes a difference: the second does suggest total annihilation, while the first, I think, suggests a plant that is still holding on to life.

13. The NRSV, making the conventional assumption that the fig tree stands for the obsoleteness of the Temple, finds this confusing. The comment reads: "The leaves showed the possibility of green fruit. Jesus' meaning, probably symbolic, is not clear." But if the fig tree is understood as a symbol of Israel's and humanity's seasonal cycles of sin and grace, the meaning is transparent.

14. J. Duncan M. Derrett comments that the point of Jesus' remark to Peter is not to impart the trick of cursing fig trees but something quite different: i.e., "When you are ready for the New Age, it will bear fruit for you when you are hungry." He also connects the casting of the mountain into the sea with the "immensely optimistic and trusting Psalm 46": "Therefore we will not fear though the earth should change / Though the mountains shake in the heart of the sea." See "Figtrees in the New Testament," *Heythrop Journal* 14, 3 (1973): 255.

15. It is worth noting that parts of the "Our Father" are scattered throughout Mark, beginning with this phrase. It is also worth noting the parallel here to a passage in Sirach: "Forgive your neighbor the wrong he has done, and then your sins will be pardoned when you pray" (Sir. 28:2). This fact is not surprising, of course, when one realizes that every phrase in the "Our Father" comes from one prayer or another in the *Siddur*, the Jewish Daily Prayer Book, which contains many prayers that antedate the time of Jesus. Jakob Petuchowski notes that although there was no fixed prayer book until the tenth century C.E., "many of the prayers went back to the first century and beyond." See "The Liturgy of the Synagogue," in *The Lord's Prayer and Jewish Liturgy* (New York: Seabury Press, 1978), 47. That the phrases contained in the "Our Father" were among them is suggested by the New Testament use of them. (One can hardly imagine the rabbis copying them afterward!) For a whole anthology of Jewish and Christian scholars discussing the Jewish character of the "Our Father," see Petuchowski and Brocke, *The Lord's Prayer and Jewish Liturgy*.

16. *Saint Mark*, 276.

17. There is a Rabbinic parallel cited by Jon Levenson in which God as a "king" leases land to a succession of unworthy tenants—who include Abraham and Isaac (!)—until Jacob appears, the man of integrity through whom God can claim his portion. See *The Death and Resurrection of the Beloved Son* (New Haven: Yale University Press, 1993), 230–31. The point of this late midrash, however, is probably to undermine the Christian claim—via Paul—of inheriting the Covenant through Abraham and Isaac. There is certainly no evidence for Jews of the first century C.E. disowning Abraham and Isaac. (Indeed if they had, Paul's appeal to Abraham's faith would have had no point.)

18. See note 11 earlier. Beasley-Murray's identification here is, unfortunately, typical. He identifies the "wicked tenants" as "Israel's leaders" but fails to make any distinction between those leaders who were truly concerned with keeping the Torah and those who had sold out to Roman power. Evidence of this lack of discrimination appears in the following sentence: "So follow the controversies of ch. 12, wherein the rulers seek in vain to discredit Jesus." (See *Jesus and the Last Days*, 381.) What this observation omits is Jesus' colloquy with the righteous scribe with whom he is in perfect agreement (Mark 12:28–34).

19. Such a thesis may seem untenable to modern Jews and Christians alike. But Mark portrays Jesus as a righteous Jew, not a renegade one. Mark does indicate, to be sure, that Jesus' ways did not always conform to every religious practice, but Mark does not describe these actions as being in conflict with the Torah, simply as a new way of understanding it. Again we need to remember that Early Judaism tolerated many new and different interpretations and that it was Rabbinic Judaism that later defined the parameters of Jewish orthodoxy that excommunicated the followers of Jesus. To those early Jewish followers who considered themselves both "Torah-observant" and "in the school of Jesus," this

excommunication would have been intolerable. Moreover, it would have provided the occasion for protest that, on the contrary, the teachings of Jesus constituted authentic Torah—indeed a "fulfillment" of it. Mark's Gospel, which shows Jesus giving wholehearted approval to the Shema (12:28–34) and yet making careful distinctions between the righteous scribe and the unrighteous one, would seem to reflect a time when members of the Jewish community were divided in their perception of Jesus. In respect to the retrenchment of Rabbinic orthodoxy, one may find a modern parallel in the tightening of orthodox Judaism after the Shoah—especially in Israel, where there continues to be intense and ongoing controversy over "who is a Jew." If this comparison is still considered far-fetched, consider that Rabbi Pinchas Lapide, in dialogue with Hans Kung, is reported to have said, "Is not this rabbi, bleeding on the cross, the authentic incarnation of his suffering people?" See Kung, *Signposts for the Future* (Garden City, N.Y.: Doubleday, 1978), 70. I am not suggesting that Lapide sees this symbolism in exactly the same way that Mark does, but nonetheless I think that this modern Jewish view of Jesus as Israel supports the possibility of a similar identification in Early Judaism.

20. Levenson, *The Death and Resurrection*, gives evidence for the first three applications. In the next chapter I take up his thesis in more detail. Levenson also argues for the necessity of reading the New Testament as midrashic exegesis, and although I disagree with the particulars of his argument, I welcome his conclusion: "Their [the Christian] effort to dispossess the community of the Torah bears eloquent and enduring witness of the Torah to the early Church and to the thoroughly intertextual, indeed midrashic character of the most basic elements of the Christian message—a point with which most Christians, even most New Testament scholars, have failed to reckon" (230).

21. Such an anti-Jewish reading has recently been proposed by Levenson. See *The Death and Resurrection*, 226. But he, too—like many Christian scholars—seems predisposed to read Mark in the context of later Jewish–Christian polemic and to ignore the possibility of an earlier time when dividing lines were neither clear nor fixed. Levenson, moreover, relates the parable to places in Hebrew Scripture where one brother killed or dispossessed another—Cain and Abel, Isaac and Ishmael, and the parable of the wise woman of Tekoa in 2 Sam. 14:4–11. But such a reading seems to ignore the fact that those who kill the son are *not* members of his family. Indeed, as I read the parable, that is the *main* point, and it is what makes it difficult to identify the killers with Jesus' fellow Jews. Surely the venal tenants, commercial occupiers of a territory to which they claim no blood relationship, are more obviously the occupying Romans and their collaborators. Following that premise I cannot agree with Levenson's further attempt to read Mark in the light of Paul and relate the Vineyard parable to the allegory of Hagar and Sarah. In my thinking the analogy does not hold because Paul is explicitly engaged in a polemic against "Judaizers," while Mark's polemic is directed toward Romans and "Herodians." Finally, as already noted, the Rabbinic parable Levenson quotes as a parallel seems clearly to have been constructed as a polemical response to later Christian interpretation of the Vineyard parable in the Gospels. Some may argue that this later interpretation is already in Matthew when he quotes Jesus saying "Therefore I tell you, the kingdom of God will be taken away from you and given to a people producing the fruits of it" (Matt. 21:43). I think that Matthew, like Mark, is contrasting the Jewish people (with whom he identifies himself and Jesus) with the foreign occupiers of Jerusa-

lem and their cohorts. (Incidentally, I think the Gospel of Thomas should be perceived as a *corruption* of the Synoptic Gospels, not a predecessor. In the history of literature it is evident that so-called primitive forms of a narrative or poem often followed sophisticated renditions, not the other way round. In any case, the parable as it appears in Thomas omits the planting of the vineyard, the hedge, and the "beloved" nature of the son—all of which I take as evidence that the composer was unacquainted with the primary sources in Jewish tradition.)

22. Indeed, when I took courses at Jewish Theological Seminary, I found the same method of study going on.

23. Josephus says: "The Pharisees have delivered to the people a great many observances by succession from their fathers, which are not written in the law of Moses; and for that reason it is that the Sadducees reject them and say that we are to esteem those observances to be obligatory which are in the written word, but are not to observe what are derived from the tradition of our forefathers" (*Jewish Antiquities*, 13.6).

24. David Daube notes that the coupling of the two greatest commandments can be found in several pre-Christian sources: The Testament of the Twelve Patriarchs, Issachar 5:2, 7:5, Dan. 5:3, and Micah 6:8. He adds that "[t]he actual credo, 'The Lord is one' occurs in none of them." At the same time he notes, however, that "Long before the New Testament period, the section from Deuteronomy beginning 'Hear, O Israel' had acquired a central place in Jewish life and worship." (See *The New Testament and Rabbinic Judaism* [1956; reprint, Peabody, Mass.: Hendrickson, 1994], 247–48). From these comments I infer that the combination in Mark probably existed in the oral tradition, but we have no prior textual record of it. I am aware, incidentally, that Jews do not usually speak of a "creed," but it is sometimes helpful to Christian understanding of Jewish religion to see it phrased in analogous terms. Petuchowski says: "There is no public recitation of a formulated 'creed' in the synagogue service in the way in which there is a recital of various Creeds in the services of the Christian Church. But the recitation of 'the *Shema* and its Benedictions' can be said to represent the 'credal' element of Jewish worship." ("The Liturgy of the Synagogue," in *The Lord's Prayer and Jewish Liturgy*, 49–50.)

25. *Saint Mark*, 291.

26. *New Testament and Rabbinic Judaism*, 163.

27. *New Testament and Rabbinic Judaism*, 158–63.

28. Daube asserts that this Midrash "is very old." *New Testament and Rabbinic Judaism*, 165. See his whole discussion of the relationship between the Haggadah and the Gospels, 166–69.

29. *New Testament and Rabbinic Judaism*, 166–69.

30. See "The Hermeneutics of Midrash," in *The Book and the Text*, edited by Regina Schwartz (Oxford: Blackwell, 1990), 200.

31. "Markus 14, 55–64: Christologie und Zerstorung des Tempels im Markusevangelium," *NTS* 27 (1980–81): 459–60, cited by Brown in *The Death of the Messiah* (Garden City, N.Y.: Doubleday, 1994), 447. Even John Townsend, who is critical of Brown for accepting the idea of Jewish involvement in the death of Jesus, does not think the witnesses are entirely false. Citing 13:1–2 and 13:14 as evidence, he seems to imply an equation between Jesus *prophesying* the destruction of the Temple and *planning* it. (See "The Tradition Behind Mark's Narrative," Society of Biblical Literature Seminar Paper, 1989.) This seems to be a popular equation: Howard Clark Kee also thinks Jesus predicts the destruc-

tion of the Temple without regret (see "Christology in Mark's Gospel," in *Judaisms and Their Messiahs at the Turn of the Christian Era*, edited by Jacob Neusner, William Scott Green, and Ernest S. Frerichs [Cambridge, England: Cambridge University Press, 1987], 199), while Paul Achtemeier (*Mark* [Philadelphia: Fortress Press, 1986]) goes further. Agreeing with Donald Juel (*Messiah and Temple: The Trial of Jesus in the Gospel of Mark* [Missoula, Mont.: Scholars Press, 1977]) that the Markan Jesus sees himself as the *replacement* of the Temple, Achtemeier comments: "It would be attractive to suggest that it was the destruction of the temple under the Roman general Titus in A.D. 70 that prompted an outburst of speculation among Christians that now in fact the end was at at hand since God had ratified Jesus' judgment on the temple and had destroyed any possibility of a Jewish religious alternative to faith in Jesus as the Messiah" (119). Such statements are evidence that an atmosphere of Christian triumphalism has so infected church thinking that it has touched even its most careful (and ordinarily least triumphalist) scholars. It is perhaps that infectious tradition that has disposed so many Christian readers to accept the false witnesses as somehow true. A notable exception to this tendency can be found in James Dunn, *The Partings of the Ways Between Christianity and Judaism and Their Significance for the Character of Christianity* (Philadelphia: Trinity Press International, 1991): in his chapters on the Temple (37–73) he observes the positive attitude of both Jesus and the early Christians toward the Temple.

32. Discussing the question of the false witnesses, Brown asks "In what precise point in 14:58 is the falsity found?" and then answers his question as follows: "In my judgment all such approaches that find the flaw solely in the witnessing (rather than in the statement itself) are refuted by Mark 15:29, where those who pass by the cross mock Jesus about destroying and building the sanctuary. That suggests a claim widely attributed to Jesus and not dependent on a few false hearers." It is particularly puzzling that Brown, who insists throughout his work that the evangelists use Scripture to provide a theological framework, should read this particular passage as historical. (See *The Death*, 445–46.)

33. It seems to me that if we persist in saying that Jesus did make a threat against the Temple, we actually perpetuate that slander.

34. It may be worth recalling that this attempt at harmonizing the Gospels was deemed heresy in the second century.

35. The word *schizō* itself appears in the LXX version of Isaiah. It is translating an equally unusual word in the Hebrew version: *qara*, meaning "sever" or "divide."

36. This understanding is clearly what also underlies the comment in John: "But he was speaking of the temple of his body" (2:21).

Chapter 5

1. See, for example, where Justin says scornfully to Trypho the Jew (who appears to be a fictitious partner set up like the "straw man" in the Socratic dialogues): "But you were never shown to be possessed of friendship or love either towards God, or towards the prophets, or towards yourselves, but, as is evident, you are ever found to be idolaters and murderers of righteous men, so that you laid hands even on Christ himself; and to this very day you abide in your wickedness, execrating those who prove that this man who was crucified by you is

the Christ. Nay, more than this, you suppose that he was crucified as hostile to and cursed by God, which supposition is the product of your most irrational mind. For though you have the means of understanding that this man is Christ from the signs given by Moses, yet you will not." (ch. 93). Justin proceeeds to interpret passage after passage from the Hebrew Bible as a direct and explicit prediction of specific details in the life of Jesus. Thus, for example, every verse of Psalm 22 is turned into prophecy and proof-text: "But when he says, 'I am a worm, and no man; a reproach of men, and despised of the people,' he prophesied the things which do exist, and which happen to him. For we who believe on him are everywhere a reproach, 'despised of the people'; for, rejected and dishonoured by your nation, he suffered those indignities which you planned against him" (ch. 101). Justin's examples go on and on. Reading him today, it is clear how arbitrary and biased such interpretations are and, sadly, how much they influenced mainstream exegesis in the church.

2. *Judaisms and Their Messiahs at the Turn of the Christian Era*, edited by Jacob Neusner, William Scott Green, and Ernest S. Frerichs (Cambridge, England: Cambridge University Press, 1987); *The Messiah: Developments in Earliest Judaism and Christianity*, The First Princeton Symposium on Judaism and Christian Origins, edited by James H. Charlesworth, James Brownson, M. T. Davis, Steven J. Kraftchick, and Alan F. Segal (Minneapolis: Fortress Press, 1992).

3. The growing consensus is amply represented by the findings of the Princeton symposium, in Charlesworth et al., *The Messiah*. Charlesworth says flatly: "No member of the Princeton Symposium on the Messiah holds that a critical historian can refer to a common Jewish messianic hope during the time of Jesus or in the sayings of Jesus" (*The Messiah*, 5). He sums up the consensus as follows: "Scholars concurred that there was no single, discernible role description for a 'Messiah' into which a historical figure like Jesus could be fit. Rather, each group which entertained a messianic hope interpreted 'Messiah' in light of its historical experiences and reinterpeted Scripture accordingly. This position was unanimously endorsed" (*The Messiah*, xv).

4. Some add "the Son of Man" to their considerations, but since this is a controversial and complex topic in its own right, I take it up separately later in this chapter (pp. 134–44).

5. For a discussion of how a tensive symbol works in the New Testament, see Norman Perrin, "Eschatology and Hermeneutics: Reflections on Method in the Interpretation of the New Testament," *JBL* 93 (1974): 3–14. In this article he focuses on "the kingdom of God." Perrin contrasts this with "apocalyptic" symbols, which he sees as one-dimensional, prompting John J. Collins to comment: "Such a contrast shows little appreciation for the allusive and evocative power of apocalyptic symbolism." In support of his argument Collins cites Ricoeur's "protest against the tendency to identify apocalyptic symbols in too univocal a way." He concludes: "In short, Ricoeur suggests that we should sometimes 'allow several concurrent identifications play,' and that the text may on occasion achieve its effect precisely through the elements of uncertainty." *The Apocalyptic Imagination* (New York: Crossroad, 1984), 13.

6. "Introduction: Messiah in Judaism: Rethinking the Question," in Neusner et al., *Judaisms*, 2.

7. The middle section, which is excepted—the Parables or Similitudes—is generally considered a later interpolation.

8. "Introduction: Messiah," 3.

9. "Introduction: Messiah," 4.

10. See his article "Messianism in the Maccabean Period," in Neusner et al., *Judaisms*, 97–106. Also see *The Apocalyptic Imagination*.

11. "Salvation Without and With a Messiah: Developing Beliefs in Writings Ascribed to Enoch," in Neusner et al., *Judaisms*, 49–69. The Enoch material is thought to have been composed over a period of 350 years.

12. "Salvation," 56.

13. "The Question of the Messiah in 4 Ezra," in Neusner et al., *Judaisms*, 209–25.

14. "Wisdom Makes a Difference," in Neusner et al., *Judaisms*, 15–48.

15. "Wisdom," 41.

16. "Christology in Mark's Gospel," in Neusner et al., *Judaisms*, 188.

17. "Christology," 190.

18. There are images of a suffering messiah in Rabbinic literature, but scholars tend to think that these images came into Jewish literature *after* Christianity (and to some extent because of it).

19. For example, one of the prayers for the morning service in the *Siddur* reads: "Our Father who art in heaven, deal kindly with us for the sake of thy great name by which we are called."

20. It could also be rendered: "Are you *an* anointed son of the Blessed?" Greek syntax requires linking nouns that belong together with a definite article; the definite article in such cases does not therefore necessarily indicate a title.

21. In 9:40 there is another passing reference to *christos*, but it occurs in a phrase that scholars have consistently found puzzling. There Mark quotes Jesus saying, "Whoever gives you to drink a cup of water in the name of *christos*, truly I say to you that he will not lose his reward." The phrase itself is a peculiar one: literally, "in the name that you are Christ's." D. E. Nineham observes that it is "a phrase as odd in Greek as it is in English." (See his *St. Mark* [New York: Penguin Books Ltd., 1963], 257.) He—like Hooker and most commentators—thinks the phrase is a church formula because the word *christos* is not used as a proper name without the article anywhere else in the Gospels or Acts. This fact might also suggest, it seems to me, that it was interpolated—like 16:9–20—by a later hand.

22. For a comprehensive treatment of the importance of the Isaac story within Judaism, see Jon Levenson, *The Death and Resurrection of the Beloved Son* (New Haven: Yale University Press, 1993).

23. This is observed by Geza Vermes in *Scripture and Tradition* (Leiden: Brill, 1961), 203.

24. John Bowker, *The Targums and Rabbinic Literature* (Cambridge, England: Cambridge University Press, 1969), 224.

25. Bowker, *The Targums*, 225.

26. Bowker, *The Targums*, 225, 230.

27. Bowker, *The Targums*, 227.

28. Aharon Agus, *The Binding of Isaac and Messiah: Law, Martyrdom and Deliverance in Early Rabbinic Religiosity* (Albany: SUNY Press, 1988), 39. Multiple midrashic connections are cited by Vermes in *Scripture and Tradition*, 202–7. Also see Roger Le Deaut, "Paque Juive et Nouveau Testament," in *Studies on the Background of the New Testament* (Assen: Van Gorcum, 1969), 38–43.

29. Agus, *The Binding*, 36.

30. Agus, *The Binding*, 55.

31. See Bowker, *The Targums*, 227, and Martin McNamara, *Targum and*

Testament. Aramaic Paraphrases of the Hebrew Bible: A Light on the New Testament (Grand Rapids, Mich.: Eerdmans, 1972), 114.

32. H. C. Kee gives 137–107 B.C.E. as the probable date for this work, and while he acknowledges the possibility of some later Christian interpolations, he does not cite as one of them "the Father's voice as from Abraham to Isaac." See *The Old Testament Pseudepigrapha*, vol. I, edited by James Charlesworth (Garden City, N.Y.: Doubleday,1983), 777. Stegner argues that whether the passage is Jewish or Christian, it still gives evidence of a tradition that connects the baptism of Jesus with Gen. 22. *Narrative Theology in Early Christianity* (Louisville, Ky.: Westminster Press, 1989), 26.

33. Some scholars suspect a later Christian hand might have interpolated some of this language.

34. See *Death and Resurrection*, 67.

35. *Death and Resurrection*, 67.

36. *Death and Resurrection*, 173–99.

37. *Death and Resurrection*, 199.

38. *Death and Resurrection*, 218. While Levenson's work is the most recent and by far the most comprehensive, other scholars, both Jewish and Christian, have offered similar reflections. See, for example, Vermes, *Scripture and Tradition*, 194–227, and Robert Daly, "The Soteriological Significance of the Sacrifice of Isaac," *CBQ* 39, 1 (1977): 45–75.

39. *Death and Resurrection*, 192.

40. *Death and Resurrection*, 145. The story of David goes on in ways that also fit the pattern, albeit somewhat differently—namely, the narrative of David's sin, the death of his first love-child, and God's gift of another "beloved" son.

41. *Death and Resurrection*, 145.

42. *Death and Resurrection*, 168.

43. *Death and Resurrection*, 154.

44. Levenson, unfortunately, does just that. See, in particular, his discussion of the parable of the Vineyard in *Death and Resurrection*, 226–30.

45. My argument here runs directly counter to that of Dominic Crossan in *Who Killed Jesus?* (San Francisco: Harper and Row, 1995) and also to Elaine Pagels in *The Origin of Satan* (New York: Random House, 1995). It is interesting to note that we are all agreed, however, in the goal of fostering a better relationship between modern Christians and Jews.

46. *Saint Mark*, 89.

47. See "Further Reflections on 'The Son of Man': The Origins and Development of the Title," in Charlesworth et al., *The Messiah*, 130–44.

48. For a similar reading of this meaning of "son of man" in Daniel, see Collins, *The Apocalyptic Imagination*, 82.

49. E. Isaac dates the Similitudes c. 105–64 B.C.E. See Charlesworth, *The Old Testament Pseudepigrapha*, vol. 1, 7.

50. Martha Himmelfarb comments: "The Similitudes uses participation in the heavenly liturgy as a way of expressing the visionary's angelic state (39:9–13) and like them it refers to 'garments of glory'—also called 'garment[s] of life'—for the righteous when they achieve an angelic state, after death (62:15–16)." See *Ascent to Heaven in Jewish and Christian Apocalypses* (New York: Oxford University Press, 1993), 60.

51. Isaac translates the phrase as a title, "the Son of Man," and then acknowledges in a footnote: "*Man* in this context means *people* or *human beings*. Though

this passage could be rendered *Son of human beings,* to avoid unnecessary confusion, I have used *Son of Man,* which has become an accepted and standard expression among scholars for a long time." (See Charlesworth, *The Old Testament Pseudepigrapha,* vol. 1, 34 n. 46e.) Of course, given the controversy over the use and meaning of "the son of man," Isaac's choice has unfortunately *added* to the confusion, because it appears to supply a precedent for New Testament usage where it does not exist.

52. See Bruce M. Metzger's introduction to the Fourth Book of Ezra, in Charlesworth, *The Old Testament Pseudepigrapha,* vol. 1, 517–523.

53. "Further Reflections," in Charlesworth et al., *The Messiah,* 140.

54. See Geza Vermes, *Jesus the Jew* (London: Collins, 1973), 162, and *Jesus and the World of Judaism* (Philadelphia: Fortress Press, 1983), 89.

55. "Further Reflections," 140.

56. "Further Reflections," 139.

57. See *Ascent,* 18.

58. *Ascent,* 50.

59. A. Yarbro Collins expresses this kind of puzzlement. See her chapter on Mark 13 in *The Beginning of the Gospel: Probings of Mark in Context* (Minneapolis: Fortress Press, 1992).

60. For discussion that supports this point, see John Meier, *A Marginal Jew: Rethinking the Historical Jesus* (New York: Doubleday, 1991): 217–25 and 352. Morna Hooker makes an even stronger point: "It was an insult in Jewish society to describe anyone as the son of his mother alone, and it is possible that the phrase reflects rumours that Jesus' birth was illegitimate, in which case the objection to Jesus is not merely that he was a local boy" (see *Saint Mark,* 153). Hooker speaks of the Gospel here as though it were primarily a historical account. Since I see it primarily as theological interpretation, I do not agree that the phrase reflects historical rumors, but I do think her comment underlines the theological point Mark was trying to make.

61. See "A Love Story Gone Awry," in *God and the Rhetoric of Sexuality* (Philadelphia: Fortress Press, 1978): 94–105.

62. This certainly included many of the church fathers. Paul, one assumes, knew the Hebrew text as well, but he may have chosen to follow the Greek.

63. Schüssler Fiorenza wants "full humanity" to be the interpretive framework for biblical criticism (see *Jesus, Miriam's Child, Sophia's Prophet* (New York: Continuum, 1994), ch. 2) but rejects the phrase "son of man" as exclusively male. She has not, however, considered the phrase in its original Hebrew context, where *'adam* refers to human beings before their division into sexual genders (see note 61 earlier). John Townsend tries to overcome the overtones of exclusivity by translating the term as "child of humanity"—a term that is certainly accurate but unfortunately awkward. I think Mark has anticipated modern feminist concerns by paralleling *ben 'adam* with *ben Miriam.* Perhaps if the extant text were in Hebrew or Aramaic, as many scholars think the original compositon must have been, the parallel and its significance would seem more obvious.

64. See *Jesus, Miriam's Child,* 133–50.

65. For this insight and for these translations of the daughters' names, see Ellen F. Davis, "Job and Jacob: The Integrity of Faith," in *Reading Between the Texts: Intertextuality and the Hebrew Bible,* edited by Danna Nolan Fewell (Louisville, Ky.: Westminster Press, 1992), 220.

66. In a recent article Walter Brueggemann traces the history of critical interest in Creation theology and outlines the current scholarly consensus asserting its importance in the Hebrew Bible. He notes the convergence between this development and a renewed interest in the traditions of Wisdom. In particular he cites von Rad's 1972 work *Wisdom in Israel*: "In von Rad's general analysis, wisdom theology has as its subject the ongoing, generative order of creation, which is nourishing, sustaining, and reliable." See "The Loss and Recovery of Creation in OT Theology," in *Theology Today* 53, 2 (July 1996): 183.

67. In his opening chapter, "The Origin of the Story of Creation," Calum Carmichael notes how often the Bible poses an antithesis between idolatry and God's act of creation, and he suggests that this antithesis underlies both Genesis and Exodus. See *The Story of Creation* (Ithaca, N.Y.: Cornell University Press, 1996), 1–31.

68. To read "son of Mary" as a historically accurate reporting of the townsfolk's appellation results in speculation on Mary's uncertain status as a mother; to read it within the context of Wisdom is to understand that it is pointing not to a social reality but to a theologically informed violation of literary convention.

69. Both Elizabeth Schüssler Fiorenza, in *Jesus, Miriam's Child*, and Elizabeth A. Johnson, in *She Who Is* (New York: Crossroad, 1998), speak of Jesus as being "Wisdom incarnate" in the Gospels. Perhaps a case for that can be made in the Gospel of John, but not, I think, in the Gospel of Mark. Seeing how Mark makes use of the feminine aspects of Wisdom in his characterization of Jesus, however, is suggestive of the process whereby a later community and more Hellenized culture might have shifted style and meaning. Even so, I think the references to "Sophia" are misleading, suggesting a Greek goddess who is quite unlike the various female personifications of Wisdom in the Jewish writings. (I also think the designation *Lady* Wisdom is anachronistic, suggesting an aristocratic society rather than the context of Early Judaism.)

70. See Genesis Rabbah (Ber. 8.10): "R. Hoshaya said: When the Holy One, blessed be He, created *'adam*, the ministering angels mistook him [for a divine being] and wished to exclaim 'Holy' before him." The text of this Midrash is several centuries later than the text of Mark, so some scholars will argue that it cannot be used to illumine it. On the other hand, it seems fair to note that midrashic hermeneutic coexisted with Mark in oral tradition and that there is good reason to conjecture that what was ultimately written down reflects the nature of earlier theological thinking. Another, perhaps even more striking Midrash on human beings reflecting God's image is found in the Sifra to Leviticus 26:12, "I will be ever in your midst." The exegesis reads as follows: "It is to be expressed by means of parable; to what may this be likened? To a king who went out to stroll in his orchard (*pardes*) with his tenant farmer, and [out of respect] that tenant kept hiding himself from the presence of the king. So the king said to that tenant, 'Why do you hide from me? Behold, I, you—we're alike.' Similarly in the Age to Come the Holy One, blessed be he, will stroll with the righteous in the Garden of Eden, but when the righteous see Him they will tremble before him; and the Holy One, blessed be he, will say to him, 'Why is it that you tremble before Me? Behold, I, you—we're alike!'" This is cited by Judah Goldin in his article "Of Midrash and the Messianic Theme," in *Studies in Midrash and Related Literature*, edited by B. L. Eichler and J. H. Tigay (New York: Jewish Publication Society, 1988), 360.

71. Also consider the warning of Psalm 95:8: "Harden not your hearts as at Meribah."

72. Gerhardsson discusses various ways the Jewish oral tradition condensed teachings in order to facilitate memorizing. In particular, he mentions the *kelal*, a form which he defines as "a summarizing, inclusive, condensed statement," and he cites R. Simeon ben Azzai on "the great *kelal*." See *Memory and Manuscript* (Uppsala: C. W. Gleerup-Luna, 1961), 138.

73. *A Midrash Reader* (Minneapolis: Fortress Press, 1990), 140.

74. *Parables in Midrash* (Cambridge: Harvard University Press, 1991), 93.

75. *A Midrash Reader*, 162.

76. *The Gospel in Parable* (Philadelphia: Fortress Press, 1988), 9. Similarly, Stephen Moore comments that "parable" in chapter 4 of Mark "may mean more than just a traditional teaching device taken over by the historical Jesus. The term may encompass Jesus' enigmatic ministry as such, a fusion of word and deed." See "Deconstructive Criticism: The Gospel of Mark," in *Mark and Method: New Approaches in Biblical Studies*, edited by Janice Capel Anderson and Stephen D. Moore (Minneapolis: Fortress Press, 1992): 87–88.

77. See "Canon and Christology" in *Christian Engagements With Judaism* (Harrisburg, Pa.: Trinity Press International, 1999), especially 53–56.

78. It is worth noting that the idea of God as remote, perfect, and static is one that belongs to Greek philosophy but not to the Hebrew Bible. For a recent Jewish discussion of God in Genesis, see Jon Levenson, *Creation and the Persistence of Evil* (Princeton: Princeton University Press, 1988), where he argues that the Bible does not show God creating out of nothing but rather holding chaos at bay by reshaping its raw materials. For a full discussion of the differences between the Jewish and the Greek metaphors for God and how the shift from one to the other involved a shift in christology, see Bernard Lee, *Jesus and the Metaphors of God: The Christs of the New Testament* (Mahwah, N.J.: Paulist Press, 1993).

79. For a concurring view—although based on "the historical Jesus" rather than the midrashic model—see John Meier, who states that Jesus "eludes all our neat theological programs" and is "a bulwark against the reduction of Christian faith in general and christology in particular to 'relevant' ideology of any stripe. His refusal to be held fast by any given school of thought is what drives theologians onward into new paths; hence the historical Jesus remains a constant stimulus to theological renewal." See *A Marginal Jew: Rethinking the Historical Jesus* (New York: Doubleday, 1991), 199–200.

80. *The Gospel in Parable*, 16.

81. See David Stern, "Rhetoric and Midrash," *Prooftexts* 1 (1981): 26–91, where he notes that "it is like" is the standard formula that introduces the *mashal* (267). Also see *Parables in Midrash*, where Stern speaks of "as it were" (*kivyakhol*) as the typical midrashic introduction to anthropomorphic imagery for God (165). Fishbane elaborates on the significance of *kivyakhol* in *The Garments of Torah* (Bloomington: University of Indiana Press, 1989), 27. For the significance of this kind of phrasing in Christian theology, see Garrett Green, *Imagining God* (San Francisco: Harper and Row, 1989). In the context of describing Scripture as "a work of imagination" (106), he says: "The religious imagination does not 'image' God (i.e., construct some kind of picture of God) but imagines God (i.e., thinks of God according to a paradigm). The paradigmatic imagination is not mimetic but analogical; it shows us not

what God is but what God is *like*. (Idolatry, reduced to an epigram, confuses the 'is' with the 'as')" (93). Chapter 5 of Green's book is devoted to Jesus himself as the image of God.

82. "From Christ to God: The Christian Perspective," in *Jews and Christians Speak of Jesus*, edited by Arthur E. Zannoni (Minneapolis: Fortress Press, 1994): 139. Hellwig offers as a particular example the contrast between the Jewish rhetoric of Peter when he says, in Acts 2:36, "God has made him both Lord and Messiah" and "one of the earliest gentile statements of the same claim" by Ignatius of Antioch, in which he speaks of "Jesus Christ our God" (138). Similarly, Bernard Lee takes as his starting point our need to separate ourselves from our culturally conditioned images of Christ. He notes that he is not proposing "a substitute theology" but "trying to introduce into the christological conversation a new participant [i.e., the original Jewish way of seeing Jesus], one which earlier history excluded." *The Galilean Jewishness of Jesus* (Mahwah, N.J.: Paulist Press, 1988), 9. Later he observes the essential differences between the Jewish and Greek paradigms of God: he observes that the Greek paradigm emphasized reason as the highest human faculty and thus logically posited God as a perfect being who does not change, while the emphasis in the Hebrew Bible is not on a static God but on God of relationship and action (23). He cites (133) Abraham Heschel on the Jewish belief in the *pathos* of God: "Pathos denotes, not an idea of goodness, but a living care; not an immutable example, but an ongoing challenge, a dynamic relation between God and Man . . . no mere contemplative survey of the world, but a passionate summons." *The Prophets*, vol. 2 (New York: Harper and Row, 1975), 5.

83. "From Christ to God," 138.

84. In this regard she also refers to the famous statement of Irenaeus: "The glory of God is man fully alive." "From Christ to God," 144.

85. "From Christ to God," 142.

86. "From Christ to God," 143.

Chapter 6

1. The actual phrase, *hoi par' autou*, literally just means "those with him." It has generally been interpreted as a reference to Jesus' family—most plausibly because of their explicit appearance at the end of the chapter. See Vincent Taylor, *The Gospel According to St. Mark* (London: Macmillan, 1963), 236.

2. See Taylor, *Mark*, 256.

3. The NRSV has replaced "is" with "comes."

4. After the Christian church was established, this assertion unfortunately gave itself to the interpretation of exclusivity, but if considered in the context of early and fluid Judaism, it is an open invitation. Particularly when read in the context of the Wisdom writings, it is clearly inclusive in its intent. Given that understanding of v. 11, then other readings also shift. The final comment in v. 34 might then be translated and punctuated differently. Instead of "he did not speak to them [the crowd] except in parables, but he explained everything in private to his disciples" (NRSV), the pronoun "them" might be taken as reference to the disciples and the phrasing restructured so that it would read: "he did not speak in private to them [his disciples] apart from parables; on the contrary, to his disciples he interpreted everything." The implication would then be that Jesus was constantly interpreting Torah to his disciples in parabolic form, sometimes

through speech and sometimes through action. The contrast being presented in chapter 4, then, would be seen not as a contrast between public and private communication, or between direct and indirect meaning, but rather between a purely intellectual interpretation of Scripture and the enacted interpretation set forth in the life of Jesus. For those on the "outside," "everything takes place in parables" (v. 11), but for "his own"—that is, whoever has eyes to see and ears to hear—the interpretation of Scripture is being lived out before them.

5. Mark describes the woman's touching of Jesus as an act of faith: "For she said, If I should touch even his garments, I will be saved" (v. 28). He also describes Jesus perceiving her touch as a holy and healing act: "And straightway Jesus, recognizing in himself that out of him power had gone forth, having turned around in the crowd, said, 'Who touched me?'" (v. 30). (The idea of sacramentality, incidentally, was Jewish before it was Christian: the word "sacramental" belongs to the church, but the notion that God touches human lives through concrete things pervades the Hebrew Bible.)

6. Still another way of reading the text, moreover, might be in terms of the Rabbinic idiom that designated certain sacred texts as those that "soiled the hands"—meaning that they would defile those who were not holy enough to read them. Since "bread" was also a figurative way of referring to God's word, the question might be paraphrased, "Why do your disciples not observe *halakhah* but come to Scripture unworthily?" The question could then be taken to imply that the disciples' violation of the Sabbath laws makes them unfit to be interpreters of Scripture. The challenge of the Pharisees here would then be shown to be aimed at scriptural interpretation—a reading that is also supported by Jesus' reply.

7. Does the consistent parallelism indicate that Jesus' disciples are themselves members of the Pharisaic sect? Such a conclusion seems quite plausible. Others have suggested that Jesus' continual debates with the Pharisees imply that they were indeed his associates.

8. John Drury treats the statement of Jesus here as a "riddle" that only becomes clear after the Passover supper when Jesus equates the bread with his body. (See "Understanding the Bread: Disruption and Aggregation, Secrecy and Revelation in Mark's Gospel," in *Not in Heaven: Coherence and Complexity in Biblical Narrative*, edited by Jason P. Rosenblatt and Joseph C. Sitterson Jr. [Bloomington: University of Indiana Press, 1991], 98–119.) He suggests that the reader does not initially understand Jesus' words here any more than his disciples did (100), and he further suggests that Mark intends the reader's confusion: "The bread riddle was Mark's attempt to get his readers to use their own wit and resources" (115). While I agree that Mark in general intends his hearers to identify with the obtuse disciples, I think that in this particular instance, the reader has been given definite clues to understanding.

9. The *eutheias-euthus* tally has been obscured by translations seeking variety rather than echoes, but it is striking in the Greek. A probing of the two words discloses, moreover, that they both have the same root meaning of "straight": the relationship in Greek would be best preserved in English by translating *euthus* as "straightway." (As far as I know, the King James Bible is the only English version that so translates it.) The result is a linking word that is also a relevant theological pun: Isaiah's voice calls to "make straight the ways" of the Lord, and Jesus responds "straightway"—the word conveys not mere temporal speed but moral urgency. The fact that Mark connects the word with Jesus no less than eighteen times in his Gospel is a clue to the significance Mark assigns to it—the

actions of Jesus actualize the traditions in the immediate present and effect the straightened way called for by Isaiah.

10. In Mark this person is simply described as "one of those standing by," but in context, one of the disciples seems to be implied.

11. This detail may also be linked to Amos 2:16: "And he who is stout of heart among the mighty shall flee away naked in that day" (a point noted by Raymond Brown in *The Death of the Messiah* [Garden City, N.Y.: Doubleday, 1994], 303), but the connection with chapter 13 seems closer. Of course, both passages are using the imagery of eschatological devastation.

12. See Walter Bauer, *A Greek-English Lexicon of the New Testament* (Chicago: University of Chicago Press, 1958), 290.

13. "The Twelve," Taylor notes, "are not identical with the disciples nor with the apostles, who represent a circle wider than that of the Twelve" (*Mark*, 230).

14. The same word appears in 4:41 and 16:8. The NRSV translates it as "filled with great awe" in the former instance, where it is applied to the male disciples, but "afraid" here in chapter 16.

15. See the work of Judith Plaskow, Bernadette Broonton, and Ross Kraemer, all of which show that women were beginning to achieve a new status in Judaism, even beginning to act as leaders in the synagogues. Shaye Cohen also takes note of this phenomenon. (See "Women in Synagogues of Antiquity," *Conservative Judaism* 34, 2 (1980): 23–29.) I see the attitude toward women exhibited by the Markan Jesus to be reflective of this emerging trend in Early Judaism. I agree with Schüssler Fiorenza that if so, then "Underlining this renewal aspect of the Jesus movement does not imply anti-Judaism." (See *In Memory of Her*, 141.) What it should provide instead is a deeper bond between Jewish and Christian women.

16. See Bauer, *Greek-English Lexicon*, 411.

17. In fact, most translations obscure its significance. Both the King James and the NRSV, for example, translate it as "*lifted* her up," while the Jerusalem Bible and the New American Bible say Jesus "*helped* her up."

18. It probably did not carry a full ecclesial meaning at the time of Mark's composition, because "the church," as such, was not officially established. Yet the sacramental language I have noted elsewhere indicates evolving liturgical structures. It is also worth pondering Schüssler Fiorenza's observation that whenever the word *diakonos* is applied to a man in New Testament writing, it has been translated "deacon," whereas whenever it is used for a woman, it has been given as "servant" or "helper."

19. In Rabbinic law a menstruating woman was considered unfit for either sexual or religious intercourse until the menstruation had ceased and the woman had undergone a ritual bath; righteous men were forbidden to touch a menstruating woman for fear of contamination. Similar proscriptions were adopted by the later Christian church when it instituted a "churching" or cleansing ceremony for new mothers. The ceremony has now been dropped—an acknowledgment, perhaps, that it did not exist in early Christianity. In general, it is important to state that the sympathetic view given here should not be taken as a contrast between Christianity and Judaism per se but rather between different attitudes within Judaism. The Gospel representation of women undoubtedly reflects the consciousness of the Early Judaism that formed its matrix.

20. Just as translators have made women "servants" and men "deacons," so they have habitually translated these words to make women sound weak and men

sound reverential. In terms of common Greek usage, they should always be interpreted as connoting the experience of *mysterium tremendum.*

21. See Taylor, *Mark,* 293.

22. Ironically, the word "straightway" here is omitted in many translations and poorly translated when it is included. The NRSV translates it "immediately"; the King James and the New American Bible omit it. The Jerusalem Bible, however, does include it as "straightaway."

23. One might also note the exclusion in the book of Revelation of "sorcerers and dogs" (22:15).

24. Bauer states (662): "In later writers *pistikos* means that which belongs to *pistis,* faithful, trustworthy." He does not appear to see the relevance of that meaning to this description in Mark, nor do any of the commentaries.

25. The words themselves are different: in 13:2, the word describing the end of the Temple is *kataluthē,* aorist passive subjunctive of *kataluō.* The meaning, in each case, however, is "total destruction." It is one more small verbal effect that serves to make the demolition of the Temple and the death of Jesus analogies for one another.

26. The root of both these words is *cheō.*

27. See Bauer, *Greek-English Lexicon,* 307.

28. See Taylor's discussion of the Jewish practice, *Mark,* 533.

29. In her first work retrieving the role of women hidden in Scripture, *In Memory of Her* (New York: Crossroad, 1984), Schüssler Fiorenza made brilliant and ironic use of this phrase, suggesting that far from being remembered, this woman has been so totally forgotten that no one even knows her name. She thus uses this incident to symbolize women's forgotten place in the Gospel. I am suggesting that a full retrieval of the woman's actions here would mean recognition that she performs the key liturgical act of eucharistic celebration.

30. Similar insights are expressed by Schüssler Fiorenza: see *In Memory of Her,* 320, and *Discipleship of Equals* (New York: Crossroad, 1993), 113.

31. The NRSV actually gives the name of Herod's daughter as *Herodias* (see Mark 6:22) but also notes that "other ancient authorities read 'the daughter of Herodias herself.'" Taylor states that most commentators accept this second reading (315). The name *Salome* is not provided by the evangelists but by Josephus (*Antiquities* 18.5.4), so perhaps my point here is too fragile to hold up: it assumes that the name of Herod's daughter was so widely known that it would have been assumed by Mark's audience.

32. See the *Siddur,* or *Authorized Daily Prayer Book,* edited by Joseph H. Hertz (New York: Bloch, 1974), 747, for one version of this prayer and some explanations of it.

33. See Taylor, *Mark,* 606.

34. See Gen. 9:2, Ex. 15:16, Dt. 2:25.

35. Bauer (*Greek-English Lexicon,* 245) notes that while *ekstasis* may be translated "distraction, confusion, astonishment, terror," it also has the meaning of "trance" or "ecstasy"—that is, "a state of being brought about by God, in which consciousness is wholly or partially suspended." The NRSV translates the word as "amazement" but concedes that the word "fear" in the last phrase is "probably in the sense of overwhelming awe." The church fathers and Morna Hooker are all silent about this possible meaning. I have pondered why there are virtually no translations of Mark that use the obvious word "ecstasy." (One excep-

tion is Donald Senior, *The Passion of Jesus in the Gospel of Mark* (Wilmington, Del.: Michael Glazier, 1984. Reprint Collegeville, Minn.: The Liturgical Press, 1991, 137.) I can only speculate that it might be because of the Montanist sect of the second century (eventually deemed heretical) in which women are said to have prophesied by going into an ecstatic trance.

36. Consider the band of prophets who greet Saul with musical instruments and change him "into another person" (1 Sam. 10:6). The NRSV comments: "To *be in a prophetic frenzy . . . and be turned into another person* means here to dance ecstatically and be out of one's head, in the fashion of the so-called ecstatic prophecy of those days." This ecstatic prophecy was accompanied by "the Spirit of God" coming upon the person. Schüssler Fiorenza also discusses "the world experience [of prophecy] common to the ancient Mediterranean civilization" as ecstasy. See *In Memory of Her*, 296.

37. '*Adam* before this point in Genesis means simply "earthling" or "of the earth"; sexuality itself is created here. See Phyllis Trible, "A Love Story Gone Astray" in *God and the Rhetoric of Sexuality* (Philadelphia: Fortress Press, 1978), 94–100.

38. *The Gospel of St. Mark* (New York: Penguin Books Ltd., 1963), 441. Nineham suggests throughout his commentary his belief that Mark intends to convey feelings of reverence in his ending. Nonetheless he translates the final phrase simply as "trembling and astonishment" (442).

39. Donahue concludes: "Mark's readers are left not even with the assurance of a resurrection vision but simply with numinous fear in the face of divine promise. These reactions of wonder and surprise accompany the revelation of God in Jesus, and they signify the power of this revelation to unsettle and challenge human existence. At the same time, this wonder is fascinating and attracting; it invites people to confront mystery. Such motifs call for a parabolic reading of Mark: for an approach to Mark with a sense of wonder, awe, and holy fear." *The Gospel in Parable* (Philadelphia: Fortress Press, 1988), 196–97.

40. Gerard S. Sloyan, *The Gospel of Saint Mark* (Collegeville, Minn.: The Liturgical Press, 1960), 120.

41. Donald Senior, *The Passion of Jesus in the Gospel of Mark* (Wilmington, Del.: Michael Glazier, 1984. Reprint Collegeville, Minn.: The Liturgical Press, 1991), 137.

42. *Mark: A Commentary on His Apology for the Cross* (Grand Rapids, Mich.: Eerdmans, 1993), 1015.

Chapter 7

1. In the sacramental churches it is this false text that is used in Cycle B for the feast of the Ascension and every year on the feast of Saint Mark!

2. Donald Juel is a notable exception: "The stubborn refusal of commentators to accept sound text-critical arguments in their interpretation of Mark and the continuing creation of hypothetical conclusions, say more about the commentators than about Mark." *A Master of Surprise: Mark Interpreted* (Minneapolis: Fortress Press, 1994), 109. Dale Allison is also an exception, asking incredulously, "Where is the commentator who regards Mark 16:9–20 as secondary and yet still employs it to interpret Mark?" *The New Moses* (Minneapolis: Fortress Press, 1993), 5. Unfortunately, the answer to that question is that many have. The point I am trying to make, moreoever, is that this spurious ending *is in itself* an interpretation.

3. Translation taken from Kurt Aland, ed., *Synopsis of the Four Gospels* (8th ed.: Stuttgart: German Bible Society, 1987), 334.

4. *Gospel Parallels: A Synopsis of the First Three Gospels*, 4th ed., edited by Burton H. Throckmorton, Jr. (New York: Thomas Nelson, 1979), v–vi.

5. *Gospel Parallels*, vi. Throckmorton also notes that Jerome's fourth-century Latin text—the Vulgate—was intended to present a purified substitute for the multiple, conflicting, and erroneous Old Latin versions then in use. To that end Jerome went back to the original languages—both Hebrew and Greek—and apparently to the Alexandrine text of the New Testament. This text became the standard one used by the Christian church in the eighth century. Unfortunately, as time went on, this text was again corrupted by the Old Latin versions and had to be revised again in both the ninth and sixteenth centuries. Throckmorton states that the 1598 Vulgate "is still the official Latin text of the Bible of the Roman Catholic Church" (xii), but this comment of course overlooks the numerous modern Catholic translations in the vernacular that have emanated from Vatican II—not to mention the Catholic acceptance of Protestant translations and the collaboration of Catholic biblical scholars with Jewish and Protestant ones. In regard to this kind of cross-fertilization it is worth noting that both the Gutenberg Bible (1455) and the Wycliffe Bible were translations from the Vulgate (xiii). Throckmorton considers the Vulgate to be the most influential in the Western church (xii), but surely the King James, because of the beauty of its language and its consequent use by preachers and poets, has dominated the English-speaking world. In both ways the European tradition has been shortchanged in respect to theology, because both the Vulgate and the King James derive from "contaminated" texts.

6. From the Codex Ephraemi (C).

7. *Gospel Parallels*, vi–vii.

8. *Gospel Parallels*, vii.

9. This name is not descriptive (although it could be)—it is simply the name of the museum in Washington, D.C., where it is kept. It reads: "This age of lawlessness and unbelief is under Satan who by means of unclean spirits does not allow men to comprehend the true power of God. . . . Christ answered them: 'The limit of the years of the authority of Satan is fulfilled; but other afflictions draw near, even for those sinners on whose behalf I was delivered up to death, that they might return to the truth and sin no more; that they might inherit the spiritual and incorruptible glory of righteousness which is in heaven.'" Vincent Taylor, *The Gospel According to St. Mark* (London: Macmillan, 1963), sees this ending as the work of a scribe who "desired to soften the severe condemnation of the Eleven" (615) in the longer ending. He does not comment on all its vocabulary, images, or ideas but does note that the image of Satan's power reaching "fulfillment" and the emphasis on "incorruptible glory" for the righteous are not characteristic of Mark.

10. This shorter ending appears in so few and such inferior manuscripts and is so radically at odds with Markan style that few scholars take note of it at all. It reads: "But they reported briefly to Peter and those with him all that they had been told. And after this, Jesus himself sent out by means of them, from east to west, the sacred and imperishable proclamation of eternal salvation." Morna Hooker notes that it is found only in a few late Greek manuscripts and a few of the versions (*Saint Mark*, 387–88). Taylor notes that it mostly contains words

and phrases never found in Mark; in fact, he can verify only the opening phrase, "all that had been commanded them" (*Saint Mark*, 614).

11. *Synopsis*, 334.

12. *The New Oxford Annotated Bible With the Apocrypha*, edited by Herbert G. May and Bruce M. Metzger (New York: Oxford University Press, 1977), 1238.

13. *The New Oxford Annotated Bible With the Apocrypha*, edited by Bruce M. Metzger and Roland M. Murphy (New York: Oxford University Press, 1994), NT 74.

14. Taylor, *Mark*, 610. The "two traces" Hort refers to are in Justin Martyr and Irenaeus. The passages he cites, however, are uncertain allusions: Justin speaks of the apostles "preaching everywhere" (*The First Apology*, 45); Irenaeus says that Mark declared that Jesus was "received in heaven and sat at the right hand of the Father" (Irenaeus, *Against Heresies*, Book III, Ch. 10:5). Although Irenaeus says he is quoting Mark, the phrase is not necessarily an allusion to verses 9–20. Mark does mention the preaching of the gospel "to all the nations" as the context for the disciples' future trials (13:10) and quotes Jesus saying he will be "seated at the right hand of the power" (14:62) in the context of his response to the condemning high priest. The phrasing used by Justin and Irenaeus suggest that either or both might have been thinking of Matt. 28:19 or Acts 1:8.

15. The editors write: "scholars usually give preference to those that are preserved in the older manuscripts" and "preference is also given to the shorter reading, for scribes were much more prone to make additions than deliberately to omit. Another scribal tendency was harmonization of divergent accounts" (NT, v). In addition, the basic editorial principle of *lectio difficultor* points to verse 8 as the earliest.

16. NT, 47.

17. In his book on the formation of the canon, Metzger states that the longer ending "was known to Justin Martyr and to Tatian, who incorporated it into his *Diatesseron*," and he adds: "There seems to be good reason, therefore, to conclude that, though external and internal evidence is conclusive against the authenticity of the last twelve verses as coming from the same pen as the rest of the Gospel, the passage ought to be accepted as part of the canonical text of Mark." See *The Canon of the New Testament* (New York: Oxford University Press, 1987), 270. It is hard to understand how Metzger can both acknowledge that harmonization was one of the ways scribes corrupted the early texts and at the same time speak approvingly of the *Diatesseron* and of the longer ending of Mark! It is also hard to reconcile his approval of the longer ending with his later remarks about the need to recognize the "theological pluralism within the primitive Christian communities themselves" (*The Canon*, 279–80).

18. Taylor, *Mark*, 611–14.

19. See Taylor (*Mark*, 455) for a lengthy discussion of possible interpretations. Taylor himself thinks the reference here is not to Jesus but to the owner of the colt. Hooker also comments: "The title used here—*ho kurios*—is used in the LXX in the sense of 'the Lord' to refer to God, but this meaning hardly fits the context. One possibility is that it means 'the owner.'" She acknowledges that the Christian community later used 'Lord' as a title for Jesus himself but points out that "nowhere else . . . does Mark allow the title to slip into his narrative in this anachronistic way" (*Saint Mark*, 258).

20. Taylor, *Mark*, 613.

21. Taylor, *Mark*, 613.

22. This statement needs to be qualified by the acknowledgment that the *Diatesseron* was accepted for some time by the Syriac-speaking churches, although eventually Origen's insistence on four separate Gospels prevailed in the East— as that of Irenaeus in the West. Raymond Brown suggests that the acceptance of four Gospels was a reaction to the exclusivity of certain groups (e.g., Gnostics and Jewish Christians) who focused on a particular Gospel in order to use it as a polemical weapon. See *An Introduction to the New Testament* (New York: Doubleday, 1997), 13.

23, *Against Heresies* 2.27.2, ANF. They may have been given an implicitly equal status earlier through the liturgical practice of reading from both sources alternately or interchangeably. Justin Martyr indicates such a practice in his first Apology. See *The First Apology*, 67.3–5.

24. Metzger observes that Clement of Alexandria "uses the word 'canon' some twenty-one times, but he does not apply it to a collection of books. At the same time, he makes a marked difference between those books which he accepts as authoritative and those he does not." See *The Canon*, 131.

25. *Festal Letter* 39, 11–12. Translation of Athanasius taken from Lee Martin McDonald, *The Formation of the Christian Canon* (Nashville, Tenn.: Abingdon Press, 1988), 141.

26. Marcion's plan to cut out the whole of the Hebrew Bible, and indeed to retain only an adapted version of Luke and ten letters of Paul, was an extreme that was speedily condemned as heresy.

27. *Festal Letter* 39, 12.

28. See *The Canon*, 75.

29. McDonald, in citing Eusebius's *History of the Church* (3:66), observes: "It is clear from Eusebius that Constantine could tolerate no rivals to the rule of peace and harmony either in his empire or in the churches. . . . [I]t is a fact that he wanted 'harmony' (uniformity) at all costs. Those whose doctrines were not in keeping with the 'orthodoxy' of the day were banished into exile, their writings burned, and their meeting places confiscated" (*The Formation*, 113).

30. Metzger opposes the view that the development of the canon was "haphazard" rather than a "special gift of God" (*The Canon*, 285). Yet his own meticulous scholarship gives evidence of the multiple human elements involved in the canonical process. In respect to Eusebius's list he notes: "In the absence of any official list of the canonical writings of the NT, Eusebius finds it simplest to count the votes of his witnesses, and by this means to classify all the apostolic or pretended apostolic writings into three categories" (*The Canon*, 203).

31. Marcion, of course, is again an exception, and Justin, writing around 160 C.E., seems to have omitted Mark. All the other church fathers of the second century, however—Irenaeus, Tertullian, Clement of Alexandria, and Origen— mention Mark, Matthew, Luke, and John. Eusebius's *History of the Church* (325– 30 C.E.) also mentions the four Gospels among the twenty undisputed writings of the New Testament.

32. See *Unity and Diversity in the New Testament* (Philadelphia: Westminster Press, 1977), 377.

33. See McDonald, *The Formation*, 146–63, and Metzger, *The Canon*, 251– 57. Metzger does not accept "inspiration" as a criterion, arguing that "while the Fathers certainly agreed that the Scriptures of the Old and the New Testaments were inspired, they did not seem to have regarded inspiration as the ground

of the Bible's uniqueness." He goes on to suggest that the Fathers saw many sources of inspiration: "Not only do the early ecclesiastical writers view themselves to be, in some degree at least, inspired, but also others affirm, in a rather broad sense, the inspiration of their predecessors, if not their contemporaries." He cites, by way of example, Augustine referring both to Jerome and to himself as "inspired." (*The Canon*, 255.) Metzger does not relate this view of the Fathers to their Jewish legacy, but I would like to point out that the tendency to acknowledge that the commentary on Scripture is as inspired as Scripture itself is congenial with the view articulated by Fishbane: "Do we in fact cross a great divide from Hebrew Bible to its rabbinic interpreters?" ("Inner-Biblical Exegesis," in *Midrash and Literature*, edited by Geoffrey Hartman and Sanford Budick [New Haven: Yale University Press, 1986], 20).

34. Oscar Cullmann has aptly pointed out that many Christian scholars have had difficulty with the idea of many Gospels because they have seen them as *biography* instead of *theology*. He observes: "Four biographies of the same life could not be set alongside one another as of equal value, but would have to be harmonized and reduced to a single biography in some way or other. Four Gospels, that is, four books dealing with the content of faith, cannot be harmonized, but required by their very nature to be set alongside one another. And in any case the faith cried out for manifold witness." See "The Return of Christ," in *The Early Church: Studies in Early Christian History and Theology*, edited by A. J. B. Higgins (Philadelphia: Westminster Press, 1956), 52–54. This observation is cited approvingly by Metzger in *The Canon*, 263–64. Again one wonders how he can both approve this statement and not disapprove of the longer ending of Mark. To me it appears to be a total contradiction to this view of Cullmann's to say, as Metzger does in a later chapter, that because Tatian incorporated the longer ending into his *Diatesseron*, "there seems to be good reason to conclude that . . . the passage ought to be accepted as part of the canonical text of Mark." See *The Canon*, 270. Still later in his book, Metzger argues for recognition of "theological pluralism with the primitive Christian communities themselves" and for the "presence of diversity within and among the apostolic witnesses" (*The Canon*, 279–80). If that point of view prevails, then Mark must be given his own voice!

35. Like Metzger, Brevard Childs has argued the opposite: namely, that verses 9–20 should be read as the canonical ending of Mark precisely because they are made up of phrases taken from the other Gospels; he values this patchwork because he thinks it prevents readings that would make Mark unduly different from the others. See his *Introduction to the New Testament as Canon* (Philadelphia: Fortress Press, 1985), 94–95. His comment here is consistent with his general argument that the church should value the final form of a text over its earliest version. Child's momentous scholarship cannot be ignored, but there is a central issue here with which I must respectfully disagree: I do not think that the canon—in either testament—provides homogeneity. The fourth-century church's attempt to arrrive at uniformity is severely compromised, it seems to me, by the political influences that shaped this decision and overwhelmingly counterbalanced by the second-century church's refusal to allow Tatian's gospel harmonization. As I have been arguing throughout, I think the gospel writers knowingly composed in the tradition of Bible and midrash—which is a tradition that values counterpointing theological voices. James Sanders, who has argued at length with Childs over the meaning and function of the canon, has spoken of the value of biblical diversity in the way that I find most compelling: "The Bible is

a monotheizing literature displaying the struggles of generations over some fifteen to eighteen centuries to pursue the Integrity of reality. In this sense the Bible is a paradigm: it conjugates the nouns and verbs of the divine Integrity in a plethora of different kinds of situations and conditions." *Canon and Community* (Philadelphia: Fortress Press, 1984), 52.

36. *Sense and Absence* (Atlanta: Scholars Press, 1986).

37. *Locality and Doctrine in the Gospels* (New York: Harper and Brothers, 1938), 1–48, and *The Gospel Message of St. Mark* (Oxford: Clarendon, 1950), 80–97. Lightfoot's work is routinely cited by most commentators: see, for example, Taylor, *Mark*, 609, and Hooker, *Saint Mark*, 391. Nineham, *The Gospel of St. Mark* (New York: Penguin Books Ltd., 1963), 440, seems to allude to it. Curiously, C. S. Mann, in *Mark: Translation and Commentary* (Garden City, N.Y.: Doubleday, 1986), makes the opposite comment: "It is grammatically far more harsh in Greek" (670).

38. *Mark: A Commentary on His Apology for the Cross* (Grand Rapids, Mich.: Eerdmans, 1993), 1011. Gundry himself does not note that the word always connotes purposeful action, but that is what clearly emerges from the examples he chooses: 1:38—Jesus suggests going on to preach in other towns "*for* that is why I came out"; 3:35—"*for* whoever does the will of God is my brother, and sister, and mother"; 6:52—"*for* they did not understand about the loaves"; 10:45—"*for* the son of man also came not be served but to serve"; 11:18—"*for* they feared him"; 12:44—"*for* they contributed out of their abundance." It should be noted, however, that in none of these other examples is *gar* the last word of the sentence.

39. *Mark: A Commentary on His Apology for the Cross*, 1011.

40. "The Narrative Technique of Mark 16:8," *JBL* 100 (1981): 213–23.

41. *Saint Mark*, 393–94. Brown takes note of this possible interpretation in connection with the work of Magness, *Sense and Absence* (Atlanta: Scholars Press, 1986), but he does not endorse it: "This [Mark 16:8] may be a suspended ending, however, where the readers are expected to complete the story from the hint in the text. Then Mark would be affirming and communicating a post-resurrection reunion without narrating it. . . . Opponents respond that this is an attractive answer, but one that supposes considerable subtlety." (*Introduction to the New Testament* (New York: Doubleday, 1997), 148, n. 57.)

42. Gundry cites him, pointing out the difference between this ending and the one which Aristotle describes *(Mark, 1014)*.

43. *Jesus, the Messiah* (London: Hodder and Stoughton, 1943), 94.

44. *In Memory of Her* (New York: Crossroad, 1984), 322.

45. "The Promise and the Failure: Mark 16:7, 8," *JBL* 108 (1979): 285–87.

46. "Discipleship in the New Testament," Papers at Marquette University Symposium, edited by Fernando F. Segovia (Philadelphia: Fortress Press, 1985), 31–40.

47. *The Genesis of Secrecy: On the Interpretation of Narrative* (Cambridge: Harvard University Press, 1979), 68.

48. *A Master of Surprise* (Minneapolis: Fortress Press, 1994), 112–116. Juel even praises one of his students who confessed that the ending left her in tears (112).

49. For a survey of these comments, see P. L. Danove, *The End of Mark's Story: A Methodological Study* (Leiden: Brill, 1993).

50. *Saint Mark*, 385.

51. *Saint Mark*, 387.

52. *Mark*, 1013.

53. See Taylor, *Mark*, 609. This is the translation given by the NRSV and also by many commentaries—e.g., that of Nineham. Hooker, however, tranlates it "terrified"—consistent with her thesis that Mark is stressing "terror." These facts simply confirm the vicious circularity of interpretation and translation.

54. Gerard Sloyan observes the same connection between the word applied to the disciples in the transfiguration scene and to the women here. See his commentary *The Gospel of Saint Mark* (Collegeville, Minn.: Liturgical Press, 1960), 120. Most translations, however—e.g., the NRSV and the King James—translate *ephobounto* in Mark 9 as "exceedingly afraid" or "terrified," leaving the impression of fearfulness. But the phrase follows on Peter proclaiming "it is good for us to be here" (9:6), which expresses a feeling of well-being. Peter's simultaneous desire to put up three "booths" or tents—as in the Feast of Booths—suggests that he is in a state of gladness and gratitude.

55. For those who are still unpersuaded, it is worth noting that when Mark wants to express the idea of being frightened or scared (rather than awed) he uses an entirely different word; when the disciples think they have seen a ghost, Mark indicates their fear through a form of the verb *tarassō* (6:50).

56. Allison notes the same tendency in the reading of Matthew: "The concerns of Paul and John are unconsciously read into Matthew." *The New Moses* (Minneapolis: Fortress Press, 1993), 275.

57. Brown takes up the theological consequences of positing Mark as dependent on Matthew and Luke and in the process suggests the richness of granting each evangelist his own voice. (*Introduction to the New Testament*, 164–66.)

58. It is interesting to note that here is another place where a form of the verb *ephobounto* is used, together with an adverb, *ophodra*, which means "exceedingly." Here, however, commentators do not speak of "the centurion and those with him" as being scared to death but rather as being "filled with awe."

59. A similiar suggestion is made by Brown in respect to John's description of the tomb: "She saw two angels in white, sitting where the body of Jesus had lain, one at the head and one at the feet" (20:12). Admittedly that description is more graphically precise than the one in Luke, but I think that given Luke's liturgical context, it has a similar effect.

60. It is worth noting that Luke's words to express "fright," as at a ghost, are very different from Mark's words to express "fear," as in reverence. Luke uses two words that do not appear in Mark: *emphobos*, which means "full of fear," and *ptseō*, which means "to be "terrified." The difference in words underscores the difference in meanings: Luke is describing those who think they have seen a ghost—they are appropriately *scared*; Mark is describing women who have unexpectedly been given a new vision—they are appropriately *filled with awe*.

61. For a brilliant exposition of the use of Philo's Creation theology in John, see Calum Carmichael, *The Story of Creation: Its Origin and Its Interpretation in Philo and the Fourth Gospel* (Ithaca, N.Y.: Cornell University Press, 1996).

Bibliography

Achtemeier, Paul J. *Mark*. Philadelphia: Fortress Press, 1986.

Agus, Aharon. *The Binding of Isaac and Messiah: Law, Martyrdom and Deliverance in Early Rabbinic Religiosity*. Albany: SUNY Press, 1988.

Aland, Kurt, ed. *Synopsis of the Four Gospels*. 8th ed. Stuttgart: German Bible Society, 1987.

Albeck, C. *Einleitung und Register zum Bereshiyt Rabba*. 2 vols. 2nd ed. Jerusalem: Wahrmann Books, 1965.

Alexander, Philip S. "Pre-Emptive Exegesis: Genesis Rabba's Reading of the Story of Creation." *Journal of Jewish Studies* 43, 2 (autumn 1992): 230–45.

Allison, Dale C., Jr. *The New Moses: A Matthean Typology*. Minneapolis: Fortress Press, 1993.

Alter, Robert. *The Art of Biblical Narrative*. New York: Basic Books, 1981.

———. *The Art of Biblical Poetry*. New York: Basic Books, 1985.

———. *Genesis: Translation and Commentary*. New York: Norton, 1996.

———. *The World of Biblical Literature*. New York: Basic Books, 1962.

Alter, Robert, and Frank Kermode, eds. *The Literary Guide to the Bible*. Cambridge: Harvard University Press, 1987.

Anderson, Hugh. "A Future for Apocalyptic?" In *Biblical Studies in Honour of William Barclay*, edited by Johnston R. McKay and James F. Miller. London: Collins, 1976, 56–72.

Anderson, Janice Capel, and Stephen D. Moore, eds. *Mark and Method: New Approaches in Biblical Studies,* Minneapolis: Fortress Press, 1992.

Barr, James. *Fundamentalism*. London: SCM Press, 1981.

———. *Holy Scripture: Canon, Authority, Criticism*. Oxford: Oxford University Press, 1983.

Barth, Karl. *Church Dogmatics: The Doctrine of the Word of God.* Vol. 1, pt. 2. Edinburgh: T. and T. Clark, 1956.

Bauer, Walter, ed. *A Greek-English Lexicon of the New Testament.* Chicago: University of Chicago Press, 1958.

Beasley-Murray, G. R. *A Commentary on Mark Thirteen.* London: Macmillan, 1957.

———. *Jesus and the Last Days: The Interpretation of the Olivet Discourse.* Peabody, Mass.: Hendrikson, 1993.

———. "Second Thoughts on the Composition of Mark 13." *NTS* 29 (1983): 414–20.

Beavis, Mary Ann. *Mark's Audience: The Literary and Social Setting of Mark 4:11–12.* Sheffield, England: JSOT, 1989.

Berger, Peter L. *The Sacred Canopy.* Garden City, N.Y.: Doubleday, 1969.

Best, E. *Following Jesus: Discipleship in the Gospel of Mark.* Sheffield, England: Sheffield Academic Press, 1981.

Black, Matthew. *An Aramaic Approach to the Gospels and Acts.* 3rd ed. Oxford: Oxford University Press, 1967.

Boomershine, T. E., "The Narrative Technique of Mark 16:8," in *Journal of Biblical Literature* 100, 2 (1981): 213–23.

Borsch, F. H. "Further Reflections on 'The Son of Man.'" In *The Messiah,* edited by James H. Charlesworth, J. Brownson, M. T. Davis, S. J. Kraftchick, and A. Segal. Minneapolis: Augsburg, 1992, 130–44.

Bourke, Joseph. "The Historical Jesus and the Kerygmatic Christ." In *Who Is Jesus of Nazareth?* edited by E. Schillebeeckx and B. Wilhelms. New York: Paulist Press, 1965, 27–46.

Bowker, John. *The Targums and Rabbinic Literature.* Cambridge, England: Cambridge University Press, 1969.

Bowman, John. *The Gospel of Mark: The New Christian Jewish Passover Haggadah.* Leiden: Brill, 1965.

Boyarin, Daniel. *Intertextuality and the Reading of Midrash.* Bloomington: University of Indiana Press, 1990.

———. "The Song of Songs: Lock or Key?" In *The Book and the Text,* edited by Regina Schwartz. Oxford: Blackwell, 1990, 214–230.

Braude, William G. (Gershon Zev), trans. and ed. *Midrash on the Psalms.* New Haven: Yale University Press, 1959.

———, trans. *Pesiqta Rabbati.* New Haven: Yale University Press, 1968.

Brooks, Roger, and John J. Collins, eds. *Hebrew Bible or Old Testament?* South Bend, Ind.: Notre Dame University Press, 1990.

Brooten, Bernadette. *Women Leaders in the Ancient Synagogue.* Chico, Calif.: Scholars Press, 1982.

Brown, Raymond. *The Birth of the Messiah.* Garden City, N.Y.: Doubleday, 1977.

———. *The Churches the Apostles Left Behind.* Mahwah, N.J.: Paulist Press, 1984.

———. *The Death of the Messiah.* 2 vols. Garden City, N.Y.: Doubleday, 1994.

———. *The Gospel According to John.* 2 vols. Garden City, N.Y.: Doubleday, 1970.

———. *Introduction to the New Testament.* New York: Doubleday, 1997.

———. *The Semitic Background of the Term "Mystery" in the New Testament.* Philadelphia: Fortress Press, 1968.

Brueggemann, Walter. "The Loss and Recovery of Creation in Old Testament Theology." *Theology Today* 53 (July 1996): 177–90.

————. *The Message of the Psalms: A Theological Commentary.* Minneapolis: Augsburg, 1984.

————. *Theology of the Old Testament.* Minneapolis: Augsburg Fortress Press, 1997.

Bruns, Gerald L. "The Hermeneutics of Midrash." In *The Book and the Text,* edited by Regina Schwartz. Oxford: Blackwell, 1990, 189–213.

————. "Midrash and Allegory." In *The Literary Guide to the Bible,* edited by Robert Alter and Frank Kermode. Cambridge: Harvard University Press, 1987, 625–46.

Bultmann, Rudolf. *The History of the Synoptic Tradition.* Translated by John Marsh. New York: Harper and Row, 1963.

————. *Jesus and the Word.* New York: Scribners, 1934.

————. *Theology of the New Testament.* New York: Scribners, 1951.

Burridge, Richard A. *What Are the Gospels? A Comparison With Graeco-Roman Biography.* Cambridge, England: Cambridge University Press, 1992.

Burtchaell, James. *From Synagogue to Church.* Cambridge, England: Cambridge University Press, 1992.

Bryan, Christopher. *A Preface to Mark.* New York: Oxford University Press, 1993.

Caird, G. B. "Eschatology and Politics." In *Biblical Studies in Honour of William Barclay.* London: Collins, 1976, 72–86.

————. *The Language and Imagery of the Bible.* Grand Rapids, Mich.: Eerdmans, 1980.

Carmichael, Calum. *The Story of Creation: Its Origin and Its Interpretation in Philo and the Fourth Gospel.* Ithaca, N.Y.: Cornell University Press, 1996.

Carrington, Philip. *The Primitive Christian Calendar: A Study in the Making of the Marcan Gospel.* Cambridge, England: Cambridge University Press, 1952.

Carson, D. A., and H. G. M. Williamson, eds. *It Is Written: Scripture Citing Scripture. Essays in Honour of Barnabas Lindars.* Cambridge, England: Cambridge University Press, 1988.

Charlesworth, James H., ed. *Jesus' Jewishness: Exploring the Place of Jesus in Early Judaism.* New York: Crossroad, 1991.

————. *Jesus Within Judaism: New Light From Exciting Archaeological Discoveries.* New York: Doubleday, 1988.

————. *The Old Testament Pseudepigrapha.* 2 vols. Garden City, N.Y.: Doubleday, 1983, 1985.

Charlesworth, James H., James Brownson, M. T. Davis, Steven J. Kraftchick, and Alan Segal, eds. *The Messiah: Developments in Earliest Judaism and Christianity.* The First Princeton Symposium on Judaism and Christian Origins. Minneapolis: Fortress Press, 1992.

Childs, Brevard. *Introduction to the New Testament as Canon.* Philadelphia: Fortress Press, 1985.

————. *Introduction to the Old Testament as Scripture.* Philadelphia: Fortress Press, 1979.

Chilton, Bruce D. *A Galilean Rabbi and His Bible: Jesus' Use of the Interpreted Scripture of His Time.* Wilmington, Del.: Michael Glazier, 1984.

————, trans. and ed. *The Isaiah Targum.* Wilmington, Del.: Michael Glazier, 1987.

Chilton, Bruce D., and Jacob Neusner. *God in the World* (Harrisburg, Pa.: Trinity Press International, 1997.

———, *Judaism in the New Testament: Practices and Beliefs*. New York: Routledge, 1995.

———. *Revelation: The Torah and the Bible* (Valley Forge, Pa.: Trinity Press International, 1995.

Cohen, Shaye. *From the Maccabees to the Mishnah*. Philadelphia: Westminster Press, 1989.

———. "Were Pharisees and Rabbis the Leaders of Communal Prayer and Torah Study in Antiquity? The Evidence of the New Testament, Josephus, and the Early Church Fathers." In *Evolution of the Synagogue*, edited by Howard Clark Kee and Lynn H. Conick. Harrisburg, Pa.: Trinity Press International, 1999, 89–105.

———. "Women in the Synagogues of Antiquity." *Conservative Judaism* 34, 2 (1980): 23–29.

Colani, Timothée. *Jesus-Christ et les croyances messianiques de son temps*. Strasbourg: Treuttel and Wertz, 1964.

Collins, John J. *The Apocalyptic Imagination: An Introduction to the Jewish Matrix of Christianity*. New York: Crossroad, 1984.

———. "Messianism in the Maccabean Period." In *Judaisms and Their Messiahs at the Turn of the Christian Era*, edited by Jacob Neusner, William Scott Green, and Ernest S. Frerichs. Cambridge, England: Cambridge University Press, 1987, 97–109.

Crossan, Dominic. *In Parables: The Challenge of the Historical Jesus*. New York: Harper and Row, 1973.

———. *Who Killed Jesus?* San Francisco: Harper and Row, 1995.

Cullmann, Oscar. "The Return of Christ." In *Studies in Early Christian History and Theology*, edited by A. J. B. Higgins. Philadelphia: Westminster Press, 1956.

Daly, Robert J. "The Soteriological Significance of the Sacrifice of Isaac." *CBQ* 39, 1 (1977): 45–75.

Daube, David. *The New Testament and Rabbinic Judaism*. London: University of London Press, 1956. Reprint, Peabody, Mass: Hendrickson, 1994.

Davies, W. D. *Christian Engagements With Judaism*. Harrisburg, Pa.: Trinity Press International, 1999.

———. *Christian Origins and Judaism*. Philadelphia: Westminster Press, 1962.

———. *The Setting for the Sermon on the Mount*. Cambridge, England: Cambridge University Press, 1963.

Davis, Ellen. "Job and Jacob: The Integrity of Faith." In *Reading Between the Texts: Intertextuality and the Hebrew Bible*, edited by Danna Nolan Fewell. Louisville, Ky.: Westminster Press, 1992, 203–24.

———. *Swallowing the Scroll*. Sheffield, England: Sheffield Academic Press, 1989.

Davis, Philip G. "Mark's Christological Paradox." *JSNT* 35 (1989): 3–18.

De Jonge, Marinus. *Jesus, the Servant-Messiah*. New Haven: Yale University Press, 1991.

Derrett, J. Duncan M. "Figtrees in the New Testament." *Heythrop Journal* 14, 3 (1973): 249–65.

———. "Judaica in St. Mark." In *Studies in the New Testament*. Vol. 1. Leiden: Brill, 1977, 85–101.

———. *The Making of Mark: The Scriptural Bases of the Earliest Gospel*. 2 vols. Shipston-on-Stour: Drinkwater, 1985.

Deutsch, Celia. *Lady Wisdom, Jesus, and the Sages.* Valley Forge, Pa: Trinity Press International, 1996.

Dewey, Joanna. *Markan Public Debate.* Chico, Calif.: Scholars Press, 1980.

Dodd, C. H. *The Parables of the Kingdom.* London: Nisbet Press, 1935.

Donahue, John. *The Gospel in Parable.* Philadelphia: Fortress Press, 1988.

Drury, John. "Mark." In *The Literary Guide to the Bible,* edited by Robert Alter and Frank Kermode. Cambridge: Harvard University Press, 1987, 402–17.

———. "Mark 1:1–15. An Interpretation." In *AANT,* edited by A. E. Harvey. London: SPCK, 1985, 25–37.

———. "Understanding the Bread: Disruption and Aggregation, Secrecy and Revelation in Mark's Gospel." In *Not in Heaven: Coherence and Complexity in Biblical Narrative,* edited by Jason P. Rosenblatt and Joseph C. Sitteron, Jr. Bloomington: University of Indiana Press, 1991, 98–119.

Dunn, James D. G. *Jesus, Paul, and the Law: Studies in Mark and Galatians.* Louisville, Ky.: Westminster Press, 1990.

———. *The Partings of the Ways Between Christianity and Judaism and Their Significance for the Character of Christianity.* Philadelphia: Trinity Press International, 1991.

———. *Unity and Diversity in the New Testament.* Philadelphia: Westminster Press, 1977.

Eagleton, Terry. *Literary Theory: An Introduction.* Minneapolis: University of Minnesota Press, 1983.

Eisenbaum, Pamela. *The Jewish Heroes of Christian History: Hebrews 11 in Literary Context.* Atlanta: Scholars Press, 1998.

Ellis, Earle E. *The Old Testament in Early Christianity: Canon and Interpretation in the Light of Modern Research.* Tubingen: J. C. B. Mohr, 1991.

Farmer, William R. *The Last Twelve Verses of Mark.* Cambridge, England: Cambridge University Press, 1974.

Fewell, Danna Nolan, ed. *Reading Between the Texts: Intertextuality and the Hebrew Bible.* Louisville, Ky.: Westminster Press, 1992.

Fishbane, Michael. *Biblical Interpretation in Ancient Israel.* Oxford: Oxford University Press, 1985.

———. *The Garments of Torah: Essays in Biblical Hermeneutics.* Bloomington: University of Indiana Press, 1989.

———. "Inner-Biblical Exegesis." In *Midrash and Literature,* edited by Geoffrey Hartman and Sanford Budick. New Haven: Yale University Press, 1986, 19–37.

———. *The Midrashic Imagination: Jewish Exegesis, Thought, and History.* Albany: SUNY Press, 1993.

———. *Text and Texture.* New York: Schocken Books, 1979.

Ford, J. M., ed. *The Book of Revelation.* Anchor Bible Commentary. Garden City, N.Y.: Doubleday, 1975.

Fowler, R. M. *Let the Reader Understand: Reader-Response Criticism and the Gospel of Mark,* Minneapolis: Fortress Press, 1991.

Frei, H. W. *The Eclipse of Biblical Narrative: A Study in Eighteenth and Nineteenth Century Hermeneutics.* New Haven: Yale University Press, 1974.

Froelich, Karlfried. *Biblical Interpretation in the Early Church.* Philadelphia: Fortress Press, 1984.

Garrett, Susan R. *The Temptations of Jesus in Mark's Gospel.* Grand Rapids, Mich.: Eerdmanns, 1998.

Gaston, Lloyd. *No Stone on Another: Studies in the Significance of the Fall of Jerusalem in the Synoptic Gospels.* Leiden: Brill, 1970.

Gerhardsson, Birger. *Memory and Manuscript: Oral Tradition and Written Transmission in Rabbinic Judaism and Early Christianity.* Uppsala: C. W. K. Gleerup-Lund, 1961.

———. *The Testing of God's Son.* Uppsala: C. W. K. Gleerup-Lund, 1966.

Goldberg, A. "Form Analysis of Midrashic Literature as a Method of Description." *Journal of Jewish Studies,* 36, 2 (1985): 159–74.

Goldin, Judah. "Of Midrash and the Messianic Theme." In *Studies in Midrash and Related Literature,* edited by B. L. Eichler and J. H. Tigay. New York: Jewish Publication Society, 1988, 359–79.

Goldingay, John. *Models for Scripture.* Grand Rapids, Mich.: Eerdmans, 1994.

Goulder, Michael D. "Exegesis of Gen. 1–3 in the NT." *Journal of Jewish Studies,* 43, 2 (1992), 226–29.

———. *Midrash and Lection in Matthew.* London: SPCK, 1974.

Grant, Robert M., and David Tracy. *A Short History of the Interpretation of the Bible.* 2nd ed. Minneapolis: Fortress Press, 1984.

Green, Garrett. *Imagining God.* San Francisco: Harper and Row, 1989.

Green, William Scott. "Introduction: Messiah in Judaism, Rethinking the Question." In *Judaisms and Their Messiahs at the Turn of the Century,* edited by Jacob Neusner, W. S. Green, and Ernest S. Frerichs. Cambridge: Cambridge University Press, 1987, 1–14.

Guelich, Robert A. "The Beginning of the Gospel: Mark 1:1–15." *Biblical Research* 27 (1982): 5–15.

———. "Mark 4." *Word Biblical Commentary* 34 (1989): 247–52.

Gundry, Robert H. *Mark: A Commentary on His Apology for the Cross.* Grand Rapids, Mich.: Eerdmans, 1993.

Handelman, Susan. *The Slayers of Moses.* New York: SUNY Press, 1982.

Hanson, Paul. *The Dawn of Apocalyptic.* Philadelphia: Fortress Press, 1979.

Hartman, Geoffrey, and Sanford Budick, eds. *Midrash and Literature.* New Haven: Yale University Press, 1991.

Hartman, Lars. *Prophecy Interpreted.* Uppsala: Almqvist and Wiksalls, 1966.

Hays, Richard B. *Echoes of Scripture in the Letters of Paul.* New Haven: Yale University Press, 1989.

Heinemann, Joseph. "Profile of a Midrash." *Journal of the American Academy of Religion* 39 (1971): 142–50.

———. "The Triennial Lectionary Cycle." *Journal for Jewish Studies,,* 19 (1968): 41–48.

Hellholm, David, ed. *Apocalypticism in the Mediterranean World and the Near East.* Tubingen: J. C. B. Mohr, 1983.

Hellwig, Monika. "From Christ to God: The Christian Perspective." In *Jews and Christians Speak of Jesus,* edited by Arthur E. Zannoni. Minneapolis: Fortress Press, 1994, 137–48.

———. *Jesus the Compassion of God: New Perspectives on the Tradition of Christianity.* Collegeville, Minn.: Liturgical Press, 1983.

Hengel, Martin. *Judaism and Hellenism: Studies in their Encounter in Palestine During the Early Hellenistic Period.* 2 vols. Translated by John Bowden. Philadelphia: Fortress Press, 1974.

———. *Studies in the Gospel of Mark.* Translated by John Bowden. Philadelphia: Fortress Press, 1985.

Hertz, Joseph H., ed. *The Authorized Daily Prayer Book* (*The Siddur*). New York: Bloch, 1974 [1948].

Hiers, Richard H. "Not the Season for Figs." *Journal of Biblical Literature*, 87 (1968): 394–400.

Himmelfarb, Martha. *Ascent to Heaven in Jewish and Christian Apocalypses*. New York: Oxford University Press, 1993.

Hoffman, Lawrence. "A Symbol of Salvation in the Passover Haggadah." *Worship* 53, 6 (1979): 519–37.

Holtz, Barry W. *Back to the Sources: Reading the Classic Jewish Texts*. New York: Summit Books, 1984.

Hooker, Morna D. *The Gospel According to Saint Mark*. Black's New Testament Commentaries 2. Peabody, Mass.: Hendrickson, 1991.

———. "Mark." In *It Is Written: Scripture Citing Scripture. Essays in Honour of Barnabas Lindars*, edited by D. A. Carson and H. G. M. Williamson. Cambridge, England: Cambridge University Press, 1988, 220–30.

Horsley, R. A., and J. S. Hanson. *Bandits, Prophets and Messiahs: Popular Movements at the Time of Jesus*. San Francisco: Harper and Row, 1985.

Hurtado, Larry W. *Mark*. New International Biblical Commentary. Peabody, Mass.: Hendrikson, 1989.

Isaac, E., ed. "1 Enoch." In *The Old Testament Pseudepigrapha*, edited by James Charlesworth. Vol. 1. Garden City, N.Y.: Doubleday, 1983, 5–89.

Jensen, Anne. *God's Self-Confident Daughters: Early Christianity and the Liberation of Women*. Translated by O. C. Dean, Jr. Louisiville, Ky.: Westminster Press, 1996.

Jeremias, J. *The Parables of Jesus*. New York: Scribner's, 1963.

———. *Rediscovering the Parables*. New York: Scribner's, 1966.

Johnson, Elizabeth A. *She Who Is*. New York: Crossroad, 1998.

Johnson, Paul. *History of the Jews*. New York: Harper and Row, 1987.

Juel, Donald. *A Master of Surprise: Mark Interpreted*. Minneapolis: Fortress Press, 1994.

———. *Messiah and Temple: The Trial of Jesus in the Gospel of Mark*. Missoula, Mont.: Scholars Press, 1977.

Kahler, Martin. *The So-Called Historical Jesus and the Historical Biblical Christ*, translated and edited by Carl E. Braaten. Philadelphia: Fortress Press, 1988.

Kasemann, E. "The Beginning of Christian Theology." *Journal of Theology and Church* 6 (1969): 17–46.

Kee, Howard Clark. "Christology in Mark's Gospel." In *Judaisms and Their Messiahs at the Turn of the Christian Era*, edited by Jacob Neusner, William Scott Green, and Ernest S. Frerichs. Cambridge, England: Cambridge University Press, 1987, 187–208.

———, *Community of the New Age: Studies in Mark's Gospel*. Philadelphia: Westminster Press, 1977.

———, ed. *The Bible in the Twenty-First Century*. Philadelphia: Trinity Press International, 1993.

———, and Lynn H. Cohick, eds. *Evolution of the Synagogue*. Harrisburg, Pa.: Trinity Press International, 1999.

Kelber, W. H. "Apostolic Tradition and the Form of the Gospel." In *Discipleship in the New Testament*, edited by F. Segovia. Philadelphia: Fortress Press, 1985, 24–46.

————. "Discipleship in the New Testament." Papers given at Marquette University Symposium, edited by Fernando F. Segovia. Philadelphia: Fortress Press, 1994, 31–40.

————. *Mark's Story of Jesus*. Philadelphia: Fortress Press, 1979.

————. *The Oral and Written Gospel: The Hermeneutics of Speaking and Writing in the Synoptic Tradition, Mark, Paul, and Q*. Philadelphia: Fortress Press, 1983.

Kelsey, David H. *The Uses of Scripture in Recent Theology*. Philadelphia: Fortress Press, 1975.

Kermode, Frank. *The Genesis of Secrecy: On the Interpretation of Narrative*. Cambridge: Harvard University Press, 1979.

Kingsbury, J. D. *The Christology of Mark's Gospel*. Philadelphia: Fortress Press, 1983.

————. *Jesus Christ in Matthew, Mark, and Luke*. Philadelphia: Fortress Press, 1981.

Klausner, Joseph. *The Messianic Idea in Israel: From Its Beginning to the Completion of the Mishnah*. New York: Macmillan, 1953.

Kraemer, Ross. *Her Share of the Blessings: Women's Religions Among Pagans, Jews, and Christians in the Greco-Roman World*. New York: Oxford University Press, 1992.

Kugel, James. *The Bible As It Was*. Cambridge: Harvard University Press, 1997.

————. "Two Introductions to Midrash." In *Midrash and Literature*, edited by Geoffrey Hartman and Sanford Budick. New Haven: Yale University Press, 1991, 77–103.

————, and R. A. Greer, eds. *Early Biblical Interpretation*. Philadelphia: Westminster Press, 1986.

Kung, Hans. *Signposts for the Future*. Garden City, N.Y.: Doubleday, 1978.

Lane, W. L. *The Gospel of Mark*. Grand Rapids, Mich.: Eerdmans, 1974.

Lapide, Pinchas. *The Resurrection of Jesus: A Jewish Perspective*. Translated by Wilhelm C. Linss. Minneapolis: Augsburg, 1983.

Laws, Sophie. *In the Light of the Lamb: Imagery, Parody, and Theology in the Apocalypse of John*. Wilmington, Del.: Michael Glazier, 1988.

Le Deaut, Roger. "Paque Juive et Nouveau Testament." In *Studies on the Background of the New Testament*. Assen: Van Gorcum, 1969, 22–24.

Lee, Bernard. *The Galilean Jewishness of Jesus*. Mahwah, N.J.: Paulist Press, 1988.

————. *Jesus and the Metaphors for God: The Christs of the New Testament*. Mahwah, N.J.: Paulist Press, 1993.

Levenson, Jon D. *Creation and the Persistence of Evil*. Princeton: Princeton University Press, 1994.

————. *The Death and Resurrection of the Beloved Son*. New Haven: Yale University Press, 1993.

————. *The Hebrew Bible, the Old Testament, and Historical Criticism*. Louisville, Ky.: Westminster Press, 1993.

Lightfoot, R. H. *The Gospel Message of St. Mark*. Oxford: Clarendon, 1950.

————. *Locality and Doctrine in the Gospels*. New York: Harper and Brothers, 1938.

Lincoln, A. "The Promise and the Failure: Mark 16:7, 8." *Journal of Biblical Literature* 108, 2 (1989): 283–300.

Luhrmann, D. "Markus 14, 55–64: Christologie und Zerstorung des Tempels im Markusevangelium." *NTS* 27 (1980–81): 459–60.

Mack, Burton. *A Myth of Innocence: Mark and Christian Origins*. Philadelphia: Fortress Press, 1988.

——. *Wisdom and the Hebrew Epic*. Chicago: University of Chicago Press, 1985.

——. "Wisdom Makes a Difference." In *Judaisms and their Messiahs at the Turn of the Christian Era*, edited by Jacob Neusner, W. S. Green, and E. S. Frerichs. Cambridge, England: Cambridge University Press, 1987, 15–48.

Magness, J. Lee. *Sense and Absence: Structure and Suspension in the Ending of Mark's Gospel*. Atlanta: Scholars Press, 1986.

Mann, C. S. *Mark: Translation and Commentary*. Anchor Bible. Vol. 27. Garden City, N.Y.: Doubleday, 1986.

Mann, Jacob. *The Bible as Read and Preached in the Old Synagogue: A Study in the Cycles of the Readings From Torah and Prophets, as Well as From Psalms, and in the Structure of the Midrashic Homilies*. New York: Ktav, 1971.

Manson, T. W. *Jesus the Messiah*. London: Hodder and Stoughton, 1943.

Marcus, Joel. *The Mystery of the Kingdom of God*. Atlanta: Scholars Press, 1986.

——. *The Way of the Lord: Christological Exegesis of the Old Testament in the Gospel of Mark*. Louisville, Ky.: Westminster Press, 1992.

Matera, Frank J. "The Incomprehension of the Disciples and Peter's Confession (Mark 6:14 and 8:30)." *Biblica* 70 (1989): 153–72.

McDonald, Lee Martin. *The Formation of the Christian Biblical Canon*. Nashville, Tenn.: Abingdon Press, 1988.

McKim, Donald K., ed. *A Guide to Contemporary Hermeneutics: Major Trends in Biblical Interpretation*. Grand Rapids, Mich.: Eerdmans, 1986.

McNamara, Martin. *Targum and Testament. Aramaic Paraphrases of the Hebrew Bible: A Light on the New Testament*. Grand Rapids, Mich.: Eerdmans, 1972.

Meagher, J. C. *Clumsy Construction in Mark's Gospel*. New York: Edwin Mellon Press, 1979.

Meeks, Wayne A. *The First Urban Christians*. New Haven: Yale University Press, 1983.

Meier, John. *A Marginal Jew: Rethinking the Historical Jesus*. New York: Doubleday, 1991.

Metzger, Bruce. *The Canon of the New Testament*. New York: Oxford University Press, 1987.

Michaels, J. Ramsey. *Interpreting the Book of Revelation*. Grand Rapids, Mich.: Baker Book House, 1992.

Milavec, Aaron A. "Mark's Parable of the Wicked Husbandmen as Reaffirming God's Predilection for Israel," *Journal of Ecumenical Studies* 26, 2 (Spring, 1989): 295–311.

Millar, Alan, and John Riches. "Conceptual Change in the Synoptic Tradition." In *AANT*, edited by A. E. Harvey. London: SPCK, 1985, 37–61.

Miller, D., and P. Miller. *The Gospel of Mark as Midrash on Earlier Jewish and New Testament Literature*. Lewiston, N.Y.: Edwin Mellon Press, 1990.

Miller, Merrill P. "Targum, Midrash, and the Use of the Old Testament in the New Testament." *Journal for the Study of Judaism* 2 (1971): 29–82.

Montefiore, C. G., and H. Loewe, eds. *A Rabbinic Anthology*. New York: Schocken Books, 1974.

Morgan, Donn F. *Between Text and Community: The "Writings" in Canonical Interpretation*. Minneapolis: Augsburg Fortress Press, 1990.

Mowinckel, S. *He That Cometh*. Nashville, Tenn.: Abingdon Press, 1954.

Mullder, M. J., ed. *Mikra: Text, Translation, Reading and Interpretation of the Hebrew Bible in Ancient Judaism and Early Christianity.* Minneapolis: Fortress Press, 1988.

Myers, Allen C., ed. *The Eerdman's Bible Dictionary.* Grand Rapids, Mich.: Eerdmans, 1987.

Neusner, Jacob. *Judaism in the Beginning of Christianity.* Philadelphia: Fortress Press, 1984.

————. Preface to *Introduction to the Talmud and Midrash,* edited by H. L. Strack and G. Stemberger. Minneapolis: Fortress Press, 1992.

————, ed. *A Midrash Reader.* Minneapolis: Fortress Press, 1990.

Neusner, Jacob, and Bruce Chilton. *God in the World.* Harrisburg, Pa.: Trinity Press International, 1997.

————. *Judaism in the New Testament.* New York: Routledge, 1995.

————. *Revelation: The Torah and the Bible.* Valley Forge, Pa.: Trinity Press International, 1995.

Neusner, Jacob, William Scott Green, and Ernest S. Frerichs, eds. *Judaisms and Their Messiahs at the Turn of the Christian Era.* Cambridge, England: Cambridge University Press, 1987.

Nicklesburg, George. "Salvation Without and With a Messiah: Developing Beliefs in Writings Ascribed to Enoch." In *Judaisms and their Messiahs at the Turn of the Christian Era,* edited by Jacob Neusner, William Scott Green, and Ernest S. Frerichs. Cambridge, England: Cambridge University Press, 1987, 49–68.

Nineham, D. E. *The Gospel of St. Mark.* New York: Penguin Books, Ltd., 1963.

Norris, Richard A., Jr. *The Christological Controversy.* Philadelphia: Fortress Press, 1980.

O'Connor, Kathleen. "Wisdom Literature and the Experience of the Divine." In *Biblical Theology: Problems and Perspectives,* edited by Steven J. Kraftchick, Charles D. Meyers, Jr., and Ben C. Ollenburger. Nashville, Tenn.: Abingdon Press, 1995, 183–95.

Oden, Thomas C., and Christopher A. Hall, eds. *Mark, II, Ancient Christian Commentary on Scripture.* Downers Grove, Ill.: InterVarsity Press, 1998.

Pagels, Elaine. *The Origin of Satan.* New York: Random House, 1995.

Patai, Raphael. *The Messiah Texts.* Detroit: Wayne State University Press, 1979.

Patte, Daniel. *Early Jewish Hermeneutic in Palestine.* Society of Biblical Literature Dissertation Series 22 (1975): 41–45.

Pelikan, Jaroslav. *Jesus Through the Centuries: His Place in the History of Culture.* New Haven: Yale University Press, 1985.

Perdue, Leo G., B. B. Scott, and W. J. Wiseman, eds. *In Search of Wisdom.* Louisville, Ky.: Westminster Press, 1993.

Perrin, Norman. "Eschatology and Hermeneutics: Reflections on Method in the Interpretation of the New Testament." In *JBL* 93 (1974): 3–14.

————. *Jesus and the Language of the Kingdom.* Philadelphia: Fortress Press, 1976.

Perrot, Charles. "The Reading of the Bible in the Ancient Synagogue." In *Mikra: Text, Translation, Reading and Interpretation of the Hebrew Bible in Ancient Judaism and Early Christianity,* edited by M. J. Mullder. Minneapolis: Fortress Press, 1998, 149–59.

Petuchowski, Jakob J. *Our Masters Taught: Rabbinic Sayings and Stories.* New York: Crossroad, 1982.

Petuchowski, Jakob J., and Michael Brocke. *The Lord's Prayer and Jewish Liturgy*. New York: Seabury Press, 1978.

Plaskow, Judith. "Anti-Judaism in Feminist Christian Interpretation." In *Searching the Scriptures*, edited by Elisabeth Schüssler Fiorenza. New York: Crossroad, 1993, 117–29.

———. *Standing Again at Sinai: Judaism From a Feminist Perspective*. San Francisco: Harper and Row, 1990.

Pontifical Biblical Commission. *The Interpretation of the Bible in the Church*. Rome: Librera Editrice Vatican, 1993.

Raisanen, Heikki. *The "Messianic Secret" in Mark*. Translated by Christopher Tuckett. Edinburgh: T. and T. Clark, 1990.

Rendtorff, Rolf. "Old Testament Theology, Tanankh Theology, or Biblical Theology? Reflections in an Ecumenical Context." *Biblica* 73, 3 (1992): 441–51.

Rhoads, D., and D. Michie. *Mark as Story: An Introduction to the Narrative of a Gospel*. Philadelphia: Fortress Press, 1982.

Ritschl, D. "A Plea for the Maxim: Scripture and Tradition." *Interpretation* 25 (1971): 126.

Rosenblatt, Jason P., and Joseph C. Sitteron, Jr., eds. *Not in Heaven: Coherence and Complexity in Biblical Narrative*. Bloomington: University of Indiana Press, 1991.

Roth, W. *Hebrew Gospel: Cracking the Code of Mark*. Oak Park, Ill.: Meyer-Stone Books, 1988.

Rowland, Christopher. *The Open Heaven: A Study of Apocalyptic in Judaism and Early Christianity*. London: SPCK, 1982.

Russell, D. S. *Apocalyptic: Ancient and Modern*. Philadelphia: Fortress Press, 1968.

Saldarini, Anthony. *Matthew's Christian-Jewish Community*. Chicago: University of Chicago Press, 1994.

Sanders, E. P. *Jesus and Judaism*. Philadelphia: Fortress Press, 1985.

Sanders, James. *Canon and Community*. Philadelphia: Fortress Press, 1984.

———. *From Sacred Story to Sacred Text*. Philadelphia: Fortress Press, 1987.

Schmithals, W. *Das Evangelium nach Markus*. Gutersloher: Verlaghous Mohn, 1979.

Schnackenburg, R. *The Gospel According to St. Mark*, translated from the German by Werner Krupps. London: Sheed and Ward, 1971.

Schüssler Fiorenza, Elisabeth. *Discipleship of Equals*. New York: Crossroad, 1993.

———. *In Memory of Her*. New York: Crossroad, 1984.

———. *Invitation to the Book of Revelation*. Garden City, N.Y.: Doubleday, 1966.

———. *Jesus, Miriam's Child, Sophia's Prophet*. New York: Continuum, 1994.

———. "The Phenomenon of Early Christian Apocalypse. Some Reflections on Method." In *Apocalypticism in the Mediterranean World and the Near East*, edited by David Hellholm. Tubingen: J. C. B. Mohr, 1983, 295–316.

———, ed. *Searching the Scriptures*. New York: Crossroad, 1993.

Schwartz, Regina, ed. *The Book and the Text*. Oxford: Blackwell, 1990.

Schweitzer, Albert. *The Quest for the Historical Jesus*, translated from the German by W. Montgomery. New York: Macmillan, 1950.

Schweizer, Eduard. *The Good News According to Mark*, translated from the German by Donald H. Madvig. Richmond, Va.: John Knox Press, 1970.

Segal, Alan. *Rebecca's Children: Judaism and Christianity in a Roman World.* Cambridge: Harvard University Press, 1986.

———. *Two Powers in Heaven: Early Rabbinic Reports About Christianity and Gnosticism.* Leiden: Brill, 1977.

Senior, Donald. *The Passion of Jesus in the Gospel of Mark.* Wilmington, Del.: Michael Glazier, 1984.

Sloyan, Gerard. *The Gospel of Saint Mark.* New Testament Reading Guide. Collegeville, Minn.: Liturgical Press, 1960.

Sneen, Donald. *Visions of Hope: Apocalyptic Themes From Biblical Times.* Minneapolis: Augsburg, 1978.

Stegner, William. *Narrative Theology in Early Christianity.* Louisville, Ky.: Westminster Press, 1989.

Stendahl, Krister. *The School of St. Matthew.* Philadelphia: Fortress Press, 1968.

Stern, David. "Midrash and the Language of Exegesis: A Study of Vayikra Rabbah, Chapter 1." In *Midrash and Literature,* edited by Geoffrey Hartman and Sanford Budick. New Haven: Yale University Press, 1986, 105–24.

———. *Parables in Midrash: Narrative and Exegesis in Rabbinic Literature.* Cambridge: Harvard Univerity Press, 1991.

———. "Rhetoric and Midrash: The Case of the Mashal." *Prooftexts* 1 (1981): 261–91.

Stone, Michael. "The Question of the Messiah in 4 Ezra." In *Judaisms and Their Messiahs at the Turn of the Christian Era,* edited by Jacob Neusner, William Scott Green, and Ernest S. Frerichs. Cambridge, England: Cambridge University Press, 1987, 209–24.

Strack, H. L., and G. Stemberger, eds. *Introduction to the Talmud and Midrash.* Minneapolis: Fortress Press, 1992.

Strauss, D. F. *The Life of Jesus Critically Examined,* translated from the German by George Eliot and edited by Peter C. Hodgson. Philadelphia: Fortress Press, 1972.

Talmon, Shemaryahu. "Waiting for the Messiah: The Spiritual Universe of the Qumran Covenanters." In *Judaisms and Their Messiahs at the Turn of the Christian Era,* edited by Jacob Neusner, William Scott Green, and Ernest S. Frerichs. Cambridge, England: Cambridge University Press, 1987, 111–37.

Taylor, Vincent. *The Gospel According to St. Mark.* London: Macmillan, 1963.

Telford, W. R. *The Barren Temple and the Withered Tree.* Sheffield, England: Sheffield Academic Press, 1980.

———. *The Theology of the Gospel of Mark.* Cambridge, England: Cambridge University Press, 1999.

Throckmorton, Burton H., Jr., ed. *Gospel Parallels: A Synopsis of the First Three Gospels.* New York: Thomas Nelson, 1979.

Tolbert, Mary Ann. *Sowing the Gospel: Mark's World in Literary-Historical Perspective.* Minneapolis: Fortress Press, 1989.

Torrey, C. C. *Documents of the Primitive Church.* New York: Harper, 1941.

Townsend, John T. "The Tradition Behind Mark's Narrative." Society of Biblical Literature Seminar Paper, 1989.

Tracy, David. *Plurality and Ambiguity: Hermeneutics, Religion, Hope.* San Francisco: Harper and Row, 1987.

———, and Robert M. Grant. *A Short History of the Interpretation of the Bible.* 2nd ed. Minneapolis: Fortress Press, 1984.

Trible, Phyllis. *God and the Rhetoric of Sexuality.* Philadelphia: Fortress Press, 1978.

———. "Genesis 22: The Sacrifice of Sarah." In *Not in Heaven: Coherence and Complexity in Biblical Narrative,* edited by Jason P. Rosenblatt and Joseph C. Sitteron, Jr. Bloomington: Indiana University Press, 1991, 170–91.

Van Buren, Paul. *According to the Scriptures.* Grand Rapids, Mich.: Eerdmans, 1998.

———. *A Theology of the Jewish-Christian Reality.* 3 vols. San Francisco: Harper and Row, 1980, 1983, 1988.

Vermes, Geza. *Jesus and the World of Judaism.* Philadelphia: Fortress Press, 1984.

———. *Jesus the Jew: A Historian's Reading of the Gospels.* London: Collins, 1973.

———. *The Religion of Jesus the Jew.* Minneapolis: Fortress Press, 1993.

———. *Scripture and Tradition.* Leiden: Brill, 1961.

———, trans. and ed. *The Dead Sea Scrolls in English.* New York: Penguin, 1975.

Wacholder, Ben Zion. "Prolegomen" to Jacob Mann, *The Bible as Read and Preached in the Old Synagogue.* New York: Ktav, 1971.

Weeden, T. *Traditions in Conflict.* Philadelphia: Fortress Press, 1971.

Williams, J. G. *Gospel Against Parable: Mark's Language of Mystery.* Sheffield, England: *Journal for the Study of the Old Testament,* 1985.

Wrede, William. *The Messianic Secret.* Translated by J. C. Grieg. Greenwood, S.C.: Attic Press, 1971.

Wright, N. T. *Christian Origins and the Question of God.* Vol. 1. Minneapolis: Fortress Press, 1993.

Yarbro, Adele Collins. *The Beginning of the Gospel: Probings of Mark in Context.* Minneapolis: Fortress Press, 1992.

Young, Brad. *Jesus and His Jewish Parables.* Mahwah, N.J.: Paulist Press, 1989.

Zannoni, Arthur E., ed. *Jews and Christians Speak of Jesus.* Minneapolis: Fortress Press, 1994.

Index of Ancient Texts

Index of Authors and Subjects

Midrash
  and "birth pangs" imagery,
    238 n. 17
  as context for Mark, 31–32, 169–
    70
  on Deuteronomy, 36, 127–28
  in Early Judaism, 12–21, 126
  on Exodus, 127, 140
  on the fig tree, 83
  in fourfold scheme of questioning,
    99
  on Genesis 1:26, 163, 165–66,
    249 n. 70
  and the Gospels, 21–22
  as hermeneutical method, 90, 93,
    242 n. 20
  and history, 14, 30
  and homilies, 19, 21
  on Isaac, 126–30
  in Jesus' teaching, 50–51, 93–98,
    160–61
  at Jewish Theological Seminary, ix
  and Mark's open ending, 202, 223
  and Mark's structure, 79, 83, 90,
    106, 109–110
  in Matthew's treatment of Mark,
    216
  in Nehemiah, 12
  and New Testament canon, 210
  school of, 21, 90, 99
  as theological imagination, 14–16
  and Wisdom, 201
Mishnah, messianic references in,
  112
Moore, Stephen, 250 n. 76
Muffs, Yohanan, viii
Mysterion as "mystery," not "secret,"
  235 n. 11

Nebuchadnezzar, 48–49
Nehemiah, 12
Neusner, Jacob, xi, 113, 165–66,
  232 n. 60
New Year, Jewish rituals of, 141
Nickelsburg, George, 113
Nimshal, 42
Nineham, D. E., 240 n. 9, 246 n. 21
Novatian of Rome, 135–36
NRSV, treatment of Markan ending,
  206–7

Oden, Thomas, 228 n. 3
"Old Testament," 35
"Oral Torah"
  and Christian origins, xi
  Jesus as, 166
  in Judaism, 13
  and Pharisees, 93
Origen
  on the Antichrist, 64–65, 148–49
  on the "Beloved Son," 124–25
  on false witnesses against Jesus,
    103
  hermeneutic of, 25–26
  on Mark 1:1, 35, 38
  on Mark 13, 53–54
  on Papias tradition, 4
"Our Father," 241 n. 15
Oxford Study Bible and Markan
  ending, 206

Pagels, Elaine, 247 n. 45
Papias on Mark's link to Peter, 3–5,
  9, 12, 22–23
Parable. *See also* Mashal
  as exegetical form, 41, 45
  of the Fig Tree, 69–70, 82–83,
    109
  function of, 51, 235–36 n. 11
  Jesus as, 165–66, 168–70
  of the Mustard Seed, 44–51
  of the Returning Householder,
    59–61, 71
  of the Seed Growing Secretly, 44–
    51
  of the Sower, 39–44
  of the Vineyard, 40, 42, 84–90,
    109, 133–34
Passover
  and anointing of Jesus, 194
  and the Eucharist, 194
  in Mark's vocabulary, 8
  and Psalm 118, 88, 90
Patte, Daniel, 232 n. 30
Paul, attitudes toward Judaism, 23,
  24, 231, 242 n. 21
Perrin, Norman, 245 n. 5
Perrot, Charles, 233
Peter
  "alter ego" of, 193, 196
  and fig tree, 81, 84

9 780199 895748